| DATE | | | |
|---|---|---|---|
| | | | |
| | | | |
| | | | |
| | | | |
| | | | |
| | | | |
| | | | |
| | | | |
| | | | |
| | | | |
| | | | |
| | | | |

# *Voices from the Margin*

## INTERPRETING THE BIBLE
## IN THE THIRD WORLD

*Edited by*

R. S. Sugirtharajah

ORBIS BOOKS

**Maryknoll, New York 10545**

*872 72434*

The Catholic Foreign Mission Society of America (Maryknoll) recruits
and trains people for overseas missionary service. Through Orbis Books
Maryknoll aims to foster the international dialogue that is essential to
mission. The books published, however, reflect the opinions of their
authors and are not meant to represent the official position of the Society.

*BS
476
.V65
1991*

Published in the United States of America
by Orbis Books, Maryknoll NY 10545

Compilation and introduction © R. S. Sugirtharajah 1991

Manufactured in Great Britain

**Library of Congress Cataloging-in-Publication Data**

Voices from the margin/edited by R. S. Sugirtharajah,
p.    cm.
Includes bibliographical references and indexes.
ISBN 0-88344-770-3 (pbk.): $19.95
1. Bible—Hermeneutics—Comparative studies.    2. Christianity—
Developing countries.    3. Christianity and culture.    4. Bible.
O.T. Exodus—Hermeneutics—Comparative studies.    I. Sugirtharajah,
R. S. (Rasiah S.)
BS476.V65    1991
220.6'01—dc20        91-7323 CIP

# Contents

Acknowledgements                                                    viii

1   Introduction   *R. S. Sugirtharajah (Sri Lanka)*                  1

**Part One    Use of the Bible: Methods, Principles
and Issues**                                                         7

2   Hermeneutics: Constitution of Theological
    Pertinency   *Clodovis Boff (Brazil)*                             9
3   The Asian Context: Sources and Trends   *Stanley J.
    Samartha (India)*                                                36
4   The Use of the Bible in Black Theology   *Itumeleng J.
    Mosala (South Africa)*                                           50
5   Women's Rereading of the Bible   *Elsa Tamez (Costa Rica)*       61
6   Marxist Critical Tools: Are They Helpful in Breaking
    the Stranglehold of Idealist Hermeneutics?   *José
    Miguez-Bonino (Argentina)*                                       71

**Part Two    Re-use of the Bible: Examples of
Hermeneutical Explorations**                                         83

7   Jesus and the Minjung in the Gospel of Mark   *Ahn
    Byung-Mu (South Korea)*                                          85
8   Biblical Hermeneutics of Liberation: The Case of
    Micah   *Itumeleng J. Mosala (South Africa)*                    104
9   Water – God's Extravaganza: John 2.1–11   *Sr Vandana
    (India)*                                                        117
10  Song and Deliverance – *Gustavo Gutierrez (Peru)*               129
11  Class in the Bible: The Biblical Poor a Social
    Class?   *George M. Soares-Prabhu (India)*                      147
12  Racial Motifs in the Biblical Narratives   *Cain Hope
    Felder (USA)*                                                   172

13  The David–Bathsheba Story and the Parable of Nathan
    *Archie C. C. Lee (Hong Kong)*                                    189
14  The Equality of Women: Form or Substance
    (1 Corinthians 11.2–16)  *Christine Amjad-Ali (Pakistan)*         205
15  A Solomonic Model of Peace   *Helen R. Graham
    (Philippines)*                                                    214

**Part Three   The Exodus: One Theme, Many
Perspectives**                                                        227

16  A Latin American Perspective: The Option for the Poor
    in the Old Testament   *George V. Pixley (Nicaragua)*             229
17  A Korean Minjung Perspective: The Hebrews and the
    Exodus   *Cyris H. S. Moon (South Korea)*                         241
18  A Black African Perspective: An African Reading of
    Exodus   *Jean-Marc Ela (Cameroun)*                               256
19  An Asian Feminist Perspective: The Exodus Story
    (Exodus 1.8–22, 2.1–10)   *An Asian Group Work*                   267
20  A Palestinian Perspective: The Bible and Liberation
    *Naim Stifan Ateek (Israel)*                                      280
21  A Native American Perspective: Canaanites, Cowboys,
    and Indians   *Robert Allen Warrior (USA)*                        287

**Part Four   One Reality, Many Texts: Examples of
Multi-faith Hermeneutics**                                            297

22  Discovering the Bible in the Non-biblical World   *Kwok
    Pui Lan (Hong Kong)*                                              299
23  The Bible in Self-renewal and Church-renewal for
    Service to Society   *D. S. Amalorpavadass (India)*               316
24  'I' in the Words of Jesus   *Seiichi Yagi (Japan)*                330
25  Inter-faith Hermeneutics: An Example and Some
    Implications   *R. S. Sugirtharajah (Sri Lanka)*                  352
26  Creation of Man: Theological Reflections Based on
    Northern Thai Folktales   *Maen Pongudom (Thailand)*              364
27  Liberation in Indian Scriptures   *Jacob Kattackal (India)*       372
28  On Developing Liberation Theology in Islam   *Asghar
    Ali Engineer (India)*                                             385

**Part Five   People as Exegetes**                                    395

29  A Malawian Example: The Bible and Non-literate
    Communities   *Patrick A. Kalilombe*                              397

# Contents

30  A Nicaraguan Example: The Alabaster Bottle   Matthew
    26. 6–13                                                      412

31  An Indonesian Example: The Miraculous Catch   Luke
    5.1–11                                                        420

32  A South African Example: Jesus' Teaching at Nazareth
    Luke 4.14–30                                                  423

33  A Chinese Example: 'The Silences of the Bible'
    K. H. Ting                                                    431

Postscript: Achievements and Items for a Future Agenda
R. S. Sugirtharajah (Sri Lanka)                                  434

Index of Scripture References                                    445

Select Index of Names and Subjects                               454

# Acknowledgements

Like most things in life, producing a book is a corporate activity and one has to depend on many people. I would like to express my gratitude to the following for their invaluable help: Bas Wielenga, a former colleague at Tamilnadu Theological Seminary, Madurai, South India, for helping to remove the archaic exegetical scales from my eyes; Daniel O'Connor, Principal of the College of the Ascension, Selly Oak, for his insightful comments on this draft, for many hours of stimulating and sparkling conversations about several aspects of contextual theologies, but much more for his continual friendship and encouragement; all Mission Department course participants in the 'Bible in Context' class who helped significantly to widen and enrich the hermeneutical circle; the Central Library Staff at the Selly Oak Colleges – Meline Nielsen, Beverley Lambeth-Angell, Katrina Youster, Willemina Morton and Patrick Lambe, for bending their own rules to accede to my persistent and often unreasonable requests; Judith Longman of SPCK, for readily accepting my draft outline and for seeing the project through with drive and enthusiasm; all the copyright holders of the articles for their kind permission to reprint them; and finally, my wife Sharada, for constantly reminding me of the need for inter-religious hermeneutics.

*R. S. Sugirtharajah*
Selly Oak Colleges
Birmingham
May Day 1990

viii

# Publisher's Acknowledgements

We are grateful to the following for permission to reproduce copyright material:

*Bible Bhashayam*, India for ch. 27.

Burns & Oates, Tunbridge Wells for ch. 16.

The Christian Study Centre and 'Women in Reflection and Action', Rawalpindi Cantt., Pakistan for ch. 14.

*Christianity and Crisis*, New York for ch. 21.

Christian Literature Society, Madras, India for ch. 9.

Claretian Publications Inc., Manila, Philippines for chs 2 and 10.

Commission on Theological Concerns of Asia, New York for ch. 7.

*East Asia Journal of Theology*, Singapore for chs 13 and 26.

*Focus*, Multan, Pakistan for ch. 28.

Forum for Interdisciplinary Endeavours and Studies (FIDES), Manila, Philippines for ch. 15.

*In God's Image*, Hong Kong for ch. 19.

International Association for Mission Studies (IAMS) Secretariat, Hamburg for ch. 25.

*International Review of Mission*, Geneva for chs 31 and 32.

Orbis Books, Maryknoll, New York for chs 2, 4, 5, 7, 8, 10, 12, 16, 17, 18, 20, 24 and 30.

Plough Publications, Hong Kong for ch. 17.

SCM Press, London for chs 6 and 24.

*Semeia*, c/o Jewish Theological Society, New York for chs 4 and 8.

Skotaville Publishers, Braamfontein, South Africa for chs 4 and 8.

Tao Fong Ecumenical Centre, Hong Kong for ch. 33.

*Vidyajyoti Journal*, Delhi, India for ch. 11.

*Voices from the Third World*, Colombo, Sri Lanka for ch. 23.

Zed Press, London for ch. 7.

# 1
# Introduction

R. S. SUGIRTHARAJAH

Currently, Christian Scripture is at the centre of the theological agenda. This has been by and large due to the hermeneutical endeavours of Latin American liberation theologians. It was they who developed a new way of interpreting biblical data, and rescued the Bible from abstract, individualized and 'neutralized' reading. The day-to-day struggle to survive in a situation of injustice and oppression prompted them to scrutinize scriptural texts in the light of their awareness of their own social context.

Expanding on the insights of Latin American liberation hermeneutics, Asians, Africans, Afro-Americans and Native Americans have gone on to develop their own interpretative styles and strategies. While Latin Americans bring the critique of class to the texts, blacks from North America and Africa introduce an awareness of racial and cultural factors into the enterprise. The Asians add their multi-religious perspectives to it. Latin American, Asian and black women work out their own discourses, utilizing 'the hermeneutics of suspicion' – a method vigorously pursued by their Euro-American counterparts – but at the same time injecting their particular feminine and cultural insights into the hermeneutical arena.

This volume of essays by Latin American, Asian and black biblical scholars is a testimony to that enterprise.

A word about the title – *Voices from the Margin*. It indicates two things. First, it highlights the struggles and exegetical concerns of those who are on the periphery of society. Generally, the dominant biblical scholarship has shied away from the needs of the weak and the needy. Very rarely has it focused on people's experience of hunger, sickness and exploitation. These essays embody the needs and aspirations of those who are not normally at the forefront of things.

Secondly, it points to the marginalization of Asian, Latin American,

1

black and other biblical scholars by mainline biblical scholarship. This is an experience that is very familiar to Euro-American feminist Scripture scholars.[1] Most of the essayists are invisible in Euro-American academic circles, and one seldom finds their discourses in the journals produced in them. These scholars are marginal to a great deal of scholarly thinking, and their presence and their exegetical output receive hardly any attention. For instance, *A Dictionary of Biblical Interpretation*,[2] which is proudly presented as the work of distinguished scholars, does not carry a single entry by an Asian, Latin American or black biblical interpreter. More revealingly, it has only one reference to the work of a non Euro-American scholar.

To date, biblical interpretation has been exclusively in the hands of male Euro-American scholars. Their academies and scholarly guilds have been the arena where hermeneutical theories, interpretative constructs and exegetical discourses were worked out, and from where they were exported to other cultures and contexts as having universal validity. Asians, Latin Americans, Africans, Afro-Americans and Native Americans were excluded both for their concerns and as producers of knowledge. This volume seeks to rectify this imbalance and to introduce exegetical discourse 'from the margin', the work both of those who have had formal exegetical training and of those who have had none. Both of these groups endeavour to work out new paradigms and approaches that are vastly different from those of the dominant biblical scholarship.

An explanation is also needed on the use of the words 'Third World' in the sub-title. Its negative connotations cause a lot of resentment, especially among those who come from these countries. Its origin, subsequent usage and precise meaning are, like most biblical narratives, shrouded in ambiguity. In popular parlance it refers to the countries in the southern hemisphere, those that are not among (though within the sphere of influence of) the capitalist and industrialist nations of Europe and North America. The word also carries political overtones. Its origin belongs to political history, and goes back to the Cold War period of the 1950s. At a time when two superpowers, the USA and Russia, by espousing two different modes of economy (capitalist, Marxist) and two different political systems (democracy and socialism), were polarizing the world community, the countries that had recently been freed from colonial shackles meeting at Bandung, Indonesia, in 1955 opted to stay outside these powerful blocs and forge a third, alternative political and economic system.

But today the term 'Third World' has acquired another meaning. It is a designation for a people who have been excluded from power, from the authority to mould and shape their own future – racial minorities, the poor, women, and the marginalized peoples of the world. For Aloysius Pieris, the Sri Lankan theologian, the term has effectively the same connotation as 'oppressed'. It is also, consequently, for him, a theological statement:

> The term 'Third World' is a theological neologism for God's own people. It stands for the starving sons and daughters of Jacob – of all places and all times – who go in search of bread to a rich country, only to become its slaves. In other words, the Third World is not merely the story of the South in relation to the North or of the East in relation to the West. It is something that happens wherever and whenever socio-economic dependence in terms of race, class, or sex generates political and cultural slavery, fermenting thereby a new peoplehood.[3]

'Third worldness' is, then, no longer merely a geographical connotation referring to the countries of Asia, Africa and Latin America. Nor is it about a third political force. It is a description of a people who face harassment and exploitation wherever they are. This volume is a representative documentation of the hermeneutical efforts of such people. They emanate from a variety of cultural, social and geographical contexts. They wrestle with diverse issues such as racism, classism, sexism and religious triumphalism. But the common factor in their hermeneutical efforts is that they speak from a shared perspective of total solidarity with people and a recurrent experience of alienation and ghettoization.

The literature on contextual hermeneutics is vibrant, vast and ever growing. It was not easy to choose from the mass of materials now available. In selecting the pieces for this volume only three simple rules were applied: (1) whether the professional exegetes compassionately identify with contextual concerns and take them seriously in their biblical reflection, (2) whether they transcend the traditional historical–critical tools or employ indigenous tools to release the text, and (3) whether the 'people's commentaries' speak from the realities of the vulnerable and the underprivileged. I have come across many discourses that meet these requirements. Those omitted were because of limitations of space, or non-availability in English, or because they had already found a wider readership.

## FORMAT OF THE VOLUME

Briefly, an explanation of the arrangement of these essays. They are arranged thematically rather than under geographical location (Asia, Africa, Latin America) or in terms of gender. Placing them according to themes enables the reader to see how the issues and approaches differ from context to context, but it also underlines the fact that all of these hermeneutical cogitations are contextual and are responses to specific needs.

The essays are divided into five main themes. Part One is entitled 'Use of the Bible: Methods, Principles and Issues'. The essayists here challenge the epistemological and interpretative starting points of Euro-American uses of the Bible, and in the light of their critique re-envision tentative hermeneutical norms and proposals that are suitable to their own social and cultural milieux.

The second set of essays, in Part Two, is captioned 'Re-Use of the Bible: Examples of Hermeneutical Explorations'. It consists of samples of the work of Asian, Latin American, African and Afro-American exegetes who use traditional methods as well as indigenous tools to look at the scriptural revelation anew and to resurrect the biblical message. At a time when there is despair and loss of confidence in the effectiveness of historical–critical tools among Euro-American biblical scholars, these essayists show how these tools, which were developed by the bourgeois class to maintain its class interests, can be liberative and offer solace to the powerless. What these essays indicate is that historical–critical methods are not defunct, as Walter Wink once lamented, but that they have been in the hands of people whose social bias has placed a limitation on their use. Their exegetical findings show that the problem is not with the tools, but with those who use them.

This section also contains examples of how traditional cultural tools can illuminate the sacred text.

The essays that are assembled in Part Three, 'The Exodus: One Theme, Many Perspectives', demonstrate that a narrative can lend itself to several readings. The Exodus episode, a key event in the life of Israel, was recounted differently at different stages in the life of the Jewish people, and also later by the followers of the Jesus movement, who appropriated it for their own affirmation. The discourses that are gathered here not only reiterate the von Radian thesis that interpretation is renewal of old tradition in the light of new situations, but also reinforce the view that diverse readings do not exhaust the meaning of

4

the event. They enhance the text, and can enrich it with new shades of meaning when approached from a variety of cultural, social and gender perspectives.

This section also contains two exegetical discourses that challenge the emancipatory potential of the Exodus model as a valid biblical paradigm for liberation for all people and contexts.

The next set of essays, in Part Four, 'One Reality, Many Texts: Examples of Multi-faith Hermeneutics', deal with the key issues most acutely faced by Asian and African Christians, who as minorities live amidst people who possess their own revered sacred books. The most radical critique of Christian theology and Christian Scripture comes at present from the theological challenges posed by adherents of other faith traditions. Their scriptural texts, like the *Bhagavad Gita*, the Qur'an and the Granth, raise questions about the uniqueness, normativeness and finality of the Christian canon, the place and function of sacred stories of other faith traditions, and, more pressingly, how to handle some of the biblical texts that exude Christian triumphalism. These essays illustrate some of the ways in which these questions and challenges are being addressed by Christian biblical interpreters who feel the presence of this context. This section also contains examples of a liberative message discerned in the sacred literature of Hindus and Muslims.

The last collection of essays, in Part Five, is entitled 'People as Exegetes'. As the title indicates, this section contains unique contributions to hermeneutical discourse by ordinary people in Asia, Africa and Latin America. Basically, biblical hermeneutics in Asia, Africa and Latin America functions at two levels. One is that of those professionally trained biblical scholars whom the Boff brothers describe as having 'one foot in centers of study, but their other foot is in the community'.[4] These hermeneuts see their interpretative function in the light of what the sages of old urged: 'Open your mouth for the dumb, for the rights of those who are left desolate; open your mouth, judge righteously, maintain the rights of the poor and needy' (Prov. 31.8,9). The other is that of the interpretation undertaken at the grassroots level by ordinary people who see their task as recovering the biblical texts from other-worldly, ahistorical and apolitical readings for the empowerment of the community. It was the peasants in Solentiname in Nicaragua who set the trend, and, as the examples here show, others have followed this hermeneutical lead. The exegetical efforts of these ordinary people are exciting not only because they violate all the norms and ground-rules established by the learned academies, but also because they break away from the dominant hermeneutical practice of individual engagement with the text. The interpretative efforts of the ordinary people highlight the exciting possibilities of corporate exegetical enterprise.

The essays are printed as they appeared in their original form with little editorial emendation. Thus, some of the articles retain the terms 'OT' and 'NT' indicating a triumphalist perspective; some continue to use BC/AD rather than the neutral terms such as BCE (Before the Common Era) or CE (Common Era), and some preserve sexist language. The essayists would probably be the first to acknowledge the archaism of these terms. But these are all retained as historical indicators to show the sort of ideological and gender blinkers one has as one wrestles through one's faith.

Finally, as one who has learned much from the work of the contributors to this volume, I would like to conclude with one thought. These exegetical discourses are not so much a coming-of-age of 'Third World' hermeneutics, as a coming-to-terms hermeneutics – coming to terms, that is, with a world that is racially, economically and sexually divided and exploited. By hermeneutically reflecting on these issues, these hermeneuts have initiated a discussion about the sort of society we live in and dream for. This, I believe, should be the purpose of all hermeneutics.

## NOTES

1 See D. C. Bass, 'Women's Studies and Biblical Studies: An Historical Perspective' (*Journal for the Study of the Old Testament*, 22, 1982), pp. 6–12.

2 R. J. Coggins and J. L. Houlden (eds), *A Dictionary of Biblical Interpretation* (London, SCM Press, 1990; Philadelphia, Trinity Press International, 1990).

3 A. Pieris, *An Asian Theology of Liberation* (Edinburgh, T & T Clark, 1988; Maryknoll, NY, Orbis Books, 1988), p. 87.

4 L. Boff and C. Boff, *Introducing Liberation Theology* (Tunbridge Wells, Kent, Burns & Oates; Maryknoll, NY, Orbis Books, 1987), p. 19.

# PART ONE

# *Use of the Bible: Methods, Principles and Issues*

People ask us for bread and we offer them a handful of theories about each verse of John 6. They ask questions about God and we offer them three theories about the literary form of one Psalm. They thirst for justice and we offer them discussions about the root of the word *sedaga* ('justice' in Hebrew). I am examining my conscience out loud, and the reply I hear is: the one must be done without neglecting the other.

(L. Alonso Schöckel)

# 2

# Hermeneutics: Constitution of Theological Pertinency

## CLODOVIS BOFF

The popular understanding of Latin American hermeneutics is that it uses the Bible uncritically to suit its own theological agenda. This essay dispels such a notion. Clodovis Boff, a Servite priest from Brazil, points out that there are two different ways of reading the Bible – one through seeking a 'correspondence of terms' and the other a 'correspondence of relationships'. The former, often mistaken for liberation exegesis, is critiqued and rejected. The latter is not only presented as the proper approach to Latin American liberation theology, but also as consistent with the methods of interpretation practised by the biblical writers.

This piece forms part of a larger work of Boff's, *Theology and Praxis: Epistemological Foundations* (Maryknoll, NY, Orbis Books, 1987), where he tries to work out a true theology of the political which goes beyond what the author calls the 'first phase of liberation theology'. For a more popular reflection on biblical hermeneutics, see his *Introducing Liberation Theology* (Maryknoll, NY, Orbis Books, 1987), especially pp. 32–7, which he co-authored with his brother, Leonardo, who is one of the most influential and controversial Latin American liberation theologians.

## THREE ACCEPTATIONS OF HERMENEUTICS

I have defined theological pertinency as the essential reference effectuated by a determinate theoretical practice, called 'theology,' to revelation. I have likewise stated that such pertinency operates theoretically in and by the formal disposition of a second generality. In the present chapter I must sketch the theoretical constitution of this identifying instance of theological thought.

I shall begin by asserting that the activity of this instance belongs to the order of *hermeneutics*, as indeed my definition of theological pertinency indicates. Whether it be formulated as 'reflection in the light of God's word,' or 'reflection in the perspective of faith,' or even 'theory from the viewpoint of revelation,' or the like, it always refers to

9

*Christian positivity* – that is, to the objective (dogmatic, historical) aspect of faith, with its ties to the order of the 'given,' the 'right there.'

This positivity does not float in the air as an abstraction. It is found inscribed, witnessed, translated, and deposited in the corpus of the canonical writings of the ecclesial community, the *Christian scriptures.*

The series of canonical texts whose scope is 'fontal,' inasmuch as they constitute the font of all other Christian writings, consists of the Old and New Testaments. The superiority of their value for the Christian community is indicated in the very name they customarily receive: 'Bible' or sacred 'scripture.'

Other texts or fonts of Christian positivity must be seen under the ordination of the writings just mentioned, which always occupy a central place and perform a cardinal function. At the same time, however, within the Bible itself, a certain hierarchy can be discerned. The New Testament takes precedence over the Old. Within the New Testament, the gospels hold the primacy over the other writings. Scripture, then, must be conceived as an articulated whole, and this is a fact carefully to be taken into account in hermeneutic practice. I shall have occasion to return to this point.

The foundational texts of faith are subjected to a process of interpretation. Their sense is not simply open and plain. Time has interposed a distance between them and us. The process of decoding that seeks to overcome this distance, and thus reappropriate the original sense of the written message, goes by the name of 'hermeneutics.'

I take 'hermeneutics' here in the sense of an interpretive activity bearing on *written* texts. I thus take up a position in the ongoing 'war of hermeneutics.' Below, I shall add greater detail to my position.

From the outset, we are in the theological area. The hermeneutics I speak of is *theological.* It bears upon the Christian scriptures. In the theological area, the notion of 'hermeneutics' can have three distinct acceptations, in increasing degrees of extension:

1 Hermeneutics may be understood as a set of *canons of exegetical interpretation.* Here we have the etymological sense of the term *hermeneutike techne.*

2 Hermeneutics may be understood as *interpretation as such:* exegesis itself, as the operation of decoding, along with its result. Here we may speak of a *hermeneia*, in contradistinction to *hermeneutike techne.*

3 Finally, hermeneutics can be simply considered as synonymous

with *theology*, inasmuch as theology has the task of understanding an original sense today and for today. In this maximal acceptation, theological hermeneutics would correspond to what I have called 'theological theory.' Thus, for example, there would be a hermeneutics of the 'signs of the times,' a hermeneutics of history, a 'political hermeneutics,' and so forth.

When I speak here of 'hermeneutic mediation' of a theology of the political, I refer to senses 1 and 2 – although a theology of the political can always be considered as a hermeneutics in the third sense, in virtue of the fact that it designates a theory of the 'Christian' sense of politics – that is, in virtue of its quest of an understanding of (political) praxis in the light of faith.

By 'hermeneutic mediation' I mean the necessary relationship of a theology of the political with the Christian 'fonts,' which furnish this theology of the political with its proper identity. In this perspective, the Christian scriptures constitute an *obligatory and constitutive theoretical resource of any theological process*.

But let us recall once more that hermeneutic mediation is not constitutive of a theology of the political *ex aequo* with socio-analytic mediation. Obviously, these two mediations must have an interlocution. It is for us to delineate this interlocution, this articulation. Their relationship is governed by a logic: the logic of theoretical practice in general. In accordance with this logic as I have described it, socio-analytic mediation occupies the position of a first generality, and hermeneutic mediation that of a second generality, whereas the theology of the political will be considered a third generality. Thus, in the expression 'theology of the political,' socio-analytic mediation takes charge of the 'political' side, and hermeneutic mediation takes charge of the 'theology' side, with the 'of' indicating the articulation between the mediations.

This, then, is my position with respect to the sense and scope of hermeneutic mediation. This too is how my position is to be distinguished from that of others.

I shall now point out other positions taken with regard to hermeneutics, very sketchily, and at the risk of a certain oversimplification.

First there is the position of H. G. Gadamer, who conceives hermeneutics as a sort of ontology. His important *Wahreit und Methode* (1960) bears the subtitle, *Grundzüge einer philosophischen Hermeneutik.* The criticism to which this conception is vulnerable is that of its arrogation of universality, by which it exempts itself a priori from all analytical criticism. Gadamer permits a teeming anarchy of every sort of reading. Too much meaning is terribly strong light.

Rather too broad as well is Aristotle's conception of *hermeneia* in his work *Peri Hermeneias*. It is applied to any linguistic enunciation affirming or denying anything of anything. Here, hermeneutics has the extension of language itself.

Then there is the undertaking of Wilhelm Dilthey, who attempted to base an epistemology of *Geistwissenschaften* on the notion of 'comprehension,' which, he held, makes it possible for us to apprehend a human sense or meaning in the actions and deeds of human beings. Thus we have the 'hermeneutic sciences,' of which one is theology. This epistemology is losing ground, however, and today is considered obsolescent or passé.

Coming to Paul Ricoeur, we find interpretation assigned the task of deciphering the 'double-meaning' language that constitutes the language of symbol. Thus interpretation will bear on 'texts,' in a broad, even analogous sense: a myth, a dream, or even a whole culture. Here we have a conceptualization that obviously extends far beyond the notion of a theological hermeneutic.

Finally, we have the conceptualization, already referred to, that identifies theology with hermeneutics, in a tradition coming down to us from Friedrich Schleiermacher.

In the present chapter, I shall limit the sense of hermeneutics on two sides: on the side of its *object*, a (theological) hermeneutics will bear solely upon the Christian scriptures; on the side of its *method*, a (theological) hermeneutics will be limited to the exegetical interpretation of these Christian scriptures.

To be sure, the (original) exegetical sense of these scriptures is animated from within by a thrust that continues into the present, and this justifies the use of the term 'hermeneutics' in another sense as well – that of the recovery of meaning not just within the actual bounds of the text, as *techne hermeneutike*, but beyond them as theological theory. However, I deem it preferable to restrict its scope to that of hermeneutic *mediation*. Thus, hermeneutics, as I employ the term, will not correspond to the totality of (political) theology, although it will still be an essential part of (all) theology.

When all is said and done, the important thing will be a precise grasp of the distinct acceptations covered by the notion of hermeneutics, lest we confuse them.

# THE HERMENEUTIC CIRCLE

It will be in order to take a glance at theological hermeneutics as such, in order to determine both its scope and the manner of its use in the development of a faith datum.

To this purpose, I shall be guided by the notion of the 'hermeneutic circle.' I begin by noting that 'positive theology,' taken as final result of a labor of hermeneutics and exegesis, can be developed only if there is a relationship, however implicit, between itself and 'speculative theology,' and *e converso.*

This inescapable circle does not contradict – indeed it actually explains – my attempt in the foregoing sections to sketch a theoretical version of the key concepts of theology – notions originating with the Bible, but thereupon coming to be organized in a specific conceptual network.

Now it can be seen that we are involved in a full hermeneutic circle. In the following sections, this circle will appear and reappear in various forms.

It does not suffice, however, simply to point out the existence of this circle. We have yet to analyze the actual form of its presentation, so as to be able to 'insert ourselves into it in precise fashion' (Heidegger). For this circle subsists according to particular rules. It is not a perfectly circular trajectory between homogeneous terms. On the contrary, the constitutive relationship of the hermeneutic circle is of a dialectical nature. We are dealing with a tense, critical, indeed dramatic relationship, effectuated under the governance of one of its terms, which rules the rhythm of the dialectical movement. After all, there is dialectic and there is dialectic – one must always identify the rules of its process.

There are many forms in which the hermeneutic circle can appear, once we have set about theological, and especially biblical, deciphering. Among the manifold forms it can take, I would single out those that obtain between the following pairs of terms:

word of God – scripture
creation of meaning – acceptance of meaning
structure – meaning
present – past
technique – interpretation

Let us examine these forms one by one.

## Hermeneutic circle: scripture and the word of God

The terms of the first relationship to be considered are often simply identified. But they are on different levels, and we must recognize the difference between them. It is not for nothing that, in the determination of the *regula fidei*, the meaning context, or pragmatics, within which scripture has its value, is explicitly named: 'The norm of faith is scripture read *in the church.*' The prepositional phrase at the end of the formula inserts the biblical text into church tradition. This means that its sense can be apprehended only in relationship with the *sensus fidelium* – the living spirit of the living community.

Scripture is surely the *norma normans* of faith. But it is likewise in some manner a *norma normata*. This is clear from a study of its historico-literary genesis, as well as from its 'canonization' by the charismatic authority of the church. I shall have occasion to return to this point later on.

And so, strictly speaking, the word of God is not to be found in the letter of scripture. Nor is it in the spirit of the hearing or reading community. It is precisely *between* these two, in their mutual, dynamic relationship, in a back-and-forth that is never perfectly objectifiable.

## Hermeneutic circle: creation and perception of meaning

To clarify the dialectic operative between creation and the perception of meaning, let me cite the two extremes to which nondialectical, or dogmatist, thinking leads: hermeneutic improvisation and semantic positivism.

By *hermeneutic improvisation* I mean the attitude, and corresponding practice, that consists in taking from scripture simply whatever serves one's own interest, without any concern but that of making use of biblical passages as 'proofs' for a preestablished theoretical project or practice. This is precisely the way of *bricolage* (improvisation or tinkering or makeshift): it makes use of the tools at hand for the needs of the moment. The relationship it sees between the store of 'useful pieces' at hand and a work plan is purely utilitarian. It can be a forced relationship.

Hermeneutic improvisation translates into pragmatism in the interpretation of texts. The right meaning is the useful one. Obviously, this is an open door to a riotous carnival of meanings.

At the other end of the spectrum from hermeneutic improvisation is *semantic positivism*. Semantic positivism endeavors simply to gain control of meanings, catalogue them, and store them, so as to be able to use them at will

It is not difficult to perceive what interest these two extreme positions have in common: control of meaning and its utilization at whim.

The danger for Christian theology – less today than yesterday, it is true – is precisely that of transforming Christian positivity into textual positivism. This creates a 'meaning metaphysics,' or semantic dogmatism, that freezes any living meaning in its tracks. The images that spontaneously arise in association with semantic positivism are those of the refrigerator, the museum, and the cemetery.

Both of these hermeneutical tendencies, instead of dialecticizing their terms, flee to the extremes. My own position is that meaning can arise only from a sustained relationship between reader and text, between questions and answers.

## Hermeneutic circle: structure and meaning

Now let us consider the hermeneutic circle between explanation and comprehension with respect to a written text – here, with respect to the Christian scriptures. Various linguistic theories can offer us a particular service here, precisely in the order of a structural explanation of texts.

Inasmuch as the letter of a text, like any sign, has its titles of nobility, it is important to grasp exactly what the autonomous structure of this letter is before attempting to gather its sense and meaning. Meaning needs structure for support. Structure serves meaning as its vehicle of communication, thus imposing upon it the confinement of its own determinations.

In the case at hand, dialectic proceeds in such a way that explanation becomes a preliminary moment, whereupon the work of 'comprehensive reading,' a reading with understanding, supervenes.

The same type of relationship is operative between cause and meaning, fact and meaning, the law and meaning – all modalities of the same fundamental pair of structure and sense, structure and meaning.

## Hermeneutic circle: present and past

The text never ceases to be open to the world and history. It dispatches all its readers, real or potential, on one assignment after another.

Indeed, this is why there is such a thing as writing. It exists to last, to be read and reread.

The written text is the channel of a meaning through a succession of historical moments. This is the case with any text, and especially with the Christian scriptures.

But the Bible does not enjoy such a special and important place in the eyes of believers in its status as a literary text. It does so by reason of the meaning it simultaneously conceals and reveals. The reason it invests in faith is that faith has already been invested in it. And the circle returns.

At bottom, the ultimate reference of the Bible is to the present, to the reader's current history. The biblical sense regards precisely this. It is the reader, then, who occupies the center of attention of the text.

Thus, although in a first moment, a basic one, to be sure, sense or meaning is obtained under sign, word under writing, spirit under letter – now, in another moment, sense is obtained in the present, word in time, spirit in history. But all of this comes through the meaning of scripture. The hermeneutic circle is not broken.

This means that the entire work of exegesis can and should be conceived as a moment in a complex process bearing upon the hearer's or reader's present moment. Now word ceases to be simply text to be interpreted, and itself becomes interpretative code. *Now word is no longer world to be seen but eyes to see, no longer landscape but gaze, no longer thing but light.*

The theory that seeks to take account of this reading is called 'theology.' If we are dealing with politics, then we are of course in the presence of a theology of the political.

## Hermeneutic circle: *Techne Hermeneutike and Hermeneia*

The hermeneutic circle, whose modalities have just been described, shows how impossible it would be to construct an interpretative technique such that its application to a text would lay utterly bare, once and for all, its integral meaning, and obviate all further questions a priori, as hermeneutical positivism dreams of doing. All we would need would be 'interpreting machines'!

It so happens that the very openness of ex-sistence is an irreducible fact, one that is always 'there,' like a wound that never scars over, or a leak that cannot be plugged. The human modality of being-in-the-world is one of comprehension, of endless interrogation – an interrogation that places the world in the balance of a critique, one that seeks to deal with the very Absolute.

This 'analytic' may not, however, be allowed to furnish a pretext for the notion that the hermeneutic effort falls back to zero. The objective of the awareness furnished by this 'analytic' is only to deliver the interpreter from any kind of 'hermeneutical millenarianism' – the illusion of having exhausted, or of even being able to exhaust, the signification of the positivity of faith.

Sense arises in the interstices of the relationship between the twin poles of the decoding process. Sense cannot be seen directly. It can be seen only out of the corner of the eye when the pupil is focusing on its sign.

Thus the hermeneutic circle functions subject to the following restrictions: (1) meaning cannot be fixed once and for all; but (2) neither can meaning be random.

In principle, hermeneutic technique has the capacity to fix the spatial limits of the appearance of meaning or sense. There are incompatibilities, impossibilities – in a word, thresholds impossible to cross.

At the same time, however, hermeneutic alone, with its own tools, however perfected these may be, is incapable of deciding what the 'right' meaning is. At this point, an act of creation is performed: a *Sinngebung.* For the 'bestowal of meaning' is not to be understood as capricious invention, but as a decision and determination of meaning in the space that 'hermeneutic reason' has opened and circumscribed.

This is what occurs, for example, in the relationship between scripture and the reading community. This relationship must be conceived as one of *communication.* Scripture evokes an appeal, an invitation, a provocation, an interrogation. Its text is persuasive. It persuades acceptance, openness, availability. But there remains the task of the one invited – personal response. For meaning is realized only in and by response. Further: it is only in concrete life that meaning unfolds, and 'comes to itself.' And here hermeneutics flowers into ethics.

Thus there is no escaping the fact that all interpretation is innovative, more or less arbitrary, and always personal – without, however, the necessary exclusion of the contraries of these qualifications.

Here, then, in strokes that are still abstract, and perhaps individualistic, I have set forth the lines of a general hermeneutics, drawn from the notion of the 'circle,' and developed especially with an eye to biblical reading.

## A HERMENEUTICS FOR THEOLOGY OF THE POLITICAL: POSSIBILITY AND NECESSITY

I have now set forth the principles of interpretation of Christian writings – principles located within the force field of hermeneutic circularity. We have seen that this circle is of such a nature as to be able to include historical currency. Let us now take the present, the political present, expressly as the term of hermeneutics.

What are the implications of reading Christian writings from a point of departure in a determinate political situation? What exactly does it mean to define theology as a 'reading of the praxis of Christians in the light of God's word'?

In order to respond to questions of this kind, we shall have to transcend the phase of a simple posing of the problem and move into the area of propositions and hypotheses – to the extent of our means and capabilities, of course.

The questions just posed can be rephrased: How may we establish a hermeneutic mediation for a theology of the political?

First, however, let me delimit the problem and its conceptualization. When I speak of 'hermeneutic mediation' here, my direct and primary intent is a hermeneutic mediation with regard to sacred scripture; secondarily, I intend Christian tradition generally, inasmuch as its texts refer to sacred scripture. It is this conjunct that I denote by the expression 'Christian writings.'

Plainly, it is impossible simply to leap with both feet into the original sense of sacred scripture. It is absolutely necessary to go by way of Christian tradition. Further, any hermeneutic practice supposes a tradition, and takes a position within the flow of that tradition. This being the case, a hermeneutic of the Bible may not neglect dogmatic tradition. Its modus operandi – the hermeneutic circle – forbids it.

It is within these parameters that hermeneutics is to be understood when hermeneutic mediation is spoken of.

Before going further into these considerations, certain difficulties arising from the nature of Christian positivity should be addressed.

Method is a function of its object. We may well ask, then, whether Christian positivity indeed lends itself to an actualizing type of interpretation, such as a theology of the political aspires to, without having its nature distorted.

There are questions that no hermeneutics worthy of the name can sidestep. Especially, in our case, there is the question of the *ephapax* (the 'one-and-only' quality) of the salvific event, with its eschatological sense of the consummation of history. And then of course there is the related question of the *clausura*, '*closure*,' of revelation.

We shall see that such difficulties become insoluble only for an immobilistic, antidialectical approach, which raises them in such a way as to falsify their terms from the outset and thus preclude a correct response.

I have asserted above that the written text remains open to future readings, and that it is illusory to think that one has direct access to the original sense of a text. This is a notion that comes to us from myth. Myth, of course, takes itself for a secret witness to the genesis of a meaning *in illo tempore*, and pretends to make present that original meaning.

What is valid for any text is all the more valid, for specific dogmatic reasons, for Christian writing. These cry out in every word for their own effacement, erasure, *Aufhebung*, sending us back to the Risen One, whose currency renders the sense of these scriptures current as well. They send us to the voice of the Spirit present in the community.

At the same time, we know very well that the writings that make up the Bible, in the phase in which we find them and in which they can be analyzed, are themselves the result of an 'updating,' a going-beyond the 'letter' in favour of a free amplification of the 'spirit.'

Revelation, of course, is never closed. But it is *canonized* – fixed as an exemplar, model, or code. *Revelation is closed only and solely in order to render possible a multiplicity of readings in later historical moments.*

The closure of scripture is a closure of its *script*-ure alone. Closure does not imply a prescriptive meaning, but only a *negative* meaning (prohibitive of a certain meaning), or at most an *inductive* ('allusive') meaning.

Strictly speaking, we ought to say that scripture is to its interpretations as a language is to its various possible discourses. 'Hermeneutic competency' is analogous to Chomsky's 'linguistic competency.' The only difference is that scripture is a code only in the form of a *paradigmatic message.* Scripture is obviously not a set of formal rules with a view to a set of virtual interpretations. Scripture appears as a model interpretation, and thus as an *interpreting interpretation*, a *norma normans ut normata.* The hermeneutic circle works from the inside out, in the sense that *this hermeneutic paradigm grows richer as such through the interpretations that it permits.* Its 'letter,' in its very unchangeability, is in some sense *further determined* by the significations that it has itself engendered. This is the very meaning of tradition. We see, then, that the 'circle' is inescapable. It reappears at every turn in the hermeneutic process.

The concept of scripture as a *norma non normata*, then, must be transcended, first of all by exegesis, inasmuch as our current exegesis takes no account of the complex archeology of scripture, and then by hermeneutics, inasmuch as our standard hermeneutics is a one-sided, dogmatic tool that kills instead of giving life.

Scripture is therefore made to be taken up and given currency, and this is a principle woven into the very writing of scripture itself. This circularity – this 'virtuous circle' – lays waste with one fell stroke the myth of a 'return to the beginnings' as a resumption of the original sense of scripture in all its morning freshness. The present is entirely in the reader's eyes. Indeed, this is why the reader does not realize it. The present is not only that which is read, it is also that *by which* the reading is done. This fact is the *condition of the possibility* of any reading, not its obstacle, as historicism, or any other type of empiricism, would have it.

The obstacle, if such there be, consists in this sort of prejudicial presupposition, which dogmatically anticipates the sense to be produced. On the other hand, presuppositions that open out upon comprehension, such as interrogation, intuition, hypothesis – resource tools that remain subject to the reading process – are presuppositions only so long as interpretation itself allows them to be. The first kind, the prejudicial kind, should be minimalized. The latter kind should be enriched to the maximum.

The primacy to be conferred on the present, with its questions about the past and its texts, must be inserted in the 'circle' in such a way that the actual density of these texts (their constrictions and their inductions) will be rigorously secured, thus avoiding all 'rerouting of scripture.' The history of Christianity is too filled with instances of an ideological and manipulative use of scripture for us to continue to be so offhanded in its regard.

Still, we must also take account of this general situation: that it is apparently impossible to install adequate theoretical precautions and sufficient technical arrangements to render a given corpus of ideas inaccessible to all 'use against nature.' Scripture is exposed to the most surprising uses. It can always become a *scriptura ex machina*, and offer excellent services as such.

But this is not an argument in favor of 'misosemy' ('hatred of [multiple] meaning'). Rather, we become persuaded of the need for a *hermeneutic watchfulness* that will be all the more on the alert. The word of God continues being what it is – a reality developing throughout history. Otherwise, a theology of the political would simply be impossible.

By this very fact, the word of God is a *historical concept*. Its objective can never be decisively determined, whether it be faith, Christ, the Father, or anything else. Scientific work on the texts is not enough.

To seek to determine *in aeternum*, the 'essence of Christianity,' or the 'essence of the faith,' or the 'essence of the church,' and so on, is to fall victim to the illusion of essentialism. Such an endeavor only succeeds in canonizing what is no more than one historical, cultural form of 'Christianity' or 'faith' or 'church.' This lack of a sense of history is actually a failing in humility. It is the sort of metaphysics that leads inevitably to inquisitorial intolerance and the spirit of domination.

Far from yielding to the tendency to control and dominate the pretended 'essence' of a text, we ought to conceptualize the text as a *spring* of meaning rather than a *cistern*, a focus of energy rather than a traffic light. The text of Christian scripture is pregnant with all the virtual senses that will come to light upon contact with historical currency. I repeat, therefore: these senses are to be taken as an integral part of the text itself, a demonstration of its kairological virtuality.

## TWO UNACCEPTABLE MODELS OF HERMENEUTIC MEDIATION

Having established the possibility of hermeneutic mediation, we must now take some steps in the direction of a concrete use of written matter, both sacred scripture and Christian writings in the broad sense.

As long as we are dealing with general prescriptions, everything seems to proceed without major difficulties. We have been moving among abstract entities – 'Christian positivity' simply, 'the' political situation, 'the Bible' as such, 'the' theology of the political, and so on. Problems begin to abound, however, from the moment the 'virtue' of these prescriptions begins to be felt – that is, when we move on to concrete determinations such as a particular Christian truth, a given political situation, or this or that biblical text. For what we are now asking is: What theology can be practised upon such and such a political situation? And this is not such an easy question.

What I am about to say has meaning only in terms of this passage from the abstract to the concrete.

At the same time, let it be noted that until now I have accorded a primacy to the relationship of faith to politics in terms of *sense*, or meaning, using the equation form, oppression = sin, or liberation = salvation. But the question of *value*, which is gathered from *sense* with a view to *action*, has scarcely been considered at all. I hope, then, that the practico-theoretical aspect of ethics and strategy will become a little clearer in the course of this section and the next.

In order to have a better circumscription of the difficult terrain over which we are moving, I shall work with some diagrams. What I need to do first, then, is to develop models. In the present section, I shall discuss an interpretation model that I shall call the 'classic model.' Actually, it is a relatively recent one – but it has become so generally used in 'political theology' that it can have this title by right. I shall make some critical observations in its regard, because, as it seems to me, it is open to criticism in its very foundations, and I shall take a moment to say why.

### The gospel/politics 'model'

But first let me quickly describe another 'model' – not really a model, because, as will be seen, it is too unnuanced to deserve prolonged consideration, but the claims that have been made for it are so strident that I have to refer to it, even if only briefly. This is the gospel/politics 'model.'

This 'model' is cast in the general mode of the relationship of 'rule to application.' But such a relationship is mechanical, automatic, and antidialectical. Here the gospel is conceived as a code of norms to be *applied*, and suddenly we are back with a 'rabbinical' conception of the gospel, with its essence as the good news completely negated, and Jesus a political *Moises Moississimus!*

Referring to this construct in terms of 'scripture/diary' or 'God's word/history' fails to confer upon it any greater heuristic and operative substantiveness. It is actually so vague and general that, in seeking to 'say it all,' it finally says absolutely nothing. It is powerless to respond to the elementary requirements of articulate theological thinking. It dismisses out of hand both the internal complexity of scripture – which requires hermeneutic mediation – and the complexity of the historical situation in which this scripture is to be 'applied' and lived – which needs socio-analytic mediation.

In terms of theoretical practice, we may well ask how a 'model' of this sort can posit a relationship between a system of biblical significations, whose consistency is at least problematic, with the continuous flow of historical events, whose unity is anything but a matter of prima facie evidence. It is easy to see how open this 'model' is to abusive, uncontrollable manipulation of the gospel, and to the 'mystification' of the political. In other words, in matters of hermeneutics, it is obliged to plunge headlong one way or the other into improvisation or positivism.

If we analyze the history of Christianity in search of lessons for our own time, we easily see that the 'model' in question can equally well be perceived as a map for social organization, or as something politically impracticable.

This vague, limp manner of positing the problem of the relationship between gospel and politics is therefore not so much to be rejected, as to be transcended – all the more so in view of the fact that this 'application model' passes over in the most complete silence the *historical context* of each of the two terms of the relationship.

### The model of 'correspondence of terms'

I now turn to the model that has become the classic one. It has the merit of being *richer* than the other, in virtue of including just what was missing before – historical context. It might be called the model of 'correspondence of terms.'

In the simplest of schematic terms, I could say that this model seeks to establish the following proportionality (see Figure 1).

*Figure 1*

$$\frac{\text{scripture}}{\text{its political context}} = \frac{\text{theology of the political}}{\text{our political context}}$$

The exodus theme has been developed similarly (see Figure 2).

*Figure 2*

$$\frac{\text{exodus}}{\text{enslavement of the Hebrews}} = \frac{\text{(theology of) liberation}}{\text{oppression of the people}}$$

More recently, liberation theology has taken up the exploration of the theme of captivity, with regard to the current, seemingly insoluble, situation in Latin America. Here is an equation for this pursuit (Figure 3).

*Figure 3*

$$\frac{\text{Babylon}}{\text{Israel}} = \frac{\text{(theology of) captivity}}{\text{people of Latin America}}$$

In conformity with an analogous schema, still another effort has been launched, this time to read the New Testament with an eye to the problem of Jesus and the politics of his time. This undertaking might be formalized in the equation in Figure 4.

*Figure 4*

$$\frac{\text{Jesus}}{\text{his political context}} = \frac{\text{Christian community}}{\text{current political context}}$$

In the model of a 'correspondence of terms,' two ratios are set up and equivalated. Then the sense of the first ratio is transferred to the second, by a sort of *hermeneutical switch*.

I shall not discuss here the various theological elaborations that have implicitly followed such a model. In my opinion, the majority of these elaborations, even apart from their contradictory findings or ideo-political position, have basically been worked out under the sign of the double correspondence I have just cited. All seek to establish an 'equal sign' between the two 'ratios,' each with its bi-level pair of terms. It seems to me that, on the level of a theology of the political, the place and function of this equal sign presents problems that call into question the validity of the model of 'correspondence of terms.'

Let us take the special case of 'Jesus and the politics of his time.' There are two extreme positions here: that of *pacifism*, advanced mainly by Oscar Cullman and Martin Hengel, and that of *zealotism*, maintained especially by Robert Eisler and S. G. F. Brandon.

To my view, both positions have been conditioned by the political situation of the historical moment in which they have been developed. True, each set of investigations appears to bracket its respective political situation. Their conclusions, however, or their manner of evaluating them, show that this is not exactly the case. At all events, each reading assumes an undeniable parallel between its respective 'ratios': if Jesus can really be shown to have been a Zealot, the

Christian participation in a revolutionary process is justified; if, on the contrary, he can be shown to have been an out-and-out pacifist, then 'revolutionary Christianity' does not have a leg to stand on. Let it be noted, however, that in either case the mode of inference, in terms of 'political theology,' is the same: it is based on a parallelism model, or better, that of a 'correspondence of terms.'

My hypothesis, therefore, is that the substance of the exegetical and theological discussions provoked by these studies has not really been of the order of *historical cognition*, but rather of the order of the *political results* that might be obtained in terms of Christian social behavior.

I think that my hypothesis gains further credit from the fact that this polemical situation has been implicitly or explicitly supported by the 'evident' correspondence between the situation at the time of Jesus and that of the critical period of the moment, especially at certain moments (as in World War II, or the upheavals of the 1960s) and in certain countries (such as Germany or the Third World).

Here are some of the summary parallels that have been drawn to support the model in question:

| Roman power | = imperialism |
|---|---|
| Sadducees' power | = power of dependent bourgeoisies |
| Zealots | = revolutionaries |
| Jewish people | = oppressed peoples |
| Jesus | = Christians |

And the list could be lengthened.

This type of correlation seems to me problematic and vulnerable in the extreme. I shall now raise certain questions with respect to this model, with the objective of preparing to propose an alternative.

## Questions leveled at the 'correspondence of terms' model

*As to the figure of Jesus*

Has due consideration been given to the singularity of Jesus' earthly career – to the special character of his human, historical destiny?

Have the historical, cultural, political, ideological, and especially religious conditions (for example, the influence of apocalypticism) influencing Jesus been respected?

What might have been the degree of politicization of Jesus' human consciousness?

Was the political context in which Jesus lived really as much like ours as would at first appear?

Has the figure of Jesus not perhaps been taken in a mythical, ahistorical way?

*As to the type of relationship between Jesus' political stance and ours*

Does the model of 'correspondence of terms' not perhaps suppose that Jesus is the 'model' for Christians in the sense of an example to copy in every last detail?

Can a model of political conduct valid for today be deduced exclusively from an analysis of Jesus' political conduct?

Supposing that it could be shown, incontestably, that Jesus was indeed a revolutionary – will this, simply of itself, legitimate participation by Christians in a revolutionary process?

Supposing, instead, that it could be clearly shown that Jesus positively renounced all recourse to violence – as would appear to have been the case – will this fact alone make all recourse to violence on the part of the Christian 'nonevangelical'?

Finally, supposing that it might be shown (as the 'eschatological school' claims to have done) that Jesus had no interest in politics whatever – would this constitute a motive for the Christian to do exactly the same at all times and in all places?

*As to the basis of the model in question*

Is the comportment of Christians linked to the behavior, teachings, examples, and occurrences found in the Bible in such a way that there must be, as it were, a 'term-for-term' correspondence between the Bible and the situation in which Christians live?

Has due consideration been accorded the extreme complexity of our society, and the degree of development of political awareness to which we have attained, on the level of analysis and on the level of ideology, during the twenty centuries that separate us from the gospel events?

Can our political context be so closely identified, thematically, with the political contexts of the Bible that resemble them, that we should read 'oppression' for 'Egypt,' 'liberation' for 'exodus,' and 'political assassination' for 'cross'?

Will the correlation that this model attempts to posit be a sufficient criterion for the selection of biblical passages that can be inserted into the relationship laid down?

Will it be necessary to prescribe a precise relationship between such and such a pericope from the gospels and such and such a political fact of our history, or again a particular event and such and such a political text? Will such a one-for-one correspondence be the sine qua non of the functioning of the proportionality?

These questions show the direction I would take in criticism of the model of 'correspondence of terms.'

## ALTERNATIVE MODEL: CORRESPONDENCE OF RELATIONSHIPS

The alternative model that I here seek to present is suggested both by the hermeneutic practice of the primitive or apostolic church and by that of Christian communities generally.

A number of writings of the primitive church came to constitute the canon of Christian faith, or foundational message of Christianity. The work of the *Formgeschichte* and the *Redaktionsgeschichte* schools has taught us that the biblical writings, in their final form, are the result of the superimposition of successive redactional layers – a fact that introduces a distance between the texts as actually presented and the *ipsissima verba Jesu* in consequence of the concrete situations and needs of the various Christian communities, or what is customarily called the *Sitz im Leben* of these texts.

Further, we know that these texts, once they had been fixed, kept on being lived and commented upon by Christian communities, and that this is a phenomenon that continued down to our own day. In fact, this is precisely what constitutes the work of tradition.

We realize, then, that there are at least two great phenomena separating us from the original deeds of Jesus, in the very act of bringing us in contact with them: the Christian scriptures, and the tradition of the faith.

That the very text of the gospel constitutes the product of a tradition – that is, that it is the result of a labor of reading on the part of the primitive community – is a datum that, although not written into the gospel text itself in just these terms, is nevertheless the *external vehicle* of the gospel message, and this in its entirety. Besides its considerable dogmatic importance, therefore – with respect to the value of tradition, the authenticity of the church, the role of the Apostles, and so on – this fact has a very special hermeneutic scope all its own, and this is the aspect that is of interest to me here.

This hermeneutic scope can be represented in the model depicted in Figure 5.

*Figure 5* '*Correspondence of relationship' model*

$$\frac{\text{Jesus of Nazareth}}{\text{his context}} = \frac{\text{Christ + the church}}{\text{context of the church}} = \frac{\text{church tradition}}{\text{historical context}} = \frac{\text{ourselves (a theology of the political)}}{\text{our context}}$$

reduced: $\dfrac{\text{scripture}}{\text{its context}} = \dfrac{\text{ourselves (a theology of the political)}}{\text{our context}}$

Let me explain the relationships operative in this model. The model itself takes its inspiration especially from the manner in which the primitive church understood, interpreted, and committed to writing Jesus' original words and deeds. Hence the towering interest of the work of exegesis, which permits us to adopt, with respect to scripture, an attitude analogous to that of the first community with respect to the words and behavior of Jesus of Nazareth. Their attitude was one of creative fidelity – as they attributed to Jesus even later developments undergone by his message and work, based on the identity of the Christ of glory with the historical Jesus.

Provided, therefore, that they be accompanied by a hermeneutic concern giving priority to questions of the historical present, studies of the 'form history' type can help us to reconstitute the articulation represented by the first two ratios in the model (Figure 5). This articulation could then serve as a hermeneutic model for us today in our use of scripture.

Moving on to the third ratio – representing the relationship between church tradition and historical context – the articulation between the first and second ratio is repeated between the second and third – that is, between scripture and the later tradition of the church. This, by the way, is easily recognized as something that happens in current, indeed daily, *hermeneutic practice* of Christian communities. This hermeneutic practice is expressed in homilies, catechesis, liturgy, and other discursive or symbolic practices, even with little or no explicit intent.

This brings me to the second point of reference in my attempts to draw up an alternative model – in my attempt to 'solve the equation' in Figure 5. What do we observe in the ongoing hermeneutic practice in our communities? We observe that Christian communities seek to 'apply' the gospel to their particular situation, just as the primitive community sought to do. We further observe that, in this effort, both the text, and the situation to which they are to be 'applied,' are taken *in their respective autonomy*.

At the same time, for an ordinary hermeneutic, the 'transposition of sense' from text to life proceeds in spontaneous fashion, so that, even when the 'application' becomes difficult, the *need* for the 'application' is always felt by Christian communities as normal. As a consequence, here too, as for the primitive community, a kind of creative fidelity reigns, with the result that a genuine 'spiritual sense' continues in substantial identity in the most diverse experiential contexts. Perhaps this is the 'spirit' of the gospel. It is not meaningless, then, for these communities to call these 'applications' – as they do so call them – 'word of God,' or 'message of salvation,' or the like. Thus, meaning transpires, 'comes to light,' in historical currency, through and beyond the letter of the text of the past.

To be sure, a hermeneutic practice of this type has been and continues to be subjected to abuses. But this cannot constitute a motive for its abandonment. On the contrary, it constitutes an invitation, and a challenge. This hermeneutic practice must become the subject of greater theoretical interest, with the objective of furnishing it with the tools that will enable it to overcome these abuses.

At all events, the effort of the church community to be faithful to the gospel in a diversity of historical situations indicates that a *basic identity of significations* obtains throughout the successive readings. It is this identity that I represent by the equal sign (=). The sign does not designate an equality between *terms* of the hermeneutic equation, but precisely between the respective *relationships* between pairs of terms. The equal sign refers neither to the oral, nor to the textual, nor to the transmitted words of the message, nor even to the situations that correspond to them. It refers to the relationship between them.

We are dealing with a *relationship of relationships* (see Figure 6).

*Figure 6*

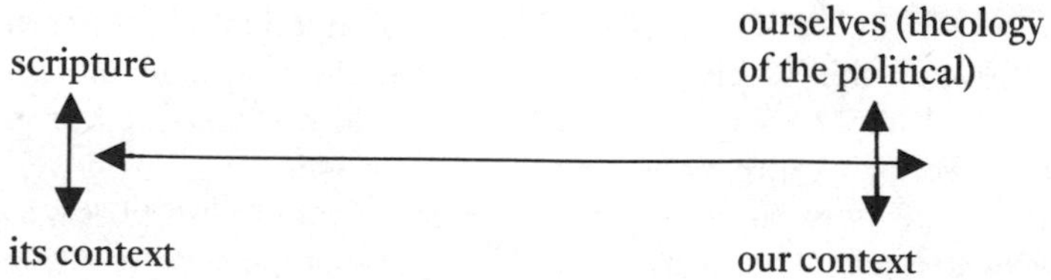

An identity of senses, then, is not to be sought on the level of context, nor, consequently, on the level of the message as such – but rather on the level of the *relationship* between context and message on each side respectively. It is this homological relationship that is the vehicle of sense. It is this relationship that produces a 'homosemy,' by virtue of serving as the vehicle of the same 'spiritual' sense. This is why I have called the model the 'correspondence of relationships' model.

The key element in this model, then, is not this or that particular text of scripture, in correspondence with such and such a precise situation. Still less is it a number of texts to be produced with a view to this or that particular behavior, or this or that particular meaning. The key element here is the global, and at the same time particular, 'spirit.' This 'spirit' may, of course, lead to the selection of a particular passage from scripture – but without invoking a correspondence of terms, or a fortiori, a relationship of application. These two models, as we have seen, are insufficiently flexible to effectuate an adequate articulation.

It seems to me that the basic hermeneutical principle called the 'analogy of faith,' or 'principle of totality,' or even 'canon of the canon,' functions and can only function along the lines of the correspondence of relationships model.

We need not, then, look for formulas to 'copy,' or techniques to 'apply,' from scripture. What scripture will offer us are rather something like orientations, models, types, directives, principles, inspirations – elements permitting us to acquire, on our own initiative, a 'hermeneutic competency,' and thus the capacity to judge – on our own initiative, in our own right – 'according to the mind of Christ,' or 'according to the Spirit,' the new, unpredictable situations with which we are continually confronted. The Christian writings offer us not a *what*, but a *how* – a manner, a style, a spirit.

Such a hermeneutic comportment is equidistant from a metaphysics of meaning (positivism) and a surfeit of meanings (improvisation *ad libitum*). It lets the hermeneutic circle have free play, which is the only way to arouse meaning.

After all, the hermeneutical equation I have drawn does not 'travel a one-way street,' or 'read from left to right,' from scripture to ourselves. The relationship is circular, like any genuine hermeneutic relationship. I might speak, then, of a 'dialectical hermeneutic,' or vice versa – were the expressions not indeed pleonastic.

But, once more: this circularity functions within an *articulation with a dominant term*. The thrust of the dialectic–hermeneutic movement comes from *scripture* and is measured, in the last instance, upon scripture as *norma normans*.

At thus juncture, let me return to the familiar model of theoretical practice, which I may seem to have allowed to fall by the wayside, in favor of other models. In fact, however, these other models have been no more than concretizations of the other, more basic one.

The first term of my equation (Figure 5, reduced) – scripture/its context – occupies the position of a second generality (as hermeneutic mediation), whereas the second term – a theology of the political/our context – holds partly the place of a first generality (in socio-analytic mediation) and partly that of a third generality with respect to the first of its elements (a theology of the political to be produced).

This, then, is the functioning of theological in the production of meaning. But there has never been, nor will there ever be, a *historical* effectuation of a so-called *sensus plenior*. This is the preserve of the eschatological. What we have is a 'plentifying' sense, a fulfilling sense, a development of unfolding of meaning – at best, because there is nothing to prevent a 'repression' of sense, either.

In any case, the advantages of hermeneutical dialectic scarcely dispense one from pursuing normal investigations and applying classic techniques, with all their advantages (material means, team or joint research, and the like). At the same time, the functioning of hermeneutical dialectic implies a 'pneumatic' reading of scripture, consisting in the agent's compenetration with the meaning that informs scripture, and a sustained familiarity with the word dwelling in it – whose enigmatic syntax is anything but connatural with our own at first.

# TWO ATTITUDES TOWARD HERMENEUTIC PRACTICE

A correct articulation between scripture and a given human situation – in other words, the correct relationship of hermeneutic mediation with socio-analytic mediation – cannot be constructed on the model of a correspondence of terms, so that our relationship to politics would be parallel to Jesus' relationship to the politics of his time, or so that our relationship to an oppressive power would correspond to the relationship of the Hebrews to the pharaoh's slaveholding regime. And so I have given methodological indications for an alternative model, which I have defined as a 'relationship of relationships' obtaining between the terms of a hermeneutic equation and bearing upon the 'homosemy' or 'pneumatic sense' of scripture in terms of a determinate situation.

For the sake of even more concreteness, I here suggest two basic attitudes of guidance in the solution of the hermeneutic question.

## Priority of the Christian community

*Priority is to be accorded to the value of the real practice of the community over that of any theoretical elaboration.*

The 'political theologian' should be more alert to what is occurring in the community and in society in general than to the past meaning of the pages of scripture. For this theologian, it is more important to theorize 'what the Spirit says in the churches' than to apprehend what the Spirit said 'once upon a time.'

To be sure, theologians cannot do this without having recourse to scripture itself – to the thesaurus of the principles of their theoretical practice. At the same time, this undertaking, in its very roots, is charged with the intent to decipher the historical *present* – to read *kata graphas*, and not the *graphai* as such. Indeed, this is how the church of the New Testament acted with respect to the Old Testament. We can speak, then, with all justice, of the 'hermeneutic value of the work of the Holy Spirit.'

As a consequence, the theoretical solution sought by the 'political theologian' for a determinate situation is in some sort already given in the actual practice of Christians, who, like other human beings, endeavor to bring an adequate solution to the problems with which they find themselves confronted. The theologian need only take account, in the element of theory, of the solutions already in process in the element of practice. These questions have been 'solved' by an analysis of the de facto practices of Christians, who, of course, do not wait upon the verdict of the theologian in order to set to work.

Then, too: even the most cursory glance at history will show from what direction the Holy Spirit comes. Without any doubt, the Spirit comes from the direction of Christian (and other christic) practices, and not – at least not principally – from that of theological research, however serious this research may be. And even if such practices are contradictory, their real object – God's salvation – continues to operate in history, thanks simply to not being tied to theology.

This is valid, I should be careful to note, not as a methodological principle, but as a basic directive, or fundamental orientation, on the level of the *attitude of mind* accompanying hermeneutic practice. The priority of practice is a practical, not a theoretical, priority. Therefore, it is not and cannot be a principle of theory, governing the theological process. Indeed, when theologians undertake to theologize the consciousness and practice of the community, they obey only the norms of theological practice – norms that, after all, exist in virtue of a 'breach' with those of the spontaneous language of this same community, as I have stated and demonstrated.

I must admit, however, that the word of revelation is bestowed upon believers in its immediacy in virtue precisely of the presence of the presence of the risen Christ, and of the ever living word of his gospel. The awareness, especially the theoretical awareness, of this practical fact is only a second phenomenon (not, of course, a secondary one).

This observation supposes, and simultaneously demands, that theologians work in close relationship with their own local community. They should live its concrete life in concrete political terms. It is their office to fashion its theory.


## Pursuit of hermeneutic prowess

*The relationship with scripture, and with Christian positivity in general, ought to tend more to the acquisition of a hermeneutic* habitus *than to immediate practical applications.*

Here I call for a hermeneutic *habitus* – prowess, skill – paralleling the socio-analytic *habitus* of socio-analytic mediation.

Thus exegetical studies, meditation, or the reading of scripture and the Christian fonts, cannot be conducted with an exclusive view to concerns of immediate, practical application, or with a direct view to a repertory of defined problems. Otherwise, there lurks the danger of one or the other of two extremes – improvisation *ad libitum* or hermeneutic positivism.

At the same time, one may legitimately search out, for purposes of a general directive, texts that clearly manifest a strict or proximate relationship with the situation in question. But this is as far as it is legitimate to go in the direction of a one-to-one correspondence; nor may these particular applications be invoked as incontestable in the face of other interpretations. It may be that we should admit, as a principle of hermeneutic practice, a basic suspicion when it comes to parallels between the Bible and politics that are too obvious and too facile. Such parallels are often deceptive, and fail to reflect the thematic unities of the Bible. As I have said, the Bible must always be taken as a complex hermeneutic totality, and the same thing applies to the body of the other Christian writings, the writings of tradition.

Reference to scripture should be by way of *creative* memory, and the readings of scripture should be a *productive* reading. Instead of being a technical relationship of application, reference to scripture should, at bottom, be a *pedagogical* relationship, in the sense of having the purpose of forming in the community the *nous Christou* (1 Cor. 2.16), or the *diakrisis pneumaton* (1 Cor. 12.10).

In any case, Christian consciousness – that vital element of theology – can be maintained as such only if it is steeped in the *memoria Jesu*, if it is activated by his 'dangerous memory.'

Further: the toil of exegesis, the inquiries of history, and the investigation of Christian fonts generally, must continue, if we are to guarantee theology an *objective basis* in hermeneutic mediation. This is all that these efforts can furnish, but it is a great deal. For want of this secure base, the Christian corpus risks becoming a kind of cafeteria, where everyone can find something or other to suit her or his particular taste. There are limits within which theology must keep lest it seek to be 'anything and everything.'

And yet, a theology of the political cannot rest content with registering, or simply gathering, the results of such studies, or with broadening their conclusions and nothing more. It must actually produce the relationship (third generality: a theology of the political) of the concrete situation in question (first generality: socio-analytic mediation) to the content that these studies disengage (second generality: hermeneutic mediation).

Theologians can never be completely equal to their task. Their office is that of setting in confrontation, in the field of the *logos*, the positivity of faith and the course of the world. After they have exercised this office, they shall have to make their own the words spoken by Jesus: 'We are useless servants. We have done no more than our duty' (Luke 17.10).

## A SELECT BIBLIOGRAPHY

The copious notes of the original article have been omitted; appended below is the list of books to which Boff refers, citing only the theological works published in England or the United States.

Belo, F., *A Materialist Reading of the Gospel of Mark* (Maryknoll, NY, Orbis Books, 1981).

Brandon, S. G. F., *Jesus and the Zealots* (Manchester, Manchester University Press, 1967).

Brandon, S. G. F., *The Trail of Jesus of Nazareth* (New York, Stein & Day, 1968).

Bultmann, R., *Jesus and the Word* (New York, Scribner's, 1962).

Bultmann, R., *Faith and Understanding* (New York, Harper & Row, 1969; London, SCM Press, 1969).

Bultmann, R., *Theology of New Testament*, vols 1 and 2 (New York, Scribner's, 1970; London, SCM Press, 1952 and 1955).

Cullmann, O., *Jesus and the Revolutionaries* (New York, Harper & Row, 1970).

Gadamer, H. G., *Truth and Method* (New York, Seabury Press, 1975).

Heidegger, M., *Basic Writings* (New York/London, Harper & Row, 1977).

Heidegger, M., *Being and Time* (New York, Harper & Row, 1962).

Hengel, M., *Was Jesus a Revolutionist?* (Philadelphia, Fortress Press, 1971).

Marle, R., *Introduction to Hermeneutics* (New York, Herder & Herder, 1967).

Moltmann, J., *The Crucified God* (New York, Harper & Row, 1974; London, SCM Press, 1974).

Ricoeur, P., *Freud and Philosophy: An Essay on Interpretation* (New Haven/London, Yale University Press, 1970).

Ricoeur, P., *The Conflict of Interpretations: Essays in Hermeneutics* (Evanston, Northwestern University Press, 1974).

Robinson, J. M., and Cobb, J. B. Jr (eds), *The New Hermeneutic* (New York, Harper & Row, 1964).

Von Rad, G., *Old Testament Theology*, vol. 1: *Theology of Israel's Historical Traditions*, and vol. 2: *The Theology of Israel's Prophetic Traditions* (New York, Harper & Row, 1962 and 1965; Edinburgh, Oliver & Boyd, 1962 and 1965).

# 3

# The Asian Context:
# Sources and Trends

## STANLEY J. SAMARTHA

---

In a multi-religious continent like Asia, where each religious community has its own sacred scripture, any claim for the supreme authority of one scriptural text is bound to face claims and counter-claims. Samartha's contention is that, in the face of such claims, the task of hermeneutics is to work out a larger framework of neighbourly relationships within which the insights of different sacred texts can be related to each other for mutual enrichment, without denying their particularities.

This essay is from the author's *The Search for New Hermeneutic in Asian Christian Theology* (Madras, The Christian Literature Society, 1987), pp. 1–14 and 45–50.

Stanley J. Samartha, an Indian, was a former Director of the Dialogue Programme of the World Council of Churches, Geneva. He has published extensively on inter-faith matters.

---

The quest for new ways to interpret the Bible is an important part of Asian Christian Theology. To claim that 'a new hermeneutics' is emerging in Asia today may be to say both too much and too little. Too much, because if one uses the criteria taken from the history of Biblical criticism in the West there is little 'systematic' effort to expound principles of interpretation. Too little, because, if one takes into account not only the limitations in human resources but also the fact that among cultures and religions going back to several thousands of years Christianity is very much a late arrival in Asia, the insights that one discovers in the Asian scene are by no means insignificant. During the last two decades, although 'hermeneutics' as such has not received sustained attention by Asian theologians and Biblical scholars, there are enough hints that help to shape a new framework in which fresh discussions could take place in the coming years.

# I

There are several reasons why this hermeneutical task is important to the life of the churches in Asia. The most obvious, but not the most important reason, is the need to avoid dependence on sources of authority outside Asia. This desire to build methods of interpreting the Bible from within the cultural context of Asia is not a manifestation of misplaced nationalistic zeal. Two thousand years of Christian heritage of the West and the enormous contribution of Western Christian scholars to theological reflection cannot and should not be dismissed as of no consequence to the growing life of the churches in Asia. To do so for any reason is to repudiate our citizenship responsibilities in the household of God. Therefore this quest is not in a spirit of unwillingness to learn from insights gained by others living in different areas of the *oikoumene*. It is a sign of growth in maturity. The shifting sands of Biblical criticism in Europe have proved undependable foundations for theology even in the West. Why should churches in Asia be bound to them? There are Western scholars themselves who feel that historical criticism of the Bible, seeking to uncover 'the immersion of Biblical texts in the myriad contingencies of history has now come to the end of its usefulness to theology'.[1] Every time a Biblical scholar in Europe sneezes theologians in Asia should not catch a cold and manifest the symptoms all over the footnotes! To depend on rules of interpretation developed in countries alien to Asian life is a hindrance to the Church's growth in maturity. It reduces our credibility, diminishes our spirit, and distorts the universality of Jesus Christ to whom the scriptures bear witness.

Further, the life of the people in Asia has been nourished for a few thousand years by the scriptures of other religions. The Hindus have their *prasthānatrayā* (triple canon) of the *Upanishads*, *Brahmasūtra* and the *Bhagavadgītā*. The Buddhists have the *tripitaka* (the three baskets of the canon), the Chinese have their classics of Confucianism and Taoism. Over and over again in the history of Asian people where powerful renewal movements emerged somehow they have been nourished by profound reinterpretations of their scriptures. It is the *Bhāṣyas* (commentaries) that have pointed out new directions to the *Sampradāyas* (ways, traditions, movements) in India. Sankara and Ramanuja did not write treatises on theology, but commentaries on the triple canon, bringing out fresh meanings out of the texts. During more recent times Radhakrishnan (1888–1975), the Indian philosopher president, in addition to his other works, produced his own translations and commentaries on the *Upanishads*, and *Brahma Sūtra* and the *Bhagavadgītā*. During the days of India's freedom struggle almost every Hindu nationalist leader – Tilak, Bhave, Gandhi and many others – wrote commentaries on the *Bhagavadgītā*. In fact, the *Gītā* became the gospel of action supporting a *dharma yuddha* (righteous war) against the British. One must also add to these the vast number of books on the *Gītā* in Indian languages inaccessible to those who use only English.

During nearly a thousand years of Muslim presence in India, Pakistan and Bangladesh, Muslim scholars of the *Qur'an* have produced important volumes on the interpretation and exposition of texts. Over the years these scholars have gained a reputation in the world of Islam that gives them recognition for their distinctive hermeneutic contribution of the *Qur'an*. In Indonesia too, which has the largest Muslim population in the world, works on the *Qur'an* have continued to nourish the lives of Muslims over the centuries. Perhaps one should note that Islam, as a religion belonging to the Semitic family, is different in its approach to hermeneutics than the ancient religions of India and China.

Without sufficient information it is difficult to make convincing observations about the religious situation in China. But there is no reason to believe that in spite of decades of Maoist ideology the classics of Confucianism, Taoism and Buddhism have lost their hold on the hearts and minds of people. Confucius (born 551 BC) deeply influenced the life and thought of the Chinese as a transmitter, teacher, and creative interpreter of ancient culture and literature. The Confucian classics, including the *Analects*, 'are not the canon of a particular sect but the literary heritage of a whole people'.[2] The book *Lao Tzu*, translated into English as *I Ching*, the Book of Changes, goes back to the third century BC and is the foundation of Taoism. Although little is known of the two fathers of the Sect, Lao Tzu and Chung Tzu, what is important is the book which is 'one of the shortest, most provocative, and inspired works in all Chinese literature . . . the quietism, mysticism, and the love of paradox that distinguish this work probably represent very old strains in Chinese thought. . . .'[3]

Buddhism originated in India but in terms of its influence in China and Japan the Lotus school is important. It is based on a text from North India, the *Saddharma Pundarīka* or the *Lotus of the Good Law*. It is the interpretation given to this text by the great Chinese monk Chih k'ai (or Chih-i, AD 538–97) that forms the basis of this school. He lectured for years on its written text, 'minutely examining every detail of language and subtlety of meaning, and giving special attention to the methods of religious practice embodied in the *Lotus*'.[4] In recent years the *Rissho-kosei kai*, one of the most powerful new religious movements in Japan, is based on the *Lotus*, and a number of commentaries on it have been published recently in Japanese and in English.

What is the relevance of all this to a Christian quest for hermeneutics in Asia? There are at least two considerations which Christians cannot ignore so easily as they seem to have done so far. One is the long and persistent attention given to the study of scriptures in the *original* languages, the meticulous attention given to texts, their interpretation in particular contexts, and the exposition of meanings (*artha, tātparya*) in the life of the people. Scholarly works have not been rejected. They have been 'popular' in the sense that for long centuries they have influenced the view of life and the way of life of societies in the midst of which they emerged. The time span involved is not the lifetime of a few individual expositors, or even a couple of generations or 'a period' in history arbitrarily determined by certain happenings. It is the long-range view, the continuing stream of life, the horizon of time receding to infinity.

Second, Christians must recognise that our neighbours of other faiths in Asia, whether it is our Hindu and Buddhist neighbours in India or our Confucian, Taoist and Buddhist neighbours in China, have developed their own distinctive hermeneutics in their own setting and without depending on external sources. The question of 'foreign' influence was raised in China many centuries ago. One of the frequent objections raised by Confucianists and Taoists against Buddhism was: why should a Chinese allow himself to be influenced by Indian ways? Chinese Buddhists answered this question in various ways. Mou Tzu said, 'If a gentleman-scholar dwells in their midst, what business can there be among them? ... According to the Buddhist scriptures, above, below and all around, all beings containing blood belong to the Buddhist clan. Therefore I revere and study these scriptures. Why should I reject the way of Yao, Shan, Confucius, and the Duke of Chou? Gold and jade do not harm each other. Crystal and amber do not cheapen each other. You say that another is in error when it is you yourself who err'.[5]

According to official tradition, Buddhism reached China from India in the first century AD. In spite of Chinese aversion to foreign languages, Buddhist texts were translated into Chinese. The book

*Disposition of Error*, or *Li-hoc-lun* as it is known in Chinese, written probably AD 420–587, appears to be an apologia for Buddhism. 'The author takes the stand that there is no fundamental conflict between the Chinese and Buddhist ways of life and that the great truths of Buddhism are preached in somewhat different languages, by Confucianism and Taoism as well'.[6] Since Christians cannot, and should not, opt out of the cultural streams of Asia of which they are a part, it is necessary to remember that 'hermeneutics' as a disciplined study and interpretation of scriptures is neither recent in Asia nor the monopoly of Western Biblical scholars. Obviously, Christians in Asia cannot ignore this heritage. But whether it does or should influence the Asian Christian quest for new hermeneutics, and, if so, in what ways, are questions to which answers need to be sought in the coming years.

There is a deeper reason, however, why a Christian hermeneutics in Asia needs to develop its own distinctive character and direction. If one considers the long histories and the abiding influences of Hindu, Buddhist, Confucian and Taoist attitudes to their respective scriptures, one striking feature emerges. The basic question here is not so much about rules of interpretation as the perception of Truth or *Sat* or Reality or *Dharma* or the Tao itself. How is Reality to be perceived is a concern prior to the question, what are the rules of interpreting the scriptures which point to or explain or communicate the experience of that Reality? To the Hindu *Śruti*, that which is heard is prior to and more authoritative than *Smriti*, that which is remembered and written. The perception of Truth through *Anubhava*, inadequately translated as 'intuition' or 'experience', is basic to any knowledge to which the scriptures bear witness. The Sanskrit word for 'word' is *Śabda* (from which is derived *Śabda pramāṇa*, one of the three Hindu criteria for interpretation) means both *sound*- that which is *heard*- and *word*- that which conveys *meaning*. Thus by instantly attracting one's attention through hearing and in communicating a particular meaning through words, a relationship is established between the source of the word and word itself. In the sacred syllable *AUM* the *sound* produced by uttering it is as important, if not more, than the word itself. It overcomes the dichotomy between the knower and the known between the subject and the object. Communication therefore becomes communion. 'He who knows the Brahman becomes the Brahman'.[7]

Confucius speaks of one unitary principle that runs through everything (*Analecta*, IV, 15; XV, 2). The teaching of *Lao Tzu* is based upon the way of Tao, the one great underlying principle which is 'the source of all being which must remain essentially indescribable and known only through a kind of mystic intuition'. 'The Tao that can be told of is not the eternal Tao; the name that can be named is not the eternal name. . . . It is the Mystery of all mysteries! The door of all subtleties.'[8] The 'uncarved block' is a favourite figure in Taoism which refers to the original state of complete simplicity which is its highest ideal. *Lao Tzu* says, 'Truly a great cutter does not cut.'[9] There is an underlying mood or feeling or attitude which recognises that true knowledge (*Satyasya Satvam* – the truth of the truth, *Brihad.* I, 16) is not a matter of exegesis of scriptures in accordance with rules of interpretation, although these are recognised as important. True knowledge is a transformation of the knowing subject. *Tarka* (logic) does not lead to truth. It is the person whose mind is purified through discipline who can *hear* or *see* the Truth. In spite of all the traditions of scriptural interpretation developed with meticulous care over the centuries in India, China, Sri Lanka and other countries of Asia, one essential point is constantly affirmed, namely, that no hermeneutics by itself will yield truth in its fullness without purification of the mind, transformation of the heart and discipline of the body.

## II

The sources where one recognises hints and suggestions for Biblical interpretation in Asia are many. That in spite of the diversity and complexity of Asian countries and people, one can still talk about an 'Asianness' and therefore of *Asian* Christian theology is now recognised, and need not be further debated here. 'When Asian Christians theologise as part of the Universal Church responding to its situation in Asia, there is a contribution to Christian theology which may rightly be called Asian theology.'[10] Quite a bit of Christian reflection is going on in the three distinctive areas of Asia, the North East, comprising of Korea, Japan and the Philippines, the South East with countries like Singapore, Indonesia, Thailand and Burma, and the South with India, Sri Lanka, Burma, Pakistan and Bangladesh. There are many journals which publish articles by individual thinkers. There are national and regional consultations and conferences of which Bible studies form an important part. There are associations of theological schools which from time to time focus disciplined attention on how to teach the

Bible. The Christian Conference of Asia holds conferences and consultations strongly supported by careful Bible studies.

In addition, one should look for Asian Christian contributions in the conferences of the Ecumenical Association of Third World Theologians (EATWOT) and in the larger ecumenical world gatherings. There are theological works by Roman Catholic, Orthodox and Protestant authors which provide important sources for this enquiry. Looking at the limitations of resources, and recognising the difficulties in writing and publishing in Asia compared with the ease and facility with which it is done in the West, one is struck by the volume and variety of Asian Christian writing. Never, indeed, was so much produced by so many in so short a time and with so little resources! Some of these are repetitive; some imitations; some passing fancies; some dead ends; but some however, are significant contributions that are important for their boldness and imagination. The suggestions they contain and the directions they point to invite careful attention and critical reflection.

Certain tendencies in Biblical interpretation in Asia can be identified. One starts by affirming that the Bible is the only source of authority. The life situations to which the Bible addresses itself are accepted as pretty much the same as now because, it is claimed, human nature does not change, and that therefore the texts of the Bible provide guidance for all people at all times. One should be careful not to caricature this position, but it is necessary to indicate that this view which accepts verbal inspiration of the scripture and the literal meaning of texts is not particularly Asian, either in its origin or in its application. There is the strong call for Asian theology 'to be biblically based' because the Bible, it is claimed, is the *only* written witness to God's deeds in history.[11] It is claimed further that because the context and background of Biblical times are very similar to life situations in Asia today, 'Asians are in a better position than those in the West to develop biblical scholarships'.[12] Moreover, on the basis of what the Bible says on Israel's relation to the surrouding people and their culture, one should look to the Bible for guidance to shape indigenous expressions of thought. Describing the use of the Bible in developing a people's theology (Minjung) in Korea, Kim Yong Bok points out that Biblical resources such as the Deuteronomic Code or the Covenant code or the message of Jesus to the oppressed people of his time help Christians today 'to approach the reality of the people in the framework of their social biography and socio-economic history'.[13] This calls for the 'lifting' of texts from Biblical contexts and placing them in contemporary situations to bring out their relevance to people today. Many other examples can be given, but the general characteristics of this approach to the Bible are clear and familiar.

It is doubtful whether this attitude would indeed help Asian Christians to develop 'their own hermeneutics'. In a continent like that of Asia a claim for the supreme authority of *one* scripture can be met by a counter claim for similar authority of *another* scripture. It does not grapple sufficiently with the question of the relation between 'words' and 'events', spoken languages and written texts, the text and what or who is behind the text. 'Biblicism' should not be equated with being 'Biblical'. Further, the notion of 'correspondence' between our situations and Biblical situations ignores the gap between 'then' and 'now' and results in alienating the text both from its own historical context and ours today. What if there are situations that obviously do *not* correspond to those in the present? Is the limited and narrow experience of Israel with the surrounding nations, for example, or just one sermon by Paul to the Athenians, sufficient ground to pass heavily negative theological judgements on neighbours of other faiths in Asia today? One gets the impression that too often the search for 'similar situations' and 'applicability' of texts reduces 'the Kerygmatic content' of the word of God to which Biblical writings bear witness.

It is impatience with this kind of literalist interpretation that has led others in Asia to take a different attitude to the Bible. There are people who maintain that the Bible is indeed one of the important sources of authority for Christians, not just in Asia but everywhere. But this should not be regarded as a *formal* authority. It is not enough to say that the Bible is authoritative; it must *become* authoritative to us in our life as we grapple with our problems today. The situations in Biblical times are indeed important, but human limitations make it difficult to reconstruct them in any degree of accuracy. What we should look for is not so much correspondence between situations but the meaning of texts to us now. The Bible should not be treated as 'a deposit of truth' to be selectively used and applied. It should become true to us as we open ourselves and listen to the word of God. The crucial problem is how to *interpret* the text in our context. 'Hermeneutics might appear to be a catch word of the modern theological enterprise, but renewed interest in it is indicative of the fact that methods of Bible study followed in the past within the church *have become irrelevant*.'[14]

The motivation here is very clear and obvious: *how to use* the Bible for a particular purpose, namely, *Christian Social Action in India*. This governs both the selection of texts and the manner in which they are interpreted. 'When the Bible is approached with this situational urgency, as "a model of obedience", it is claimed, "the materials within it come alive, *they will become authoritative* for our life in community as much as for our personal lives'.[15] K. C. Abraham points out that 'the dynamism of Biblical insights when brought into contact with our situation can provide new directions for Christian obedience in the modern Indian context'.[16] As a mode of interpretation this view rejects verbal inspiration and biblicism, seeks no 'parallel' situations between Biblical times and ours, deliberately avoids 'spiritualisation' of texts which ignore harsh economic and political realities, and constantly emphasises the *usefulness* of the Bible for Christian social action. It results in taking up a selective view both of the Bible and of contemporary situations. Its hermeneutics is minimal. How Biblical texts *become* authoritative in a particular situation or country for a particular form of Christian action remains very largely subjective.[17]

One should be careful not to isolate and narrowly define these tendencies that emphasise either the text or the situation. In the life of the Churches in Asia, as Christians respond to the leading of the Holy Spirit, there are yet undiscovered meeting points between texts and contemporary human situations. What brings these together to make the 'word' come *alive* is not always easy to discover. Maybe a rational recognition is not necessary. Undoubtedly, the poor and the oppressed as they hear or read the Bible will respond to its message in very different ways than the rich, the powerful and the comfortable. It looks pretty obvious that both in the Old Testament and the New the poor and the oppressed are of special concern to God. In emphasising this point, most liberation theologians, however, tend to isolate this concern within the totality of the Bible. This leads to a kind of 'selection' and 'exclusivism', that is, selecting another group of people as 'the new Israel' and investing them with a theological significance that is too narrowly defined. God's *tilt* towards the poor, to which pointed attention is rightly being given as a matter of urgency today, however, should be regarded as part of God's *total* concern for the whole of humanity even as God's redeeming process of mending the broken creation goes on.

## III

The hermeneutic question may be stated thus. How can the Bible, a semitic book, formed through oral and written traditions in an entirely different geographic, historical and cultural context, appropriated and interpreted for so many centuries by the West through hermeneutic tools designed to meet different needs and shaped by different historical factors, be now interpreted in Asia by Asian Christians for their own people? It is a striking fact, but seldom recognised, that none of the revelations about which Christians in Asia theologise in the English language took place within a Western European culture or was recorded in a European language. The imposition of a foreign language on another people is a means of control and domination. Language and speech have a great deal to do with the cultural identity and spiritual freedom of a people. 'No clues are so helpful as those of language in pointing to ultimate, unconscious, psychological attitudes.'[18] Therefore the question of language, speech, writing and translations, and the manner in which Asia's own scriptures have been interpreted over the centuries, become important for Asian theologians. 'It is an ironic thing', writes Kraft, 'that the West which is most concerned with the spread of Christianity in the world today, and is financially best able to undertake the task of worldwide evangelism, is culturally least suited for its task because of the way in which it has specialised itself to a point where it is difficult for it to have an adequate understanding of other peoples'.[19] If the implications of this insight are seriously accepted both by Western and Asian scholars, then the quest for *new* hermeneutics in Asian Christian theology becomes more important and urgent.

The vast majority of people in Asia read or listen to the Bible not in the original language nor in English, but in their own languages to which the Bible has been translated. In Asia, unlike the West, the language of hermeneutics and the languages of the people are different. This creates a great gulf between interpretation and understanding. Translations seldom help people to encounter the experience and vision behind the texts. 'Anyone who has struggled with translation is made to realise that there is more to a language than its dictionary'.[20] Furthermore, since the Bible and its translations were brought to Asia by people from the West during the colonial period, this very movement has consequences for interpretation. Sociologically, what is worth careful attention is that 'each form of transport such as roads, canals, bridges, rivers and sea routes not only carries but translates and transforms the sender, the receiver and the message. The use of any kind of medium or extension of man alters the patterns of inter-dependence among people, as it alters the ratios among our senses'.[21] People in Asia are conscious of the fact that the Bible and the *Qur'an* are 'foreign' books in the sense that unlike the scriptures of Hinduism and Buddhism or Taoism they were brought into the country from outside. The bridge between 'outside' and 'inside' cannot be built too easily or too soon. Therefore the matter of transposition of metaphors and symbols and visions from one context to another becomes a necessity in Asia rather than the search for the exact meanings of texts. Too often the 'meaning' of a text depends not so much on the form advocated by the source as the content perceived by the receptor.

The question of translating the scriptures also becomes more than a matter of 'translation'. 'Committees' cannot translate; individuals can. Seldom have the translations of the Bible into Asian languages become part of the living culture of the people, as for example St James's version of the Bible in English or Luther's translation into German. The Hindu scriptures in India have been 'translated' into every Indian language, and over the centuries they have ceased to be translations, but have become part of the cultural and religious life of the people. The *Rāmāyaṇa* of Tulsidas or Kamba are not translations of Valmiki, they are independent works, unmistakably about the same theme, but with their own integrity and flavour. Maybe Christian scholars in Asia need to go beyond hermeneutics, and produce poems, stories, narratives about the great themes of the Bible in order that the story of God's redeeming activity in Christ does not remain the exclusive property of Christians to be selectively communicated to their neighbours, but becomes part of God's inclusive concern for all people in Asia. Faith creates community, but the community should take care that it does not imprison faith.[22]

The presence of scriptures of other faiths creates a situation for Christians in Asia fundamentally different from that which Christians in the West had to face over the years. They did not have such powerful other scriptures to contend with and therefore found no need to be open to different religious and cultural insights in the matter of interpreting the texts. Christians in the West 'co-opted' the Hebrew scriptures, and over the years have interpreted it in their own way as the 'old testament', almost wholly ignoring or rejecting the Jewish interpretations of their own scriptures. But the Jews surely have not surrendered their scriptures to the Christians. The *Torah* is very much alive, sustaining the life of a persecuted people. Only during recent years has the Jewish interpretation of their own scriptures slowly come to be recognised, at least by some Christian Biblical scholars. Admittedly, the relationship between the Hebrew scriptures and the Christian faith is far more intimate and theologically significant than that between the Christian faith and the scriptures of other faiths in Asia. No serious Asian scholar has denied this fact. But few Asian scholars have asked the question, in what ways might the hermeneutical tools of our neighbours be of help in interpreting the Bible to our people in our own cultural context, particularly when our daily life is so inextricably mixed up with theirs? Furthermore, we need to recognise that in a multi-religious society the criteria derived on the basis of one particular scripture of one particular community of faith cannot be used to pass negative judgements on other scriptures regarded as equally authoritative by communities of other faiths living side by side with Christians.

The question of inspiration, authority and interpretation of the scriptures has to be discussed in Asia in a very different manner than in the West. Asian scholars should not be bound by the opinions of these matters expressed by a previous generation of Western Biblical scholars who had little knowledge of and no personal experience whatsoever of living together with people of other faiths. Renewed discussion on these matters is necessary for the sake of spiritual nourishment, theological credibility and pastoral care of the Christian community in Asian countries. Further, any claim for the exclusive truth of the Bible and the rejection of other scriptures as false sounds hollow in Asia. In the context of growing relationships between Christians and their neighbours of other faiths, such claims and counter claims do not take us too far. Therefore even as the task of hermeneutics should continue *within* each community of faith, it is equally important to work out a larger framework of *neighbourly relationships* within which the insights of different scriptures can be related to each other for mutual enrichment without denying their particularities. After all, today the scriptures of one faith can no more be regarded as the exclusive possession of one group of people. They belong to the heritage of *all* humankind in the larger life of the *oikoumene*.

And finally, even as Christians in Asia continue their quest for new hermeneutics, they need to become sensitive to a pervasive feeling or a conviction which is more than an intellectual assent in the Asian religious heart. This is the inward feeling that even as necessity is laid upon the believing community to be constantly engaged in the hermeneutical task, no hermeneutics by itself will yield Truth in its fullness. Mere scholarship does not yield Truth or reach God. God is not sitting behind the texts waiting to be recognised at the end of long and patient hermeneutic exercise. God is never the object of human knowledge. God always remains the eternal subject. Therefore, without a faith-response to God all hermeneutics remains an exercise in scholarly futility. True knowledge is the transformation of the knowing subject. Without disciplining the body, focusing the mind, purifying the emotions, and controlling the will no one can *hear* the sound of Truth or *see* the vision of God. 'Blessed are the pure in heart, for they shall see God' (Matt. 5.8).

## NOTES

1  C. Davies, 'The Theological Career of Historical Criticism of the Bible' (*Cross Currents*, 32, 3, Fall 1982), p. 282.

2  *The Sources of Chinese Tradition*, compiled by T. de Bary (New York, Columbia University Press, third printing, 1961), p. 17.

3  ibid., p. 50. See also H. Glessner Creel, *The Birth of China, A Survey of the Formative Period of Chinese Civilization* (New York, Frederick Unger Publishing Co., 1961, fourth printing), section on 'Literature', pp. 254 ff. *The Book of Changes* was probably the first complete work of Chinese Literature (p. 267). See also P. N. Gregory, 'Chinese Buddhist Hermeneutics' (*Journal of the American Academy of Religion*, 51, 2, January 1983), pp. 231 ff.

4  de Bary, p. 350.

5  Quoted in de Bary, pp. 317–18.

6  From *Hung ming chi* in *Raisho daizokvo* L II 1–7, quoted by de Bary, p. 14.

7  *Mundaka*, III, ii, 9.

8  Selections quoted by de Bary, pp. 53 ff.

9  ibid., p. 56.

10  See, for example, D. J. Elwood (ed.), *Asian Christian Theology* (Philadelphia, Westminster Press, 1980, rev. edn), p. 24.

11  S. P. Athyal, 'Towards an Asian Christian Theology', in Elwood, p. 69, italics mine.

12  ibid., p. 69.

13  'Doing Theology in Asia Today: A Korean Perspective', in Elwood, p. 317. See also K. Arayaprateep, 'The Convenant: An Effective Tool in Bible Study' (*The South East Asia Journal of Theology*, 18, 1, 1977), pp. 21–31; and

P. S. H. Liao, 'The Meaning of Galatians, 4: 21–31: A New Perspective' (*The Northeast Asia Journal of Theology*, 22/23, March–September 1979), pp. 115–32.

14  Editorial in *Religion and Society*, Christian Institute for Study of Religion and Society, Bangalore (21, 1, March 1974), p. 3, italics mine. This is one of the few consultations organized by the CISRS specifically on 'The Authority and use of the Bible for Christian Action in India'.

15  ibid., p. 6, italics mine.

16  ibid., p. 44.

17  There are personal statements in this issue of *Religion and Society* in which individual Christians testify how the Bible helps them in their personal lives and work. Thus Mark Sunder Rao claims that for him personal experience (*anubhava*) is the seat of authority for looking at the Bible, pp. 66 ff. S. P. Raju says that the Bible gives him directions for his work to be a good Christian engineer, pp. 67 ff. To B. M. Pulimood, a Christian physician, Christ's model of training disciples is the model for training medical doctors, p. 81. T. K. Thomas says, 'I do not any longer consciously *use* the Bible. But I claim I try to live by the light it sheds on my path. And this light for me is almost wholly the life and work of Jesus the Messiah,' p. 75. *Selectivity* seems to be the most obvious principle of interpretation here both for personal guidance and group action.

18  Quoted by K. Kanjilal Chaudhari, 'Communication – Information Revolution: Model for India and The Third World' (*Mainstream*, 27 October 1984), p. 21.

19  C. Kraft and T. N. Wisley (eds), *Readings in Dynamic Indigeneity* (Pasadena, CA, William Carey Library, 1979), p. 277.

20  Kanjilal Chaudhari, p. 21.

21  ibid., p. 23.

22  One may draw attention to some of the recent works in India; for example, P. C. Devasia, a Christian poet in Kerala, has written *Kristu Bhagavatam*, Trivandrum, 1977, the first long poem in Sanskrit with an English commentary on each verse (33 cantos and 1581 stanzas) on the life of Jesus Christ. Dr Gopal Singh, a Sikh scholar, has written a poem on the life of Christ under the title 'The Man who Never Died' (London, Macmillan, 1969). This has been translated into English, German and French. Manjeshwar Govinda Pai, a Hindu scholar, winner of the National Academy Award, has published in Kannada (one of the languages of South India) a long poem on the crucifixion and death of Jesus Christ entitled 'Golgotha' (Mysore, Kavyalaya Publishers, 1936 and 1981).

# 4

# The Use of the Bible in Black Theology

## ITUMELENG J. MOSALA

This essay, which appeared in a volume co-edited by Mosala, entitled *The Unquestionable Right to be Free* (Maryknoll, NY, Orbis Books, 1986), is in two sections. In the first section, which is found below, the author points out the need for black theology to work out its own black biblical hermeneutics that will identify with the social, political and cultural struggles of the black working class. In the second section of the essay, which is included in Part Two, he uses a materialist hermeneutics, which sees the Bible as the product and record of class struggle, as a possible liberative appropriation of the Bible. The Book of Micah is analysed in this way as an example of a biblical hermeneutics of liberation.

For an expanded version of the issues referred to here, and also for Mosala's critique of the use of social-science methods in biblical studies, see his *Biblical Hermeneutics and Black Theology in South Africa* (Grand Rapids, W. B. Eerdmans, 1989).

Itumeleng J. Mosala teaches in the Department of Religious Studies, University of Cape Town, Republic of South Africa.

## INTRODUCTION

This paper presupposes the contribution of Black Theology to human knowledge in general and to the black struggle for liberation in particular. No attempt will, therefore, be made to catalogue the virtues of this theology. Suffice it to recall that among its key contributions is its insistence on the necessary ideological rootedness of all theology. This, black theologians may not have pointed to in an explicit way. The fact, however, that they exposed the cultural assumptions of white theology and showed their link with white society and white values exploded the myth of rational objectivity in theology.

The paper will, however, take issue with Black Theology for not taking its own criticism of white theology seriously enough. It will be shown that this is particularly the case with regard to the use of the

Bible. The first part of the paper will, therefore, extrapolate features of Black Theology which, it will be argued, represent an ideological captivity to the hermeneutical principles of a theology of oppression. It will further be maintained that it is precisely this slavery to the hermeneutics of white theology which is responsible for the inability of Black Theology to become a theoretical weapon of struggle in the hands of the exploited masses themselves. In this respect we will take our cue from the words of Marx when he writes:

> The weapon of criticism cannot, of course, replace criticism of the weapon; material force must be overthrown by material force; but theory also becomes a material force as soon as it has gripped the masses. Theory is capable of gripping the masses as soon as it demonstrates *ad hominem*, and it demonstrates *ad hominem* as soon as it becomes radical. To be radical is to grasp the root of the matter. But for man the root is man himself.[1]

It cannot be contested that although Black Theology has developed and is well and alive,[2] it has not yet, as a weapon of theory, become the property of the struggling black masses. To this extent it is a theory that has not yet become a *material force* because it has not gripped the masses. It has served its purpose well as a weapon of criticism against white theology and the white society. That activity, however, does not replace criticism of the weapon itself. Elsewhere I have argued that part of the reason why Black Theology has not become the property of the toiling masses may lie in the class positions and class commitments of its proponents.[3]

The second part of the paper will attempt to set out a programme for biblical hermeneutics of liberation using the Book of Micah as a case study.

## BLACK THEOLOGY'S EXEGETICAL STARTING POINT

All major black theological studies in South Africa draw, in some way, from the work of James Cone. While Cone cannot be faulted for the omissions of South African Black Theology, it is nevertheless necessary to trace the trajectory of the biblical hermeneutics of Black Theology back to its first and most outstanding exponent in order to see how it has been uncritically reproduced in this country.

Black Theology's exegetical starting point expresses itself in the notion that the Bible is the revealed 'Word of God'. The task of a black theologian is to recognize 'God's Word' and help illuminate it to those who are oppressed and humiliated in this world. For Cone, the 'Word of God', therefore, represents one structuring pole of the biblical hermeneutics of Black Theology while the black experience stands for the other.[4] He summarizes Black Theology's hermeneutical position when he asserts that:

> The Bible is the witness to God's self-disclosure in Jesus Christ. Thus the black experience requires that Scripture be a source of Black Theology. For it was Scripture that enabled slaves to affirm a view of God that differed radically from that of the slave masters. The slave masters' intention was to present a 'Jesus' who would make the slave obedient and docile. Jesus was supposed to make black people better slaves, that is, faithful servants of white masters. But many blacks rejected that view of Jesus, not only because it contradicted their African heritage, but because it contradicted the witness of Scripture.[5]

Thus the black experience of oppression and exploitation provides the epistemological lenses for perceiving the God of the Bible as the God of liberation. This process, however, does not alter Cone's perception of the nature and function of the Bible as the 'Word of God'. Rather, 'scripture', in its status as the 'Word of God', 'established limits to white people's use of Jesus Christ as a confirmation of black oppression'.[6]

Paradoxically, Black Theology's notion of the Bible as the 'Word of God' carries the implication that there is such a thing as a non-ideological appropriation of scripture. Black theologians condemn white people's view of God and Jesus Christ as apolitical and above ideologies on the one hand, but maintain a view of scripture as an absolute, non-ideological 'Word of God' which can be made ideological by being applied to the situation of oppression. This position is taken by even the most theoretically astute of black theologians, Cornel West. He argues:

> An interpretation of the black historical experience and the readings of the biblical texts that emerge out of this experience constitute the raw ingredients for the second step of black theological reflection. By trying to understand the plight of black people in the light of the Bible, black theologians claim to preserve the biblical truth that God sides with the oppressed and acts on their behalf.[7]

To be fair to West it must be added that he goes a step further than Cone and other black theologians by not resting the case at interpreting the black experience in the light of the Bible, but also advocates interpreting the Bible in the light of the black experience. Neverthe-less, West, like Cone, insists on there being a biblical truth according to which God sides with the oppressed in their struggle for liberation. This is true as far as it goes. But as any hermeneutics that derives from the crucible of class struggle will attest to, the biblical truth that God sides with the oppressed is only one of the biblical truths. The other truth is that the struggle between Yahweh and Baal is not simply an ideological warfare taking place in the minds and hearts of believers, but a struggle between the God of the Israelite landless peasants and subdued slaves and the God of the Israelite royal, noble, landlord and priestly classes. The Bible is as rent apart by the antagonistic struggles of the warring classes of Israelite society as our life is torn asunder by the class divisions of our society.

What then is meant by the Bible as the 'Word of God'? The ideological import of such a theological statement is immense. For the 'Word of God' cannot be the object of criticism. Least of all can the 'Word of God' be critiqued in the light of the black experience. The only appropriate response is *obedience.* At best the black experi-ence can be seen in the light of the 'Word of God', but not vice versa. If the Bible is the 'Word of God', therefore, the implication is that even the 'law and order' God of David and Solomon cannot be the object of criticism in the light of the black experience. The black struggle cannot be hermeneutically connected with the struggles of the oppressed and exploited Israelites against the economic and political domination of the Israelite monarchic state which was undergirded by the ideology of the Davidic-Zionist covenant (2 Sam. 7). Neither can any hermeneutic affinity be established with the landless peasants, exploited workers and destitute underclasses that made up the followers of Jesus. One cannot select one part of the 'Word of God' and neglect the other.

South African black theologians are not free from enslavement to this neo-orthodox theological problematic that regards the notion of the 'Word of God' as a hermeneutical starting point. S. Dwane displays this exegetical bondage when he writes:

> Liberation theology as an aspect of Christian theology cannot play to the gallery of secular expectations. It seeks to understand and to articulate what in the light of his revelation in the past, God is doing now for the redemption of his people. Liberation theology is theocentric and soundly biblical insofar as it points out that God does not luxuriate in his eternal bliss, but reaches out to man and to the world. . . . To say that liberation theology is not a Gospel of liberation is to state the obvious. *The Gospel, it is true, is good news*

*for all men.* And no theology, Western or African, has the right to equate itself with the Gospel. The entire theological enterprise is concerned with the interpretation of *the one Gospel for all sorts of conditions.*[8]

The attempt to claim *the whole* of the Bible in support of black theology is misdirected because it ignores the results of biblical scholarship over the last century and has its roots in ruling-class ideology. By ruling-class ideology we refer to that activity on the part of dominant classes of society by which they seek to establish hegemonic control over other classes through a rationalizing universalization of what are in effect sectional class interests. James Joll makes this point succinctly:

> The hegemony of a political class meant for Gramsci that that class had succeeded in persuading the other classes of society to accept its own moral, political and cultural values. If the ruling class is successful, then this will involve the minimum use of force, as was the case with the successful liberal regimes of the nineteenth century.[9]

Thus the insistence on the Bible as the 'Word of God' must be seen for what it is: an ideological manoeuvre whereby ruling-class interests in the Bible as in our society today are converted into a faith that transcends social, political, racial, sexual and economic divisions. In this way the Bible becomes an ahistorical interclassist document. Sergio Rostagno has exposed the ideological roots of this line of thinking when he asserts, concerning the church, that:

> Historically speaking, the church has always been a church of the bourgeoisie, even when it claimed to transcend class barriers or labored under the illusion that it pervaded all classes in the same way. Indeed, it has been a truly bourgeois church, if the notion of interclassism is taken as part of bourgeois ideology. . . . The church has been the church of the class which has identified itself with the history of the West, in which Christianity may be considered to have been a major force. Only those members of the working class who accepted this view of history attended church. But most of the working people never accepted this view and only gave the church the kind of formal allegiance subjects give to the claims of their rulers. They could not really belong to the church of another class.[10]

Just as the church has always been the church of the bourgeoisie, theology and biblical exegesis have always been bourgeois theology and exegesis. It is, therefore, a tragedy that rebel theologies like Black Theology and Liberation Theology should adopt uncritically the biblical hermeneutics of bourgeois theology. According to Rostagno, bourgeois exegesis shows the sterility of its ahistoricism in that:

> It claims to consider humanity in certain typical existential situations which provide analogies for all historical situations resulting from the human condition. It deals, therefore, with *humanity*, rather than with *workers* as they try to wrest from the dominant class its hold on the means of production and its hold over the vital spheres of human life. In this sense, it could be said that exegesis was an interclass affair. . . . This was an indication that biblical exegesis had been effectively estranged from the labor movement.[11]

The belief in the Bible as the 'Word of God' has had similar effects, that is, *pro-humanity* but anti-black working class and black women. It has, to all intents and purposes, been bourgeois exegesis applied to the working-class situation. The theoretical tragedy of such a state of affairs is that claims in that direction have been made with confidence and pride. Boesak, for instance, states unashamedly that:

> In its focus on the poor and the oppressed, the theology of liberation is not a new theology; it is simply the proclamation of the age-old gospel, but now liberated from the deadly hold of the mighty and the powerful and made relevant to the situation of the oppressed and the poor.[12]

Black Theology needs a new exegetical starting point if it is to become a material force capable of gripping the black working-class and peasant masses. Such a starting point needs to be rooted in the kind of epistemology that underlies the words of Marx and Engels when they declared: 'The task of history, therefore, once the world beyond the truth has disappeared, is to establish the truth of this world.'[13] The social, cultural, political and economic world of the black working class and peasantry constitutes the only valid hermeneutical starting point for a Black Theology of Liberation.

## THE PROBLEM OF UNIVERSALITY AND PARTICULARITY IN BLACK THEOLOGY

The abstract exegetical starting point of Black Theology leads inevitably to problems about the validity of the particularistic character of this theology. If the 'Word of God' transcends boundaries of culture, class, race, sex, etc., how can there be a theology that is concerned primarily with the issues of a particular race? Conversely, if black people are right when they claim that in their struggle for liberation

Jesus is on their side, how can the same Jesus remain the supreme *universal* disclosure of the 'Word of God'?

This simultaneous concern for a cultureless and culture-bound, classless and class-based, raceless and race-oriented Jesus manifested itself fairly early in the development of Black Theology. Thus Gqubule states:

> Black Theology is not an attempt to localize Christ in the black situation, but to make him so universal that the Red Indian, the Pigmy, the Maori, the Russian, the Hungarian, the Venda and the American, may each say: 'This man Jesus is bone of my bone; he speaks in my own accent of things that are true to me!' Viewed in this way Christianity can never be a white man's religion although it was brought to us by a white missionary. It is natural that any white artist would portray Jesus as a white man.[14]

This line of thinking is corroborated by Mgojo who sees Black Theology as contextual. By this he seems to understand that it is the application of universal theological principles to a particular situation. Consequently he traces the development of universal theology from the Age of Apology through to the period starting in 1720 which he characterizes as the era of evolving theological responses to the technological society. He then concludes:

> In looking at the history of doctrine we can see in every period theology developed in response to challenges from the larger society. This being the case there is nothing strange in a particular segment of the Christian community reflecting on the nature of God in relation to its experience of suffering and oppression. Hence today there is Black Theology.[15]

Thus Mgojo's understanding of the origins and function of Black Theology is rooted in a belief in the fundamental universality of the gospel. This understanding stems from a hermeneutical commitment to the Bible as the 'Word of God'. As a result, he sees the emergence of Black Theology as a logical historical development of Christian theology, not a rebellion against traditional western theology. Indeed Black Theology is simply *contextual* theology, that is, white theology in black clothes. It is little wonder that he applies the following strictures against James Cone:

> Cone's understanding of the theological task in his early work is in conflict with our definition of theology, in fact it is in direct opposition. His focus is on the analysis of the black man's condition, ours is on God as revealed in Jesus Christ and his relationship to the world and man. Cone's approach

here could be classified as Christian sociology rather than Christian theology.[16]

This apologetic attitude on the part of black theologians is related to their enslavement to traditional biblical hermeneutics which we discussed above.[17] There are also forms of colonization that are connected to this hermeneutical bondage. In South African Black Theology the debate between African and black theologians exemplifies this crisis of cultural identity. Gqubule, for instance, in addressing one of the points of conflict between Christianity and African religion, locates himself unproblematically in a framework that reflects at once a cultural desertion and a biblical hermeneutical position based in the dominant western culture. He argues:

> There is a widespread belief about the role of the ancestors. One view is that they are an object of worship. Another view is that they are intermediaries who, because they know our lot on earth, are better able to mediate to God on our behalf. However, for the Christian only the Triune God can be the object of worship; moreover the Christian Scriptures say: 'There is *one God*, and also *one mediator* between God and men, Christ Jesus' (1 Tim. 2.5).[18]

The most explicit and often quoted criticism of African Theology and religion, which feeds on this cultural self-hate, is the one made by Manas Buthelezi. Buthelezi's strictures are rightly directed against tendencies to reify the African past, especially African culture. However, the terms of his strictures display an uneasiness about culture which characterizes the conflict between the universal and the particular in Black Theology. He writes:

> There is a danger that the 'African past' may be romanticized and conceived in isolation from the realities of the present. Yet this 'past' seen as a world view is nothing more than a historical abstraction of 'what once was'. Rightly or wrongly, one cannot help but sense something panicky about the mood which has set the tenor and tempo of the current concerns about 'indigenous theology.'[19]

Notwithstanding this rigorously anti-abstractionist stance, Buthelezi proceeds to suggest equally abstractionist solutions to the problem of indigenous theology in South Africa:

> The shift from the 'ideological' to the 'human' expressions of ecclesiastical kinship solidarity will serve as a freeing factor for indigenous theology. Considerations of *esprit de corps* will no longer be a haunting specter for

theological freedom in Africa, since there will be another way of expressing this kinship solidarity.[20]

The abstract universalizing category of the 'human' as opposed to the concrete particularizing concept of the 'African' helps Buthelezi to maintain ties with what is 'universal' and, for him, non-ideological, while at the same time his theology is intended to address the indigenous and, therefore, ideological situation. It may even be argued that for Buthelezi the 'human' or 'anthropological' is finally given in the 'Word of God' which he asserts addresses him within the reality of his blackness.[21] That is why in his view Black Theology is no more than a methodological technique of theologizing.[22]

Bereft of a theoretical perspective that can locate both the Bible and the black experience within appropriate historical contexts, Buthelezi and other black theologians are unable to explode the myth of the inherent universality of the 'Word of God'. They have been surpassed by the largely illiterate black working class and poor peasantry who have defied the canon of scripture, with its ruling-class ideological basis, by appropriating the Bible in their own way by using the cultural tools emerging out of their struggle for survival.[23] To be able to reopen the canon of scripture in the interests of black liberation, black theologians will need to take the materialist hermeneutical significance of the black experience much more seriously.

The problem of the lack of a black biblical hermeneutics of liberation, however, has its roots in the inherent crisis of the petit bourgeoisie of all shades, but especially those of the colonized countries. Amilcar Cabral diagnoses the inherent malaise of this class when he declares:

As I said, regarding culture there are usually no important modifications at the summit of the indigenous social pyramid or pyramids (groups with a hierarchical structure). Each stratum or class retains its identity, integrated within the larger group, but distinct from the identities of other social categories. By contrast in urban centers and in urban zones of the interior where the colonial power's cultural influence is felt, the problem of identity is more complex. Whereas those at the base of the social pyramid – that is, the majority of the masses of working people from different ethnic groups – and those at the top (the foreign ruling class) keep their identities, *those in the middle range of this pyramid (the native lower middle class) – culturally rootless, alienated or more or less assimilated – flounder* in a social and cultural conflict in quest of their identity.[24]

Cornel West has raised the same question of the cultural crisis of the petit bourgeois class in relation to Latin American Liberation Theology. In the case of this theology the problem expresses itself in terms of the conspicuous absence of blacks and Indians, or the issues related to them, in Liberation Theology. He suggests that when Marxists are preoccupied with an analysis that denigrates the liberating aspects of the culture of oppressed people, the implication is that such Marxists share the ethos – not of the degraded and oppressed minorities – but of the dominant European culture. Seen from the point of view of concern with the hermeneutics of liberation this means that the dominant European culture would constitute their material hermeneutical starting point. West makes the point succinctly when he asserts that:

> Historically, a central feature of this dominant European culture has been its inability to take seriously the culture of colored people and its tendency to degrade and oppress the culture of these people. For oppressed colored people, the central problem is not only repressive capitalist regimes, but also oppressive European civilizing attitudes. And even Marxists who reject oppressive capitalist regimes often display oppressive European civilizing attitudes toward colored peoples. In this sense, such Marxists, though rightly critical of capitalism, remain captives of the worst of European culture.[25]

Thus universal abstract starting points derived presumably from the biblical message will not do for a biblical hermeneutics of liberation. Black Theology for its part will have to rediscover black working-class and poor peasant culture in order to find for itself a materialist hermeneutical starting point. The particularity of the black struggle in its different forms and phases must provide the epistemological lenses with which the Bible can be read. Only such a position seems to us to represent a theoretical break with dominant biblical hermeneutics. Anything else is a tinkering with what in fact must be destroyed.

## NOTES

1   K. Marx and F. Engels, *On Religion* (New York, Schocken Books, 1964), p. 50.

2   See J. Noko, 'The Concept of God in Black Theology', Ph.D. thesis, McGill University, 1977; L. E. Ntshebe, 'A Voice of Protest', M.A. thesis, Rhodes University; S. Mogoba, 'The Faith of Urban Blacks', M.A.

thesis, Bristol, 1978; T. A. Mofokeng, 'The Crucified among the Cross-bearers', doctoral thesis, Kampen, 1983; and numerous articles in the various issues of the *Journal of Theology for Southern Africa* (*JTSA*).

3   'Black and African Theologies', unpublished paper read at the University of Cape Town (1982). See also the 'Final Statement of the Black Theology Seminar' (*ICT News* 1, 2 September 1983), pp. 9 ff. S. Nolutshungu, writing on the political interpretation of the so-called 'Black Middle Class', corroborates this contention. He writes: 'As things stand, it is not surprising that attempts to define a modern cultural sensibility for Blacks in the late 1960s and early 1970s were so derivative in idiom and style – deep and authentic though the anguish which they expressed. "Middle class" Blacks remained, even so, firmly attached to the common culture and even in the area of religion where much was written about the need for a black theology, radical dissent was still expressed by separatist churches that were predominantly non-middle-class in following' (*Changing South Africa* (Cape Town, David Philip, 1983), p. 125).

4   See J. H. Cone, *God of the Oppressed* (New York, Seabury Press, 1975), p. 8.

5   ibid., p. 31.

6   ibid.

7   Cornel West, *Prophesy Deliverance* (Philadelphia, Westminster Press, 1982), p. 109.

8   'Christology and Liberation' (*JTSA*, 35, 1981), p. 30. Italics mine.

9   James Joll, *Gramsci* (Glasgow, Fontana Paperbacks, 1977), p. 99.

10   'The Bible: Is Interclass Reading Legitimate?', in *The Bible and Liberation*, ed. N. K. Gottwald (Maryknoll, NY, Orbis Books, 1983), p. 62.

11   ibid.

12   A. Boesak, *Farewell to Innocence* (Maryknoll, NY, Orbis Books, 1977), p. 10.

13   Marx and Engels, p. 42.

14   S. Gqubule, 'What is Black Theology' (*JTSA*, 8, 1974), p. 18.

15   E. K. M. Mgojo, 'Prolegomenon to the Study of Black Theology' (*JTSA*, 21 1977), pp. 26 f.

16   ibid.

17   See also E. K. Mosothoane, 'The Use of Scripture in Black Theology', *Scripture and the Use of Scripture* (Pretoria, Unisa, 1979), p. 32.

18   Gqubule, p. 17.

19   Manas Buthelezi, 'Toward Indigenous Theology in South Africa', in *The Emergent Gospel* (Maryknoll, NY, Orbis Books, 1978), p. 62.

20   ibid., p. 73.

21   ibid., p. 74.

22   ibid.

23   For a helpful study of this process, see J. M. Schoffeleer's 'African Christology', unpublished paper, Free University, Amsterdam, 1981, *passim*.

24   Amilcar Cabral, 'The Role of Culture in the Liberation Struggle' (*Latin American Research Unit Studies*, Toronto, 1, 3, 1977), p. 93.

25   'The North American Blacks', in *The Challenge of Basic Christian Communities* (Maryknoll, NY, Orbis Books, 1981), p. 256.

# 5

# Women's Rereading of the Bible*

## ELSA TAMEZ

The emergence of Euro-American feminist hermeneutics has raised important issues for biblical studies. Elsa Tamez, expanding on this, offers basic skills that are indispensable for a reading of the Bible from a Latin American woman's perspective.

This essay is from V. Fabella and M. A. Oduyoye (eds), *With Passion and Compassion: Third World Women Doing Theology* (Maryknoll, NY, Orbis Books, 1988). Her books include *Bible of the Oppressed* (Maryknoll, NY, Orbis Books, 1982), *Against Machismo* (Oak Park, IL, Meyer Stone Books, 1987), and a volume of essays *Through Her Eyes: Women's Theology from Latin America* (Maryknoll, NY, Orbis Books, 1989).

Elsa Tamez is from Costa Rica and is on the staff of Seminario Biblico Latinamericano, in San Jose.

## THE REDISCOVERY OF THE BIBLE

Not long ago, when the Latin American poor burst on the scene of church life in Latin America, the consciousness of a large number of people was stirred. The Bible took on new meaning. That book – read by many but until now assimilated through a safe, unidimensional interpretation controlled by a predominantly unchallenged way of thinking – became the simple text that speaks of a loving, just, liberating God who accompanies the poor in their suffering and their struggle through human history. This is not the only new development on our continent. On the contrary, it appears as one more break-through in a fast-growing movement in Latin America, a movement propelled mainly by the strong yearning of the poor for life. For multiple reasons and in many ways, the poor are today stronger than ever in their commitment. This is why we, in Latin America, speak of a new way of being church, of doing theology, of reading the Bible.

* Translated from Spanish by Alicia Partnoy.

A reading of the Scripture that truly liberates responds to the situation that has motivated the reading. It seems that, in a context of hunger, unemployment, repression, and war, creativity more than abounds in theology, hermeneutics, liturgy, and the pastoral field. At least this has been our experience. Both Catholic and Protestant grass-roots communities provide clear examples of the ways in which the Bible has been and still is being rediscovered. The study, discussion, and meditation based on the Word has become an integral part of the meetings of the Catholic grass-roots Christian communities. Everybody studies and discusses the Bible from the point of view of liberation. In the progressive Protestant communities, where the Bible has always been fundamental to the liturgy, hermeneutic keys have changed and the Bible has come to be read from the perspective of the poor. In both communities the Bible has been rediscovered.

Characteristically, their readings are strongly linked to the daily life of the members of these Christian communities. There is an unquestionable bridge between the life of the people of God in the Old Testament and that of Jesus' followers in the New Testament.

This reading of the Word from the point of view of the poor has been consolidated and has become so evident that Holy Scripture is regarded as a threatening or dangerous book by some sectors of society that do not share a preferential option for the poor. The sectors I mention might be either religious or secular, such as the government (particularly in countries where the National Security Doctrine is actively enforced). Some religious circles have even decided to avoid biblical discussions. Do they fear the Bible? The ancient book of Christianity has indeed become new and defiant when it is read from the perspective of the poor.

## 'HOWEVER . . . ,' SAY THE WOMEN

Despite this situation, women with a certain degree of female consciousness have started to raise some questions about the Bible. It is not that they don't feel included in the main liberation experiences of the Bible: the exodus and the historical role of Jesus. It is that women find clear, explicit cases of the marginalization or segregation of women in several passages of both the Old and the New Testaments. There are, then, differences between reading the Bible from the point of view of the poor and reading it from a woman's perspective. The poor find that the Word reaffirms in a clear and direct way that God is with them in their fight for life. Women who live in poverty, however, even when they are aware that the strength of the Holy Spirit is on their side, do not know how to confront the texts that openly segregate them. These texts sound strange and surprising to someone who is not familiar with the culture of the biblical world and believes in a just and liberating God.

This concrete problem has not been regarded as such until recently. First, the discovery of the Bible as 'historical memory of the poor' was greeted with great enthusiasm by both men and women. This discovery implied that it was necessary to discuss a significant number of biblical texts essential to the history of salvation from a new perspective, starting with those texts where the liberation of the oppressed is most apparent (Exodus, the Prophets, the Gospels). Up until now texts that segregate women have been disregarded and subordinated because the main criterion has been to experience God as a God of life who has a preferential option for the oppressed, including women. Second, only in recent years has a feminine consciousness gained some strength in the theological and ecclesiastical worlds. There have, of course, always been women who have openly questioned the church and theology. This is happening to an increasing degree in our days, especially with the upsurge of liberation theology and the proliferation of grass-roots Christian communities where women are the majority and their participation is key.

For several reasons this problem of the marginalization, or segregation, of women is harder to solve than it appears to be. One of the reasons is that our society is extremely sexist – a phenomenon that can be detected at both a tacit and an explicit level. Nor are grass-roots Christian communities free from this sexist ideology, which has deep historico-cultural roots that are hard to pull out in a single tug. To the extent that there is an easy correspondence between two cultures that marginalize women, it becomes even harder to discuss the biblical texts that reaffirm women's marginality.

Furthermore, it is a well-known fact that throughout history this correspondence of two patriarchal sexist societies has resulted in their mutual consolidation. On one hand, old-time antiwomen customs of Hebrew culture have been declared sacred; on the other hand, certain texts have consequently been held up as biblical principles to prove that women's marginalization is natural in daily life. It is in this sense that the Hebrew–Jewish lifestyle presented by the Bible is perpetuated

precisely because 'thus is written the word of God.' This explains why
the Bible has been used to reinforce the position of inferiority in which
society and culture have placed women for centuries. Today this
attitude is not so apparent as in the past, but in some churches it still
manifests itself, albeit in disguise.

Something different takes place in grass-roots Christian communities. They react in different ways to difficult biblical texts. Sometimes
they disregard antiwomen texts, at other times they juggle them to
come out with a positive side or they soften the oppressive nature of the
content. On other occasions they wisely simplify the problem by stating
that those were other times, that reality should be different today, that
God is a God of life and therefore he cannot favor discrimination
against women.

Having experienced all of these attitudes in the context of different
religious communities I have never taken this problem seriously. In
truth, the problem would not be serious if everybody considered the
Bible for what it really is: a testimony of a Judeo-Christian people with
a particular culture, for whom holy revelation works always in favor of
those who have least. Women would then feel included among the
oppressed and they would contextualize those texts that segregate
them. I believe this is what happens in many communities.

However, I have come to think that the problem is serious. Its
seriousness comes, first, from the effects that these antiwomen biblical
readings have produced on so many women and men who have
internalized, as sacred natural law, the inferiority of women. Second,
there is an inherent difficulty in interpreting texts that not only
legitimate but also legislate the marginalization of women. Third, and
this is mainly for Protestants, the problem is the principle of biblical
authority as it is traditionally perceived. These are three difficulties
that women are consciously confronting. Let us look at them in detail.

## MYTHS, TEXTS, AND BIBLICAL AUTHORITY

After working with some biblical texts, like the famous narration in
Genesis 3, it is easy to perceive that between the text and its current
interpretation is a long series of ideologizing (or mythologizing)
readings of this narration that are more harmful to women than the
actual texts are.

Genesis 3 and the second account about creation have been the basis for creating a mythical framework that legitimizes women's inferiority and their submission to men. Myths – ideologies that distort reality – have been created based on these texts, not so much because of information contained in the story *per se*, but because of the conditions imposed by a society structured around men as its center; and by a particular way of reading the story, which places emphasis on its peripheral aspects; and by a story-telling technique that employs literal description and repetition as literary devices.

There are also other texts in which the example of a patriarchal culture has been brought in for a specific purpose. However, on many occasions, the readers of these texts have elevated the example to the category of divine law. The result is thus a legitimation and legislation, as if it were holy, of an order unfavorable to women.

Women are called, therefore, to deny the authority of those readings that harm them. It is here, then, that the collaboration of women experts in the Bible or of male exegetes with feminist perspectives is needed to reinterpret the texts, using a new hermeneutic approach.

Thus it would finally be possible for women to do a liberation-oriented reading of a text that for centuries had been used against them. However, on occasion there will be no other way to interpret the text except as a putdown of women. Its exegesis will show only the patriarchal ideology of the author, the commentator, the culture, and the historic moment in which the text was elaborated. This is the other Bible-related problem that women confront.

The tendency of some First World radical feminists to reject the Bible is, it seems to me, an exaggerated reaction. I think that by assigning too much importance to these peripheral texts, many leave aside the central message, which is profoundly liberating. From my point of view, it is precisely the Gospel's spirit of justice and freedom that neutralizes antifemale texts. A reading of the Bible that attempts to be faithful to the word of the Lord will achieve that goal best when it is done in a way that reflects the liberating meaning of the Gospel, even when sometimes fidelity to the Gospel forces the reader to distance herself or himself from the text. Therefore, a time has come to acknowledge that those biblical texts that reflect patriarchal culture and proclaim women's inferiority and their submission to men are not normative; neither are those texts that legitimize slavery normative. The rationale behind this statement is essentially the same as that offered by the Scriptures: the proclamation of the gospel of Jesus calls us to life and announces the coming of the kingdom of justice.

German theologian Elisabeth Schüssler Fiorenza, who lives in the United States, proposes a new hermeneutic approach. She tries to reconstruct the beginnings of Christianity from a feminist perspective. Using this method she finds very interesting situations that explain women's active participation in the beginnings of the church. She also discovers contradictions in some of St Paul's writings, which eventually were used to promote the submission of women. From an exegetical point of view, this is one of the best and newest approaches to the Bible. We must admit that, for Third World women, this is an important contribution regarding the analysis of the text from a woman's point of view. However, it is likely that in some communities, mainly Protestant, it will be hard to accept the idea of questioning a biblical author, not to mention an apostle, as is the case with Paul.

This presents us with the third problem: the classic formulation of the doctrine of biblical authority. I shall refer here to Protestant churches because I know them a bit better.

Women with a certain degree of female consciousness, who move in conservative sectors, at times confront the difficulties of the principle implied in the idea of inspiration, namely, being without error, or God's word in a literal sense. I stress that they confront it *at times*, because, according to my experience, a curious phenomenon takes place in real life: there is a mismatch between belief in the traditionally formulated principle of biblical authority and daily-life practice. Women in both traditional and grass-roots Protestant churches have achieved an important degree of participation in the liturgy and other areas and – except in the case of extremely conservative churches – this has not been a problem even though it is clear to these institutions that St Paul called for 'women to keep silent' in church. The issue is not even under discussion; in practice there is a tacit acceptance of women's participation and an increasing recurrence of texts that suggest the active participation of women. However, in some more traditional churches, when a woman becomes dangerously active or threatening to those in powerful positions, aid is found in the classic Pauline texts to demand women's submission to men. It is in moments like these that some women do not know how to respond. This is because they either lack the proper hermeneutic tools or have a mistaken interpretation of the principle of biblical authority.

On the other hand, when at meetings of Christian women there is an attempt to study texts such as Ephesians 5.22–4 or 1 Corinthians 14.34, the discussion frequently winds up on a dead-end street. The conflict arises because women, although not in accord with the texts nor practising such behavior in everyday life, yet do concede at the same time that the Bible has all the authority of the word of God. Thus they find themselves trapped within a framework of literal translations, forgetting that the word of God is much more than that.

This situation tells us that it is about time to reformulate the principle of biblical authority, from the point of departure of our Latin American reality. From a woman's perspective it is time to look for new hermeneutic criteria, patterns that not only will help us to handle patriarchal texts but also will illuminate our re-reading of the whole Bible from a feminine perspective, even texts that do not explicitly refer to women. I shall discuss now some matters that come from my own experience.

## GUIDES TOWARD READING THE BIBLE FROM A LATIN AMERICAN WOMAN'S PERSPECTIVE

### Gaining distance and coming closer

To counteract myth-laden readings of biblical texts and to avoid the risk of repeating the interpretations of other readers, I believe in the importance of gaining distance from the text, mainly from those parts that have been frequently read and therefore have become overly familiar to our ears. When I say 'gaining distance' I mean picking up the book and ignoring the interpretations that almost automatically come to mind even before reading the actual text. To distance oneself means to be new to the text (to be a stranger, a first-time visitor to the text), to be amazed by everything, especially by those details that repeated readings have made seem so logical and natural. It is necessary to take up the Bible as a new book, a book that has never been heard or read before. This demands a conscious effort that implies reading the texts a thousand times and very carefully.

This way of reading is going to be conditioned by or embedded in the life experience of the Latin American reader. Her or his experiences must be very consciously taken into account at the time of the reading. It is this experience, in the end, that will facilitate the distancing of oneself from the all-too-familiar interpretation of the common suppositions in the text, and will help to uncover keys to a liberation-oriented reading. This is the process of coming closer to daily life, which implies the experiences of pain, joy, hope, hunger, celebration, and struggle. It is clear from this process of gaining distance and coming closer that in Latin America the Bible is not read as an intellectual or academic exercise; it is read with the goal of giving meaning to our lives today. In the confusing situation we find ourselves, we want to discern God's will and how it is present in our history. We think that the written word offers us criteria for discerning. Already this is a way of reformulating the principle of biblical authority.

The process I call 'gaining distance' and 'coming closer' is not only geared to finding a woman's perspective. Every Latin American reading of the Bible needs to shake off rote readings that cloud the text. We must approach it with questions coming from life. However, considering that a reading of the Scriptures from a woman's angle is very new for us, considering that it is mandatory to discern between 'macho' cultures and the gospel of life, the process of gaining distance from 'macho' readings and texts and coming closer to the experience of Latin American women gains relevance for all women.

## The reading of the Bible with the poor as a point of departure

Every liberation reading from the perspective of Latin American women must be understood within the framework that arises from the situation of the poor. In a context of misery, malnutrition, repression, torture, Indian genocide, and war – in other words, in a context of death – there is no greater priority than framing and articulating the readings according to these situations. The poor (men, women, blacks, Indians) comprise the large majority, and it is because of their discontent that repression and mass killings generally take place. They are in a privileged place, hermeneutically speaking, because we conceive of the God of life and One who has a preferential option for the poor. Besides, the mystery of God's reign is with them because it has been revealed to them (Matt. 11.25). Therefore, a reading from a woman's perspective has to go through this world of the poor. This will be a guarantee that it has a core theme of liberation, and it will shed light on other faces of the poor, such as blacks and native peoples. This kind of reading will also give us methods to develop specific approaches to salvation in each of their situations.

Besides, this reading key, which has as a synonymous parallel 'God is on the side of the oppressed,' is the key to cancel and disallow those – really very few in number – antiwomen texts that promote the submission of women to men and affirm the inferiority of certain human beings because of their gender.

It should be remembered that a reading of the Bible from the perspective of the poor is a hermeneutic key offered by the Scriptures themselves, mainly through 'events that create meaning' such as the exodus and the historical praxis of Jesus. Much has been said about this, and it is not my aim to discuss it more extensively here.

## A clear feminist consciousness

To read the Bible from a woman's perspective, we must read it with women's eyes, that is to say, conscious of the existence of individuals who are cast aside because of their sex. This procedure includes not only women. Men who feel identified with this specific struggle might also be able to read the Bible from this approach. This simple step is fundamental to achieve a reading that attempts to include other oppressed sectors besides the poor. It is a stamp that will distinguish this reading from others that consider the oppressed in general.

This approach, as noted above, is recent in Latin America. Therefore, even we women are not entirely conscious of it yet. For this reason, our reading does not come out spontaneously, and a conscious effort is needed to discover new women-liberating aspects, or even elements in the text that other perspectives would not bring to light.

Women, as victims of sexist oppression, will obviously perceive with less difficulty those aspects that directly affect them. Their experiences, their bodies, their social upbringing, their suffering and specific struggles give them keys (insights) to this reading.

Some liberation theologians agree that to the degree women actively engage themselves as readers of Scriptures and participants in other theological activities they offer important contributions to exegesis, hermeneutics, and theology.

It must remain clear that when I speak of reading the Bible from a woman's perspective, I am not referring specifically to texts that mention female subjects, but to the whole Bible. It is here where an enriching contribution from a perspective long absent until now can be made.

The novelty of such readings comes from reflection on the experiences of women. Women, for example, due to their experiences of oppression, can pose new 'ideological suspicions' not only to the culture that reads the text but also to the heart of the text itself by reason of its being a product of a patriarchal culture. Furthermore, their 'ideological suspicions' are also applied to biblical tools, such as dictionaries, commentaries, and concordances, tools that are regarded as objective because they are scientific, but that are undoubtedly susceptible to being biased by sexism. This fact has been proved true by female exegetic scholars.

If to the oppression women endure we add the fact that they live a particular experience as women – in the sense that they are closer to vital processes, and have a unique stance in their view of the world – we shall see new contributions reflected in their readings (in recent years much has been discussed about women's identity).

In conclusion, the 'gaining distance' from and 'coming closer' to the Bible, the retrieval of liberation keys from the perspective of the poor, and a feminist consciousness are three basic skills indispensable to reading the Bible from a Latin American woman's perspective.

We are just taking the first steps. We are rediscovering new duties that will benefit Latin American women, and we are yearning to learn more. Consequently, this meeting in Mexico attended by Third World women from Asia and Africa, women who share concerns and hopes similar to ours, is for us an event of immeasurable value.

# 6

# Marxist Critical Tools: Are They Helpful in Breaking the Stranglehold of Idealist Hermeneutics?

## JOSÉ MIGUEZ-BONINO

Down through the history of interpretation, exegetes have used diverse external sources from philosophy and so on to illuminate biblical texts. Here is an attempt to use Marxist analysis to free biblical interpretation from its idealist imprisonment. It is a helpful method to awaken an interpreter to his or her context. Though Miguez-Bonino sees it as the 'best instrument' for social analysis, in some of his other writings he also draws attention to its short-comings.

This essay first appeared in a pamphlet (*Holy Bible: The Politics of Bible Study*, issued by the Student Christian Movement, London, in 1974). For his further reflections on biblical hermeneutics, see his *Doing Theology in a Revolutionary Context* (Philadelphia, Fortress Press, 1975), pp. 85–105.

José Miguez-Bonino is an Argentinian and is one of the leading Protestant exponents of Latin American liberation theology.

The question of the title, given to me by the editor, is both puzzling and tempting. Marxism presents itself, whether as scientific analysis or as revolutionary theory and ideology, as a blunt negation (or overcoming) of religion in general and of the Christian religion in particular. The acceptance of a Marxist vision should logically result, therefore, not in the interpretation of the Biblical message but in its dissolution. On the other hand, Marx and his followers have offered an interpretation of the Christian religion and even of the Biblical (particularly but not exclusively the New Testament) writings. Is there anything in this interpretation which could help a Christian today to a better grasp of his own faith? Or, coming more specifically to our question: is there in the way in which Marx and some of his followers come to the interpretation of Christian origins and development anything that a Christian interpreter can learn when he faces the Scriptures? My subtitle tries to summarize my answer to this question. It is offered here very tentatively, as comments and questions to be discussed and pursued rather than as an elaborate analysis. And it is offered out of the concrete context of Christians who are engaged in the struggle for the liberation of man and society, and who are engaged in that struggle together with many Marxists in a common – though not undifferentiated – socialist commitment. It seems to me that, translated to the area of Biblical study, the Marxist insights are a powerful instrument to free interpretation from its idealist captivity. This is what I shall try to illustrate.

## TRACKING DOWN 'IDEOLOGY': THE CRITICISM OF INTERPRETATION

It is well known that Marxism places religion in the area of ideologies – the intellectual constructions whose real significance is in the economic and social relations which they reflect (or hide). Among the criticisms that Marx directs against Christianity within this framework is the accusation that it provides religious sanction to the oppressive capitalist bourgeois system (in fact, that 'Christian principles' have justified all forms of exploitation and oppression). The concrete form to which he points is the Christian buttressing of the Prussian absolutist state.

Whatever qualifications one might have to make concerning this interpretation, I submit that 'ideological suspicion' is a fundamental critical tool for interpretation. I think the first application has to do with the 'history of interpretation' because, as a matter of fact, our study of the Bible is always placed within a stream of interpretations. We modify, correct, qualify, even reverse, 'meanings' which have already been given, traditioned, almost incorporated into the texts. It is, therefore, crucial to ask about the ideological presuppositions and functions which such interpretations may have had.

Marx said, for instance, that Protestant ethics had reflected the capitalist bourgeois ideology by substituting 'having' for 'being': man had to forgo all aesthetic, material and social enhancement of the self in order to work and save – 'the more you save . . . the greater will become your treasure which neither moss or rust will corrupt – your capital'. We know that – although in a different way – Max Weber's sociological studies have borne out the operation (if not the reasoning) of this interpretation. But if this is so, should not we ask how has this affected Biblical interpretation? How has, in fact, Biblical interpretation dealt with the texts which relate being and having?

1 The first thing that comes to mind are Jesus' sayings about 'riches' and 'the rich'. Even a cursory look to Biblical commentaries in the Protestant tradition shows the almost uniform ideological train of thought: riches (in themselves) are good – therefore Jesus could not have condemned them as such, nor rich people as such – consequently the text must mean something else – this something else must be found in the 'subjective' sphere (intention, attitudes, motivations). Once this framework of interpretation is in operation, all texts gather around it in one coherent whole. Exegesis follows suit: Luke's version of the Beatitude of the poor, for instance, is interpreted through Matthew's 'in spirit'; this is in time disconnected from the prophetic-Psalmic relation of 'poor' and 'oppressed' or the whole is 'spiritualized' as devotion (humility before God). The ideological function of such interpretation is evident (however different the intention of the interpreter may have been), you can rest assured in your capitalist accumulation of wealth (or your attempt to reach it); religion (reverence for God) legitimizes and blesses your effort! The persistence of such ideological stereotypes is forcefully attested in the interpretation of such an honest and responsible exegete as J. Jeremias. He – perhaps correctly – argues that in the parable of the rich man and Lazarus, 'Jesus does not want to comment on a social problem'. But when verse 25 (Luke 16.19–31) poses the question of the reversal of the condition of the poor, Jeremias argues from the 'ideological supposition' and asks: 'Where had Jesus ever suggested that wealth in itself merits hell and that poverty in itself is rewarded by paradise?' To which, clearly, there are at least two answers that an interpretation free from the bourgeois presupposition could not have failed to see. One: that Jesus never speaks of wealth *in itself* or poverty *in itself* but of rich and poor as they are, historically. The 'in itself' abstraction is clearly a piece of liberal ideology. Secondly: a whole number of texts, or rather practically all texts dealing with the subject (with the exception of Matthew 13.12 and parallels if interpreted in this connection), point in the clear direction of this reversal, whatever explanation we may want to give them. Moreover, its relation to one trend of the prophetic tradition – to

which Jesus is evidently related in several other aspects of his teaching – makes it all the more clear. We reach the real ground of Jeremias' interpretation in the strange affirmation that 'Jesus does not intend to take a position on the question of rich and poor'.

2 A host of other examples could easily be given. The problem is not one of particular texts but of the total framework into which interpretation is cast. Once the 'mythical' cosmic dimension in which traditional interpretation had projected the Biblical story began to slip away at the advent of the modern world, the peculiar atmosphere of liberal bourgeois 'spirituality', individualistic and subjective, became normative for interpretation. Thus, historical and political events like the death of Jesus, the Parousia, or mission, were decoded out of their cosmic representation into an individualistic and inward 'existential' moment, experience or appropriation. A reinterpretation of the texts requires the explosion of the ideological straitjacket in which they have been imprisoned.

## THE SOCIO-ECONOMIC MATRIX: THE CRITICISM OF THE SOURCES

Deeper than the discovery of the ideological functions of religion is Marx's understanding of it as the projection of man's 'misery', of his suffering from and protest against an unjust and oppressive world. In this line, Engels, Kautsky and others have understood the emergence of Christianity as the 'slave's' protest against oppression, finding a (substitutionary) satisfaction in the hope of an apocalyptic (and later otherworldly) vindication. Lately Ernst Bloch has called attention to the dynamism of that hope. A dynamism that can only find historic realisation when the religious 'heritage' is wrenched from its transcendent-mythical and incorporated into a historic-scientific (Marxist) projection.

We need not concern ourselves with the details of this interpretation. They suffer from serious historical oversimplifications and inaccuracies. Moreover, we must reject – even on Marxist grounds – all simplistic and mechanistic explanation of religion as a mere 'reflex' of economic conditions. The religious reality is a complex phenomenon which has its own laws and internal coherence. It would be ridiculous – though a wooden orthodox Marxism sometimes has tried it – to explain the biblical texts as a direct consequence of economic and social situations. But it is quite another thing to ask for the socio-economic matrix in which these texts were born. This is more than the already established determination of the *Sitz im Leben* in order to illumine a text. It is the question of whether and in what form a religious outlook which finds expression in texts expresses the socio-economic relations and circumstances of a given society.

1 The 'social' prophets offer a good illustration. Socially engaged and progressive Christians rightly appeal to them. Their scathing denunciation of exploitation and oppression, their condemnation of a religion which covers up injustice with ritual, their call to repentance and their announcement of judgement are all relevant to our present situation. But one may wonder whether the prophets can be so directly 'enrolled' for socio-economic revolution. As conservative exegetes are always ready to point out, most prophets are actually opposed to progress and change; they rather dream of a former (perhaps never existent) society in which every family freely cultivated its field, cared for its cattle and enjoyed a self-sufficient situation. In fact, sometimes they even go back to a pre-agricultural, nomadic ideal. The real crisis which prompts their message is the 'progress' to a more differentiated society in which class differences become accentuated and the structural class-relationships (landowner and labourer, producer and tradesman, the intermediation of business, and the corresponding political differentiations) take the place of face-to-face and intra-familial ones. Their prophecy is indeed 'the sigh of the oppressed creature' alienated in this change and 'the protest' of that creature. But it is cast in the form of an utopic projection of a previous real or imagined harmony.

What is the importance of this distinction? It is this: that unless we identify the utopian character of the prophetic projection, we run the risk (to which most 'progressive' interpretation succumb) of merely *moralizing* the prophetic message into a well-meaning admonition to those in power to repent and put an end to injustice. The real question posed by the prophetic message so understood is not how to translate into modern terms the prophetic demands. This can only result in a new set of idealistic principles. The question is: how can we, in the present historical conditions, give adequate expression to the prophetic protest against the disruption of human life created by the conditions of our capitalist society and how can we in the present historical conditions give adequate expression to the prophetic hope of a reintegration of human life and society in justice and solidarity?

2   Again, there is no need to provide many illustrations of the point we are trying to make. In one sense, what we are saying is that Biblical texts – like all texts – can be (and at one level must be) seen (as Marxism indicates) as an expression of the human misery and hope generated by the socio-economic conditions and finding expression in mythical or utopian projections. The 'eschatological reversal' of rich and poor to which we alluded previously, the thaumaturgic (healing) expectations and performances, the forms of communal solidarity which we find both in the Old and the New Testament, cannot be exempted from this level of analysis.

3   The previous affirmation will immediately prompt a question: is not God's reality and power evacuated in this interpretation? Because it seems clear that it is precisely in this 'mythical' or 'utopic' space where the Bible locates God's presence: God raises the Assyrian to punish Israel, he appoints Cyrus to bring his people back, he strikes down with sickness the wicked king. Jesus miraculously heals the sick, feeds the hungry, raises the dead – i.e. brings the signs of the coming Kingdom. A divinely ordained catastrophic event ushers in the new age. It seems to me that this question points to a deeper level of Biblical interpretation in several ways.

Firstly, it is this question which helps us to see one peculiarity of the Biblical witness: its own tendency to historicize the space of God's intervention: thus, God judges and liberates 'in, with and under' historical, worldly events. Jesus relativizes his own role as thaumaturg by relating it to faith on the one hand and subordinating it to his message of the Kingdom on the other. Paul historicizes the eschatological expectation by demanding in the Christian community the reality of the eschatological reversal (no more woman and man, Jew or Greek, slave or master). Using the terms of the Marxist analysis: the Bible is not satisfied with expressing human misery, nor with other worldly or subjective realm – it announces, narrates and demands historical events which, at least in principle and initially, *overcome in reality* this misery. Biblical interpretation looks for the presence of these pointers not by denying the socio-economic matrix but by bringing it to light.

## PRAXIS AND INTERPRETATION: WHAT IS THE 'TRUTH' OF THE BIBLE?

Are we really entitled to take the step indicated in the last paragraph? Is this not a dissolution of God's message into human activism, an unwarranted secularization of the Gospel? The answer to this question hinges on the understanding of the character of God's Word. If it is understood as a *statement* of what God is or does, then the mythical or utopian frameworks (or the subjectivistic inversion of reality of liberal hermeneutics) has the last word. But if the Biblical message is a *call, an announcement-proclamation (kerygma)* which is given in order to put in motion certain actions and to produce certain situations, then God is not the *content* of the message but the *wherefrom* and the *whereto*, the originator and the impulse of this course of action and these conditions. Then, *hearing* the message can mean no other than becoming involved in this action and this creation of conditions and situations. By defining an event as 'God's action', the Bible is not withdrawing it from history – even if the ideological framework used is mythical – but pointing to the divinely wrought and revealed background and power of the human action demanded. This is even so in the New Testament references to Christ's resurrection: mission, the new life, community active love, are the human historical content of which Christ's resurrection is the ground and power.

1  In this perspective we are forced to transform our understanding of interpretation itself. Even in the Bible-study renewal which has been so significant for the SCM and the ecumenical movement, we have been used to the 'idealist' method of trying to establish the meaning of the text in the first place and then to relate it to our historical conditions and to listen to what the text will say to us. There are two misunderstandings in this procedure. The first is that it does not take seriously enough the fact that the text itself is an 'action', the record of an involvement in God's call. We are not faced with a naked divine word but with a human obedience or disobedience in which God's Word is made present to us. We enter into these courses of action.

But – and this is even more important – we always read the texts 'out of' a praxis and 'into' a praxis. As Christian citizens, workers, intellectuals, husbands or wives, we already have an 'enacted interpretation' of the text which will be confirmed, deepened, challenged or rejected in the confrontation – but which will set the terms of that confrontation. The relation between theory and praxis – to which Marxist thinking has called our attention – is by no means simple. It does not deny that any course of action already incorporates (conscious or unconscious) theoretical presuppositions. It underlines the importance of theoretical thinking which examines the practical course of action in terms of its relevance to the direction of the process and criticizes the theoretical presuppositions in terms of the development of the process. There is, in this respect, a constant relation between theory and praxis. We cannot and need not at this point enter further into this discussion. But we need to stress the importance of this basic understanding for Biblical interpretation.

2 Let me take an illustration from a very controversial person and situation in my continent: the Colombian priest Camilo Torres. When he reads in the Gospel: 'If you are offering your gift at the altar and then remember that your brother has something against you, leave your gift before the altar and go; first be reconciled to your brother, and then come and offer your gift' (Matt. 5.23–4). He asks himself – using all the tools of knowledge available to him: who is my brother who has something against me? Not merely in an individual and subjective sense but as a priest who belongs to a particular historical structure of religious and political power, as an intellectual who belongs to a group who has played a role in history, as a member of a (economically powerful and dominating) class. The answer is clear: the poor, the worker, the peasant, he 'has something against me'. Furthermore, what he has against me is objectively real – my action in the solidarity of the institution, the group, the class to which I belong is an oppressive action. Therefore, if I interpret the text as merely affecting my subjective interpersonal relation to those whom I know personally (within the circle of my relations) I am rejecting and denying the real estrangement. My interpretation in such a case is an ideological occultation, bound to the interests of my class. I can only read the text authentically from within the recognition of the class conflict in which my relation to the largest number of my brothers places me. The command to 'reconcile myself with my brother' can only be understood, therefore, as objectively demanding me to remove the objective alienation between my brother and myself.

We can perhaps question the course of action taken by Camilo Torres as he moves into political action and finally into the guerrilla. But this discussion misses (or eludes) the point; Camilo reads the text in and out of the explicit recognition of his total involvement as an historical man and re-acts his praxis out of the total impact of the text on his involvement. He refuses to take refuge in a 'normative' course of behaviour which would be found in the text without exposing himself to it, without bringing to it his total present reality. Otherwise he might have been satisfied to fulfill the 'normative requirement' within the self-understood limits of his un-exposed and therefore unchallenged sociological condition (i.e. resolve the personal quarrel he may have had with a fellow-priest or a colleague-professor). And he refuses to let the command hover over the concrete historical circumstances in which his actions take place. Otherwise he might have been satisfied with an action of charity – which leaves the objective conflict untouched. Only by incorporating his action within a total 'praxis' in which the cause of 'offense' might be objectively removed could the reading of Jesus' word be actually 'heard.' Naturally, the relation between interpretation and praxis understood in this way, requires the use of all the analytical tools at our disposal – both in the understanding of our present praxis, of the text and of the conditions for a new praxis. This is precisely the 'theoretical' work. And this is the only justification for doing theology . . . when it fulfills its task!

3　This is, in fact, the kind of theology that we meet in the Biblical 'reading of the Bible'. Modern scholarship has shown us, for instance, how the story of creation, or the exodus, is 'read' in the course of the tradition of Israel. When Deutero-Isaiah, for instance, tells the 'exodus' in chapter 35, he reads it as the exile who mourns in captivity far from the Promised Land and who waits for the return. The road in the desert, the springs of water, the power that comes to the weary, is *the new road* to the return from exile. He does not 'deduce' from the Exodus story a 'moral' for his time: he is invited to enter the exodus *now*, the first exodus as God's action is the *wherefrom* and the *power* of this call. This is what happens when people in the Third World receive today this same story. As a Latin-American theologian puts it: 'If our reading of the Biblical kerygma has any purpose, the "memory" of the Exodus becomes for us – oppressed people of the Third World – a pro-vocative Word, an announcement of liberation. . . . It is our call to prolong the exodus, because it was not an exclusive Hebrew event but God's liberating purpose for all peoples. In an hermeneutic line it is perfectly legitimate to understand ourselves *out of* the Biblical exodus and, above all, to understand it *out of* our situation as peoples living in political, social, economic or cultural "slavery"' (J. Croatto).

## God's Word: the limitations of the tools

An interpretation which would limit itself to a Marxist analysis could not, certainly, make sense of what we have been saying, particularly in the last section. There is no 'wherefrom' and no 'power' in such interpretation, except in man's own action. Anything else is a human projection, the reification of relationships which man has not yet understood or wants to mystify. The Bible can – at best – record this dynamism of human action. Marxism gives it its real name. At this point no doubt there is a basic divergence. What for a Christian is the ultimate ground and power of his praxis is for an orthodox Marxist an ultimate alienation. This divergence cannot be solved in discussion or through argument. The faithfulness of his commitment is the only verification – not certainly proof – that a Christian can offer for the reality of the source and the power which sustains it. But a few brief theological points may be in order for a Christian who intends to take seriously the critical tools that Marxism has developed.

1 The overcoming of an idealist interpretation, far from being a surrender to a materialistic conception of reality, seems to me – to use a Marxist analogy – placing the Biblical perspective 'back on its head'. Idealist interpretation, in fact, particularly in its modern subjectivist form, inverted the direction of the Biblical message by projecting the historical events of God's action into consciousness as subjective events. This is precisely the reverse of the Incarnation: while God's Word becomes history, idealist interpretation replaces history by words. God in the flesh is the rejection of the idealist resolution of objective conflict and liberation into subjective transactions.

2 God's Word – the power of the Risen Lord – is a dynamic reality. It cannot be tied down to the merely logical continuity of dogmatic formulae but it impinges creatively on historical circumstances. Jesus Christ is the same yesterday, today and forever not in the static identity of a thing or a formulation, but in the dynamic unity of his redemptive purpose working itself out within the conditions and possibilities of a human history which itself is in movement. As a normative witness of that purpose, the Biblical record has a 'reserve of meaning' which becomes concrete as men read it in obedience, within the conditions of their own history. To claim normativity for the sociological limitations of understanding and action of the eighth-century prophets or the First-century Apostles is to stultify the Word of God. This is certainly not to surrender to arbitrary interpretation. There is a direction and

a congruity in God's purpose – and the tools of historical and literary criticism cannot be underestimated in helping to clarify this direction and congruity. But to look for a direct unmediated transposition is to deny the reality of the Holy Spirit.

3 'Discernment of the spirits' is not, therefore, a purely analytical process. Analytical processes (which are indispensable both in relation to the reading of the text and our relation to them) are assumed into and have their place within a synthetic act of commitment. Not the mere 'hearer' but only the 'doer' can understand God's Word.

# PART TWO

# *Re-use of the Bible:*
# *Examples of Hermeneutical*
# *Explorations*

The more I wrote the more deeply I felt that in writing I was struggling, not for beauty, but for deliverance.

(Nikos Kazantzakis *Report to Greco*)

# 7

# Jesus and the Minjung in the Gospel of Mark

## AHN BYUNG-MU

Minjung theology is one of the most provocative and challenging theologies to emerge from Asia. As its starting-point for doing theology and reading the Bible, it takes the minjung, the people who are politically oppressed, socially alienated, economically exploited and kept uneducated in cultural and intellectual matters. Ahn Byung-Mu's piece is an example of such an enterprise. In this essay, he attempts to re-read 'the crowd' – the *ochlos* – in Mark's Gospel from the perspective of Korean minjung theology. His approach also demonstrates how historical–critical tools can be used to liberate biblical texts.

This article forms a chapter in a volume on minjung theology, *Minjung Theology: People as the Subjects of History*, edited by the Commission on Theological Concerns of the Christian Conference of Asia (Maryknoll, NY, Orbis Books, 1981; London, Zed Press).

Ahn Byung-Mu is one of the pioneers of minjung theology and has written extensively from a biblical perspective.

Although New Testament scholarship has focused a great deal of attention on the people who were the audience and the object of Jesus' teaching, not much attention has been paid to the social character of his audience. Consequently, the words and deeds of Jesus have been desocialized. Whom did Jesus address and what was the character of what he said? This question will clarify the historical character of Jesus' words. The social characteristics of the 'whom' can be clarified by investigating the economic, political, and cultural make-up of the people. To understand this subject more comprehensively we need to see the total social structure and the place of the people surrounding Jesus. This is what this chapter will seek to do on the basis of the editorial phrases in the Gospel of Mark and the words of Jesus himself.

## *OCHLOS* IN THE GOSPEL ACCORDING TO MARK

From the beginning, the Gospel according to Mark mentions the crowds surrounding Jesus. Form critics view the editorial sections about the people surrounding Jesus as only the framework for the words of Jesus or for the kerygma that Jesus is the Christ. Therefore the people have been excluded and, as a result, a very important aspect has been lost.

In contrast to the approach of form critics, redaction critics consider the redactional framework important both for understanding the viewpoint of the author and the import of Jesus' sayings in context. However, surprisingly, these too have paid little attention to the audience of Jesus, preferring to concentrate on 'the theology' of the author as found in his redactional statements and redactional arrangements. Redaction critics also seem to have missed the point that the authors of the Gospels put so much emphasis on 'the people' because they considered the relationship between Jesus and the people to be crucial for understanding the identity and mission of Jesus. Therefore, while this paper will reflect essentially the approach of redaction criticism, it will pay greater attention to the reality of 'the people' and their relationship to Jesus.

As early as Mark 1.22 the crowd is mentioned, and it continually appears on the scene. At the beginning, 'the people,' or the third person plural, 'all,' is used to refer to them. In this way attention is drawn to the people (Mark 1.22, 30, 32, 33, 37, 44, 45; 2.2). However, their identity does not become clear. This kind of descriptive method makes the readers pay attention to the social composition of the people. Eventually the concept which represents the many people (*polloi*) appears on the stage: this is *ochlos* (2.4). In the Gospel according to Mark, without counting the indicative pronouns, there are thirty-six occurrences of the word *ochlos*. This indicates a definite intention in the use of the word.[1]

Besides the frequency in the use of the word, there is another reason why our attention is drawn to this word. For we would normally expect the term *laos* rather than *ochlos* to be used for the people, since the term *laos* occurs far more frequently in the language of the biblical writers. The term *laos* is used around 2,000 times in the Septuagint. This word consistently indicates the people of Israel as the people of God.[2] However, in the Gospel according to Mark, there is no use of the word *laos* except in a quotation from the Old Testament in 7.6 and in the words of the chief priests and lawyers (14.2).

Besides these two uses of *laos*, there is one occurrence of *plethos* as a noun, and 'the many' as an adjective, which do not describe any characteristic group (3.8).

It is certain that in the New Testament, Mark is the first writer to introduce the term *ochlos*. It does not appear in any New Testament writing before Mark, but the documents written after Mark, such as the other Gospels and Acts, contain this word many times, proving the influence of Mark. *Ochlos* appears three times in Revelation, which we know to have been written during the persecution of Christians (7.9; 19.1, 6). It is noteworthy that in the Epistles of Paul, which were written before Mark, this word does not appear even once.

All these facts indicate that we must pay close attention to Mark's use of the word *ochlos*. A comparison of the contexts and intentions of Paul's writings and those of Mark will indicate in a preliminary way Mark's predilection for this term.

The Epistles of Paul were written ten years before Mark's Gospel, that is, about AD 50–60. Paul's writings were intended to explicate the mission to the Gentiles and were addressed to the Gentile churches to exhort and to teach them the faith. These concentrate on Christology and soteriology, and therefore have an apologetic and a didactic character. For his purpose, Paul does not think it important to mention anything about the historical Jesus. In fact, he declares that he does not really want to know about the historical Jesus (2 Cor. 5.16).

In contrast, the Gospel of Mark was written when the Jewish War had already started, or when Jerusalem was already occupied in AD 70 (I believe the latter) and the Jews were being expelled *en masse* from the land of Judea.[3] Unlike Paul, Mark concentrates on the traditions of the historical Jesus. Although Mark's basic position is similar to that of Paul, namely, that Jesus is the Christ (the kerygma), his concern is to present the historical Jesus prior to the Resurrection. Hence the kerygmatic materials that were already established as the basis for Christology were insufficient. He uses other materials of a historical nature. Therefore, we cannot agree with Bultmann that Mark is only an expanded kerygma. Thus Mark, unlike Paul, is not apologetic, and neither is he interested in developing a Christology or a soteriology, which are abstract and idealistic. His descriptive style is simple and folksy, containing historical facts.

In the above comparison we can see certain factors that are related to our subject matter. Mark was in a different social situation from Paul's. Therefore, not only could Mark not accept the highly concentrated kerygmatic theology, but it seems he also consciously had to maintain a certain distance from Paul. Such a position made Mark move toward a historical rather than kerygmatic Jesus. Under such a premise, the term *ochlos*, which Mark introduces, has a very important function which was demanded by Mark's historical situation. During Mark's time, the Jewish people, including the Jewish Christians, were expelled from their land and were on the way to exile like lost sheep without a shepherd.

## THE CHARACTERISTICS OF *OCHLOS* IN THE GOSPEL ACCORDING TO MARK

Normally, we would begin with a semantic and conceptual clarification of a term and then see how this is reflected in a writing. We are not going to follow this procedure. Rather, we will first determine the character of the *ochlos* by examining the occurrences of this term in Mark. By so doing we will reduce to a minimum the subjective interpretation of this term. We will later examine its semantic field and usage in other literature.

### The characteristics of *ochlos*

1 Wherever Jesus went, there were always people who gathered around him. They are called the *ochlos* (2.4, 13; 3.9, 20, 32; 4.1; 5.21, 24, 31; 8.1; 10.1). In most instances, there is no clear reason as to why these people followed Jesus. They form the background of Jesus' activities.

2 These people were the so-called sinners, who stood condemned in their society. Especially at the beginning of his Gospel, Mark applies the term *ochlos* in a typical way to the tax collectors and sinners. As we shall show more fully later, Mark describes in this scene how the dogmatic legalists criticize Jesus for meeting with these people, who are the outcasts of society (2.13–17).

3 There are cases where they (the *ochlos*) are differentiated from the disciples (8.34; 9.14; 10.46). In some instances Jesus teaches only the disciples (4.36; 6.46; 7.17, 33). Thus it seems that Jesus placed the disciples above the *ochlos*. However, we must note that Jesus often fiercely criticized the disciples.[4] On the contrary, there are no instances of Jesus rebuking the *ochlos*. Matthew and Luke either boldly suppress the criticism of the disciples or beautify Jesus' attitude toward the disciples. This fact should be remembered when we view the disciples as representatives of the church.[5]

4 The *ochlos* are contrasted with the ruling class from Jerusalem who attack and criticize Jesus as their enemy. The *ochlos* took an anti-Jerusalem position and were clearly on the side of Jesus (2.4–6; 3.2–21; 4.1; 11.18, 27, 32). In this connection, it is important to note that they were the minjung of Galilee.[6]

5 Because the *ochlos* were against the rulers, the rulers were afraid of them and tried not to arouse their anger (11.18, 32; 12.12; 15.8, 15). Accordingly, to get the *ochlos* on their side, the rulers had to bribe them. For instance, when Jesus was arrested the rulers are said to have given money to mobilize the *ochlos* – a fact which indicates the strength of the *ochlos*. However, the fact that they were mobilized in such a way does not mean that they were necessarily anti-Jesus, but that they could be manipulated.[7]

## The attitude of Jesus toward the *ochlos*

1 'Jesus had compassion on them, because they were like sheep without a shepherd' (6.34). The expression 'sheep without a shepherd' comes from the Old Testament. Such an expression implies a tradition of criticism against the rulers, who had a responsibility to take care of the people (for example, Ezek, 34.5), as well as against the crowd, who were cursed with directionlessness because of their betrayal of Yahweh. The latter tradition, however, does not appear in the Gospels. In the prayer of Moses requesting a successor, he says, 'Please do not abandon the congregation of Yahweh like lost sheep without a shepherd' (Num. 27.17). Moses regards the *ochlos*, who were hungry and following him, as a crowd without leaders. At the same time, he seems to suggest that they were also alienated from the rulers.

2 After the brief narration in Mark 3.34 ('And looking around on those who sat about him . . .'), Jesus announces that they (the people) were his mother and brothers. Previously in verse 32, it is written, 'A crowd was sitting about him . . .' This editorial phrase specifically refers to the *ochlos*. The announcement indicates, on the one hand, a deliberate extrication of Jesus from the ties and demands of kinship and, on the other, it announces that the *ochlos* are the members of a new community (family). This statement was not easily accepted in those days. Therefore, in Matthew we have *mathetai* (disciples) instead of *ochlos*, and in Luke it has been eliminated.

3 'As was his custom, Jesus taught the *ochlos*' (10.1; see also 2.13; 4.11–12; 7.4; 11.18). This means that the *ochlos* were fascinated with

his teachings (13.18b). In Matthew and Luke the instances noted above of Jesus teaching the *ochlos* have either been partially eliminated or altered. Such alteration certainly weakens the position of the *ochlos* as the people whom Jesus taught and as the object of his teachings. Although the *ochlos* is not totally ignored in the other Gospels, there is evidence of the expanding authority of the apostles and the church.

### Synthesis

Taking into consideration all these factors, we may state the following:

1 There is no evidence of a qualitative evaluation of the *ochlos*. In other words, there is no attempt to evaluate the *ochlos* either in terms of an established religious or ethical standard or in terms of a new ethic. (Mark 3.35 is patently a later addition.)

2 Those who were the *ochlos* gathered around Jesus and followed him: if Jesus was the *Wanderprediger*, they were the *Wanderochlos*. In 8.2 we see that they followed Jesus for three days without eating. This shows us that they had neither an established position in their society nor were they members of an identifiable economic class.

3 When we consider the fact that the *ochlos* are contrasted with the ruling class of that time and that Jesus was criticized for associating with the *ochlos*, it becomes evident that the *ochlos* were the condemned and alienated class.

4 Finally, there is a consistent attitude of Jesus toward the *ochlos*. He accepted and supported them without making any conditions. He received them as they were. He also promised them the future (the Kingdom of God). Such action was unacceptable to the leaders – the Pharisees and the Sadducees – and even to the religious groups who were anti-Jerusalem, i.e. the Essenes and the followers of John the Baptist.

### THE COMPOSITION OF THE *OCHLOS* – THOSE WHO FOLLOWED JESUS

There are a variety of people who followed Jesus and about whom Jesus spoke. However, socially all these are seen as belonging to one social class, namely, the *ochlos*. In Mark 2.13–17, the *ochlos* is presented in a paradigmatic way, as we shall see in the following analysis.

Mark 2.13–17 can be divided into two parts: (1) verses 13–14 and (2) verses 15–17. The first part is concerned with the invitation 'Follow me!' addressed to Levi (14b); and the second focuses on the joy of sharing a meal in which Levi does not have a major role. These two parts were transmitted independently, as is particularly evident in Luke 5.29 where Luke clarifies the link Mark makes in 2.15a by saying that Levi invited Jesus and his disciples for a meal.

It is important to make a connection between these two passages without which it is not possible to see the significance of the two. If we keep the two separate, we do not really get the significance of Levi being a tax collector and the meaning of the meal also becomes vague. When we combine these two, the dinner becomes a joyful feast celebrating the fact that certain types of people were called to be the disciples of Jesus.

To make this connection, Mark does not rely simply on the connection he makes in 2.15a, which Luke amplifies. He perceives and states a more substantial connection in verses 13 and 15c, which scholars agree are Mark's own editorial compositions. In verse 13b Mark says that those who followed Jesus and listened to his teaching were 'the whole crowd' (*pas ho ochlos*); and in verse 15a he says that many tax collectors and sinners sat at the meal with Jesus and his disciples. In so saying, he sees the tax collectors and sinners as part of those who followed him. In other words, the 'many who followed him' are the very *ochlos* referred to in verse 13 (cf. 2.2–4).

The presence of the *ochlos* is what provides a substantial connection between these two parts, i.e. verses 13–14 and 15–17, and indeed provides the overall connection and background for Jesus' teaching and ministry. We will now turn to an examination of the composition of the *ochlos*.

The sinners and tax collectors already referred to are mentioned in the old so-called Q source (Matt. 11.19) and in Luke's special source. There is thus early and convincing agreement that 'tax collectors and sinners' were a part of the *ochlos*. In Matthew the category of prostitutes is also mentioned in 'tax collectors and prostitutes' (Matt. 21.32) so this category too formed a part of the designation 'sinners.' Although there are many references to the sick (fifteen times), to the hungry (6.34–5; 8.1ff), and to widows (12.41ff) who appear more often in Luke as part of the *ochlos*, the category 'tax-collectors and sinners' seems to be a more pervasive group in the *ochlos*. Hence, a clarification, in particular, of the concept of sinners and the social composition of tax collectors, identified in terms of their occupation, would provide us with a good idea of the contours of this amorphous group of people called the *ochlos*.

## Sinners (*Hamartolos*)

There is no argument about the fact that Jesus associated with sinners. The question is who are the types of people called sinners, or what is the meaning of sinner?

A sinner in the Judaic tradition primarily signified one who is a criminal before God. Concretely, it is an overall designation for people who cannot accomplish the duty of the law. From the time the Pharisees appeared on the religious scene, the law of cleanliness, previously limited to the priests, was applied to the Israelites as a whole.[8] This raised a new problem *vis-à-vis* the classification of sinners.

In discussing this problem, Jeremias points out that the sinner in Jewish society was defined in two ways.[9] One was a publicly recognized criminal (offender against the law), and the other was a person in a lowly, i.e. a socially unacceptable, occupation as defined in those days. He differentiates these two and says that the latter was despised because of 'immoral conduct of life' or 'dishonorable occupation.' But the reason why the occupation made a person a sinner was because the occupation violated the law, either directly or indirectly, and not because of the occupation itself. These were persons who could not rest on the Sabbath day because of the character of their occupations (boatmen, shepherds, and prostitutes). Or, persons who were ill-smelling or those who had to handle things defined as impure (leather-makers, coppersmiths, and butchers). They were alienated and could not participate in worship. While drawing attention to these categories of sinners, Jeremias overlooked another important group. Even persons who could not fulfill the requirements of the law because of sickness or poverty were also designated sinners.

The notion that sickness was the result of crime was pervasive in Judaism. Such a notion appears continually not only among the orthodox in the Old Testament (for example, Psalm 73, Job, etc.), but also in the New Testament (John 9.1 f). In particular, lepers, hemophiliacs, and the mentally ill were regarded either as unclean according to the law or as those upon whom the wrath of God had come. These are not really criminals, but were forced into these situations because of outside pressures and religious–social thinking. Poverty also brought about this condition for it prevented people from keeping the Sabbath or the law of cleanliness.

These persons were different from those who violated the law on purpose. But in effect they were also branded as sinners by the law which upheld a particular system.

The tradition of the three Gospels views the scholars of religious and civil law and the Pharisees as Jesus' antagonists. These understood sinners in terms of the categories given above. As we have already noted, in Pharisaic thinking the label 'sinner' was applied widely, especially to those who infringed the law of cleanliness, so that the realm of the law was expanded. This brought about the social alienation of those in humble occupations, the poor, and the sick. Therefore, both persons defined according to their occupations and those who were criminals were forcibly marginalized and alienated by the system. They were sinners because they violated the law or could not adapt themselves to the system of the law. From this standpoint, religious sin and social alienation were really two sides of the same coin.

### Tax collectors

Tax collectors are not included in the comprehensive category of sinners, but are another conspicuous parallel category. As already noted, the usage 'tax collectors and sinners' can be seen in the Q source (Matt. 11.19), in the special source of Luke (15.1), and in the Gospel of Mark.

If the tax collectors were regarded as Jesus' people (minjung), the minjung cannot be limited just to politically and economically alienated people. For the tax collectors were agents of the Roman Empire and cannot be characterized as the poor class. Mark dares to describe the tax collector Levi as a person who could afford to give a dinner. But there is a difficulty in characterizing tax collectors as a group because among them too there were the rich and the poor. There was a class which received contracts from the Roman Empire to collect taxes and these exploited the people. There were also a number of others who worked under these people as their employees. Among the employee category, there were many people who worked part-time. All of them were treated as tax collectors in that society and were alienated. This can be seen in the fact that they were often referred to like Gentiles (Matt. 5.46–8; cf. 6.7, 32; 10.5).

When the anti-Roman movement eventually became a guerrilla movement, an attempt was made to get a general nationalist response. In order to do this the people rose in revolt at the time of a census for the purpose of tax-collection. They made Galilee their stronghold and made the refusal to pay taxes the beginning of their struggle. This fact indicates the general animosity towards tax collectors. Even in the Rabbinic tradition, they convicted the tax collectors and arrayed them with murderers and burglars.[10]

Why did Mark include them in the category of *ochlos*? First of all, it is precisely because of the tradition that Jesus associated with them (Matt. 11.9). The distinguishing character of this tradition about Jesus is that, no matter what, he unconditionally embraced the alienated and despised class in the community. It is clear that tax collectors were excluded not only by the nationalists, but also by the religious ruling class, landowners, and merchants. The tax collectors were denied the right to make offerings for the poor (Baba Qamma 10.1, 2), and they were not permitted as witnesses in the Judaic court (*Babylonian Talmud*).

Jesus' attitude to the tax collectors is implied in the saying 'those who are well have no need of a physician, but those who are sick; I came not to call the righteous, but sinners' (16b–17), which was given in answer to the question 'Why does he eat with tax collectors and sinners?' As already indicated, Jesus includes tax collectors with sinners and says that he has come to call the sinners.

Here it is necessary to note the meaning of *kalesai* (to call) in order to understand Jesus' attitude to tax collectors. Unlike Mark, Luke speaks of making one repent or the sinner who repents (Luke 15.7–10, 18). This idea is not present in Mark; and he uses the word *kalesai*, which is used to call one as a disciple.

Jesus shows this basic attitude also to other groups, that is, the ill, fishermen, women, and children. Though tax collectors were different in some respects from these people, they have something in common. They too were alienated from the system and were therefore despised. Taking into account the fact that Zealots were also included with tax collectors among Jesus' disciples (Mark 3.18), we know that Jesus' attitude toward the minjung was never limited to people who were politically oppressed.

## The sick

In Judaism, sickness like other forms of ill fortune was considered to be punishment for sin. There are evidences of this notion also in the Gospels (cf. John 9.1; Luke 13.2; Mark 2.5, etc.). This idea became even more dominant when the Pharisees applied the law of cleanliness to the common people. Consequently, in particular, lepers, the mentally ill and hemophiliacs were also alienated. The sick appear many times in the Gospels, and in many cases it seems that they have already been deserted by their family and neighbors. The reason why the sick were socially alienated was because they were poor and their condition contrary to the law of cleanliness. They were thus also alienated on religious grounds. The belief that their unfortunate lot was punishment for crime made it possible to exclude them from the community.

Some people feel that, according to Mark 2.5b, Jesus also had such an idea, but this is wrong. Mark speaks of belief here, but he does not speak about the belief of the patient himself, but of the people who carried the sick person on their shoulders. There are two more cases like this (5.36; 9.23) where belief is seen as a precondition for healing. We must recognize the fact that here belief means pure trust, regardless of belief about redemption. If this text gives weight to the idea of absolution from sin, the advent of the Kingdom of God must be regarded as bringing liberation not just from sins but rather from the whole dominating system and from the ideas upon which it is founded.[11]

In this connection, we must take note of two things regarding the character of the healing story. One is that most of the sick had already left their dwelling houses and were in the alienated situation of wanderers. The other is that, in most cases, Jesus sent them to their homes after curing them.

A good illustration of this character of the healing story, namely, the restoration of lost rights, occurs in those stories concerning lepers, who were typical of persons alienated by the law of cleanliness (cf. Bill. I, 474). Furthermore, lepers were isolated from places where others lived. Hence, an important aspect of the restoration is for the cured leper to show himself to the priest to prove that he is cured and to offer the sacrifice that Moses ordered. Except for cases where the sick were children (5.35 ff; 7.24 ff) and where healing stories have another purpose (3.1 ff), Jesus says, 'Go back home!' or 'Go!' (2.11; 5.19; 5.34; 8.26; 10.52). The phrase in 5.19 that 'the cured man wanted to follow Jesus' emphasizes the fact that Jesus sent him home in spite of the fact that he wanted to remain with Jesus. The restoration here is different from 'to call him' (*kalesai*), which was a different process for the restoration of rights of people in the society.

## SAYINGS IN MARK ABOUT JESUS' ATTITUDE TO THE *OCHLOS*

1 'I came not to call the righteous, but sinners' (2.17b). In this logion we have an indication of Jesus' basic attitude of love. We must not overlook in this logion the terms 'not' and 'but.' It cannot be interpreted as saying 'not only . . . but also . . .' Jesus never showed what may be called universal love. He loved people with partiality. He always stood on the side of the oppressed, the aggrieved, and the weak. This fact is clarified in the Q source, as for example in the parable in Luke 15.2 ff (Q). It says, 'He leaves the other ninety-nine sheep in the pasture and goes looking for the one that got lost until he finds it.'

As we have already said, Mark views sinners as the *ochlos* and says definitely that Jesus came to the world for the *ochlos*.

Then it is necessary to clarify whether the sinners were defined from Jesus' standpoint or defined by the society. Luke, in using Mark, adds at the end 'who repent,' so that they are sinners from the point of view of Jesus. The King James version adds this phrase to the text of Mark and understands it from Luke's standpoint. But 'who repent' is Luke's, not Mark's. However, Luke's understanding of 'sinners who repent' is clarified in Luke 15 in the parables of the lost sheep, lost coin, and lost son. The sinner who repents is the one who is lost and is returned to the place to which he or she belongs. Therefore Luke 15 also reflects in some measure Jesus' attitude to the *ochlos* as found in Mark. Hence, 'sinner' must be given the added prefix 'so-called.' For Jesus, those labeled sinners by the current ideology of the rulers were the victims who were robbed and oppressed.

2 'There is nothing outside a man which by going into him can defile him; but the things which come out of a man are what defile him' (7.15). This is Jesus' saying about the law of cleanliness. This logion reflects situational language related to verses 1, 2, 5, 14b, 15. The original meaning became unclear because of the insertion of verses 6–14, which are unrelated to the original content. When this section is bracketed out, the original speech shows a stand opposing the law of

cleanliness as generalized in the Pharisaic system which, as noted above, alienated many people. Incidentally, the speech of Jesus opposes the absolute rule of cult over life. Most people have discussed this revolutionary declaration in terms of Judaism and anti-Judaism, but have not asked the question as to why he made it.

The situation which provided the background for this speech was that of the Pharisees and the scholars of law from Jerusalem criticizing Jesus' disciples for eating with unwashed hands. Eating with unwashed hands contravened the law of cleanliness. In Jewish society of that time, people who violated the law of cleanliness were branded as *'am ha'aretz*.[12] In his editorial phrases (7.14a), Mark confirms the important fact that the hearers are the *ochlos*. They demonstrate their liberation from the system by disregarding the law of cleanliness which is a heavy burden on the *ochlos* – a fact which is confirmed in the saying in 7.15. Like this saying, the statement 'The sabbath was made for man, not man for the sabbath' (2.27) also is a declaration which liberates the people oppressed by the Sabbath law. In the Gospel of Matthew, it is for 'all who labor and are heavy-laden' (11.28).

3  The saying, in 9.37 and 10.13–15, requires respect for children. In 9.37 children are identified with Jesus and through him with God. In 10.13–15 he says that the Kingdom of God belongs to children. It is said that Judaism is the religion of adults because there is the responsibility to know the law and to keep it. In this situation women and children were treated contemptuously. There are many arguments about what the words 'with children' mean. In the context of the quarrel over who is higher or who is the first, Mark makes children the symbol of low persons (9.37). Mark 10.13–15 is the same because Jesus reacts to the bad attitude of the disciples toward the children. Luke (9.48) adds to the text of Mark the words 'for he who is least among you all is the one who is great' and indicates that a child is the symbol of a person who is treated coldly by society. In fact, the children stand in common with the minority (*mikroi*).[13]

Bultmann considers Luke 17.1–2 to be the basic source reflecting this attitude of Jesus which was later Christianized by identifying 'little ones' with '*ton pisteuonton*' (believers) (Matt. 18.6–7). Kummel identifies the little ones with 'the poor in spirit' (Matt. 5.3). However, 'little ones' does not designate a modest attitude, but a social position. It is proper that they are understood in relation to the poor, the crying, and the hungry and as participants in the Kingdom of God. The attitude of Jesus to the children is similar to his attitude toward the crowd, *ochlos*.

## THE LINGUISTIC MEANING OF *OCHLOS*

We have noted that Mark introduced the term *ochlos* into the New Testament and that he identified the followers of Jesus and the persons whom Jesus loved with partiality as the *ochlos*. We must now inquire into the linguistic tradition of this word. By so doing, we will be able to discover Mark's understanding of the meaning of 'minjung.' We will focus on the characteristics of the minjung (people) mainly through an analysis of materials in Kittel's New Testament dictionary.

### *Laos* and *ochlos*

1 *Before the New Testament*. The Septuagint introduces the term *laos* into Jewish usage. It translates the Hebrew term *'am* as many as 2,000 times. In Greek sources it is mostly used to denote a national group and often means belonging to some ruling community. For example, the expression 'Pharaoh's *laos*' is found in Homer, Pindar, and Herodotus. The Septuagint reflects the meaning of 'national group,' and this word especially indicates the Israelites who are referred to as *'am* in Hebrew. For non-Israelites the term *ethnos* is used in most cases. Of course, *laos* is used especially for 'God's people' (*'am*). Another characteristic usage of the Septuagint is that *laoi*, plural of *laos*, is used only 140 times, and it has the meaning of 'crowd' or *ochlos*. In this case, there is not the substantial meanings of *laos*. This is a significant characteristic, since ordinary common people hardly make an appearance in the use of *laos* in the Septuagint.

This tradition is also followed in Rabbinic documents. Usually, these documents employ *laos* also to designate non-Israelites, but the added description 'offended the law' differentiates them from the Israelites. Also epigraphic material from the Jewish diaspora often designates Israel as *laos*.

Compared with the use of *laos*, *ochlos* is used only about sixty times in the Septuagint. However, it does not occur in the ancient Old Testament documents, but in the documents of the later period. It is used to translate several Hebrew words, except *hamon*, which mean minjung. The common meaning of all these usages is 'the crowd.' But, it does not mean a particular social group or a member of a social group. Typical uses of the term are '*ochlos laou*' – a crowd of Israelites – or '*ochloi ethnou*' – a crowd of Gentiles.

After Pindar, the term *ochlos* appears in Greek documents referring to a confused majority or to the ordinary soldiers in a combat unit, but not to officers. It also refers to non-combat people who follow the army and perform menial duties. We must note that the anonymous people referred to as the *ochlos* are differentiated from the ruling class. The term *ochlos* refers to an ignorant crowd under a burden.

The Septuagint uses this Greek word with this general meaning of 'the mass.' As a descriptive term its precise meaning varies from context to context. It could mean 'insurgents,' 'tactical troops,' or just refer to the majority. It sometimes designates a crowd of children or women. Its usage in Rabbinic literature is not very different.

2 *Usage in the New Testament.* In the New Testament, unlike in the Septuagint, the term *ochlos* is used more often than *laos*. It occurs 174 times while the term *laos* occurs 141 times.

Looking at the use of the term *laos* in the New Testament, it occurs some 84 times in Luke, so that the majority of its uses are here. Luke seems to use it consciously since there are several aspects peculiar to his use of this term. First, quite often *laos* and *ochlos* are used interchangeably and carry the same meaning as *ochlos* in Mark. Second, Luke, however, seems to prefer the term *laos* for Israelites, though understood on the same lines as *ochlos* in Mark, to distinguish them from other national groups who are the *ethnoi* (Luke 19.47; 22.66; Acts 4.8; 23.5; etc.). This usage of *laos* betrays the influence of the Septuagint. It is worth noting in this connection that non-Christian Jews who oppress Christians are also called *ochlos* or *ochloi*. Third, the *laos* is in a situation of confrontation with those in power. This is similar to the use of *ochlos* in Mark. However, sometimes, Luke takes the *laos* and the ruling class together: *presbuteroi tou laou*, the elders of the *laos* (Luke 22.66). Mark never uses the term *ochlos* in relation to the Jews of the ruling class.

By and large, it is Mark's use of the term *ochlos* for people that is distinctive in the New Testament and has even influenced Luke's use of *laos*. Besides this use of *laos* in Luke, other uses of this word in the New Testament are by and large in quotations from or allusions to the Old Testament and in the language of the rulers. References to Israel as the people of God also have *laos*, following the Septuagint.

## Ochlos and the 'Am Ha'aretz

In order to understand the meaning of *'am ha'aretz*, we should look not at its usage in the whole Old Testament but rather at its everyday use at the beginning of the first century BC.

Before the Israelites were taken into exile, this term designated landowners, aristocrats, etc. who were the upper class of Israelite society. However, the meaning of this word changed during the exilic and post-exilic periods. Once the leading members of the society were taken into exile, the ownership of the land passed to the common people, including the Samaritans, who were left behind. Thus, these became the *'am ha'aretz*.

However, this term became a pejorative and was used both in a religious sense and in a 'national sense for a low class of people as the people of the land,' while the cream of the society was considered to be that which was taken into exile. From the time of Ezra onwards, it became a sociological term designating a class of people that was uneducated and ignorant of the law.

We must remember that it was during this time that Rabbinic Judaism was established; and it was Rabbinic Judaism that systematized the law and set up the social and religious system of its time. Defining the term *'am ha'aretz* in the way it did, Rabbinic Judaism made it refer to the poor and the powerless class which was despised and marginalized. According to Rabbinic Judaism, Jews were forbidden to marry the daughters of the *'am ha'aretz* or sit together with them at meals. This attitude was clearly evident during the time of Jesus.

In the *Babylonian Pesachim*, there are the following prohibitions concerning the *'am ha'aretz*. These are worth noting in relation to the *ochlos*. (1) They cannot be witnesses. (2) Their witness cannot be believed. (3) No secret is to be revealed to them. (4) They are not permitted to be the guardians of orphans. (5) They are not permitted to take charge of contributions for the poor. (6) No Jew is to travel with them.

As we have already mentioned, at least during the time of Mark, if not before, the *'am ha'aretz* designates a social status and indicates an object of contempt. It is close in meaning to *ochlos*. Geographically, Galilee symbolizes the *'am ha'aretz*. Mark selected the word *ochlos*, which was used in a negative sense at that time, to refer to the *'am ha'aretz* and took Galilee as the background to show the victims of the society of that time.

## SUMMARY

1 Mark deliberately avoided the term *loas* and used the term *ochlos* to indicate the minjung. This is different from the people of God, who

are those within the national and religious framework as defined by the Pharisees. It is also different from the *laos* in Luke, which refers to those who repent and become the new people of God. The minjung do not belong to either group, nor are they the baptized crowd. They belong to a class of society which has been marginalized and abandoned.

2 However, the term *ochlos* is not consolidated into a concept but is defined in a relational way, and is therefore a fluid notion. For example, the poor are *ochlos* in relation to the rich or the ruler. The tax collector is minjung only in relation to the Jewish nationalist establishment. Accordingly, a certain value or beautification cannot be attributed to the term.

3 The *ochlos* are feared by the unjust and powerful, but they are not organized into a power group. Therefore, we cannot regard them as a political power bloc; rather, they should be regarded existentially as a crowd. They are minjung not because they have a common destiny, but simply because they are alienated, dispossessed, and powerless. They are never represented as a class which has a power base. They yearn for something. In this sense, they are different from the people in the Gospel of John who sought to crown Jesus as a king. The *ochlos* in the Gospel of Mark follow Jesus, but they do not force Jesus to conform to a course of action set up by them. In this sense they are different from the Zealots in Galilee. The Zealots, in their social character and position, have some things in common with the *ochlos*, but the Zealots have a clear purpose which the *ochlos* do not have.

4 Jesus sides with the *ochlos* and accepts them as they are without making any conditions. Jesus never rebukes these persons who are called sinners; rather he rebukes only those who criticize and attack the *ochlos*. (This reconfirms the statement in 2 above.)

5 Jesus does not give the impression that he intends to organize the *ochlos* into a force. He does not provide a program for their movement, nor does he make them an object of his movement. He does not forcibly demand anything from them. He does not ask to be their ruler or head. He 'passively' stands with them. A relationship between Jesus and the minjung takes place and then is broken. They follow him without condition. They welcome him. They also betray him.

6 In a word, Jesus informed the minjung of the advent of God's Kingdom. Significantly, Mark summarizes Jesus' preaching thus: 'The time is fulfilled, and the kingdom of God is at hand' (1.15). This eschatological declaration announces that there is the creation of a new

world as the old world ends. And this declaration gave the *ochlos* a new way and a new hope. Jesus struggled together with the suffering minjung on the frontline of this advent. In this sense, he is the Messiah – a viewpoint Mark reflects.

7 Jesus proclaims the coming of God's Kingdom. He stands with the minjung, and promises them the future of God. The God whom Jesus presented is not like Yahweh of the Old Testament who manifests a tension between love and justice. God's will is to side with the minjung completely and unconditionally. This notion was not comprehensible within the framework of established ethics, cult, and laws. God's will is revealed in the event of Jesus being with them in which he loves the minjung.

## NOTES

1 J. Gnilka, *Das Evangelium nach Markus* in *Evangelsch-Katholischer Kommentar Zum Neuen Testament* I (Neukirchen, Neukirchen Verlag, 1978), p. 28.

2 H. Strathmann, 'Laos' in *Theological Dictionary of the New Testament* IV (Grand Rapids, MI, W. B. Eerdmans, 1967), pp. 29, 34.

3 Often chapter 13 of the Gospel of Mark is taken as the criterion for determining the date of the authorship of the Gospel, depending on whether one takes the account as a prophecy of the Fall of Jerusalem or as an expression of the reality after the Fall of Jerusalem. However, considering the situation of the *ochlos* as they appear in Mark – the four thousand people who followed Jesus for three days without food (Mark 8.1 ff) – I conclude that Mark 13 reflects the situation of the people of Israel, including Christians, who had been expelled from their homeland after the Jewish war. Even the expression in Mark 6.34 regarding Jesus' attitude to the five thousand, 'Jesus was moved with compassion as they were as sheep without a shepherd,' is a reflection of the historical reality of the people.

4 Jesus mainly rebukes their ignorance, for example, their misunderstanding of the parables (4.13; 7.18), their unbelief during the storm (4.35–41; 6.51 f), and their lack of understanding of Jesus' suffering (8.32 ff; 9.32; 10.32, etc.).

5 See especially Gnilka, p. 279.

6 The first to contrast Galilee with Jerusalem were E. Lohmeyer *Galiläa und Jerusalem* (Gottingen, Vandenhoek & Ruprecht, 1936) and W. Marxen, *Mark the Evangelist: Studies on the Redaction of the Gospels* (Nashville TN, Abingdon, 1969). But both simply note the contrasting characteristics of the two words in the light of the history of the church, but do not investigate the use of these words in terms of the socio-economic context.

7 The attempt to distinguish between the minjung of Galilee who stood by Jesus and the minjung of Jerusalem who turned against him – for example,

Lohmeyer, *Galilee* – is not tenable. The real intention of this attempt seems to be to beautify the minjung.

8   There is still much confusion about the identity of the Pharisees. This is because there is an opinion which puts Pharisees on the side of the minjung. The Pharisees originally came from the pietistic Chassidim, who fought in the Maccabean War. The Pharisees are known from the time of Simon of the house of Hasmon, who appointed himself as arch-priest and ethnarch in 140 BC. They popularized the law; therefore they conscientized the minjung. First they were in conflict with the royal family of Hasmon. But after the death of Jannai, their policies were accepted by the next ruler, who was Jannai's wife, Alexandra (76–67 BC). From then on their position changed, so that they became the defenders of the system. During the time of Herod the Great, they were in conflict with the regime, and ten Pharisees were even executed. However, after the death of Herod, they became part of the establishment. They were allowed to participate in the decision-making assemblies of the ruling regime centered around Jerusalem, i.e. the arch-priest Hannas (AD 6–15), who was appointed by the Roman governor-general, Quirinus, AD 6–11. Therefore their role changed. From working for the minjung they now became inspectors enforcing submission to the establishment. At least, this is the way the Gospel of Mark presents the Pharisees. For example, they attacked Jesus and his disciples for their violation of rules concerning fasting (2.18), and their eating without washing their hands (7.15). These rules were made by the Pharisees, and therefore express the Pharisees' attitude about the minjung. Also they called themselves Pharisees in order to distinguish themselves, as elites, from the minjung.

9   J. Jeremias, *Jerusalem in the Time of Jesus* (London, SCM Press, 1969) pp. 303 f.

10   *Nedarim*, III 4: Bill. I, 379.

11   J. Schniewind and others understand this in a similar fashion, and John 9.2–3 also clearly indicates such an attitude.

12   See also discussion of *'am ha'aretz* in this paper.

13   Mark 9.42; Matt. 10.42; 17.2 (Q). Cf. R. Bultmann, *History of the Synoptic Tradition* (Oxford, Basil Blackwell, 1963), p. 84.

# 8

# Biblical Hermeneutics of Liberation: The Case of Micah

## ITUMELENG J. MOSALA

This extract is the second part of Mosala's essay introduced in Part One. Here he gives a practical application of the use of a materialist method to read the Book of Micah for a South African context.

Biblical scholars have always been aware of the tendency in biblical literature to use older traditions to address the needs of new situations. The whole question of the reappearance of themes and motifs in different contexts at different times exemplifies this process. This creation of new traditions by means of old ones has in fact been seen as a natural order of things in the internal hermeneutics of the Bible. As Deist puts it, 'It is the primary function of tradition to explain the new in terms of the old and in that way to authorize the new,' G. Von Rad has gone further and drawn attention to the fact that in the biblical literature not only do we have a reapplication of old themes and motifs, but we are confronted with what are matter of fact historical data alongside a 'spiritualising interpretation of these data'. According to him there is a unifying principle that keeps the various traditions together:

> In the process the old disassociated traditions have been given a reference and interpretation which in most cases was foreign to their original meaning. . . . Only the reader is not aware of the tremendous process of unification lying behind the picture given in the source documents.[1]

Until recently, however, biblical scholars seem to have been eluded by the historical–ideological significance of the 'unified diversity' of biblical literature.

By this we mean that although scholars have noticed the disparate character of the material and the manner in which it has been precariously held together by what they have called 'theological interpretative themes', they have nevertheless failed to see the ideological unity that pervades most of the Bible.

In recent times new directions have emerged. N. K. Gottwald's monumental book, *The Tribes of Yahweh*, breaks new ground in a radical way. Amongst other things, Gottwald argues convincingly for the cultic–ideological origins of the texts of the Bible.

This paper intends to set out and to test the use of a materialist method in biblical hermeneutics of liberation. The most basic concept of a materialist approach is the mode of production. By the mode of production is meant the combination of the forces and relations of production. Forces of production refer to the means of production, e.g. land, cattle, trees, raw materials, tools, and factories, plus human labour. In every society human beings use their labour on the means of production in order to set in motion the process of production whereby at least basic human needs are met. The nature or level of development of the forces of production tends to differ in different historical epochs and geographical areas.

The relations of production refer to the places occupied by people in the process of production. The nature of these places is determined by the nature of the division of labour in the society. As to whether there are classes or not in the society depends on whether the process of production is characterized by a social division of labour or not. Relations of production also determine ways of disposing of the social products.

Thus the specific combination of the forces of production (means of production plus labour) with the relations of production (places in the productive process) constitute the mode of production on which societies are based. Modes of production are differentiated from one another by the way in which the surplus social products are appropriated. Hence in a communal mode of production the key characteristic is the communal method of appropriating the surplus products. Tributary modes of production have as their distinguishing feature various forms of exacting tribute. The capitalist mode of production can be differentiated through the appropriation of surplus value which is made up of unrewarded human hours in production extracted by the capitalist class from the labour power of dispossessed workers.

How a society produces and reproduces its life is fundamentally conditioned by its mode of production. The legal, religious, political and philosophical spheres of society develop on the basis of the mode of production and refer back to it.

Any approach, therefore, that seeks to employ a materialist method must inquire into (1) the nature of the mode of production (2) the constellation of classes necessitated by that mode (3) the nature of the ideological manifestations arising out of and referring back to that mode of production. This paper intends, however, to do more than simply apply a materialist method to the biblical text. Rather, it aims at developing a materialist biblical hermeneutics of liberation. For this reason the following points would seem to constitute an adequate programme for such a task:

1 Material conditions of the biblical text – mode of production, class forces and dominant ideology.

2 Ideological conditions of the text – class origins of the text and class interests of the text.

3 Material conditions of the biblical reader – mode of production, classes, dominant ideology.

4 Ideological conditions of the biblical reader – class origins of the reader and class commitments of the reader.

5 Biblical hermeneutics and the class struggle – the Bible as a site of class conflict.

6 The historical–cultural specificity of the class struggle and biblical hermeneutics – towards a Black Theology of Liberation.

## MATERIAL CONDITIONS OF THE BOOK OF MICAH

### The mode of production

Given a proper theoretical framework, it does not take much to realise that the Israelite monarchical system was based on a tributary mode of production. Since, however, the concept of a mode of production is a theoretical abstraction, we must give historical specificity to the form of such a mode of production in the Israelite monarchy.

### The forces of production

The most fundamental means of production in Palestine throughout all ancient historical epochs was the land. People needed land to settle in as families (*bēth 'āvoth*) and as associations of extended families (*mishpahoth*). But what land they settled in was determined not only by historical factors but also by ecological characteristics. Both agriculture and pastoralism depended for the form they took on the nature of the land as determined by demographical, climatological and topographical factors. The significance of land as a fundamental means of production can be appreciated even more if it is kept in mind that 'environmentally, Palestine is a conglomerate of many different ecological zones of dramatic contrast. These essentially geographical differences in the sub regions of Palestine are reflected in the patterns of settlement, as well as in economic and historical development.' Thus the struggle for the occupation and indeed possession of the more favourable portions of the land of Palestine was one of the key motors of historical development in ancient times.

Both demographical and historical factors, however, led to situations where innumerable communities had to make do with naturally unfavourable parts of the land. Settlements have been uncovered by archaeologists in desert, arid, and hilly areas which are often long distances away from sources of water.

These parts of the land required of necessity particular kinds of technological means to mediate between human labour and the means of production as a way of setting the forces of production in motion. The question of tools, therefore, as part of the means of production, indicates another level at which the historical struggles of ancient Palestine were waged. We are referring here specifically to the struggles of human beings with the natural environment as they attempted to humanize and socialize it.

The Israelite community of the period before the monarchy was forced by circumstance of formidable feudal dictatorships of the city-states of Canaan to retribalize/regroup as an alternative egalitarian society of equals in the hill country of Palestine under extremely adverse natural conditions. The general problem of agriculture, namely, the soil and water, was for them particularly accentuated. C. H. J. De Geus summarizes the situation as follows.

> The tremendous efforts of the terracing of the mountain-slopes were undertaken in order:
> a. To transform a continuous slope into a series of level surfaces or terraced planes.
> b. To prevent the run-off erosion and enhance the accumulation of soil and water.
> c. To get rid of the stones and to form a flat upper layer of cultivatable soil. The stones are used for building the terrace-walls and other structures

accompanying the terraces. This third reason is connected with ploughing.

d. To facilitate the transport and distribution of irrigation water in the case of (spring) irrigated terraces.[2]

N. K. Gottwald has recently reconstructed the specific combination of the relations and forces of production, that is the mode of production, of premonarchic Israel. He points among other things to the way in which an egalitarian communal society, arranged in large extended families which were relatively self-contained socio-economic units and political equals, took advantage of the introduction of iron implements for clearing and tilling the land and of slake lime plaster for waterproofing cisterns in order to keep reserve water during the annual dry season.

Despite the technological breakthrough that the use of iron implements represented for the Israelite communities of the hill country, it is well to remember that technical difficulties in the local production of iron imposed a slowness in the general adoption of iron for practical use. There were for instance not yet any local smiths by the time of the beginning of the monarchy (1 Sam. 13.19ff). As Jane C. Waldbaum has put it:

> In eleventh century contexts agricultural use of iron appears for the first time. Though most tool types continue to be made exclusively in bronze, such objects as a ploughshare from Gibeah, a sickle from Beth Shemesh, and a hafted ax-head from Tell el-Far'ah South – all from occupation levels – testify to the advent of iron for practical use in Palestine, though it is still far less commonly used than bronze.[3]

Archaeological evidence from some Iron Age sites in Palestine indicates that by the tenth century BC there was not only a good supply of iron in Palestine, but that some conscious manufacturing of steel was taking place in the area. Stech-Wheeler *et al.* make the point that:

> The evidence presented by the Tel Qiri axe tends to confirm observations drawn from the Taanach iron. Although an isolated object from a single site is not sufficient to permit the characterization of a regional industry, it does lend support to the contention that steel was being regularly used in the Jezreel Valley by the tenth century BC.[4]

There is, therefore, no doubt that agricultural production, which was the basis of the ancient Israelite economy, was optimized by the generalized use of iron technology. But since 'the seasonal character of the climate that sets the boundaries of the agricultural year contrasts with the aseasonal demand for food which knows no boundaries', it is necessary in a discussion of the forces of production to identify patterns of labour utilization to get a complete picture of the nature of the forces of production.

In premonarchic Israel the basic economic unit was the *bēth-'āv* or father's house. The labour of the family was differentiated on the basis of age and sex to accomplish the process of producing the basic means of subsistence. Grain and fruits were grown, and limited animal husbandry was practised where the *bēth-'āv* owned some sheep and goats and a few cattle. 'The staple crops were barley and wheat, wine and olive oil, which were produced alone or in combinations depending on the variable climate and soil from region to region.' Co-operation between the *bēth-'āvs* which made up the *mishpaha* (extended families networks) (2 Sam. 6.6; 1 Sam. 23.1, Ruth 3.2 and 1 Kings 22.10) helped to spread risk and to increase productivity particularly in view of the *great diversity* of the agricultural environment created especially by a variegated landscape overlaid by variations in rainfall, soil and vegetation.

The forces of production that took shape in the hill country of Palestine remained fundamentally the same during the period of the monarchy with differences in the degree of their development. Since, however, the area occupied by Israelites during the monarchy was far wider, covering some of the plains and valleys formerly belonging to the Canaanite city-states, we must refer to the changes brought about by this expansion in the forces.

Marvin Chaney has suggested that the expansion of the Israelite land by David's conquest of the alluvial plains and valleys brought about a change in the relations of production and ideology of pre-monarchic Israel. We concur with him in this matter. The starting point, however, for understanding a change in the social relations and ideology of a social formation is seeing how the alteration in the forces of production necessitates such a change. The availability of crown lands in the plains and valleys gave King David the political power to install a system of land tenure in them which conflicted with the older communally owned and communally tilled land of the hill country. Thus since 'rain agriculture in Palestine was subject to the vicissitudes of periodic drought, blight, and pestilence', the incorporation of the valleys and plains into Israel meant that there were inherent inequalities in the means of production. But however fertile the lands were, wealth was, then as now, a function of human labour. In themselves the crown lands of the plains and valleys could not produce the wealth that the Davidic monarchy required as a material basis of state power. To do this the incipient kingdom required a system of surplus extraction whose presupposition was unrewarded human labour. To be sure the crown lands were tilled and they yielded surpluses, but the mode of integrating human labour into those means of production must be discussed together with the question of the relations of production in the united monarchy of Israel.

## The relations of production

Although David had incurred debts and obligations to the military mercenaries that fought by his side during the period of his rise to power, it is generally agreed that the capture of the Canaanite lowlands made it possible for him to make grants of land there by way of meeting these obligations rather than from the village lands in the hill country. What is more, the surplus derived from the lowlands helped him to avoid the imposition of heavy demands on the villages in order to finance the new state bureaucracy. Hopkins has isolated four advantages of the economic situation of the period of the monarchy. First, the expansion of the Israelite borders brought about the much needed geopolitical security 'conducive to the smooth operations of agricultural systems'. Second, the monarchic tax-base was expanded, thus lightening the burden on village agriculturalists. More importantly the possession of newly acquired lands 'fueled international trade such as that developed with Tyre to supply the court with costly timber'. Third, the expansion of borders helped the agriculturalists to be less vulnerable to the vicissitudes of the Palestinian environment. Fourth, 'the expansion of borders not only meant an increase in sources of income and produce for import/export trade, but also could lead, given propitious geopolitical conditions, to an expansion of transit trade'.

The above notwithstanding, Hopkins rightly argues further that, historically, agrarian states depend more upon surpluses extracted from the agricultural base than on profits from trade. He makes the point aptly that:

> Maintaining secure borders and participating in export/import and transit trade were decisive determinants of the extent of the burden imposed by the monarchy upon the village-based agricultural systems. The literary and

archaeological record evidences plentitudinous royal-sponsored construction relating to these areas of its concern. The fiscal apparatus which supported these and other activities of the monarchy, with its facilities and personnel expenses, must have required an even greater imposition of taxes. On top of taxes of agricultural produce, Chaney is right to emphasize the pernicious effect of royal enterprise on the availability of tools and labour, both of which it siphoned away from possible involvement in the agricultural sector.[5]

There are, therefore, three main factors which precipitated changes in the social relations of production during the monarchy. First, as Marvin Chaney has stated, the unpredictable nature of the environment and climate of Palestine on the one hand, and the availability of surplus producing alluvial crown lands on the other created a situation where people incurred debts through borrowing in times of crisis. Secondly, as Gottwald argues, the question of military 'call-up on rotation to supplement David's professional army on the basis of a twelve-tribe-system (1 Chron. 27.1–21)' would have had an impact on the labour needs of the village agricultural systems. This state of affairs, whatever its extent, would surely have 'contributed to the neglect of crops and falling of surpluses'. On the basis of exegesis of a number of texts in the books of Samuel and Kings, I have argued elsewhere that the political murders and rebellions during the reign of David were a function of the dislocations brought about by structural changes in the political economy of the monarchy. Thirdly, Gottwald argues that the imposition of taxes on agriculturalists especially under Solomon marked the dominance of a new mode of production: the tributary mode of production. Gottwald summarized the fundamental character of this mode expertly when he wrote:

> We can identify the quantum leap in pressure on free agrarians by noting the offices that Solomon added to those of David's administration:
> (1) a chief administrator over the twelve regional areas for the provisioning of an enlarged court establishment with accelerated taste . . .
> (2) a large network of officers supervising forced labour operations . . .
> (3) a head steward who managed the royal household, probably including royal holdings and estates not granted to retainers . . .
> These added officers indicate a more thorough administration of the court proper, and especially a smoother, more regular, and far more abundant flow of resources *from the Israelite cultivators* to the court and royal bureaucracy, both at Jerusalem and wherever officials were installed throughout the land. In this way Solomon 'rationalized', not 'modernized',

the agricultural base of the economy, for his basic strategy was not to improve the means of production but to improve the flow of as much agricultural surplus as possible into the control of his regime.[6]

Thus the stage was set for the development of a tributary social formation. The class structure of this formation was characterized by a social division of labour resulting in antagonistic social relations of production, exchange and distribution. At the top of the class structure of the monarchy was the royal aristocracy made up of the king and the nobility, the latter consisting of the king's sons and wives. As R. De Vaux has explained, next to the royal aristocracy but within the ruling class were the *sarim* (chiefs or governors), the *horim* (non-royal nobility), the *nedibim* (members of the houses of assembly by virtue of their wealth and power deriving from their land properties and thus controlling pools of landless labour), the *gibbore hayil* (valiant men, brave warriors, etc.), and the *zeqenim* (heads of influential families that had power most probably on the basis of their property). There can be no doubt that the writer of the Book of Micah has this ruling class in mind when he writes: 'How terrible it will be for those who lie awake and plan evil! When morning comes, as soon as they have the chance, they do the evil they planned. When they want fields, they seize them; when they want houses, they take them. No man's family or property is safe' (Mic. 2.1 ff).

Next to the ruling aristocratic and propertied class was the middle class made up of the bureaucratic and state ideologists' sectors, merchants (mainly foreigners), and artisans or craftsmen. The authors of 2 Samuel 20.23 ff describe some of the elements of this class when they state that: 'Joab was in command of the army of Israel; Benaiah son of Jehoiada was in charge of David's bodyguard; Adoniram was in charge of the forced labour; Jehoshaphat son of Ahilud was in charge of the records; Sheva was the court secretary; Zadok and Abiathar were the priests, and Ira from the town of Jair was also one of David's priests.'

Marvin Chaney has estimated that the ruling class together with the middle class made up 2 per cent or less of the population while they controlled half or more of the total goods and services produced in the society. The rest of the Israelite population constituted the oppressed and exploited class. It was made up of poor peasants, debtor slaves, captured slaves, prostitutes and criminals. Micah has them in mind when he declares against the rulers of Israel, 'You skin my people alive and tear the flesh of their bones. You eat my people up. You strip off their skin, break their bones, and chop them up like meat for the pot' (Mic. 3.2 ff).

The Book of Micah, therefore, arises out of this tributary mode of production consisting of the class forces we have described. David inaugurated this social formation, Solomon pushed it to its logical conclusion and the rest of the Israelite and Judean rulers took it to its grave. For as Marx writes: 'History is thorough and goes through many phases when taking an old form to the grave.' In the Book of Micah as in other prophetic texts we find some of the evidence about the material conditions out of which these biblical texts came.

## IDEOLOGICAL CONDITIONS OF THE TEXT

### Class origins and class interests of the text

The route to this point has been a long one. There is no royal road to science. Time and space do not allow us, however, to spell out what remains of this paper in equal detail. Suffice it to indicate in general terms how, having reconstructed the material basis of the text, the biblical hermeneutics of liberation would proceed.

While the text of Micah offers sufficient indications as to the nature of the material conditions, the configuration of class forces, and the effects of class rule, it is nevertheless itself cast within an ideological framework that at the same time creates contradictions within the book and distorts the usefulness of its text for struggling classes today.

Ideology is not a lie. It is rather a harmonization of contradictions in such a way that the class interests of one group are universalized and made acceptable to other classes. Also, ideology is not a selection process or filter through which only certain facts pass. On the contrary it is a process by which the presence of certain facts is constituted by their absence.

Thus making scientific sense of the ideological condition of a text means knowing that text in a way in which it is incapable of knowing itself. Terry Eagleton makes this point expertly when he says:

> The task of criticism, then, is not to situate itself within the same space as the text, allowing it to speak or completing what it necessarily leaves unsaid. On the contrary, its function is to install itself in the very incompleteness of the work in order to *theorise* it – to explain the ideological necessity of those 'not-saids' which constitute the very principle of its identity. Its object is the unconsciousness of the work – that of which it is not, and cannot be, aware.[7]

The text of Micah is eloquent about certain issues by being silent about them. Biblical scholars have long been puzzled by the literary dysjunction between Micah 1–3 and Micah 4–7, broadly speaking. The first three chapters have been said to be genuinely Micah passages, while the others have been considered later additions. The issue that has not been faced squarely is what kind of additions are they?

Looked at ideologically these chapters fit well into the royal Zion ideology that started during the time of David, was made more sophisticated and began to be the dominant self-consciousness of the nation in the later reigns culminating in the ideological activity of the priestly class during the Babylonian exile. Bourgeois biblical scholarship has long been aware of this development, but has been unwilling or unable to perceive the political significance of such an ideological set-up. Walter Brueggemann was the first biblical scholar to elicit the political importance of ideological development in the Old Testament. He has isolated two different covenant traditions representing two different social, political and ideological tendencies, namely the Mosaic covenant tradition which is revolutionary and the Davidic covenant tradition which is status quo oriented. According to him, the 'Davidic tradition . . . is situated among the established and secure'. Brueggemann summarizes the tension in the biblical traditions when he says:

> The Davidic–Solomonic tradition with its roots in Abrahamic memory provides an important alternative theological trajectory. We may identify two theological elements which are surely linked to this movement and which are important to the subsequent faith and literature of the Bible. First, it is generally agreed that the emergence of creation faith in Israel has its setting in Jerusalem and its context in the royal consciousness. The shift of social vision is accompanied with a shifted theological method which embraces more of the imperial myths of the ancient Near East and breaks with the scandalous historical particularity of the Moses tradition. The result is a universal and comprehensive world-view which is more inclined toward social stability than toward social transformation and liberation.[8]

The central themes of this monarchic ideology are stability, grace, restoration, creation, universal peace, compassion, salvation. They contrast radically with the ideology of premonarchic Israel which has themes like justice, solidarity, struggle, vigilance.

The Book of Micah, therefore, is eloquent in its silence about the ideological struggle waged by the oppressed and exploited class of monarchic Israel. Apart from making available an otherwise un-suppressable body of information about the material situation of oppression, it simply luxuriates in an elaborate ideological statement of self-comfort by dwelling on issues like the Lord's universal reign of peace (Mich. 4.1 ff); the promise of return from exile (4.6 ff); God's promise of a ruler from Bethlehem (5.2 ff); the Lord's salvation (7.8 ff) etc. These are the dominant ideological themes of the book.

It is little wonder that dominant traditional theology has found the Bible generally politically and ideologically comfortable notwithstanding the unsuppressable evidence of a morally distorted material situation. The book itself, as indeed most of the Bible, offers no certain starting point for a theology of liberation. There is simply too much de-ideologization to be made before it can be hermeneutically straightforward in terms of the struggle for liberation. In short, it is a ruling-class document and represents the ideological and political interests of the ruling class.

Be that as it may, there are enough contradictions within the book to enable eyes that are hermeneutically trained in the struggle for liberation today to observe the kin struggles of the oppressed and exploited of the biblical communities in the very absences of those struggles in the text.

## CONCLUSIONS: TOWARDS A BLACK THEOLOGY OF LIBERATION

The point that is being made here is that the ideological condition and commitment of the reader issuing out of the class circumstances of such a reader are of immense hermeneutical significance. The biblical hermeneutics of liberation is thoroughly tied up with the political commitments of the reader. This means that not only is the Bible a product and a record of class struggles, but it is also a site of similar struggles acted out by the oppressors and oppressed, exploiters and exploited of our society even as they read the Bible.

Those, therefore, that are committed to the struggles of the black oppressed and exploited people cannot ignore the history, culture, and ideologies of the dominated black people as their primary her-meneutical starting point. There can be no Black Theology of Libera-tion and no corresponding biblical hermeneutics of liberation outside of the black struggle for both survival and liberation. Such a struggle, however, requires being as clear about issues in the black community as possible. For as Archie Mafeje has observed:

> Despite anthropology, sociology, economics . . . political science (and, let us add, theology) the oppressed peoples of the world seem to be making their choice and, like them, we shall make our choices according to our vested interests and not according to some contrived professional code . . .
> Be that as it may, very rarely would [commitment to action] take place without being accompanied or preceded by what we have called the problem of intellectual self-consciousness. Therefore clear identification of issues is as important as fighting in the streets or in the mountains.[9]

## NOTES

1    G. von Rad, *Old Testament Theology*, vol. 1 (London, SCM Press, 1975), p. 118.
2    C. H. J. De Geus, 'The Importance of Archaeological Research into the Palestine Agricultural Terraces with Excurses on the Hebrew word *gbi'* (*Palestine Exploration Quarterly*, 107, 1975), p. 67.
3    J. Waldaum, 'The First Archaeological Appearance of Iron 'in *The Coming of the Age of Iron*, ed. T. A. Wertime and J. D. Muhly (New Haven/London, Yale University Press, 1980), p. 86.
4    T. Stech-Wheeler *et al.*, 'Iron at Tannach and Early Iron Metallurgy in Eastern Mediterranean' (*American Journal of Archaeology*, 85, 1981), p. 255.
5    D. C. Hopkins, 'The Dynamics of Agriculture in Monarchical Israel', in *SBL 1983 Seminar Papers*, ed. K. H. Richards (Chico, Scholar Press, 1983), p. 187.
6    N. K. Gottwald, 'Social History of United Monarchy', a paper presented at SBL Seminar on Sociology of the Monarchy, December 1983, p. 6.
7    T. Eagleton, *Criticism and Ideology* (London, Verso, 1980), pp. 89 f.
8    W. Brueggemann, 'Trajectories in Old Testament Literature and the Sociology of Ancient Israel', in *The Bible and Liberation* ed. N. K. Gottwald (Maryknoll, NY, Orbis Books, 1983), p. 314.
9    A. Mafeje, 'The Problem of Anthropology in Historical Perspective: An Inquiry into the Growth of the Social Science' (*Canadian Journal of African Studies*, 10, 2, 1976), p. 332.

# 9

# Water – God's Extravaganza: John 2.1–11

## SR VANDANA

The historical–critical method is one among many of the tools applied to read the Bible, and its limitations are well documented. In this essay, an Indian exegete employs an indigenous tool – the *Dhvani*, a Sankristic method of exegesis – to interpret Christian texts. The *Dhvani* method stresses the 'evocative', the 'beauty' of the passage, and its emotive grip on the hearer or the reader.

This piece is one of the many expositions of St John's Gospel from her book, *Waters of Fire* (Madras, The Christian Literature Society, 1981; New York, Amity House, 1988).

For examples of *Dhvani* interpretation by other Indian biblical scholars, see *Bible Bhashyam* (5, 4, December 1979). *Bible Bhashyam* is an Indian Biblical quarterly published by St Thomas Apostolic Seminary, Vadavathoor, Kottayam 10, India.

Sister Vandana is a member of the Order of the Sacred Heart and has a great interest in Hindu spiritual tradition.

If it was in the waters of Jordan that Jesus chose to begin His public ministry by humbly going with publicans and sinners to be baptized, it was again through water that he performed the first of his 'signs.' It is one of the most charming stories in the life of Jesus. Mary, Jesus, and His disciples were invited to a wedding in Cana of Galilee. When wine – used liberally on merry-making occasions – gave out, it was Mary's presence that saved the situation. She turned to Jesus instinctively for help with the certainty of a true *bhakta* (a lover of God). When He seemed to refuse to do anything about it, with equal certainty and the equanimity of a *sthitaprajna* (one of steadfast wisdom),[1] she told the servants just to obey Him. It was at this crucial point that Jesus used His 'creature' – water. He told them to fill six large water pots with water and they filled them to the brim. It was the best wine they had ever tasted. Thus through this miracle of water, He revealed His glory and His disciples believed in Him.

## 1 WATER USED TO MANIFEST HIS GLORY

Water! An ordinary, everyday, familiar thing, usually taken for granted and unnoticed except when found absent and needed. This the Lord used as an instrument to 'manifest His glory,' or 'He let His glory be seen' through it, 'and His disciples believed in Him' (John 2.11, Jerusalem Bible translation). God often uses very ordinary things and lets His glory shine out through them. One is tempted perhaps to call water God's favorite creation! It may be worthwhile, then, to look at water in His first creation and then in St John's Gospel – as an aid to understanding better the miracle of Cana in Galilee.

## 2 WATER IN GENESIS AND ST JOHN

It is interesting to note that in the first half of John's Gospel, called 'the Book of Signs,' the seven-day structure of the original creation story is imitated, culminating in this first manifestation of Jesus' glory.[2]

Three days later there was a wedding at Cana in Galilee (2.1), that is, three days after the meeting of Jesus with Philip and Nathaniel. The opening events of the Gospel, therefore, are contained within one week, of which almost every day is noticed.[3] That John 2.1 introduces an event that occurs on 'the third day' doubtless has yet another symbolism. But for our purpose, it is interesting to see how water is treated in the original creation story.

Water appears first in Genesis 1.2 as 'the raging ocean covering everything engulfed in darkness and the power of God moving over the waters on the first day'. On the second day God said, 'Let there be a dome to divide the water' (Gen. 1.6). On the third day God commanded, 'Let the water below the sky come together in one place, so that the land will appear . . . and He named the water sea' (Gen. 1.9–10). God had not yet finished with water. He said, 'Let the water be filled with many kinds of living beings. . . . He blessed all and told the creatures that live in the water to reproduce, and to fill the sea . . . Evening passed and morning came – that was the fifth day' (Gen. 1.20–3). Thus on four out of the six days of creation, God dealt with water. 'From the waters is this universe produced.' No wonder we read this in the Vedas in the Satpatha Brahmana VI.8.2.4.

St John, while apparently alluding to the seven-day structure of the original creation story, shows the same predilection for water as God does – the way he uses it in a variety of circumstances throughout his narrative of Jesus' life – now as a 'venue' for His appearance, now for healing, now as a symbol of His life, now as a lesson in humility, now as signifying the pouring out of His Spirit. Here, in this His first miracle, Jesus used water as an instrument of his first 'sign.'

## 3 'THIS WAS THE FIRST OF THE SIGNS GIVEN BY JESUS' (JOHN 2.11)

In Israel, as in India, miracles and wonders were often looked for in prophets and saints, and were considered a seal of God on such men. There are many wonder-working 'Sai Babas' found in the Old Testament.

In fact, the term *signs* comes from the Old Testament background in which it especially meant Yahweh's wonderful works in the Exodus story (Num. 14.11). 'However, what was meaningful about these wonderful deeds was not precisely that they were beyond natural causality, but that they had been worked by the God of Israel to reveal Himself to His people. The "signs" of Jesus have exactly this meaning for John and only certain miracles are called "signs."'[4] The signs of Jesus constitute the miracles that reveal the nature of Jesus as the revelation of God: these are signs in the Johannine sense.[5] In transforming the waters into wine, this 'creative miracle' allowed us to see Jesus as the manifestation of God: 'we saw His glory . . . full of grace and truth' (John 1.14).

## 4 'AND THE MOTHER OF JESUS WAS THERE' (JOHN 2.2.)

If water were an instrument Jesus used, He also used Mary. When He first manifested His glory, Mary was present, as she was there again at His death on the cross (John 19.25–7). Both these descriptions in John 2 and 19 have several details in common, no doubt on purpose. And in both these events, together with Mary, water was present.

Mary and water have much in common. Mary, like water, was creature – ordinary, unnoticed, quiet, serviceable, lovely, and precious. As there can be no life without water, so God ordained that there would be no new life without Mary. In John, Mary is seen not only in her historical character but in her function in salvation history. The woman of the first creation was called 'Life' (Eve) because she was 'mother of all the living' (Gen. 3.20). Mary 'the woman' – as she will be called again at the foot of the cross – is mother of the new life; not only mother of the Word made flesh, but of all who live by His life. She is the figure of the Church – 'the New Eve.'[6] And although Jesus said his hour had not yet come, because of her intercession, he anticipates it and her petition is granted. Who can refuse a mother? And Mary is essentially mother.

In all ages and cultures people have sought God in a mother figure. Without making too facile connections, it is interesting to study similarities. Thus in the Vedas the waters are called 'mothers.' 'May the waters, the mothers, purify us!' The Lord is the Son of the waters, born of the waters. 'In the waters, Lord, is your seat' (Narayan, Taittiriya Samhita 1.2.2, S.B. VII 4.1.6). Both a mother and a river are venerated with special love in India. The Ganges – the most sacred of all rivers – is always *Gangamata*. When crossing her, pilgrims in the ferries cry out, '*Gangamaya-ki-jai.*' *Arati* is done to her singing:

*Om jaya Gange-mata Ekhi Bar jto teri Sharangati ata, Yamkir tras mitakar paramgati pata.*

Hail to the Mother Ganges, He who comes to take refuge in you even once will cross the difficulties of death, and find the supreme heaven.

Ganga is called the 'refuge' of the *patita* – the fallen ones – as Mary is called 'Refuge of sinners,' for did not the Lord, dispeller of all sins, dwell in her? There is a story of the Goddess Ganga appearing before King Bhagiratha (who did austere penances to propitiate her) and saying, 'All the sinners of the world come to wash away their sins and purify themselves by immersing their sinful bodies in my holy waters. Where shall I wash the immense store of sins they deposit in my watery body?' Bhagiratha replied: 'O sacred mother, holy saints will bathe in the Ganges and will purge all sins away, for the Lord Vishnu (the all-pervading one), dispeller of all sins, dwells in their heart.' If Mary is, as we have seen, 'the mother of the new life,' Gangaji is called 'the nectar of immortality that gives us salvation.' Over the radio recently I heard a song: '*Hamari zindagi, hamari roti, Gangajike dwara*' ('we receive life and bread through the Ganges'). She it is who gives to us life and bread, and Mary gives to us Jesus, who called Himself our 'Life' and 'the true Bread of life.' Some of the prayers addressed to the waters of the Ganga are reminiscent of prayers to the Virgin Mother:

Who can describe, O Mother, thy glory and splendor? O, all powerful Mother of compassion and love!

Mary and water have yet something else in common. Waters of a river can be very silent, gentle, sometimes as still as a pool; they hardly seem to move, even though the river never ceases to flow from its Source. They can be considerate, cautious as they pass by a rough rock. They are ever ready to give of themselves, to bathe or slake thirst, without ever objecting that too much is asked of them, without expecting a word of gratitude. They are a real example of *Nishkarma karma* that the Gita teaches; service without looking for any reward. They give what they have to give to those who ask or need their help, then pass on, silently, unnoticed, as unspectacularly as they came.

Mary was like that at the wedding feast in Cana – gentle, unobtrusive, quiet, yet able to secure a miracle from a seemingly reluctant Son, with apparent ease through her softly spoken words and her unfailing trust. Lao-tse has said, 'The softest substance of the world goes through the hardest; softness and gentleness are the companions of life. There is nothing weaker than water, but none is superior to it in overcoming the hard, for which there is no substitute. Weakness overcomes strength and gentleness overcomes rigidity.'

Mary, like the waters, and like Dakshinamoorthy in Shankaracharya's Hymn, taught by her *maun vyakhya* (silent discourse). She noticed the need and embarrassment of the wedding party, as the wine came to an end. No one had asked her help, yet she went to her Son and said gently, 'They have no wine' (John 2.3). Jesus answered, 'Woman' – which word in the vocative shows no disrespect, as many examples show (e.g. John 19.26 – 'You must not tell me what to do' (Good News Bible translation); 'You have no claims upon me yet' or 'my hour is not yet come' – his hour being his death and exaltation (John 7.30; 8.20; 12.23, 27; 13.1). 'What have I to do with you?' seems to draw a line between Mother and Son, especially as the words remind us of those used by demons to Jesus (Mark 1.24, 5.7, Matt. 8.29). 'You have no business with us yet.' But Jesus, as always, makes decisions only depending on His Father's will (cf. 6.38). He had refused, too, to act on his brothers' advice and instructions (John 7.6).

Without being deterred by the apparent rebuff, Mary told the servants what to do – in the words of John 2.5: 'Do whatever He tells you' – and slipped back into anonymity. She who had spent years listening to His word and pondering it in her heart knew the value of obedience. *Obaudiro:* from listening comes obedience. This had made her know her Son and be sure of His unfailing love. She advised them simply to obey. She knew He would always do what was good, or rather, best.

And 'when the steward tasted the water' it was wine. Not only that, but in great abundance and the best they had! Each stone jar, we are told, could hold twenty to thirty gallons (John 2.6).

## 5 'THEY FILLED THEM TO THE BRIM'

Though we are not told – as we are in the miracle of the loaves – how much wine was 'left over,' we may be sure there was some. Jesus, who could not refuse his mother, had told the servants, 'Fill the jars with water' – an apparently crazy thing to say and expect them to do. But they did and 'they filled them to the brim' (John 2.7). To the brim! Here we see the extravagance of water – and of love. God does nothing by half measures. Is Jesus not Himself the *pleroma* of God, the plentitude, the *Poornam?* 'In Him dwells the fullness of God corporeally' (cf. Col. 2.9; 1.19).

It is interesting that Schoonenberg bases his christology of the enhypostasis of the Word in the man Jesus, and of God's full presence in his human person, on these Pauline texts. Might one not say that Jesus, who was 'filled to the brim' with divinity, now sees the servants fill the stone pots 'to the brim,' so that through this very human act of being present at a wedding and of sensitively saving an embarrassing situation, he could show forth the divinity, with which he was filled, to the full? One begins to see a new meaning – or a new interpretation – in the *Shanti* Path of the Isa Upanishad.

*Poornamadah, Poornam idam*
Fullness there (beyond); fullness here.

That is, the fully divine (there) is fully human (here). Christ, who is God's eternal Son, is seen by some modern theologians (like Schoonenberg) as being 'threatened to become dehumanized; the man in him risks being undermined to the benefit of the divine person. John, in this miracle, however, shows Christ to be truly and utterly human, as we have seen. God in Himself as God-made-man walking the earth, is seen living Himself fully – to the full. 'Of His fullness we have all received grace upon grace' (John 1.16). The torrents of His grace flow freely on man – without 'let or stay,' for God is generosity, and what better symbolism is there for this gracious and super-abundant giving than waters released in abundance?

All through the Old Testament waters appear 'now real, now symbolic, now gentle and life-giving, now destructive and terrifying, now a trickle, now a torrent.' In Cana we see it as a torrent – freely given and flowing over. Water in the Bible is always freely given – from the first book to the last. In Genesis we read: "When all was *Tohu-tohu* (a mess) – waters were created and flowed freely. On the fifth day God said, 'Let the waters abound with life' and in Revelation we read, 'Let him receive the water of life freely – who thirsts – come!' The Garden of Eden had to abound in water. 'The desert mind, thirsting for beauty, must be told that there was water to make it a paradise, a couple of trees and the four-branched river. Even when sin becomes prevalent, waters are still abundant, and the floodgates of heaven are opened, but now to punish man.[7] Whether it is well water – or the rains sent by Yahweh – it is always in abundance – to show the greatness of His love. The floodwater covered the enemies of Israel as they tried to cross the Red Sea, until they sank into the depths like a stone: 'Horse and chariot He cast into the sea' (Exod. 15.1; 5). When Moses struck the rock, waters gushed forth in abundance – a figure, too, of the waters that would gush forth from the side of Christ and become 'waters of salvation,' which Isaiah foretold we would draw with joy from the Savior's fountains (Isa. 12.3).

The same superabundance is seen in the Gospels and in this miracle of Christ. For if Christ is the infinite self-expenditure of God,[8] was He not Himself to be 'poured out like water' for our sake?

Ratzinger, speaking of an 'excess' of seven baskets mentioned in Mark 8.8, says:

One thinks at once of a related miracle preserved in the Johannine tradition; the changing of water into wine at the marriage feast at Cana. It is true that the word *excess* does not occur here, but the fact certainly does: according to the evidence of the Gospel, the new-made wine amounted to between 130 and 190 gallons, a somewhat unusual quantity for a private banquet![9] In the Evangelist's view both stories have to do with the central element in Christian worship, the Eucharist. They show it as the divine excess or abundance, which infinitely surpasses all needs and legitimate demands. In this way both stories are concerned, through their reference to the Eucharist,[10] with Christ Himself. And both point back to the law governing the structure of creation, in which life squanders a million seeds in order to save one living one, in which a whole universe is squandered in order to prepare at one point, a place for spirit, for man. Excess is God's trademark in his creation; as the fathers put it: 'God does not reckon his gifts by the measure.' At the same time excess is also the real foundation and form of the history of salvation, which in the last analysis is nothing other than the truly breath-taking fact that God, in an incredible outpouring of himself, expends not only a universe, but his own self, in order to lead man, a speck of dust, to salvation. So excess or superfluity – let us repeat – is the real definition or mark of the history of salvation. The purely calculating mind will always find it absurd that for man, God himself would be expended. Only the lover can understand the folly of a love to which prodigality is a law, and excess alone is sufficient.[11]

## 6 'THERE WERE SIX STONE WATER JARS STANDING THERE' (JOHN 2.6)

Stone was used because, according to Jewish belief, it would not contract ritual uncleanness, just as the Hindu Dharmashastra lays down which materials are considered pure and which not. The Jewish ritual provided for numerous purifications by water – as does the Hindu ritual. Hence the water jars were for ablutions customary among the Jews. But all these purifications were powerless to bring about effectively true purity of soul until the New Covenant. Hence Jesus' changing of water into wine is symbolic. At this wedding He foretells it when He changes water (destined for symbolic cleansing) into wine, which symbolizes both spirit (John 15.3) and the purifying word (John 13.10). John sees this changing of water into wine as the replacement of the weak elements of Old Covenant by the rich wine of the New Covenant and Messianic Banquet.[12] It is interesting, too, that Jesus says that His word and teaching will henceforth purify – (rather than ritual washings) in the context of the vine (John 15). The vine being 'pruned' means again purification. 'You are pruned already by means of the Word I have spoken to you' (John 15.3). To be truly purified by God does not mean mere external washings laid down by rituals, but rather to enter into His word and teaching that leads to self-emptying and death. At the washing of the feet of His disciples, Jesus made this clear, though Peter took some time to understand that by refusing to let Jesus wash his feet, he 'would have no part' with Him; he would cut himself off from our Lord's ministry and glory if he did not share His outlook and accept the total mystery of self-emptying – even unto love and service of his betrayers.[13]

The water pots at the wedding in Cana remind one, too, of the Indian custom of water pots being piled up at the door of the house where the wedding takes place. Pots with water, as with rice, earth, etc. are symbols of a new life – the *poorna kumbha* – the full pot – filled to the brim – being a symbol of the fullness of life and joy. Laxmi, the Goddess of prosperity, often carries it in one of her four arms.

## 7 THE WINE

The wine, too, is symbolic – of joy, celebration, life, love, a new creation, whether as Dodd thinks, the story of the Cana wedding developed out of a parable, or whether, as F. E. Williams thinks, it was based on Luke 5.33–39, together with the tradition of Jesus' mother and brothers. In any case, says Barrett, it seems clear that 'John meant to show the supersession of Judaism in the glory of Jesus.'[14] It is possible that in so doing he drew material from Dionysiac sources. 'There was an exact precedent for the benefaction of Jesus in a pagan worship, doubtless known to some, at least, of John's readers. The god Dionysius was not only the discoverer of wine, but also the cause of miraculous transformation of water into wine (cf. Euripides: Bacchae 704–7, etc.).[15]

So, too, in Vedic India, *Soma* – originally a plant – was raised to the status of a God. The juice of this plant was offered three times a day in a sacrifice – as wine is offered in the Eucharistic sacrifice. If at Pentecost, the apostles, inebriated with the Divine Spirit, were suspected of having drunk too much wine, the gods were often thought to have been inspired by Soma. Thus Indra, for instance, did great and extraordinary deeds. Believed to have grown on the Mujavat mountain, Parjnya, the rain god is, interestingly enough, said to be Soma's father and the waters are his sisters.[16] We find Soma destroying towns, begetting gods, upholding the sky, prolonging mortals' lives. He is also the Lord of the tidal floods.[17] He is given all the attributes given to Indra.[18] For a Christian, wine, transformed into the Blood of Christ at a Eucharistic sacrifice, is believed to give immortality (life everlasting). He would find it interesting to read, in a Rig Vedic hymn (i.91) the prayer:

And Soma, let it be thy will
For us to live, nor let us die . . .
Thou Soma, bliss upon the old,
And on the young and pious men
Ability to live, bestowest.

Christ fulfilled 'all the scriptures' – (cf. Luke 24.27) and gave 'the best wine' – that inebriates one with love of God.

## 8 'THE SERVANTS WHO HAD DRAWN THE WATER'

Only the servants who had drawn the water knew from whence the wine had come. The steward and the bridegroom's friends were surprised that the best wine was kept to the last. Only the servants 'knew,' for they had done the work of filling those huge water pots. Only those who labor, who taste, who experience personally, really 'know,' 'I am the taste of water.' We read also in the Bhagavad Gita, 'I am the knowledge of those who know' (10.38) and again, 'I am the soul which dwells in the heart of all things' (10.20). 'He is the Lord of all, who is hidden in the heart of all things. Those who know Him through their hearts and minds become immortal.'[19] Immortality is given to those who have the knowledge that comes from having drunk of this 'immortal nectar.' And only those who labor at 'drawing' from His Heart, in the cave of their own hearts, in meditation, know from whence comes this best wine, which alone can satisfy man's thirst forever.

John, whenever dealing with water (as in 1.26; 3.25; 4.10; 7.38), shows it to be both purifying and satisfying of thirst. The Cana miracle illustrates, as already seen, 'at once the poverty of the old dispensation with its merely ceremonial cleansing and the richness of the new, in which the Blood of Christ is available both for cleansing (1.29) and for drink' (6.53). The initial reference is to the supersession of Judaism, but Bultmann is right to generalize: 'The water stands for everything that is a substitute for revelation, everything by which a man thinks he can live, and which yet fails him when put to the test.'[20]

## CONCLUSION

And through water 'his disciples came to believe in Him' (John 2.11). Thus, by working this miracle of transformation with his humble creature water, Jesus 'manifested his glory.' 'The miracle of water made into wine may in itself not appear to be an apt indication of Christ's glory; however, it must be taken as John takes it, as the first of a series, all of which are related to the life that is to be found in the word of God.'[21] 'And his disciples came to believe in Him' – through water turned into wine. And we, too, come to believe that the water of the self – the *ahamkar* or ego – if poured out in silent, unresisting surrender like Mary's – can become, at her word of intercession, the wine of the Self, who dwells in the heart of all things.

> Be praised, my Lord,
> through sister water,
> for greatly useful, lowly,
> precious, chaste is she.

> (St Francis of Assisi)

## NOTES

1   Cf. *Bhagavad Gita* 2.54 f.

2   B. Vawter, 'The Gospel According to John' in R. E. Brown *et al.* (eds), *Jerome Bible Commentary*, (London, Geoffrey Chapman, 1968), p. 424.

3   The sequence can be seen in John 1.29; 1.35; 1.39–42, 43 – four days.

4   John 2.11; 4.54; 6.14; 9.16; 12.18; also dealing with water, John 5.2–9; 6.16–21 describe them in detail but do not call them 'signs,' though they doubtless are.

5   ibid.

6   Cf. the Woman of the Apocalypse 12, who is also the Mother of Christ and of the new Israel, where the vision of John is again by the imagery of Genesis.

7   T. T. Feeney, 'Waters of Salvation', (*Bible Today*, March 1965), pp. 1097–1102.

8   J. Ratzinger, *Introduction to Christianity* (London, Search Press, 1971), p. 197.

9   Cf. the use of the figure of an abundance of wine in Amos 9.13 f; Hos. 14.7; Jer. 31.12; Enoch 10.19; Bar. 29.5.

10   C. K. Barrett, however, says: 'It remains quite uncertain whether any allusion to the Eucharist is intended' '*The Gospel According to John*', introduction and commentary (London, SPCK, 1979), p. 189.

11   Ratzinger, pp. 197–8.

12   Cf. L. Dufour, 'Water', in *Dictionary of Biblical Theology* (Bangalore, Theological Publications of India), p. 646.

13   ibid., p. 646.

14   Barrett, pp. 188 f.

15   ibid.

16  Rig Ved X.34.1; IX.98.9.
17  Rig Ved 88.24–25.
18  Cf. Motilal Pandit, *Vedic Hinduism* (Allahabad, St. Paul's), p. 76.
19  Svetasvatara Upanishad 4.15, 17.
20  Bultmann, *The Gospel of John*, quoted by Barrett.
21  Vawter, p. 428.

# 10

# Song and Deliverance

## GUSTAVO GUTIERREZ

The popular view is that Latin American liberation theology over-interprets, and works with only one biblical paradigm – the Exodus. Moving beyond that, the father of Latin American liberation theology finds in the Book of Job a hermeneutical clue to understanding the Latin American situation. Gutierrez reckons that the question of Job is still valid for Latin America: how are we to talk about God in a situation of innocent sufferings. In other words, the key theological issue is not only how to talk about God after Auschwitz, but also how to talk about God while Ayacucho lasts. Ayacucho is a city in the Peruvian mountains in which poverty and violence reign.

This extract is the concluding chapter of his book, *On Job: God-Talk and the Suffering of the Innocent* (Maryknoll, NY, Orbis Books, 1987).

Gustavo Gutierrez is from Peru and is the author of the classic *A Theology of Liberation* (Maryknoll, NY, Orbis Books, 1973, and the revised edition, 1988). His other books include *The Power of the Poor in History* (Maryknoll, NY, Orbis Books, 1983) and *We Drink from Our Own Wells* (Maryknoll, NY, Orbis Books, 1984).

The movement of the Book of Job is twofold: a forward, linear movement, and a circling movement of deepening insight into the answer to the opening question: Is it possible to believe in God without expectation of reward, or 'for nothing'? In an effort to answer this question, the poet comes upon the doctrine of temporal retribution. This, he finds, does not take into account his own experience or the experience of so many others. He therefore looks for a correct way of talking about God within the most strained and knotty of all human situations: the suffering of the innocent.

The Book of Job does not claim to have found a rational or definitive explanation of suffering; the poet is quite aware that the subject is a complex one. On the other hand, his faith prompts him to inquire into the possibility of finding an appropriate language about God that does justice to the situation of suffering. Not to make the effort is to risk succumbing to impotent resignation, a religion of calculated self-interest, a cynical outlook that forgets the suffering of others, and even despair.

Perhaps the author knew these attitudes from experience, for there are echoes of all of them in his work. But his profound sense of God and his keen sensitivity to the misfortunes of others kept him from yielding to these temptations. Despite everything, he remained resolutely disposed to look for and find a way of talking about God. He remains a deeply human and religious man who takes seriously the reality of unjust suffering and does not play down the difficulty of understanding it. His determination to seek and find – which is already a gift from the Lord – leads him through a battlefield in which, as one author puts it, the shots come at him from every side.[1] He does not avoid them, despite the danger that they may put an end to him and his hope of finding a correct way of talking about God. His personal courage and his trust in God impel him to follow paths that are a challenge to the theology of his day. At once more traditional than those who boast of being such, and more innovative than the standards of the mediocre allow them to be, the poet of the Book of Job is guided by God's hand to discover ways of talking about God.

We have followed these ways one by one. We have accompanied Job as his experience of unjust suffering broadened and he acquired a moving realization of the suffering of others. The ethical perspective inspired by consideration of the needs of others and especially of the poor made him abandon a morality of rewards and punishments, and caused a reversal in his way of speaking about God. We also accompanied him when after accepting adversity he rebelled and struggled with God but meanwhile kept hoping in God and, despite everything, finally surrendered to God's presence and unmerited love. But these two paths that we have travelled with him should not be thought of as simply parallel; in fact, they cross and enrich each other, and finally converge to yield a correct way of talking about God.

For Job to leave his own world and enter into that of the poor already meant taking the path of gratuitousness and not simply that of concern for justice. On the other hand, all prophecy has as its starting point an encounter with the Lord and the Lord's unmerited love (see the theme of the prophetic vocation in Isa. 6; Jer. 1.4–10; Ezek. 2 and 3). The result is that two languages – the prophetic and the contemplative – are required; but they must also be combined and become increasingly integrated into a single language.

Prophetic language makes it possible to draw near to a God who has a predilection for the poor precisely because divine love refuses to be confined by the categories of human justice. God has a preferential love for the poor not because they are necessarily better than others, morally or religiously, but simply because they are poor and living in an inhuman situation that is contrary to God's will. The ultimate basis for the privileged position of the poor is not in the poor themselves but in God, in the gratuitousness and universality of God's *agapeic love*. Nothing can limit or contain this love, as Yahweh makes clear to Job in the revelation of what Yahweh has established as the fulcrum of the world. Belief in God and God's gratuitous love leads to a preferential option for the poor and to solidarity with those who suffer wretched conditions, contempt, and oppression, those whom the social order ignores and exploits. The God of utter freedom and gratuitousness who has been revealed to Job can alone explain the privileged place of those whom the powerful and the self-righteous of society treat unjustly and make outcasts. In the God of Christian revelation gratuitousness and preferential love for the poor go hand in hand; they are therefore also inseparable in our contemplation of God and our concern for the disinherited of this world.

The doctrine of retribution contained a valid principle: that to be a believer requires a certain ethical behavior. But even this idea became distorted when inserted into a narrow framework of rewards and punishments.

The language of the prophets took a different approach in emphasizing the connection between God and the poor. It acknowledged the demands of ethics but it transformed their meaning, because the fulfillment of these demands was not regarded as a form of personal insurance or as a way of gaining a hold on God. Obedience was rather a matter of freely giving what we have freely received (see Matt. 10.8).

As a result, prophetic language supports and reinforces language inspired by contemplation of God. At the very beginning of the Book of Job and at the level of popular faith we saw the proper tone to be used in speaking of the Lord's actions. But the tone weakened as Job's unjust situation was prolonged and as he listened to the criticisms of his friends. The language of mysticism restores vigor to the values of popular faith by strengthening them and enabling them to resist every attempt at manipulation. It thus prevents the distortion that turns these values into fruitless resignation and passivity in the face of injustice. But conversely the language of contemplation likewise becomes more vigorous and more community-minded to the extent that it is nourished by popular faith.

Mystical language expresses the gratuitousness of God's love; prophetic language expresses the demands this love makes. The followers of Jesus and the community they form – the church – live in the space created by this gratuitousness and these demands. Both languages are necessary and therefore inseparable; they also feed and correct each other. In a passage to which I referred earlier, Jeremiah brings out the connection nicely:

> Sing to the Lord;
>> praise the Lord!
> For he has delivered the life of the needy
>> from the hand of evildoers (20.13).

*Song and deliverance*: thanksgiving for the liberation of the poor. Contemplation and practice, gratuitousness and justice. This is a central theme of the Bible (see Ps. 69.34–5; 109.30–1). After her people had been delivered from the Assyrian threat, Judith sang a song of thanksgiving:

> Begin a song to my God with tambourines,
>> sing to my Lord with cymbals.
> Raise to him a new psalm;
>> exalt him, and call upon his name (Judith 16.2).

The figure and theme of the suffering servant in Isaiah show numerous and very valuable points of contact with Job. In the first of the Isaian poems God presents the servant and describes his mission among the nations:

> Behold my servant, whom I uphold,
>> my chosen, in whom my soul delights;
> I have put my Spirit upon him,
>> he will bring forth justice to the nations.
> He will not cry or lift up his voice,
>> or make it heard in the street;
> a bruised reed he will not break,
>> and a dimly burning wick he will not quench;
>> he will faithfully bring forth justice.
> He will not fail or be discouraged
>> till he has established justice in the earth;
>> and the coastlands wait for his law (Isa. 42:1–5).

Anointed with the Spirit of the Lord, the servant has as his task to promote and bring forth justice (*mishpat*) on earth, to restore the full justice of God,[2] A little further on, and in the context of the universalist vision of Second Isaiah, we are again urged to sing to the Lord:

> Sing to the Lord a new song,
> his praise from the end of the earth!
> Let the sea roar and all that fills it,
> the coastlands and their inhabitants (Isa. 42.10).

In this 'new song' the text deals with *deliverance*, the melody adds the *thanksgiving*. Job likewise points to the combination of these two elements when he voices his hope that he will *see* his *gō'ēl* (his avenger), the protector of the poor (19.25–7). The poet of the Book of Job gives the name 'Yahweh' – the guarantor of covenantal *justice* – to the God who 'from the heart of the tempest' reveals to Job the plan of *unmerited love*.

Vision of God (final stage in Job's suit against God) and defense of the poor (a role he discovers for himself because of his own innocence) are thus combined in the experience of Job as a man of justice. They are two aspects of a single gift from the Lord and of the single road that leads to the Lord.[3]

For the same reason, emphasis on the practice of justice and on solidarity with the poor must never become an obsession and prevent our seeing that this commitment reveals its value and ultimate meaning only within the vast and mysterious horizon of God's gratuitous love.[4] Furthermore, the very building of a just society requires a stimulus and an enveloping atmosphere that gratuitousness alone can supply.[5] The point here is not to assign greater importance to the element of play and gratuitousness than to justice, but to ensure that the world of justice finds its full meaning and source in the freely given love of God.[6]

The world of unmerited love is not a place dominated by the arbitrary or the superfluous.[7] Without the prophetic dimension, the language of contemplation is in danger of having no grip on the history in which God acts and in which we meet God. Without the mystical dimension the language of prophecy can narrow its vision and weaken its perception of the God who makes all things new (Rev. 21.5). Each undergoes a distortion that isolates it and renders it unauthentic.

The journey of prophecy and the journey of contemplation are precisely that: a journey. The road must be travelled in freedom without turning from it because of its pitfalls, and without pretending ignorance of its ever new forms, for unjust human suffering continues to be heartrending and insatiable; it continually raises new questions and causes new dilemmas. It never ends; neither does protest, after the manner of Job. Although the way of talking about God has become clearer, it continues to be mysterious, as awesome and as alluring as ever.

Many difficult tasks remain to be done, many distressing questions to be answered; but an initial glimpse has been given of the path to full encounter with the loving and free God.

The language of contemplation acknowledges that everything comes from the Father's unmerited love and opens up 'new horizons of hope' (Puebla, para. 1165).[8] The language of prophecy attacks the situation – and its structural causes – of injustice and deprivation in which the poor live, because it looks for 'the suffering features of Christ the Lord' in the pain-ravaged faces of an oppressed people (Puebla, paras 31–9). Both languages arise, among the poor of Latin America as in Job, out of the suffering and hopes of the innocent. For poverty and unjust suffering are in fact the situation of the majority in Latin America. Our theological reflection thus starts from the experience of the cross and death as well as from the joy of the resurrection and life.

This twofold language is the language that Jesus, prefigured by Job, uses in speaking of the Father's love. The author of the Book of Job stammers out what Christ will say unhesitatingly. He starts from the experience of unjust human suffering, which Jesus in turn will share on the 'two sticks' of which Gonzalo Rose speaks to us with such tenderness. The author of Job reminds us of the call for justice that issues from God the liberator. The Messiah will make that same call his own as a central element in the message of love that sums up 'the ten commandments of God,' which fit into our hands 'like ten more fingers,' to cite Gonzalo Rose once again. The author of Job directs us toward that gratuitousness of the Father's love that will be the heart of the proclamation and witness of Jesus Christ. He seeks a way; he offers himself as 'the way' (John 14.6).

# A CRY OF LONELINESS AND COMMUNION

Jesus speaks to us of the Father, and in his discourses language about God achieves its greatest expressiveness. The Son of God teaches us that talk of God must be mediated by the experience of the cross. He accepts abandonment and death precisely in order to reveal God to us as love. Universal love and preference for the poor distinguish the message of the divine reign that both purifies human history and transcends it. Sin, which is the refusal to accept the message, brings Jesus to his death; the cross is the result of the resistance of those who refuse to accept the unmerited and demanding gift of God's love.

The final words of Jesus – 'My God, my God, why hast thou forsaken me?' (Matt. 27.46; Mark 15.34) – speak of the suffering and loneliness of one who feels abandoned by the hand of God.[9] But when he cries out his feeling of abandonment in the opening words of Psalm 22, he also makes the rest of the psalm his own.[10] The whole of the psalm must therefore be taken into account if we are to understand the meaning of his lament.[11]

Psalm 22 expresses the cruel loneliness experienced by a man of deep faith. In the midst of this experience he turns to his God:

> Why art thou so far from helping me, from the words
>     of my groaning?
> O my God, I cry by day, but thou dost not answer;
>     and by night, but find no rest.
> Yet thou art holy,
>     enthroned on the praises of Israel (Ps. 22.1–3).

But in the Bible complaint does not exclude hope; in fact, they go together.[12] We saw this to be so in the case of Job. The confidence of the psalmist grows as he recalls that this is a God who has delivered the people of Israel from slavery and deprivation:

> In thee our fathers trusted;
>     they trusted, and thou didst deliver them.
> To thee they cried, and were saved;
>     in thee they trusted, and were not disappointed (vv. 4–5).

The psalmist is referring to the deliverance from Egypt and to Exodus 3.7. This was the experience on which biblical faith was based. All the more reason, then, for him to describe his own pitiful situation in all its bleakness. This man who laments knows that God does not regard suffering as an ideal. His complaint is filled with a longing for life.[13]

> But I am a worm, and no man;
>   scorned by men, and despised by the people.
> All who see me mock at me,
>   they make mouths at me, they wag their heads;
> 'He committed his cause to the Lord; let him deliver
>   him,
>   let him rescue him, for he delights in him!' . . .
> I am poured out like water,
>   and all my bones are out of joint;
> my heart is like wax,
>   it is melted within my breast;
> my strength is dried up like a potsherd,
>   and my tongue cleaves to my jaws;
>   thou dost lay me in the dust of death.
> Yea, dogs are round about me;
>   a company of evildoers encircle me;
>   they have pierced my hands and feet –
> I can count all my bones (vv. 6–8, 14–17).

The person speaking in this psalm tells of his misfortune and abandonment, but he says not a word of personal faults that would have merited such adversity. He is an innocent man who has been treated unjustly. This fact makes it easier for the evangelists to apply the text to Jesus at various moments in their accounts of his death.

The psalmist sinks deeper into suffering and loneliness. His situation is due to those who harass him and mock his faith in a God who can deliver him. But he remains steadfast; he knows that his God is bent on justice, and hears and protects the poor:

> For he has not despised or abhorred
>   the affliction of the afflicted;
> and he has not hid his face from him,
>   but has heard, when he cried to him. . . .
> The afflicted shall eat and be satisfied;
>   those who seek him shall praise the Lord!
> May your hearts live for ever! (vv. 24, 26).

The God who could hear the cry of the Israelites when they were oppressed in Egypt does not disdain 'the destitution of the destitute,'[14] the poverty of the poor and the least of human beings. Verse 26 is an allusion to Deuteronomy 14.29, which says that 'the sojourner, the fatherless, and the widow' – the biblical triad used in referring to the poor and helpless – shall all 'eat and be filled.'

This solidarity with the poor and the starving, which leads to an ongoing transformation of history and requires behavior to this end, is the fruit of the gratuitous love of the God in whom the psalmist believes and hopes. This accounts for his self-surrender and praise toward the end of the poem:

> I will tell of thy name to my brethren;
>   in the midst of the congregation I will praise thee:
> You who fear the Lord, praise him!
>   all you sons of Jacob, glorify him,
>   and stand in awe of him, all you sons of Israel! . . .
> All the ends of the earth shall remember
>   and turn to the Lord;
> and all the families of the nations
>   shall worship before him.
> For dominion belongs to the Lord,
>   and he rules over the nations (vv. 22–3, 27–8).

Jesus did not compose this psalm, he inherited it. It had its origin in the suffering of a believer, perhaps someone who in some way represented his people.[15] The important thing is that Jesus made it his own and, while nailed to the cross, offered to the Father the suffering and abandonment of all humankind. This radical communion with the suffering of human beings brought him down to the deepest level of history at the very moment when his life was ending.

But in adopting this psalm Jesus also gave expression to his hope in the liberating God who with predilection defends the poor and the dispossessed.[16] Luke could therefore put on the lips of Jesus not the cry of abandonment but words of confident self-surrender: 'Father, into thy hands I commit my spirit!' (23.46; see Ps. 31.5).[17] He who has been 'abandoned' abandons himself in turn into the hands of the Father. He confronts the forces of evil and sin when, in communion with the hopes of the human race, he asserts that life, not death, has the final say.[18] All this is part of the redemptive experience of the cross.[19] It is there that Jesus experiences and proclaims the resurrection and true, unending life, and becomes 'the source of eternal salvation.' Here is how the Letter to the Hebrews speaks of the value of Jesus' death for our salvation:

In the days of his flesh, Jesus offered up prayers and supplications, with loud cries and tears, to him who was able to save him from death, and he was heard for his godly fear. Although he was a Son, he learned obedience through what he suffered; and being made perfect he became the source of eternal salvation to all who obey him, being designated by God a high priest after the order of Melchizedek (5.7–10).

Communion in suffering and in hope, in the abandonment of loneliness and in trusting self-surrender in death as in life: this is the message of the cross, which is 'folly to those who are perishing, but to us who are being saved it is the power of God' (1 Cor. 1.18). Because it is 'folly' it can pass unnoticed by those who have eyes only for wonders and manifestations of might. Paradoxically, this power of God is at the same time 'weakness' (1 Cor. 1.25). It inspires the language of the cross, which is a synthesis of the prophetic and the contemplative and the only appropriate way of talking about the God of Jesus Christ.[20]

By using this language one engages in a 'dangerous remembrance' of him who was publicly crucified at the crossroads and whom the Father raised to life.[21] This kind of talk – which the wise and understanding of this world regard as madness – calls all human beings together 'as a church' via the privileged choice of the weak and despised of human history.

For consider your call, brethren; not many of you were wise according to worldly standards, not many were powerful, not many were of noble birth; but God chose what is foolish in the world to shame the wise, God chose what is weak in the world to shame the strong, God chose what is low and despised in the world, even things that are not, to bring to nothing things that are, so that no human being might boast in the presence of God (1 Cor. 1.26–9).

At the same time, however, if we are to use the language of the cross we must have made our own the meaning of the crucifixion. Only within the following of Jesus is it possible to talk of God.[22] From the cross Jesus calls us to follow in his steps, 'for,' he tells us, 'my yoke is easy, and my burden light' (Matt. 11.30). This invitation to follow him completes the passage on the revelation to the simple. At that time I singled out the message of the gratuitousness of God's love that the passage contains. It is in the context of this gratuitousness that the way of the cross to which Jesus invites us must be set.

All these considerations do not eliminate the element of protest from the final words of Jesus; they are rather an attempt to situate it

properly. Even in his lament Jesus 'spoke correctly of God.' His cry on
the cross renders more audible and more penetrating the cries of all
the Jobs, individual and collective, of human history. To adopt a
comparison that Bonhoeffer uses in another context, the cry of Jesus is
the *cantus firmus*, the leading voice to which all the voices of those who
suffer unjustly are joined.

## 'I WILL NOT RESTRAIN MY TONGUE'

This cry cannot be muted. Those who suffer unjustly have a right to
complain and protest. Their cry expresses both their bewilderment
and their faith. It is not possible to do theology in Latin America
without taking into account the situation of the most downtrodden of
history; this means in turn that at some point the theologian must cry
out, as Jesus did, 'My God, my God, why hast thou forsaken me?'[23]
   This kind of communion in suffering demands watchfulness and
solidarity. 'Jesus will be in agony until the end of the world. There must
be no sleeping during that time.'[24] Commitment of the alleviation of
human suffering, and especially to the removal of its causes as far as
possible, is an obligation for the followers of Jesus, who took upon
himself his own 'easy yoke and light burden.' Such a commitment
presupposes genuine human compassion, as well as a measure of
understanding of human history and the factors that condition it
(consider the effort made in the documents of Medellín and Puebla to
understand the causes of the present situation of injustice in which
Latin America is living). It also requires a firm and stubborn determination to be present, regardless of the consequences, wherever the
unjust abuse the innocent.
   Human suffering, whatever its causes – social, personal, or other – is
a major question for theological reflection.[25] J. B. Metz has, with
refined human and historical sensitivity, called the attention of contemporary theologians, those of Europe in particular, to what it means
to talk about God after Auschwitz.[26] For the terrible holocaust of
millions of Jews is an inescapable challenge to the Christian conscience and an inexcusable reproach to the silence of many Christians
in the face of that dreadful event. We must therefore ask: How can we
talk about God without referring to our own age? More than that: How
can we do it without taking into account situations like the holocaust in
which God seems to be absent from immense human suffering.[27]

It needs to be realized, however, that for us Latin Americans the question is not precisely 'How are we to do theology after Auschwitz?' The reason is that in Latin America we are still experiencing every day the violation of human rights, murder, and the torture that we find so blameworthy in the Jewish holocaust of World War II. Our task here is to find the words with which to talk about God in the midst of the starvation of millions, the humiliation of races regarded as inferior, discrimination against women, especially women who are poor, systematic social injustice, a persistent high rate of infant mortality, those who simply 'disappear' or are deprived of their freedom, the sufferings of peoples who are struggling for their right to live,[28] the exiles and the refugees, terrorism of every kind, and the corpse-filled common graves of Ayacucho. What we must deal with is not the past but, unfortunately, a cruel present and a dark tunnel with no apparent end.

In Peru, therefore – but the question is perhaps symbolic of all Latin America – we must ask: How are we to do theology *while Ayacucho lasts?* How are we to speak of the God of life when cruel murder on a massive scale goes on in 'the corner of the dead'?[29] How are we to preach the love of God amid such profound contempt for human life? How are we to proclaim the resurrection of the Lord where death reigns, and especially the death of children, women, the poor, indigenes, and the 'unimportant' members of our society?

These are our questions, and this is our challenge. Job shows us a way with his vigorous protest, his discovery of concrete commitment to the poor and all who suffer unjustly, his facing up to God, and his acknowledgment of the gratuitousness that characterizes God's plan for human history. It is for us to find our own route amid the present sufferings and hopes of the poor of Latin America, to analyze its course with the requisite historical effectiveness, and, above all, to compare it anew with the word of God. This is what has been done by those, for example, who in recent years have been murdered for their witness of faith and solidarity with the poorest and most helpless, those now known as 'the Latin American martyrs.'

'That is why I cannot keep quiet: in my anguish of spirit I shall speak, in my bitterness of soul I shall complain' (Job 7.11). Nor can the poor and oppressed of Latin America remain silent.[30] For them 'day comes like a lamentation arising from the depths of the heart.'[31] What the poor and oppressed have to say may sound harsh and unpleasant to some. It is possible that they may be scandalized at hearing a frank avowal of the human and religious experience of the poor, and at seeing their clumsy attempts to relate their lives to the God in whom they have such deep faith. Perhaps those who live, and try to express, their faith and hope amid unjust suffering will some day have to say humbly, with Job, 'I spoke without understanding marvels that are beyond my grasp,' and put aside their harsh language. Yet who knows but that the Lord may tell them, to the surprise of some: 'You have spoken correctly about me.'[32]

The prophet Isaiah announces that 'the Lord God will wipe away tears from all faces, and the reproach of his people he will take away from all the earth.'[33] Woe to those whom the Lord finds dry-eyed because they could not bring themselves to solidarity with the poor and suffering of this world! If we are to receive from God the tender consolation promised by the prophet, we must make our own the needs of the oppressed; our hearts must be moved at seeing a wounded person by the wayside,[34] be attuned to the sufferings of others, and be more sensitive to persons in conflict and confusion than to 'the order of the day.'

Only if we know how to be silent and involve ourselves in the suffering of the poor will we be able to speak out of their hope. Only if we take seriously the suffering of the innocent and live the mystery of the cross amid that suffering, but in the light of Easter, can we prevent our theology from being 'windy arguments (Job 16.3). But if we do, then we shall not deserve to hear from the poor the reproach that Job threw in the faces of his friends: 'What sorry comforters you are!' (16.2).

In sending his Son, the Father 'wagered' on the possibility of faith and behavior characterized by gratuitousness and by a response to the demand that justice be established. When history's 'losers' – persons like Job – follow in the steps of Jesus, they are seeing to it that the Lord wins his wager. The risks accepted in talking about God with the suffering of the innocent in view are great. But, again like Job, we cannot keep quiet; we must humbly allow the cry of Jesus on the cross to echo through history and nourish our theological efforts.[35] As St Gregory the Great says in his commentary on Job, the cry of Jesus will not be heard 'if our tongues keep silent about what our souls believe. But lest his cry be stifled in us, let each of us make known to those who approach him the mystery by which he lives!'[36]

This mystery is the one proclaimed by the dead and risen Son of God. It is the mystery that we come to know when his Spirit impels us to say 'Abba! Father!' (Gal. 4.6).

## NOTES

1 R. de Pury, *Job ou l'homme revolté*, cited by Barth, *Church Dogmatics*, IV/3, pt 1, p. 424: 'The remarkable thing about this Book is that Job makes not a single step of flight to a better God, but stays resolutely in the field of battle under the fire of the divine wrath. Although God treats him as an enemy, through the dark night and the abyss Job does not falter, nor invoke another court, nor even appeal to the God of his friends, but calls upon this God who crushes him. He flees to the God whom he accuses. He sets his confidence in God who has disillusioned him and reduced him to despair. . . . Without deviating from the violent assertion of his innocence and God's hostility, he confesses his hope, taking as his Defender the One who judges him, as his Liberator the One who throws him in prison, and as his Friend his mortal enemy.'

2 See W. A. M. Beuker, 'Mispat. The First Servant Song and Its Context' (*Vetus Testamentum*, 22, 1972), pp. 1–30.

3 Those who follow this road may draw encouragement from the words of St Augustine to his people: 'Therefore, brothers and sisters, let us now sing, not in the delight of repose but to ease our toil. As travelers are accustomed to sing, so do you sing but journey on; comfort yourself in your toil by singing. . . . If you advance, you are continuing your journey, but advance in goodness, in true faith, in good practices; sing and journey on' (*Sermon* 256, 1, 2–3 = PL 38:1193).

4 Despite reductionist interpretations that try to deny the fact, this conviction has been part of the theology of liberation from the beginning and has always fed the spirituality that animates this theology. The theme of the gratuitousness of divine love is therefore the point of reference for determining the ultimate meaning of the emphasis on the practice of justice; see my *A Theology of Liberation* (Maryknoll, NY, Orbis Books, 1973), *passim*, and *We Drink from Our Own Wells* (Maryknoll, NY, Orbis Books, 1984), pp. 117–26.

5 See A. Heschel, *The Prophets* (New York, Harper & Row, 1962), p. 201: 'Justice dies when dehumanized. . . . Justice dies when deified, for beyond all justice is God's compassion. The logic of justice may seem impersonal, yet the concern for justice is an act of love.'

6 See John Paul II, encyclical *Rich in Mercy*, para. 7: 'This redemption is the final, definitive revelation of the holiness of God who in His very being is the absolute fullness of perfection. This means that He is the fullness of justice and love, for justice is based on love, flows from it and seeks it as its crown' (*The Pope Speaks*, 26, 1981, pp. 36–7). See also para. 14.

7 See J. M. González Ruíz, *Dios es gratuito, no superfluo* (Madrid/Barcelona, Marova/Fontanella, 1970).

8 The Puebla document is translated in J. Eagleson and P. Scharper (eds), *Puebla and Beyond: Documentation and Commentary* (Maryknoll, NY, Orbis Books, 1979). See H. Bourgeois, *Dieu selon les chrétiens* (Paris, Centurion, 1974), p. 58: 'God is for him [Jesus] the generosity behind his own generosity. He is the primal source of the potentialities that Jesus finds in himself and elicits in those around him. God is here not an explanation but a permanent

condition; a symbol for the symbolism of the human being; an image of the total gratuitousness that makes possible the limited and yet indefinitely extended gratuitousness of the human person.'

9 J. J. González Faus observes in his *La Humanidad Nueva* (Madrid, 1975), that 'these words – the only ones in which Jesus does not address God as *Abba* – reveal the deepest dimension of this death: . . . the dimension of abandonment by God' (2.131).

10 See J. Delorme, *Lecture de l'Evangile selon Saint Marc* (Paris, Cerf, 1972), p. 112: 'It is clear that although Jesus recites only the opening words of Ps. 22, the reader is to know that the entire psalm is the key to an understanding of the crucifixion. The reader knows therefore that the attitude of Jesus during this time is that expressed in the prayer of the suffering just man, according to which the ill-treatment he suffers is the condition for a rebirth and for the success of God's plan (see Ps. 22.23–31).'

11 The meaning and historical character of these final moments of Jesus have been the subject of recent studies. See in particular the fresh and penetrating observations of X. Léon-Dufour, *Face à la mort: Jésus et Paul* (Paris, Seuil, 1979), esp. pp. 149–67.

12 See W. Kasper, *Jesus the Christ* (New York, Paulist Press, 1976), p. 118: 'This psalm [22] is a lament which turns into a song of thanksgiving. The religious man's suffering is experienced as abandonment by God; but in his suffering and in the agony of death the religious man finds that God has been Lord all along, and that he saves him and brings him into a new life. The psalm uses the language of apocalyptic to put this experience into the form of a typical, paradigmatic fate. Being saved from death now becomes the way in which the eschatological kingdom of God intervenes. Consequently Jesus' words, "My God, my God, why hast thou forsaken me?" are not a cry of despair but a prayer confident of an answer; and one which hopes for the coming of God's kingdom.'

13 See I. González, 'Salmos de lamentación: Protesta ante el sufrimiento' (*Vida y Pensamiento* (San José, Costa Rica), 4/1–2, 1984), pp. 69–88. At the end of her essay the author reproduces the free translations, inspired by the situation in Latin America, that Ernesto Cardenal, Mamerto Menapace, and she herself have made of Psalm 22.

14 This ('la miseria del misero') is how the *Biblia de Jerusalén* translates verse 25. [The French *Bible de Jérusalem* has 'la pauvreté du pauvre,' the Jerusalem Bible has 'the poor man in his poverty,' and the New Jerusalm Bible has 'the poverty of the poor' – Translator M. J. O'Connell's note).

15 See P. Beauchamp, *Psaumes nuit et jour* (Paris, Seuil, 1977), pp. 233–52.

16 J. Delorme (*Lecture*) links the final words of Jesus with Job: 'The abandonment that Jesus experiences must be taken seriously, but it must be interpreted not according to our modern outlook that looks upon it as a cry of despair, but according to the biblical outlook for which the sense of abandonment is the occasion for a new outburst of faith: "I have no hope; you, God, are my only hope, and you are abandoning me. Only you can explain to me why I am in this situation; therefore I shall keep after you until you do explain it. Meanwhile I put myself in your hands no matter what happens." Neither was

the cry of Job a cry of despair: if he keeps pressing heaven with his questions, it is simply because he expects God to answer. He lays on God the obligation of answering, and not only at this moment; until he dies he will go on demanding justice (Job 19:25–7). His is the cry of a madman, for it expresses a hope his age found inconceivable. But thanks to this faith that perseveres to the end, his cry is, as it were, the revelation of a step forward' (pp. 112–13).

17  Léon-Dufour, p. 164: 'The Markan and Lukan traditions both make use of the "lamentation" pattern. . . . They have selected from these prayers of suffering and trust [Psalms 22 and 31] the words that can best serve as point of departure for a positive response from God. According to Mark, Jesus makes his own the sentiments of the suffering just man: behind his words we can hear the cry of the persecuted but trusting just man. The same holds for Luke, but with a quite different tonality and with the appeal to the "Father."'

18  This is clearly pointed out in the final report of the 1985 Synod of Bishops, which had been convoked to review the implementation of Vatican II over a period of twenty years. In Section D 2 the report reads: 'It seems to us that in the present-day difficulties God wishes to teach us more deeply the value, the importance, and the centrality of the cross of Jesus Christ. Therefore the relationship between human history and salvation history is to be explained in the light of the paschal mystery. Certainly the theology of the cross does not at all exclude the theology of the creation and incarnation, but, as is clear, it presupposes it. When we Christians speak of the cross, we do not deserve to be clear, it presupposes it. When we Christians speak of the cross, we do not deserve to be labeled pessimists, but we rather base ourselves upon the realism of Christian hope' (text printed in *East Asian Pastoral Review* (23/1, 1986), p. 22).

19  Because of my theme I am especially concerned in these pages with the element of loneliness and communion in the cross and resurrection of Christ, to the extent that these have to do with talk about God. On the comprehensive meaning of the redemptive experience of Jesus, see C. Duquoc, *Christologie*, vol. 2, *Le Messie* (Paris, Cerf, 1972), pp. 171–226; E. Schillebeeckx, *Jesus: An Experiment in Christology* (New York, Seabury Press, 1979), pp. 179–271.

20  L. Boff, 'Como predicar la cruz hoy' (*Christus* (Mexico City), 573–4, March–April 1984), p. 22, writes: 'The supreme theological art is to be able to speak of death and the cross.'

21  See J. B. Metz, 'The Future in the Memory of Suffering' (*Concilium*, 76, 1972), pp. 9–25.

22  See G. Gutierrez, *Beber en su propio pozo* (rev. and enlarged edn; Lima, CEP, 1983), p. 204.

23  See J. Moltmann, *The Crucified God: The Cross of Christ as the Foundation and Criticism of Christian Theology* (New York, Harper & Row, 1974), p. 153: 'Every theology that claims to be Christian must come to terms with Jesus' cry on the cross. Basically, every Christian theology is consciously or unconsciously answering the question, "Why hast thou forsaken me?" . . . Sharing in the sufferings of this time, Christian theology is truly contemporary theology.'

24  Pascal, *Pensées* (Baltimore, Penguin, 1968), no. 919 (p. 313).

25  I phrase my thought in this way because human suffering is not limited

to suffering caused by social injustice. It is undeniable, however, that this latter kind of suffering is found on a vast scale and marked by refined cruelty in Latin America; that many other human wants have their origin in it; that it is occasioned by a contempt for the life of the poor that has its roots in sin – that is, in the refusal to love God and other human beings; and that the responsibility for removing its causes is ours, at least in part. Throughout these pages I have tried to keep in mind the complexity of human suffering.

26  In his essay 'Facing the Jews: Christian Theology after Auschwitz,' (*Concilium*, 175, 1984), p. 26, Metz writes: 'Søren Kierkegaard: In order to experience and understand what it means to be a Christian, it is always necessary to recognize a definitive historical situation. I start with the idea that Kierkegaard is right (without being able to explain this in detail at this time). The situation without the recognition of which Christian theology does not know whereof it speaks, is for us in this country first of all "after Auschwitz."' Some years before, Metz had sketched the problem in an article entitled 'Christians and Jews after Auschwitz', which was reprinted in *Beyond Civic Religion* (Mainz/Munich, 1980), pp. 29–50. There the author points out the historical responsibility of Christians for Auschwitz. They have the same responsibility for the situation that Latin America is experiencing and to which I refer in what follows.

27  R. Rubinstein, *The Religious Imagination: A Study in Psychoanalysis and Jewish Theology* (Indianapolis, Bobbs-Merrill, 198), and A. Neher, *L'exil de la parole: Du silence biblique au silence d'Auschwitz* (Paris, Seuil, 1970), have strongly emphasized this absence of God and related it to the experience of Job. See the excellent review of these two books by P. Watte, 'Job à Auschwitz' (*Revue théologique de Louvain*, 4, 1973), pp. 173–90.

28  I am thinking of Central America in particular. In this context, see the testimonies given by the tenacious and heroic people of Nicaragua in T. Cabestrero, *Nicaragua: crónica de una sangre inocente* (Mexico City, Katun, 1985); English translation, *Blood of the Innocent* (Maryknoll, NY, Orbis Books, 1985).

29  This is the meaning of the Quechuan word 'Ayacucho'.

30  'Holy Father, we are hungry, we suffer affliction, we lack work, we are sick. Our hearts are crushed by suffering as we see our tubercular wives giving birth, our children dying, our sons and daughters growing up weak and without a future. Yet despite everything we believe in the God of life.' These were the words with which Victor and Isabel Chero greeted John Paul II when he visited one of the poorest areas of Lima. In a strongly worded, improvised response, the Pope repeated what the inhabitants had said about their hunger for bread and their hunger for God. See the texts in 'Villa El Salvador: un diálogo del Papa con los pobres' (*Páginas*, 68, April 1985) pp. 34–7.

31  From the words of the cantata 'Santa María de Iquique' by Claudio Sapian, cited in J. Míguez Bonino, 'Compromiso cristiano ante el sufrimiento' (*Christus* (Mexico City), 573–4, March–April 1984), pp. 35–41; the author has some excellent reflections on the theme.

32  Alonso Schökel says forcefully and aptly: 'God did not shut Job's mouth as soon as he ended his opening curse (ch. 3). God does not look for mute co-workers; God wants the words of Job. Because we, though a critical

people, critical even of God, lack our own words, Job is our spokesman. That is why he could not keep quiet. Beyond our criticisms of the God whom our critical minds invent, comes the voice of the ever true God. Job could not keep quiet' L. A. Schökel and J. L. Sicre, *Job* (Madrid, Cristiandad, 1983), p. 597.

33   The Apocalypse has the Lamb drying the tears of those who have come out of the great tribulation (Rev. 7.17).

34   See the remarks on Luke 10 in G. Gutierrez, *A Theology of Liberation* (Maryknoll, NY, Orbis Books, 1973), pp. 198–200.

35   See J. Sobrino, *Christology at the Crossroads: A Latin American Approach* (Maryknoll, NY, Orbis Books, 1978), p. 231: 'There is the abandonment by God that Jesus felt on the cross and the abandonment by God that we experience. There is the cry of Jesus on the cross and the cry of countless victims in history. They do not allow us to nurture an ingenuous faith in God; it must be a faith that overcomes the world (1 John 5.4).'

36   Cited in Léon-Dufour, p. 167.

# 11

# Class in the Bible:
# The Biblical Poor a Social Class?

GEORGE M. SOARES-PRABHU

Indian biblical hermeneutics has to take into account two realities of India – religious pluralism and economic poverty. This essay is an example of an Indian biblical interpreter's study of the meaning of the poor in the Bible; he sees the poor as a sociological category rather than a religious or a spiritual group.

George M. Soares-Prabhu is on the staff of Jnana Deepa Vidyapeth (Pontifical Athenaeum) Pune, India, where he teaches New Testament exegesis. For his critique of the historical method and for his own proposal, see 'The Historical Critical Method: Reflections on its Relevance for the Study of the Gospels in India Today', in M. Amaladoss *et al.* (ed.) *Theologizing in India* (Bangalore, Theological Publications in India, 1981), pp. 314–49.

This piece appeared in *Vidyajyoti* (49, 7, 1985). *Vidyajyoti* is a monthly journal of theological reflection. The address is: The Editor, *Vidyajyoti*, 23 Raj Niwas Marg, Delhi 110054 India.

Liberation Theology has made at least two significant contributions to contemporary exegesis. It has sensitized exegetes to the social, economic, and political dimensions of the Bible; and it has made them aware of the extent to which their supposedly scientific exegesis is inevitably coloured by cultural and class prejudices. Neither contribution is specific or new. What we might call *the sociological contribution* was anticipated in early Marxist studies on the Bible, notably Kautsky's study of the origins of Christianity,[1] and was a conspicuous concern of the Chicago school. But these remained marginal movements in the world of biblical scholarship, soon to be overwhelmed by the wave of 'existentialist interpretation' with its highly privatized understanding of the biblical message as a call to personal decision. It is after the appearance of liberation theology that the sociological study of the Bible begins in earnest. And while not all (nor even most) of the works which this has produced are liberationist, or have been directly inspired by liberation theology, the present burgeoning of interest in the social world of the Bible owes much more, I suspect, to the impetus of liberation theology than exegetes would care to admit.

The *hermeneutical contribution* of liberation theology too – its awareness of the extent to which the class-culture of the reader affects his interpretation of a text – is again part of a general hermeneutical awakening. No one today seriously supposes that the exegesis of the Bible, even at its most 'scientific', is really value-free or wholly 'objective'. A totally objective interpretation is no doubt possible for a text made up of *terms* (formulae expressing measurable quantitative entities). It is not possible for a text like the Bible, which consists of *words* (linguistic expressions of human experiences). Words inevitably evoke specific resonances in each reader, which are coloured by his personal experiences and shaped by his particular world-view. Each reader will thus perceive a text made up of words in his own strictly personal way. This insight of modern hermeneutics has of course developed independently of liberation theology. What liberation theology has done is to draw attention to the class character of the reader's perception of the biblical text.

In the light of liberation theology, then, a topic like 'Class in the Bible' poses two distinct questions. It raises (1) the sociological question: to what extent is the biblical narrative intelligible in terms of class and class struggle? And it raises (2) the hermeneutical question: how far does one's class culture determine one's reading of the biblical text? Both questions are significant and have been raised by the *Instruction on Certain Aspects of the 'Theology of Liberation'*, published by the Sacred Congregation for the Doctrine of the Faith in 1984. A proper appreciation of the role of class and class struggle in the Bible would require that we thoroughly discuss both; but since limitations of time and space will not allow this, I shall take up the first, the sociological question only, leaving the second, the hermeneutical one, for another occasion.

The aim of this article, then, is to determine how far the history of Israel and of Jesus, as this is told in the Old and the New Testaments, is amenable to a class analysis. How far, that is, did the biblical authors understand their history in terms of what we might today call class and class struggle.

Class and class struggle are of course ambiguous terms, variously defined in different sociological schools. But it is the Marxist understanding that is the most pertinent to us, since it is this that has influenced biblical exegesis most extensively. When the categories of class or of class struggle have been used for interpreting the Bible, this has always been done as part of a Marxist analysis. For it is only in a Marxist analysis that these categories play a significant role. Other forms of the sociological study of the Bible do not focus, or do not focus so sharply, on class. To the extent, then, that class is significant for biblical interpretation, it is class understood in the Marxist sense of the term. Understandably, then, it is precisely the alleged use or misuse of class and class struggle understood in this way that has been singled out by the *Instruction* on liberation theology for censure.

We use 'class', then, in the popularly accepted Marxist understanding of the word, taking it to be a system of social stratification based on the ownership of the means of production. Such stratification divides society into antagonistic groups of those who own the means of production (today the bourgeoisie) and those who do not (today the proletariat); and leads inevitably to a class struggle between them. The ultimate outcome of this struggle will be the expropriation of expropriators and the emergence of a classless society where the means of production will be owned by all. This is obviously a highly simplified exposition of the Marxist understanding of class – simplified some might say to the point of parody. But it does, I hope, bring out the essential factors we need to keep in mind when we speak of 'class' in the Bible.

Obviously no detailed study of the relevance of class to the biblical narrative can be attempted within the limits of this article. I shall therefore limit myself to exploring a single focal issue, the biblical understanding of the poor. There is much in the Bible to suggest that the poor there are given the same confrontational and creative historical role that Karl Marx assigns to the working class in capitalist society. Are the poor in the Bible, then, a class in the Marxist sense? Can their action in the history of Israel be described as a class struggle? To what extent can a class analysis be applied to them?

To answer such questions, we shall (A) take a quick look at what the Bible has to say about the poor, and then (B) reflect on this in the light of the Marxist understanding of class.

## A THE POOR IN THE BIBLE

The poor are a conspicuous and frequently mentioned group in the Bible, which uses a battery of more or less synonymous words to describe them.[2]

(a) The most familiar of these, a word which has deservedly become part of standard Christian language, is '*ānî* or '*ānāw* (plural: '*anîyyîm* or '*anāwîm*) which occurs 92 times in the Hebrew Bible and probably underlies most of the 34 occurrences of the Greek *ptōchos* (= 'poor, destitute') in the New. The word probably derives from the root '*nh* (II) = 'to be bent, bowed down, afflicted'. It suggests a person who is afflicted and bent, that is, dehumanized, reduced by oppression to a condition of diminished capacity or worth. By extension the word '*ānî*, particularly in its late and secondary form '*ānāw*, has been given a religious meaning and has come to stand for those whom poverty and powerlessness have taught 'to bend before God' and place their trust in him alone. In this sense '*ānāw* comes close to the 'poor in spirit' (*ptōchoi tō pneumati*) of Matthew's beatitude (Matt. 5.3), an expression which designates those who are wholly dependent on God. But this religious connotation given to '*ānî/*'*ānāw* is derived, secondary, and closely dependent on the primary sociological meaning of the word. The poor in spirit are those also who are sociologically poor; for it is precisely the powerless who learn to place their trust in God. The religious connotation of the word thus implies the sociological. The '*ānî/*'*ānāw* is thus primarily one who is sociologically poor, that is, one who has been brought to a situation of diminished capacity or worth.

(b) Closely associated with '*ānî/*'*ānāw*, specially in exilic and post-exilic psalms is '*ebyôn* from the root '*bh* (II) = 'to be willing, to consent'. Occurring 61 times in the Hebrew Bible, the word is best understood as indicating a person in need. It is sometimes spiritualized so that it can serve as a parallel to *ṣadiq* (= 'a righteous person') as in Amos 2.6 and 5.12; or to *yishrê derek* (= 'those of upright conduct') as in Psalm 37.14; but it normally indicates plain material need.

(c) So do *dal* from the root *dll* = 'to languish, to be weak, to be little', found 48 times in the Hebrew Bible, frequently as a parallel to '*ānî* (Amos 2.7; Isa. 10.2; 11.4; Prov. 22.22; Ps. 82.3; Job 34.28 – where the RSV regularly translates *dal* as 'poor' and '*ānî* as 'afflicted'); or to '*ebyôn* (Amos 4.1; 8.6; Isa 14.30; 25.4; Prov. 14.31; Ps. 113.7; 1 Sam. 2.8 – with *dal* almost always appearing as 'poor' and '*ebyôn* always as 'needy'). In its usage in the Bible *dal* keeps its root meaning of being 'low, weak, feeble', and so describes people of low social status as opposed to those who are great or noble (*gādôl* – cf. Jer. 5.4 f); people of straitened economic means as opposed to those who are wealthy ('*āshîr* – cf. Exod. 30.15), and people who are physically or socially weak as opposed to those who are powerful and strong (*ḥāzēq* – cf. 2 Sam. 3.1).

(d) A fourth synonym, *rāsh*, on the other hand, which derives from the root *rush* = 'to be in want, to be poor', and is found 21 times in the Hebrew Bible, mostly in Wisdom texts from Proverbs and Qoheleth, stands unambiguously for strictly economic poverty. The word is the proper antonym of '*āshîr* ('rich') and is frequently used in antithetical parallelism with it (2 Sam. 12.1; Prov. 14.20; 18.23; 22.2; 28.6).

(e) Finally, *miskēn*, found only 6 times in the Hebrew Bible and that too in its latest books (Qoheleth and Sirach), is a word whose etymology is very dubious. It is probably a loan word into Hebrew related possibly to the Assyrian *mushkenu* (= 'beggars'). As used in the Old Testament, however, *miskēn* denotes not so much the destitution of the beggar as the indigence of a poor man who, because he does not own property, must struggle for a living by dint of hard and painful labour.

Two points emerge from this rapid survey of the Old Testament words for the poor.

(1) Of the many partially overlapping synonyms which the Hebrew Bible uses to describe the poor, the word '*ānî/ānāw* is certainly the most significant. Not only is it the most used of these words; it is also the richest in meaning. It expresses most accurately and completely the multifaceted character of the biblical understanding of the poor. Its synonyms (*'ebyôn, dal, rāsh* and *mîskēn*) tend to take up one or other of these aspects: economic deprivation, social backwardness or physical inadequacy. That is why they are frequently used in conjunction with '*ānî* (cf. the '*ānî we' ebyôn* (poor and needy) of Deut. 24.14; Ps. 37.14; Ezek. 16.49; or the '*am 'ānî medal* (a people poor and weak) of Zeph. 3.12; or the '*ānî wārāsh* (the oppressed and the destitute) of Ps. 82.3), or in parallelism with it (*'ebyôn* in Isa. 29.19; Amos 8.4; Ps. 35.10; and *dal* in Amos 2.7; Isa. 10.2; Ps. 82.3), in order to bring out one or other aspect of this multifaceted word. It is by determining the meaning given to '*ānî/'ānāw* in the Bible that we shall arrive at the proper biblical understanding of the poor.

(2) The variety of the terms used to describe the poor in the Bible and the frequency of their occurrence is striking, and gives a unique flavour to the religiosity of the Bible. No other religious tradition I know of gives such importance to the poor or assigns to them so significant a role. For the Bible does not (as other religious texts tend to do) merely present the poor as deserving of human concern (Exod. 23.11; Lev. 19.9–10; 25.25–8; Deut. 15.7–11; 24.14–18). Nor does it (as do other expressions of popular wisdom) merely point to the plight

of the poor as warning against wastefulness and sloth (Prov. 6.6–11; 21.17; 23.21; Sir. 18.32). Such ethical and proverbial sayings are in fact marginal to the Bible's main concern, which is to reveal the theological significance of the poor, the part they have to play in saving history. Victims of human history, the poor, as the Bible defines them, are also those through whom that history is redeemed.

This specifically biblical understanding of the role of the poor can, I suggest, be spelled out in the following three propositions: (1) the poor in the Bible form *a sociological group* whose identity is defined not by their religious attitude but by their social situation (2) the poor in the Bible are *a dialectical* group whose situation is determined by antagonistic groups standing over and against them and (3) the poor in the Bible are *a dynamic group* who are not the passive victims of history but those through whom God shapes his history. Such a description of the biblical poor obviously invites comparison with the Marxists' working class – also a sociological group which is both the victim of history and its maker. We shall, then, after we have examined each of these three propositions given above, and tested its appropriateness as a description of the biblical understanding of the poor, proceed to ask how far this understanding is consonant with the Marxist understanding of class.

## 1 The poor in the Bible as a sociological group

### (a) In the Old Testament

In the Old Testament the poor (*'anîyyîm*) are primarily the sociologically poor. They are the economically destitute and the socially outcast, typified by the characteristic biblical figures of exploited powerlessness: the widow, the orphan, and the refugee (Exod. 22.21f; Deut. 10.18; Ps. 68.5; 146.9; Jer. 7.6; 22.3; Zech. 7.10; Mal. 3.5). If the *ānî* in the Bible has at times the religious connotation of one who puts his trust in God alone, this is a secondary and derived meaning, built upon the primary sociological meaning of the word. It is the sociologically poor who learn from their powerlessness to place their whole trust in God. The poor in spirit are thus also the materially poor. Sociologically, deprivation of some sort is thus the basic feature of the biblical poor.

Concretely, the poor would comprise the following more or less well-defined groups:

(a) The poor of the Old Testament would include impoverished and indebted small peasants who live in grave economic distress, without being wholly destitute or marginalized. They still own some property (Prov. 13.23) and so are both liable to taxation (Exod. 30.15; Lev. 14.21), and vulnerable to economic exploitation (Amos 5.11; Isa. 3.14; Prov. 22.22). And they still enjoy tribal or citizens' rights so that they can claim – but are frequently denied – 'justice at the gate' (Exod. 23.6–8; Amos 5.12; Isa. 10.2; 11.4; Jer. 5.28; Prov. 29.7).

(b) The poor in the Old Testament would include too the rural and the urban destitute – unemployed landless labourers, bonded labour (enslaved because of their inability to pay their debts), a city proletariat of unemployed artisan and beggars – all those who possess nothing and eke out a precarious existence through begging, or through the relief provided by a socially conscious community. These are the 'poor' (*anāwîm*) envisaged in the social legislation of Israel's great codes which prohibit the exhaustive harvesting of fields or vineyards so as to allow the poor to gather up the gleanings (Lev. 19.9f; Deut. 24.19–22), or the charging of interest on loans (Exod. 22.25; Lev. 25.36–8; Deut. 23.19f), or the ruthless exaction of pledges (Exod. 22.26f; Deut. 24.10–13; Ezek. 18.12); and which prescribe radical measures of social relief through institutions like the 'year of rest' (Exod. 23.10f; Lev. 25.1–7; Deut. 15.1–18) or the 'jubilee year' (Lev. 25.8–17). Such too are the 'poor and the needy' commended to our concern in prophetic oracles and wisdom sayings which warn us against exploiting or oppressing them (Amos 2.6; 8.6; Isa. 3.14; Ezek. 22.29; Zech. 7.10; Prov. 22.22); or which urge us to look after their need (Isa. 58.6–9; Ezek. 16.49).

(c) To a lesser extent the poor in the Old Testament are those afflicted or oppressed in any way and not just the economically needy. The poor can thus be identified with exiled Israel as a whole, so that *anāwîm* becomes synonymous with '*ammî* ('my people' as in Isa. 41.17–20; 49.13; 51.21f; 54.11–14; Ps. 72.2); or with a specially oppressed group within it the '*anwe 'ammê* ('the poor of my people') of Exod. 22.25; Isa. 10.2; Ps. 72.4.

(d) To an even smaller extent, in a limited number of texts mainly from post-exilic times, the 'poor' in the Old Testament can mean the spiritually poor, the 'poor of Yahweh', who place their trust in God alone (Isa. 66.2; Zeph. 3.12). This is specially true of some exilic and post-exilic psalms, in which the original sociological meaning of '*anāwim* has been so overlaid by the spiritual that it is often impossible now to distinguish between the two (Ps. 22.24; 34.6; 86.1; 140.12–13).

## (b) In the New Testament

This wide spectrum use of the word for 'poor' in the Old Testament, where *'ānî,' ebyôn, dal, rûsh* and *miskēn* can stand for the materially needy, the socially oppressed or the spiritually lowly, is not taken up in the New Testament, which understands the poor in a more restricted and literal way. The standard, indeed almost the exclusive, designation for the poor in the New Testament is *ptōchos* from the root *ptōssō* = 'to crouch or to cringe'. The Greek word thus describes a person who is destitute, that is, one who lacks the necessities of life, and must eke out his existence by begging. The word *ptōchos* is thus a much stronger term than its three equivalents which occur just once each in the New Testament. For both *penēs* (2 Cor. 9.9) and the related *penichros* (Luke 21.2) describe an indigent rather than a destitute person, one who lacks property and so must work painfully for his living; while *endeēs* (Acts 4.34) from the root *endeō* – 'to be in want of something', stands simply for someone in need. These etymological differences, however, do not affect the usage of these words, which are in fact used synonymously in the New Testament.

The use of *ptōchos* in the New Testament is significant:

(a) Thrice the word is used for the spiritually poor, but with its spiritual sense clearly indicated by a qualifying expression (as in the 'poor in spirit' of Matthew 5.3); a governing word (as in the 'beggarly elemental spirits' (*ptōcha stoîcheia*) of Gal. 4.9); or by the context (as in Rev. 3.17 where 'poor' stands for the spiritual emptiness of the Laodicean church, which is what the text is talking about).

(b) Of the remaining 25 occurrences of the word (parallel occurrences in Synoptic passages counting as one), fully 22 indicate merely the economically distressed or the destitute (Mark 12.42ff; Luke 16.20,22; Jas. 2.2–6) who are to be the recipients of almsgiving and aid (Mark 10.21; Luke 14.5; Luke 14.13,21; 19.8; John 13.29; Rom. 15.26; 2 Cor. 6.10; Gal. 2.10). This is true also of the three synonyms for *ptōchos* that we find in the New Testament – of the *penēs* of 2 Cor. 9.9 (in a quotation from Ps. 112 which refers to the poor Christians of Jerusalem, for whom Paul is collecting money) of the *penichros* of Luke 21.2 (which describes the widow of the widow's mite); and of the *endeēs* of Acts 4.34 (the needy, who are singularly absent in the first Christian community of Jerusalem).

(c) In only three New Testament texts (Matt. 5.11 = Luke 7.22; Luke 4.18 and Luke 6.20) is the meaning of *ptōchos* in dispute. These are texts in which Jesus announces 'the privilege of the poor'. The 'poor' have the 'good news' preached to them (Matt. 11.5; Luke 4.18), for the Kingdom of God is theirs (Luke 6.20). How then are we to understand these *ptōchoi*, the privileged beneficiaries of Jesus' preaching, to whom the Kingdom of God is exclusively promised? Are they the spiritually poor whose religious attitude of openness and trust disposes them to receive God's love? Or are they the sociologically poor whose situation of social deprivation invites God's saving action on their behalf?

Western exegesis, part of the immense ideological production of an affluent and intensely acquisitive society built on principles diametrically opposed to those of Jesus, has tended to the first option, and has tried systematically to spiritualize the gospel understanding of the poor. In his monumental three-volume study on the Beatitudes, Jacques Dupont gives quotations from four different authors which illustrate this strikingly. One is from a Roman Catholic Old Testament exegete, Albert Gelin; another from T. W. Manson an Anglican specialist in the New; a third from a conservative Lutheran theologian, Leonhardt Goppelt, and the fourth from the radical Protestant scholar, Rudolf Bultmann. All four are reluctant to identify the poor of the beatitude to whom Jesus announces the good news of the Kingdom as a social class. Rather, the poor, the hungry, and the weeping of the first three Lucan beatitudes (Luke 6.20ff) – almost certainly more original than the better-known eight beatitudes of Matthew (Matt. 5.3–10), and a good approximation of what Jesus actually said – are blessed (they believe) not because of their social situation but because of their religious attitude. They are 'poor' not because they are in need, but because they have made themselves humbly dependent on God; they hunger not for bread but for salvation; they weep not on account of the deprivations and indignities they suffer but because they long for the Kingdom.

This tendency to spiritualize the poor of the Beatitudes which cuts across all denominational differences and brings together exegetes who would otherwise agree on scarcely anything else, is a good indication of the extent to which exegetical trends are in fact determined by the spirit of the times. It may be a pointer too to the hermeneutical significance of class we have spoken of above. But in its spiritualized understanding of the poor in the gospel it is unacceptable, and is being increasingly rejected by exegetes today. Because of its growing sensitivity to social issues in a world that has been rudely awakened to social awareness (largely, I believe, because of the resounding prophetic protest of Karl Marx) Western exegesis, to its credit, has begun to rediscover the sociological content of the gospel understanding of the poor, and so to recover the specific challenge of biblical religiosity, its strongly social thrust. There may indeed still be scholars who would like to understand the poor of the New Testament, specially those to whom Jesus promises the Kingdom, as the spiritually poor. But there is a growing consensus today that in the New Testament, even more than in the Old, the word 'poor' is a sociological category even in the three good-news-to-the-poor texts mentioned above.

For the context of these texts and the way in which they have been formulated make it clear that here too *ptōchos* has been given a sociological and not a religious meaning – but a sociological meaning that is wider than the one it has elsewhere in the New Testament, where to be poor means merely to be in economic need. The *ptōchoi* to whom Jesus announces the good news of the Kingdom are a larger group. They include not only the destitute (a fast growing population in the Palestine of Jesus' time, where heavy civil and religious taxation led to large-scale rural indebtedness, the selling off of small landholdings, and the creation of a vast rural and urban proletariat, subsisting precariously on daily wage labour, begging, or banditry), but also the illiterate, the socially outcast, the physically handicapped, and the mentally ill (in gospel language: the 'poor', the 'little ones', the 'tax collectors and sinners', the 'sick' and the 'possessed') who form so large a part of the crowds that continually swarm about Jesus in the early days of his Galilean ministry (Mark 1.33,45; 5.24; 6.34; 8.1–2). All these are the 'poor' because all are seen as victims of an oppression – whether human (as with the destitute and the outcast) or demonic (as with the crippled, the sick and the possessed) – which reduces them to a condition of diminished capacity or worth. It is this diminution (whether social, physical or economic), this being 'bent' (*'ānāh*), this state of oppression, which is the specific feature defining the gospel (indeed the biblical) poor.

## (c) Conclusion

All through the Bible, then, the poor are a sociological rather than a religious group. Their identity is defined not by any spiritual attitude of openness or dependence on God, but simply by their sociological situation of powerlessness and need. This need is not necessarily economic need. For biblical poverty is a sociological category that is wider than the merely economic. Economic deprivation is of course a capital feature of the biblical understanding of the poor, since any category other than the destitute who are included in the great mass of the biblical poor (the exploited, the oppressed, the outcast, the crippled, the sick) will also, normally, be in great economic need. But such economic need does not enter into the definition, as it were, of the biblical poor. The poor of the Bible are all those who are in any way, and not just economically, deprived of the means or the dignity they need to lead a fully human existence; or who are in a situation of powerlessness which exposes them to such deprivation. The poor of the Bible are thus the 'wretched of the earth', the marginalized, the exploited, all those who are actually or potentially oppressed. In his brief but lucid survey of the vocabulary of poverty in the Old Testament, Augustine George has expressed this well:

> This vocabulary expresses an understanding of poverty quite different from our own. For our modern language, as already in Greek and Latin, poverty is the lack of goods; it is an economic idea. While Hebrew sometimes considers poverty a lack (*rāsh*) or a situation of begging (*'ebyôn*), it views it primarily as a situation of dependence (*'ānî, ānāw, miskēn*) or weakness (*dal*). In the biblical mind, the poor person is less one who is indigent and more one who is oppressed, an inferior or a lesser one. It is a social idea. This is why later, when the poor begin to spiritualize their condition, their ideal will not become detachment from the goods of this world but rather a voluntary and loving submission to the will of God.[3]

## 2 The poor in the Bible as a dialectical group

Poverty in the Bible is sometimes attributed to internal factors, that is, to the behaviour or attitude of the poor themselves. Laziness is identified as the cause of poverty in Proverbs 6.6–11 and 10.4; luxurious living in Proverbs 21.17 and Sir. 18.32; gluttony and drunkenness in Proverbs 23.21. But this way of thinking is found only in a few Wisdom texts which retail the popular wisdom of the Hellenistic world in the form of proverbial sayings. It is quite atypical of the Bible, which elsewhere consistently locates the basic cause of poverty in external factors: the exploitation of the poor by elite groups that dominate and oppress them. The poor in the Bible are thus a dialectical group, in the sense that it is a group whose situation is determined by and depends dialectically (through mutual causation) upon that of other groups which stand in opposition to it.

## (a) In the Old Testament

In the Old Testament, the poor (*ānî*) are opposed not so much to the 'rich' (*āshîr*) as to the wicked (*rāshā'* – cf. Ps. 10.2; 37.14; 82.3 f; 147.6; Job 36.6; Isa. 11.4 ff); to the 'haughty' (*rām* – cf. 2 Sam. 22.28; Ps. 18.28; Isa. 26.5 f); to the 'powerful' (*hazēq* – cf. Ps. 35.10). These exploit the poor and the needy (Amos 8.4–6; Isa. 3.14 ff; Ezek. 22.29; Ps. 12.5; 35.10); deceive them with lying words (Isa. 32.7); pervert justice to deprive them of their rights (Isa. 10.2); 'devour' them (Prov. 30.14; Hab. 3.14); swallow up their fields (Isa. 5.8–10; Prov. 13.23); oppress and crush them (Amos 4.1); sell them into slavery (Amos 8.4–6); 'pursue' them (Ps. 10.2; 109.16); and even slay them (Ps. 37.14). The overall picture, found with nuances throughout the Old Testament, is that of a powerless and harassed group, reduced to a state of indigence by the unjust and violent exploitation of the strong.

The number of the poor, their situation of destitution, the extent of the exploitation that they suffer, doubtless varied considerably in the course of Israel's history, becoming progressively worse as we pass from the relatively egalitarian tribal society of the pre-monarchical period, to the monarchy when the exploitation of the people by a nobility owning the land and controlling the apparatus of justice was greatly intensified, provoking a sharp reaction from the pre-exilic prophets. New levels of exploitation were reached in the exilic and post-exilic periods when poverty in Israel becomes so widespread that the whole people can be called Yahweh's poor (Isa. 49.13; 51.21 ff). But whatever its form, poverty in the Bible is experienced not as a natural phenomenon, the inevitable outcome of one's *karma*, or the acceptable result of the free play of market forces. It is always identified as the avoidable and undesirable consequences of injustice and exploitation. Its existence in Israel is sensed as an intolerable scandal, for God had given his people a 'good land' (Deut. 1.25,35; 3.25; 6.18 . . .), richly endowed with material wealth (Deut. 8.7–10), in order that there might be no poor (*'ebyôn*) among them (Deut. 15.4). That the poor continue to exist becomes a scandal to the conscience of Israel and a warning that it has failed to live up to its calling.

This warning is reinforced by Yahweh's attitude to the poor, in which we can distinguish several stages of commitment.

(a)  Yahweh is concerned about the poor. He is their refuge and protector (Isa. 3.13–15; 24.4 ff; Zeph. 3.12; Ps. 14.6); he responds to their needs (Isa. 41.17–20); he consoles and comforts them (Isa. 49.13).

(b)  Yahweh vindicates his poor. He pleads their cause (Isa. 51.22); he defends the 'widow, the orphan, and the refugee' (Exod. 22.21–4; Deut. 10.17–19; Ps. 69.5); and saves 'the oppressed of all the earth' (Ps. 76.9; 146.7–9); he despoils those who despoil the poor (Prov. 22.23).

(c)  Yahweh demands a like concern from his people (Exod. 22.21–4; Lev. 19.10; Deut. 15.1–11; 24.14 f, 17 f; Isa. 58.1–12; Jer. 7.5–7; Ezek. 16.49; Zech. 7.10), and from their king (Isa. 11.4; Jer. 22.16; Ps. 22.1–4); and, through a long succession of prophets, he denounces every form of oppression with unparalleled vigour (Amos 2.6–8; 4.1–3; 6.4–8; Mic. 2.1–3; Isa. 3.13–15; 10.1–4; Jer. 22.13 f; Ezek. 34.1–24).

(d)  Indeed so radical is Yahweh's concern for the poor, 'his people' (Isa. 3.15), that not only does he plead their cause but as it were identifies himself with them. 'He who oppresses the poor', Proverbs tells us, 'insults his maker' (Prov. 14.31); while to be 'kind to the poor' is to 'lend to the Lord' (Prov. 19.17).

(e)  This close identification of Yahweh with the poor leads to a *lex talionis* whereby those who oppress the poor are ultimately impoverished (Prov. 22.16); those who are deaf to the cries of the poor find their own cries unheeded (Prov. 21.13); and those who are kind to the poor prosper and are happy (Prov. 14.21; 28.8,27).

Such a *karmic* law is obviously only a parenetic formulation of Yahweh's concern for the poor, urging us to a similar concern. And Yahweh's concern is ultimately grounded in the biblical understanding of the poor as the victim of injustice and oppression. It is because the poor are a dialectical group whose situation is not of their own making, nor the result of chance or natural causes, but the avoidable effect of unjust oppression, that they have a claim on Yahweh's concern.

## (b)  In the New Testament

In the New Testament this dialectical character of the poor is less evident. The poor (*ptōchos*) are here opposed not to the 'wicked', but, more naturally, to the 'rich' (*plousios*) – cf. Mark 12.41 f; Luke 6.20–6; 14.12–14; 16.19–31; Jas. 2.1–6; 2 Cor. 6.10; 8.9; Rev. 13.16). Rich and poor do not confront each other as conflicting groups in a dialectical relationship of mutual dependence, with the rich creating, as it were, the poor through their exploitation and oppression. Indeed except in James 2.5 f and 5.1–6 and in occasional sayings of Jesus like the one reported in Mark 12.44, the New Testament does not speak of oppression and exploitation by the rich. It speaks rather of their excessive preoccupation with material wealth which leaves them indifferent to God (Luke 12.13–21) and to neighbour (Luke 16.19–31). Greed rather than exploitation is the sin of the rich in the New Testament. The opposition of rich and poor in the New Testament thus appears to be not so much the opposition of conflicting classes as the opposition of contrasting situations. The poor are (1) in a situation of need and so commended to our care more than the rich who enjoy a surfeit of goods (Luke 14.12–14); and the poor (2) are in a situation of salvation because they rather than the rich are to be the beneficiaries of God's saving action (the Kingdom of God), in the eschatological reversal which is imminent (Luke 6.20–6; 16.19–31).

Yet behind this understanding of rich/poor, the Old Testament dialectic of conflicting classes is implicit. The eschatological reversal announced in the New Testament, when the hungry will be filled (by God) with good things, and the rich sent away empty (Luke 1.52 f; 6.20–6) makes no sense unless the Old Testament understanding of poverty as a state of unjust oppression continues into the New. In the New Testament too, as in the Old, the rich/wicked are seen as the exploiters of the poor, who are the exploited and the oppressed. Only then can we understand how God takes side with the poor ('blessed are you poor') and against the rich ('Woe to you rich'). For God must redress injustice and he can only do this by bringing down the oppressor (the rich) and lifting up the oppressed (the poor). It is clear too why the New Testament proclamation of the Kingdom (God's definitive saving intervention in history) must always be 'good news' to the poor, and bad news to the rich.

*(c) Conclusion*

In spite of differences in emphasis then, the biblical understanding of the poor as a sociological and a dialectical group is basically the same throughout the Bible. If the sociological character of the poor is more evident in the New Testament than it is in the Old, their dialectical character is less evident. Rarely in the New Testament (Jas. 5.1–6;

Mark 12.44) do we find anything like the powerful prophetic denunciation of the exploitation of the poor by the wicked that is so significant a part of the Old. For where the 'wicked' of the Old Testament are defined in terms of their exploitation of the poor, the 'rich' of the New Testament are recognized primarily by their greed, their single-minded devotion to mammon (Matt. 6.24; Luke 16.10–14) which leaves them impervious to love for God or concern for their neighbour. So too when the Old Testament sees the spiritual dimension of poverty as an undivided trust in God (poor in spirit), the New Testament sees it primarily in detachment (spiritual poverty), that is, in freedom from the tyranny of material things (Luke 12.15).

Such a sociological and a dialectical understanding of the poor in the Bible precludes any romanticization of poverty. Real poverty, as distinct from metaphorical or 'spiritual poverty', is never valued in the Bible for itself. As a state of economic or social deprivation brought about by exploitation, it is an evil. Biblical teaching aims not at perpetuating such poverty but at eliminating it. So Yahweh promises to vindicate the poor so that they will be poor no more. And Jesus, who blesses not poverty but the poor, announces the dawning of the eschatological age which will bring all poverty to an end.

### 3 The poor in the Bible as a dynamic group

The deprived and the exploited group of the poor are not depicted in the Bible as a pitiable group of unfortunates of no historical significance whatever, who merely wait passively for the deliverance promised them in the prophetic and apocalyptic texts of the Old Testament, and announced as imminent by Jesus in his proclamation of the Kingdom of God. They are given a significant role in biblical history. History is of course the key category of biblical religion. For the Bible (both in its Old and New Testaments) is not primarily a book of doctrine retailing metaphysical truths about God, humankind and the universe; nor is it a book of worship, explaining complex rituals or spelling out elaborate techniques of prayer; nor even a code setting down cultic or ethical norms. Doctrinal, cultic, and legal texts do in fact abound in the Bible, but they are all integrated into the history of Israel and of Jesus. It is this history which is primary, because it is seen as the locus of God's encounter with humankind.

Obviously the history that the Bible narrates is not critical history but confessional or kerygmatic history – history interpreted as an expression of an encounter with God and narrated in such a way as to bring out the contemporary significance of this encounter as tellingly as possible. Such history 'is founded in the actual history', but so interpreted 'that the historic and factual can no longer be detached from the spiritualising interpretation which pervades them all'.[4] It is this confessional history of Israel and of Jesus that is the soul of biblical religion; and in it the poor are given a significant and dynamic role. This emerges with particular clarity in the two foundational moments of this history: the Exodus event in the Old Testament, and the coming of Jesus in the New.

## (a) In the Old Testament

The Exodus is obviously the central moment in the confessional history of Israel. The earliest and most widely used of the confessional formulae, in which Israel affirms her faith in her God, is the one in which she acknowledges Yahweh as the one 'who brings Israel out of Egypt'. Possibly the oldest Old Testament tradition we possess, the Song of Miriam (Exod. 15.20 ff), sings precisely of this liberation. And the most ancient of the cultic creeds of Israel (Deut. 26.5–9; 6.20–3; Josh. 24.2–13), while they cover a wider range of saving history (from the Patriarchs to the settlement) also focus on the Exodus as the central saving event. It would seem then that the Old Testament has grown up by the accretion of tradition round this central core. These extend the central historical core towards the past through the integration of the traditions about patriarchial and primeval history; and towards the future, through the addition of the traditions contained in the historical, prophetic, and wisdom books, which take the history of Israel from the settlement in Canaan, through the pre-monarchical and monarchical periods to its 'resettlement' after the exile. This is obviously similar to the way in which the New Testament has grown up by the accumulation of traditions about Jesus round the central proclamation of his death and resurrection.

But the Exodus is not merely the historical core of the biblical narrative: it is also its theological centre. It is in the Exodus that Israel receives her specific God-experience and is given her specific self-understanding of her role as God's people. This is brought home to us in a late but significant Old Testament text, the Priestly version of the call of Moses (Exod. 6.2–7), which gives us Israel's mature reflection on the significance of her history:

Say this to the people of Israel:
'I am Yahweh
    and I will free you from the burden
        of the Egyptians;
    and I will deliver you from their bondage,
    and I will redeem you with an outstretched arm
        and with great acts of judgment,
    and I will take you for my people,
    and I will be your God;
And you shall know that
I am Yahweh
    who has freed you from the burden
        of the Egyptians' (Exod. 6.6–7).

The text speaks of the revelation of a new name for God given to Moses, a name not revealed to the Patriarchs. Since a name in the world of the Bible is never an empty label but always the disclosure of the nature or the function of a person or thing, the revelation of a new name constitutes a new self-disclosure by God. Israel is thus constituted by a new understanding of God – not of his abstract essence (such metaphysical speculations about God himself are totally foreign to the Bible where 'no one can see God and live') – but of his relation to his people. Israel, that is, has a new and specific experience of God. She experiences God as 'Yahweh', that is, as the one who liberates her 'from under the burden of the Egyptians'. But the liberation that Yahweh brings is not just a liberation from servitude; it is also a liberation for service. If Yahweh liberates Israel from bondage in Egypt, redeems and delivers her, it is in order to make her 'his people'.

What this means is spelled out in the covenant at Sinai (Exod. 19.1–20.21) – originally an independent tradition which the compilers of the confessional history of Israel have added to the Exodus traditions, in order to explicate their meaning. The Sinai covenant spells out the new social order which Israel is to adopt in order to become Yahweh's people, that is, to form the free, just, non-exploitative community that will serve as a 'contrast community' to the oppressive, violent and power-hungry city states among which Israel lives (Exod. 19.4–6; Deut. 4.6–8).[5] The strongly social legislation of Israel's codes (the Covenant Code of Exodus 20.22–23.33; the Priestly Code of Leviticus 2–15; the Holiness Code of Leviticus 17–26; the Deuteronomist Code of Deutoronomy 12–26) is a witness of Israel's attempts to live up to this her vocation, while the passionate denunciation of the pre-exilic prophets against the scandal of poverty and oppression in Israel (Amos 2.6–8; 4.1–3; 5.7–12; 8.4–6; Mic. 2.1–3; 3.1–4; 6.9–16; Isa. 1.16ff; 3.13–15; 5.1–7; 10.1–4) witnesses poignantly to her failure to do so. For, after an initial attempt to live as a community of free, equal peasants governed by local elected leaders ('judges'), Israel succumbs to the temptations of a monarchy (1 Sam. 8.1–22), and adopts the venal oppressive structure of her neighbours.

But the dream of one day realizing this 'contrast community' remains an inalienable part of Israel's hope. This hope assumes various forms in Israel's history. Pre-exilic Israel hopes for the messianic kingdom, a world-wide community of justice and peace established by a descendant of David 'anointed' by God for the purpose (Isa. 11.2–9). Post-exilic Israel, influenced by apocalyptic, looks rather for the 'new heavens and the new earth', a new world order to be created by God to replace this corrupt satanic age which is doomed to destruction (Isa. 65.12–25). But always, Israel's remains the hope of the poor.

Biblical history thus begins with the liberation of the poor. A group of utterly powerless bonded labourers rescued by Yahweh are summoned to be the nucleus of his contrast community. This is the starting point of the whole confessional history of Israel! And when the detour of God's people into errant ways that lead them to models of society imitating the oppressive systems of their powerful neighbours (the 'Constantinian Era' of Israel) is brought to an end by the Exile, it is once more a poor remnant that becomes the bearer of Israel's hope (Zeph. 3.12 f).

## (b) In the New Testament

In the New Testament too it is the poor who continue to be the bearers of salvation and of hope. For just as Israel's history begins as a movement of the poor, so does the history of Jesus. Born into a poor though not destitute artisan family (Mark 6.3), Jesus is shown 'de-classing' himself, giving up the security of family and of home (Mark 3.31–5) to become an itinerant preacher with nowhere to lay his head (Matt. 8.20). His first followers too come from the same artisan class to which he belongs, or are drawn from the social outcasts (tax-collectors and sinners) among whom he moves (Mark 2.13–17; Luke 15.1–2). Four are fishermen (Mark 1.16–20), one an 'untouchable' toll collector collaborating with the hated Roman regime (Mark 2.13); a third is a zealot, a member of an outlawed group waging a guerilla war against Rome (Luke 6.15). We know nothing about the other close followers of Jesus, but none seems to have come from the upper or even the middle strata of society.

Jesus has indeed some rich sympathizers but they are fewer and more marginal to his movements than is generally realized. Not all the 'tax collectors' who associate with him, nor the Pharisees who invite him to dine, are necessarily rich. The chief customs tax collector of a district or a town (like Zaccheus in Luke 19.1) would no doubt be wealthy. But Zaccheus is an exception in the gospels. The tax collectors mentioned there are not such important officials but their agents, the employees (often slaves) charged with the actual collection of tolls. These were poor, despised men, who were paid a pittance and resorted to so dishonourable a profession only because they were driven to it by desperate need. The Pharisees too were a group that drew its membership mainly from the artisan and lower middle classes of Jewish society. They were influential because of the piety and the integrity of their lives; not because of the wealth they possessed or the power they wielded. Very few truly rich people meet us in the pages of the gospel; and these are either opposed to Jesus (like the Sadducees, or the Elders), or they fit rather uneasily into his company. A rich landowner who has much property is unable to accept Jesus' invitation to sell what he has and follow him (Mark 10.17–22); Nicodemus, a member of the council, visits Jesus by night because he is afraid of damaging his reputation among the upper class Jews (John 3.1); Joseph of Arimathaea, described expressly as a 'seeker' rather than a disciple of Jesus, is heard of only as one who helps out in his burial (Mark 15.43). By and large the Jesus movement begins as a movement of the poor. And whatever be the sociological complexion of the early Church (probably more varied than was once supposed), it continued to be and to think of itself as a Church of the poor (1 Cor. 1.26–8).

## (c) Conclusion

All through the Bible, then, the poor are taken to be an oppressed group of the economically and the socially deprived, who because they are the victims of oppression will be the beneficiaries of salvation and will mediate this salvation to others. The salvation they mediate is a salvation which is eschatological but not other-worldly. It transcends the world but does not attempt to deny or escape from it. Biblical eschatology is the fulfilment of history, not its negation. 'Here grows the body of the new humanity,' Vatican II announces, 'which even now is able to give a prefiguration of the new age' (*Gaudium et Spes*, n. 39). Pre-figured by the new humanity, salvation in the Bible is a communitarian, not merely an individual, enterprise. Its image is the New Jerusalem, the end-time community (Rev. 21.1–4), prefigured and prepared for by the contrast communities that we keep on struggling to build in time.

The new humanity and the communities through which it takes shape grow through conflict. The conflict results from the ethical dualism of biblical thinking, whose basic opposition of good and evil, expressed in various ways (God/Satan, life/death, reward/punishment, liberation/bondage), finds a concrete sociological expression in the conflict of poor/wicked or poor/rich. The boundaries of these proposed groups are shifting: for the 'poor' can stand for the poor in Israel (Ps. 72.4), for Israel as poor among the nations (Isa. 49.13), or for the 'oppressed of all the earth' (Ps. 76.9). The intensity of the polarization between them also varies, increasing as the biblical narratives proceed until it reaches its high point in the violent conflict of the apocalyptic texts, with one of which (the Revelation of John) the Bible, perhaps significantly, ends.

This conflict is ultimately resolved by an act of God in favour of the poor, which brings their sufferings and struggles to fruition. But God acts with and through the poor. For if the Bible is ethically dualistic it is 'metaphysically' (so to speak) holistic. It avoids the sharp distinctions, so beloved of the Greeks, between soul and body, matter and spirit, word and deed, divine grace and human freedom. God's gift does not dispense from human effort. The Kingdom comes indeed as a gift but it comes also as a responsibility inviting urgent and active response from those to whom it is given. Salvation comes from God, but it is actualized in and through the struggles of the poor.

## B THE POOR A SOCIAL CLASS?

To what extent, then, is this understanding of the poor in the Bible illuminated by the Marxist category of class? Are the biblically poor a social class in the Marxist understanding of the term? Is their history a history of class struggle? The question is a delicate one, for it is always risky to transpose categories from one discipline to another, specially across two thousand years of history.

Rather than to attempt to answer this question, then (which in any case is a task for the sociologist and not the exegete) I shall merely make a few hopefully pertinent comments, which might suggest the direction such an answer could take.

## Two approaches to class in the Bible

The question of class in the Bible can be answered at two levels. At (1) the *historical level*, one might ask whether the groups active in the history of Israel, as it actually took place, were really sociological classes in the Marxist sense of the word – (defined, that is, by their ownership or otherwise of the means of production); and whether the interaction between them took the form of a class struggle for the control of these means of production. At (2) the *theological level*, one might ask whether the Marxist category of class can be usefully applied to the poor as these are understood and presented to us in the biblical writings available to us today. Is the biblical understanding of the poor that we have spelt out above illuminated by the Marxist category of class struggle and of class?

### *1 The historical approach*

An answer to the first, the historical, question would require an investigation into the critical history of Israel; followed by a sociological analysis of this history, using models provided by current sociological theory. In spite of the rather meagre results that such critical historical investigation has yielded, significant attempts have been made to present a sociological account of the origins of Israel and of the early Church. Conspicuous among these are the works of Norman Gottwald and Gerd Theissen.[6]

Gottwald's monumental study on the 'Tribes of Yahweh' explains the Hebrew settlement of Canaan not (a) as a 'conquest', that is, as the overrunning of Canaanite civilization by fierce nomadic tribes from the desert (the traditional explanation, defended in the classical works of Albright, Wright, and Bright); nor (b) as the peaceful sedentarization of semi-nomads who infiltrated into the sparsely inhabited hill country of Palestine and settled down there (so Alt, Noth, and Weippert); but (c) as a revolt of the heavily exploited Canaanite peasants against their military overlords in the Canaanite city-states, sparked off by a 'numerically small but ideologically powerful' band of escaped bonded labourers from Egypt, whose liberative God (Yahweh) and whose blueprint for a new community (the Sinai covenant) provided the catalyst for the revolt (Mendenhall and Gottwald). Gottwald uses a Marxist framework to develop his massive explanation of Israel's origins. But this has been violently rejected by Mendenhall, the original proponent of the peasant-revolt model of Israel's origins, in a surprisingly petulant review of Gottwald's book, which accuses him of distorting facts to suit his ideological prejudice.[7] But Mendenhall's own explanation of the peasant-revolt as a 'cultural' rather than an economic and political occurrence suffers, as his own ill-tempered reaction to Gottwald's book so clearly shows, from its own unacknowledged ideological bias, and leaves too much unexplained to carry conviction. Gottwald's 'Marxist' explanation of the origins of Israel is still to be reckoned with, and may indeed provide Old Testament studies with just the paradigm-shift it needs.

Less impressive in scope, but probably more powerful in its impact, has been Theissen's attempt to explain the Jesus movement as a response to the social uprootedness that plagued Palestinian society at the time. Avoiding both the 'evasion' of the Qumran sectarians and the 'aggression' of the Zealots, Jesus and his followers founded a prophetic movement made up of itinerant preachers owning nothing and of groups of local sympathizers who supported them. The movement attempted to renew Palestinian society from within, through a version of reconciliation and of love. In his detailed and often quite sophisticated analysis of the origins of the Jesus movement, Theissen does not use Marxist categories at all. His sociological approach is basically functional.

Clearly then the Marxist categories of class struggle and of class are not necessary for the understanding of the origins of Israel and of the Church as narrated in the Bible. They may, however, be useful categories as Gottwald's pioneering study has shown. They are certainly, I believe, legitimate categories not to be dismissed out of hand because of their supposed ideological contamination. Theories of social analysis, like all theories in the physical and the human sciences, are heuristic models which are to be evaluated operationally, in terms of their usefulness and not in terms of the truth or falsehood of their supposed presupposition. The question to be asked is whether or not the model works (that is, whether or not it accounts satisfactorily for the relevant empirical data we possess); not what are the ideological pre-suppositions on which it depends. The reason for this is that a model of analysis can in fact be adapted to a wide variety of ideologies. It is not necessarily tied to any one set of pre-suppositions, not even to those of the system in which it originated. One can, after all, adopt the theory of natural selection without subscribing to Darwinism as a world-view; or use the classical mechanics of Newton without accepting the determinism of the mechanistic universe that this seems to imply; or even attempt a Freudian analysis of dreams without necessarily agreeing with Freud's understanding of the human person.

The question needs to be studied further, but I would suggest that the link between models of analysis operating at the empirical level and the ideologies which provide philosophical interpretations for these models is not univocal. The same model can be interpreted in different ways, theistically or atheistically. For models do not of themselves raise questions of ultimate meaning. When such questions arise it is because a model has already been made part of an ideology, from which it can be detached and linked to another. Scientific theories are theologically neutral. There is much truth (though not in the sense he intended it!) in Laplace's celebrated remark that 'science (as science) has no need of a God-hypothesis'.

To reject Marxist analysis on theological grounds implies, it seems to me, a confusion of two different language games. I suspect, too, that any such rejection would re-enact in sociology what once happened in physics (with Galileo), in biology (with Darwin) or in psychology (with Freud). In each case a scientific model was rejected because of its supposed theological implications, with disastrous results.

## 2  The theological approach

Our concern in this paper, however, has been not the critical history of Israel but its confessional history – the history of Israel as this has been interpreted and proclaimed by the Bible. The relevant question for us, then, is not so much the historical as the theological one. How far do the Marxist ideas of class struggle and class throw light on the biblical understanding of the poor?

There is no doubt that there are analogies between the Marxist proletariat and the sociologically deprived, oppressed and the dynamic groups of the biblical poor. But these analogies are distant and tend to become even more remote as we move from the Old Testament to the New, which understands the poor in a less dialectical and dynamic way than does the Old. The poor in the New Testament are less oppressed and a good deal more passive in the face of their oppression (Jas. 5.7) than the poor of the Old. Poverty in the Bible is indeed primarily a sociological category but it is not to be defined in purely economic, much less in Marxist, terms (non-ownership of the means of production). Biblical poverty has a broader sociological and even a religious meaning. The poor in the Bible are an oppressed group in conflict, but it is doubtful whether their conflict can be usefully described as a class struggle. Factors other than the need to control the means of production or to secure economic betterment enter into it, and give it a different colour. The poor in the Bible aspire too after a free, fraternal and non-exploitative community which does indeed call to mind the classless society of Karl Marx. But the Bible goes beyond Marx's classless society in its affirmation of a religious basis for social justice. The 'new heavens and the new earth' will be 'full of the knowledge of the Lord as the waters cover the sea' (Isa. 11.9; 65.25); and in the New Jerusalem God himself will dwell with humankind, and they will be his people and he will be with them:

> Behold the dwelling of God is with humankind.
> He will dwell with them and they will be his people,
> and God himself will be with them;
> He will wipe away every tear from their eyes,
> and death shall be no more,
> neither shall there be mourning nor crying nor pain any more,
> for the former things have passed away (Rev. 21.3–4).

## C CONCLUSION

While the usefulness of Marxist analysis as a method for investigating the social history of Israel and of the early Church (the historical problem) remains an open question, there is no doubt that the configuration of the poor as understood in the Bible does not coincide with that of a Marxist class. But neither is it altogether different from it. The relation between them, it seems to me, can best be described as one of inclusion and transcendence. Just as evangelization includes and transcends 'liberation' (*Evangelii Nuntiandi*, nn. 30–9), or as the New Jerusalem includes and transcends the classless society of Marx, so too the biblical poor include and transcend Marx's proletariat, and the conflicts of biblical history include and transcend the class struggle of Marxism – taken in a corrected form and purged from elements that are not compatible with Jesus' command to universal and non-exclusive love. Indeed it is just such love that requires of us that we do not simply reject adverse positions out of hand, but attempt to understand and interpret them!

'The truth', Oscar Wilde has observed, 'is rarely pure and never simple'. Rather than insisting on simplistic blanket oppositions between Church and World, Christianity and non-Christian religions, Gospel and Marxism, it would be more Christian (and certainly more Indian) to avoid accentuating differences by the much used technique of demonizing the opponent (whether it be Hinduism or Islam, targets of the aggressive missionaries of the past, or Marxism, the target of crusading conservative Christians today) and to look rather for positive elements in the opponent's positions that can be taken up, discussed, corrected and 'fulfilled'. This might seem too obvious to need mention. But in the increasingly polemic atmosphere engendered by the irruption of religious revivalism everywhere, it may be useful to remind ourselves of a saying of Jesus whose import reaches well beyond the context in which it is reported: 'Do not think that I have come to destroy the law and the prophets,' says Jesus, 'I have come not to destroy, but to fulfil them' (Matt. 5.17).

## NOTES

1  K. Kautsky, *Foundations of Christianity* (London, George Allen & Unwin, 1925).

2  The analysis of the biblical words on poverty that follows depends on the study of M. Schwantes, *Das Recht der Armes* (Frankfurt-am-Main, Lang, 1977).

3  A. George, 'Poverty in the Old Testament', in A. George *et al.* (eds), *Gospel Poverty* (Chicago, Franciscan Herald Press, 1977), p. 6.

4  G. von Rad, *Old Testament Theology*, vol. 1 (Edinburgh, Oliver & Boyd, 1962), p. 108.

5  I owe the idea of Israel as a 'contrast community' to an unpublished article by Norbert Lohfink.

6  N. K. Gottwald, *The Tribes of Yahweh: A Sociology of the Religion of Liberated Israel 1250–1050 BCE* (Maryknoll, NY, Orbis Books, 1979); G. Theissen, *The First Followers of Jesus* (London, SCM Press, 1978). American edition: *The Sociology of Early Palestinian Christianity* (Philadelphia, Fortress Press, 1978).

7  G. E. Mendenhall, 'Ancient Israel's Hyphenated History', in D. N. Freedman and D. F. Graf (eds), *Palestine in Transition: The Emergence of Ancient Israel* (Sheffield, Almond Press, 1983), pp. 91–103.

# 12

# Racial Motifs in the Biblical Narratives

## CAIN HOPE FELDER

While Latin American liberation theology has persuasively introduced the questions of class and ideology into the hermeneutical debate, the black theologies of North America and Africa have added the questions of race and culture. This article is an attempt to highlight the racial motifs in the Christian Scriptures and their importance for interpretation.

This piece is from his book, *Troubling Biblical Waters: Race, Class, and Family* (Maryknoll, NY, Orbis Books, 1989).

Cain Hope Felder is Professor of New Testament Language and Literature at Howard University, Washington DC.

As we have indicated, the Bible contains different, even conflicting, traditions about the precise location of ancient Sheba, although the evidence suggests that Sheba was in or very near Black Africa. The Old Testament may lack details on the race or ethnicity of the celebrated Queen of Sheba, but there are sufficient ancient extra-biblical witnesses that favour her Black identity.

We now take up the larger questions of race and racism – not in relation to a particular biblical figure, but as it pertains to a wide range of biblical narratives. We do not find any elaborate definitions or theories about race in antiquity. This means we must reckon with certain methodological problems in attempting to examine racial motifs in the Bible. Ancient authors of biblical texts did have color and race consciousness (they were aware of certain physiological differences), but this consciousness of color and race was by no means a political or ideological basis for enslaving or otherwise oppressing other peoples. In fact, the Bible contains scarcely any narratives in which the original intent was to negate the humanity of Black people or view Blacks unfavourably.

The specific racial type of the biblical Hebrews is itself quite difficult to determine.[1] Scholars today generally recognize that the biblical Hebrews most probably emerged as an amalgamation of races rather than from any pure racial stock. When they departed from Egypt, they may well have been Afroasiatics. To refer to the earliest Hebrews as 'Semites' does not take us very far, since as the eighteenth-century term does not designate a race, but a family of languages embracing Hebrew, Akkadian, Arabic, and Ethiopic (*Ge'ez*).[2] The language of 'burnt-face' Africans, for example, is as equally Semitic as the language of the Jews or the Arabs.[3] This reaffirms our earlier contention that sophisticated theories about race and the phenomenon of racism are by-products of the postbiblical era. Consequently part of the task in this chapter is to construct an interpretive framework for a range of biblical attitudes about race and to determine implications for the problem of racism and enthnocentrism that still bedevil both Church and society in many nations today, including those of the Third World.

Although the Bible primarily presents sociopolitical entities that are differentiated as empires, nations, and tribes, there are important ways in which the subject of race acquires particular significance. In the Bible, two broad processes related to racism may be operating. First there is the phenomenon of 'sacralization.' By this we mean *the transposing of an ideological concept into a tenet of religious faith in order to serve the vested interest of a particular ethnic group.* Second is the process of 'secularization' or *the diluting of a rich religious concept under the weighty influence of secular pressures (social or political).*[4] In secularization, ideas are wrenched from their original religious moorings and fall prey to nationalistic ideologies. These often cultivate patterns of ethno-centrism and even racism, which in turn can have harmful effects on certain racial groups who are scorned and marginalized.

## RACE AND SACRALIZATION IN THE OLD TESTAMENT

Several Old Testament passages are quite suitable as illustrations of sacralization, and as such, require a new kind of critical engagement. First, we shall consider the so-called curse of Ham (Gen. 9.18–27), which rabbis of the early Talmudic periods and the Church Fathers at times used to denigrate Black people. Later Europeans adopted the so-called curse of Ham as a justification for slavery and stereotypical aspersions about Blacks. Second, we shall discuss the fascinating narrative about Miriam and Aaron, who object to Moses' Ethiopian wife (Num. 12.1–16). Third, our attention will focus on the Old Testament genealogies that contributed to the Israelite and ancient Jewish perception that they constituted a most divinely favored people ('race'). Fourth, we shall take up the biblical notion of election (chosen people) as it develops as an explicit theme in the Old Testament and changes in the New Testament.

Our first example of sacralization is found in some of the earliest Jahwist ('J') traditions of the Old Testament. It is Genesis 9.18–27, which has achieved notoriety in many quarters because it contains the so-called curse of Ham. Technically, the passage should follow directly after the 'J' passage that concludes the flood narrative (Gen. 8.20–2), since critical investigations have shown that Genesis 9.1–17, 28, 29 represent the much later Priestly ('P') exilic tradition.[5] The great significance of Genesis 9.18–27 is not that it contains the so-called curse of Ham, which technically does not take place at all. Rather, these verses make it clear that, to the mind of the ancient Israelite author, 'the whole post-diluvial humanity stems from Noah's three sons.'[6] On Genesis 9.19, Claus Westermann remarks:

> The whole of humankind takes its origin from them [Shem, Ham, Japheth] . . . humanity is conceived here as a unity, in a way different from the creation; humanity in all its variety across the earth, takes its origin from these three who survived the flood. The purpose of the contrast is to underscore the amazing fact that humanity scattered in all its variety throughout the world comes from one family.[7]

Once the passage established this essential aspect of human origin (vv. 18, 19), it continued by providing what appears to be a primeval rationale for differences in the destinies or fortunes of certain groups of persons. Certainly, as one scholar notes, 'from a form critical viewpoint Genesis 9.20–7 is an ethnological etiology concerned with the theology of culture and history.'[8] This observation alerts us to the theological motives in verses 20–7 that have implications for definite interpretations regarding culture and history. It is this development that most clearly attests to the process of sacralization, where cultural and historical phenomena are recast as theological truths holding the vested interest of particular groups.

A word about the literary form of this narrative is important. In general, the narrative passages of Genesis 1–11 concern themselves with the matter of 'crime and punishment; this is particularly evident in the ("J") narratives.'[9] Westermann informs us that these narratives have antecedents and parallels in ancient African myths: 'It is beyond dispute that African myths about the primeval state and biblical stories of crime and punishment in J correspond both in their leading motifs and in their structure.'[10]

With respect to Genesis 9.18–27, the crime is Ham's seeing the nakedness of his drunken father, Noah, without immediately covering him. In error, Ham leaves his father uncovered (an act of great shamelessness and parental disrespect in Hebrew tradition) while he goes to report Noah's condition to Shem and Japheth, his brothers (v. 22). Ham's two brothers display proper respect by discreetly covering their father (v. 23). When Noah awakens (v. 24), the problems begin. Noah pronounces a curse – *not* on Ham, but on Ham's son Canaan, who has not been mentioned before. Noah also blesses Shem and Japheth, presumably as a reward for their sense of respect.

If one attempts to argue for the unity of the passage, inconsistencies and other difficulties abound. To illustrate, Ham commits the shameless act in verse 22, but Canaan is cursed in verse 25. In 9.18, the list of Noah's sons refers to Ham as being second, but in 9.24, the text – presumably referring to Ham – uses the phrase, Noah's 'youngest son.' Also, the mentioning of Canaan as cursed in verse 25 raises the possibility (albeit untenable) that Noah had a fourth son, named Canaan.

Then too, uncertainties about the precise nature of Ham's error result in a fantastic variety of suggestions, which range from Ham's having possibly castrated his father, attacked his father homosexually, committed incest with his father's wife, or having had sexual relations with his own wife while aboard the ark.[11] The matter was far less complicated: Ham violated a vital rule of respect. Many of the difficulties within this passage find a solution if we allow the possibility that the original version of Genesis 9.18–27 only referred to Ham and his error, and a later version of the story – one motivated by political developments in ancient Palestine – attempted to justify Shem's descendants (Israel) and those of Japheth (Philistines) over the subjugated Canaanites.[12]

While admitting that it is Ham who shows disrespect to Noah but Canaan, Ham's son, who is cursed, Westermann asserts:

> The same person who committed the outrage in v. 22 falls under the curse in v. 25. The Yahwist has preserved, together with the story of Ham's outrage, a curse over Canaan which could be resumed because of the

genealogical proximity of Canaan to Ham. Those who heard the story knew the descendants of Ham as identical with those of Canaan.[13]

In Westermann's view, Ham *was* cursed and presumably not just Canaan, but all the other descendants of Ham cited in Genesis 10.6: Cush, Egypt, and Put (Punt).

Although I disagree with Westermann's contention that Ham was, *in effect*, cursed in Genesis 9.18–27, he helps us see that the ambiguity of the text can lead Bible interpreters to justify their particular history, culture, and race by developing self-serving theological constructs. In one instance, the Canaanites 'deserve' subjugation; in another instance, the Hamites 'deserve' to be hewers of wood and drawers of water.

Whether or not sacralization was actually part of the original narrative, we have much evidence in the Midrashim (fifth century AD), where Noah says to Ham: 'You have prevented me from doing something in the dark (cohabitation), therefore your seed will be ugly and dark-skinned.'[14] Similarly, the Babylonian Talmud (sixth century AD) states that 'the descendants of Ham are cursed by being Black and are sinful with a degenerate progeny.'[15] The idea that the blackness of Africans was due to a curse, and thus reinforced and sanctioned enslaving Blacks, persisted into the seventeenth century.[16] Even today, in such versions of Holy Scripture as *Dake's Annotated Reference Bible*, one finds in Genesis 9.18–27 a so-called 'great racial prophecy' with the following racist hermeneutic:

> All colors and types of men came into existence after the flood. All men were white up to this point, for there was only one family line of Christ, being mentioned in Luke 3.36 with his son Shem . . . prophecy that Shem would be a chosen race and have a peculiar relationship with God. All divine revelation since Shem has come through his line . . . prophecy that Japheth would be the father of the great and enlarged races. Government, Science and Art are mainly Japhethic. . . . His descendants constitute the leading nations of civilization.[17]

Another instance of sacralization confronts us quite early in the Old Testament, within the genealogies of the descendants of Noah. It is especially useful to consider the so-called table of nations (Genesis 10) in conjunction with the much later genealogical listing of 1 Chronicles 1.1–2.55. On the one hand, these listings purport to be comprehensive catalogs. All too often they have been erroneously taken as reliable sources of ancient ethnography. Critical study of these genealogies illuminates theological motives that inevitably demonstrate a tendency to arrange different groups in priority, thereby attaching the greatest significance to the Israelites as an ethnic and national entity greater than all other peoples of the earth.

At first glance, Genesis 10 appears to be a single listing of ancient nations. However, biblical criticism has for some time demonstrated that Genesis 10 represents a combination of at least two different lists, separated by centuries: Jahwist ('J') and Priestly ('P').[18] In fact, the fusing of different traditions in Genesis 10 doubtlessly accounts for the difficulty in locating the land of Cush, and determining the relationship between Cush and Sheba or the differences between Seba and Sheba. Genesis 10.7 mentions Seba as a son of Cush, and Sheba is a grandson of Cush. Here the text clearly is identifying the descendants of Ham (*ham*). Then in Genesis 10.28, the text introduces an anomaly, mentioning Sheba as a direct descendant of Shem, not Ham. Furthermore, since the initial Samech (*s*) of *seb'a* is the equivalent of and interchangeable with the Hebrew Shin (*s*) in old South Arabic,[19] one could argue that Genesis 10 offers us two persons named Sheba as descendants of Cush, but only one person by that name as a descendant of Shem. In any case, it is not clear that the table of nations as it stands does not have the motive of delineating sharp ethnic differences between the ancient peoples of Africa, South Arabia, and Mesopotamia. The true motive lies elsewhere.

Rather than an objective historical account of genealogies, the table of nations in Genesis 10 is a theologically motivated catalog of people. The table not only ends with the descendants of Shem, but does so in a way consciously stylized to accentuate the importance of his descendants.[20] About this, the author of the genealogy in 1 Chronicles 1.17–34 is most explicit; of all the descendants of the sons of Noah, Shem's receive the most elaborate attention. Thus the most primitive 'J' listing of the nations is theologically edited centuries later according to the post-exilic Priestly tradition, in order to establish the priority of the descendants of Shem. Centuries later, a further elaboration takes place, as found in the genealogies of 1 Chronicles. In this long progression, the theological presuppositions of a particular ethnic group displace any concern for objective historiography and ethnography. The descendants of Noah not related to Shem become increasingly insignificant and are mentioned only when they serve as foils to demonstrate the priority of the Israelites.

The subtle process being described may consequently be called sacralization, because it represents an attempt on the part of one ethnic group to construe salvation history in terms that are distinctly favorable to it, as opposed to others. Here, ethnic particularity evolves with a certain divine vindication, and the dangers of rank racism lie just beneath the surface. While the genealogies do not express negative attitudes about persons of African descent, as my colleague Gene Rice has noted, it is important to clarify an aspect of his judgment in light of the way in which sacralization expresses itself in these genealogies. Consider Rice's remarks:

> Genesis 10 has to do with all the peoples of the world known to ancient Israel and since this chapter immediately follows the episode of Noah's cursing and blessing, it would have been most appropriate to express here any prejudicial feelings toward African peoples. Not only are such feelings absent, but all peoples are consciously and deliberately related to each other as brothers. *No one, not even Israel, is elevated above anyone else and no disparaging remark is made about any people, not even the enemies of Israel* [emphasis mine].[21]

Rice's contention that the genealogies do not elevate Israel above anyone else must be qualified. After all, Genesis 10.21–31 becomes the basis for amplifying the descendants of Shem and Judah (1 Chron. 2.1–55) as the distinctive *laos tou Theou* (LXX 'people of God'). Thus the entire genealogies are construed theologically to enhance the status of a particular people, and this is sacralization.

Numbers 12 attests all too well to the way individuals can quickly move from a sacred ethnic stance to racism of the worst sort. In Numbers 12.1, Moses' brother and sister castigate him for having married a Cushite woman (*hāʾišā hacū šiʿt*). Several factors point to the probability that the offensive aspect of the marriage was the woman's Black identity. In the first place, this is clearly the view expressed in the wording of the Septuagint *heneken tēs gunaikos tēs Aithiopissēs* ('on account of the Ethiopian woman').[22] Secondly, in the selection of the rather odd punishment that God unleashes on Miriam (v. 10), it can hardly be accidental that leprosy is described vividly as 'leprous, as white as snow.' Quite an intentional contrast is dramatized here: Moses' Black wife, accursed by Miriam and Aaron, is now contrasted with Miriam, who suddenly becomes 'as white as snow' in her punishment. The contrast is sharpened all the more because only Miriam is punished for an offense of which Aaron is equally guilty. The LXX witness, together with these exegetical considerations, point strongly to the probability that more than arrogance is at issue in this text. Also involved is a rebuke to the racial prejudice characterized by the attitudes of Miriam and Aaron.

God's stern rebuke of Miriam's and Aaron's incipient racial prejudice is a perennial reminder of the extraordinarily progressive racial values of the Bible in comparison to the hostile racial attitudes in the medieval and modern period.[23] At the same time, however, the Numbers 12 narrative exposes the inherent difficulties of any quick generality about the racial implications of sacralization that appear when early traditions assume, through years of refinement, an ethnic particularity that marginalizes groups outside the Torah, 'The Land of Israel' (*'ereṣ Israēl*), and the Covenant.

For theological reasons, the process of sacralization in the Old Testament largely remains racially ambiguous, especially with specific reference to Black people. The distinction the Old Testament makes is not racial. Rather, the Hebrew Scripture distinguishes groups on the basis of national identity and ethnic tribes. All who do not meet the criteria for salvation as defined by the ethnic or national 'in-groups' are relegated to an inferior status. It is therefore surprising to many that Black people are not only frequently mentioned in numerous Old Testament texts but are mentioned in ways that acknowledge their actual and potential role in the salvation history of Israel. By no means are Black people excluded from Israel's story, as long as they claim it (however secondarily) and not proclaim their own story apart from the activity of Israel's God.

Extensive lists of Old Testament passages that make favorable reference to Black people are readily accessible.[24] There are many illustrations of such provocative texts. Isaiah 37.9 and 2 Kings 19.9 refer to Tirhaka, king of the Ethiopians. This ancient Black Pharaoh was actually the fourth member of the Twenty-fifth Egyptian Dynasty that ruled all of Egypt (730–653 BC).[25] According to the biblical texts, Tirhaka was the object of the desperate hopes of Israel. In the days of Hezekiah, Israel hoped desperately that Tirhaka's armies would intervene and stave off an impending Assyrian assault by Sennacherib. More than a half-century later, another text would refer to 'men of Ethiopia and Put who handle the shield' (Jer. 46.9). The Old Testament indicates that Black people were part of the Hebrew army (2 Sam. 18.21–32) and even part of the royal court. Ebedmelech takes action to save Jeremiah's life (Jer. 38.7–13) and thereby becomes the beneficiary of a singular divine blessing (Jer. 39.15–18). The dominant portrait of the Ethiopians in the Old Testament is that of a wealthy people (Job 28.19; Isa. 45.14) who would soon experience conversion (Ps. 68.31; Isa. 11.11, 18.7, Zeph. 3.10). The reference to 'Zephaniah the son of Cushi' (Zeph. 1.1) may indicate that one of the books of the Old Testament was authored by a Black African.[26]

## ELECTION AND SACRALIZATION IN THE BIBLE

Israel's particularity loses much of its subtlety as the dubious concept of her election (*bāḥar*) begins to gain a firm footing in the Old Testament. Certainly, traces of the idea of Israel's chosenness and personal, special relationship with her deity were present in 'the pre-Jahwistic cult of the ancestors,' but the explicit concept of Jahweh's loving preference for the people of Israel develops relatively late.[27] The theologically elaborated belief that Jahweh specifically chose Israel above all other nations does not become a matter of religious ideology – and therefore an instance of sacralization – until the period of Deuteronomistic history toward the end of the seventh century BC (Deut. 7.6–8; 10.15; Jer. 2.3; compare: Isa. 43.20; 65.9).[28]

Regardless of the theological structure that attempts to support the Deuteronomistic concept of Israel's election, ambiguities engulf this concept of election. Horst Seebass, for example, insists that even among the Deuteronomistic writers, Israel's election 'only rarely stands at the center of what is meant by election.'[29] According to him, *bāḥar*, as a technical term for Israel's election, always functions as a symbol of universalism. It represents Israel in the role of 'service to the whole.'[30] Seebass is representative of those who want to de-emphasize the distinctive ethnic or racial significance of the concept in Israel's self-understanding during the Deuteronomistic period.[31]

The ethnic and racial ambiguities involved in the concept of Israel's election seem to persist. The ambiguity does not result from the fact that a universalistic history is presupposed by the biblical writers who advance the Old Testament concept of Israel's election. Rather, the ambiguities stem from the nature of the presupposed universalism. Gerhard von Rad points out that in the Deuteronomistic circles, the chosenness of Israel attains a radical form and its universal aspect is at best paradoxical.[32] Perhaps the real paradox resides in the notion that Israel's divine election seems to lead inevitably to sacralization, with the people of Israel as an ethnic group at the center. Certainly, the

Deuteronomistic authors struggle to demonstrate Jahweh's affirmation of the Davidic monarchy and, more importantly, Jahweh's selection of Jerusalem as the center of any continuing redemptive activity.[33] Although the people of Israel exhibit no extraordinary attributes or values by which they objectively merit Jahweh's election, there later develops an elaborate doctrine of merit, by which those who know and follow the Torah attempt to prove their worthiness as the chosen people.

Despite the absence of any inherent superiority of the people of Israel, the concept of election becomes inextricably bound up with ethnic particularity. Accordingly, the people of Israel claim the status of being preeminently chosen. They thereby claim to possess the Law, the Covenant, and a continuing promise of the land and the city as the 'in-group.' At the same time, all who stand outside the community or apart from the supporting religious ideology of election are relegated to the margins of Israel's 'universal' saving history. Other races and ethnic groups may, of course, subscribe to Israel's religious ideology and derive the commensurate benefits. But the criteria for such subscription always seem to be mediated through the biases of an ethnic group reinforced by elaborate genealogies and the transmission of particular legal religious traditions.

This entire development typifies the process of sacralization, and it is striking to see the different treatment of election in the New Testament. George Foot Moore provides us with a glimpse of the New Testament conception of election when he asserts that, 'Paul and the church substituted an individual election to eternal life, without regard to race or station.'[34] However, such an assertion oversimplifies New Testament ideas about election. Rudolf Bultmann provides us with a more helpful understanding of the New Testament in this regard. He argues that in the New Testament, 'the Christian Church becomes the true people of God.' In Bultmann's view, the New Testament no longer concerns itself with a preeminent ethnic group, that is, *Israēl kata sarka* (1 Cor. 10.18), but with the Israel of God (Gal. 6.16), without any exclusive ethnic or racial coordinates.[35]

In contrast to the Deuteronomistic usage of the Hebrew term *bāḥar*, the New Testament never presents the Greek verb *eklegomai* or its nominal derivatives *eklektos* ('chosen') and *eklogē* ('election') in an ethnically or racially exclusive sense. Paul wants to maintain a certain continuity with aspects of Israel's election, but that continuity is neither ethnic nor cultic (Rom. 9.11; 11.2, 11, 28, 29). For Paul, corporate election can include some Jews, but it must also embrace Gentiles (Rom. 11.25; Gal. 3.28; 1 Cor. 12.13); being 'in' and 'with' Christ becomes the new *crux interpretum.* In Paul's view, God *chose* the foolish, weak, and low (1 Cor. 1.27, 28). For James, God *chose* the poor who are rich in faith (Jas. 2.5). For Matthew, God calls many, but *chooses* only the few (Matt. 22.14). The new universalism and unity to be found in the Christian Church expresses itself further within the context of 'God's chosen ones' in the following sequence of thoughts:

> There is neither Jew nor Greek, there is neither slave nor free, there is neither male nor female; for you are all one in Christ Jesus (Gal. 3.28).

> For by one Spirit we were all baptized into one body – Jews or Greeks, slaves or free – and all were made to drink of one spirit (1 Cor. 12.13).

> Here there cannot be Greek and Jew, circumcised and uncircumcised, barbarian, Scythian, slave, free man, but Christ is all, and in all (Col. 3.11, 12).

The only New Testament text that refers to Christians as 'a chosen race' (*genos eklekton*) is 1 Peter 2.9. Yet, in this text, the phrase is manifestly metaphorical. 1 Peter 2.9 depends very heavily on the wording found in LXX Isaiah 43.20, 21, but the ethnic particularity implied in the Old Testament text has fallen away entirely in 1 Peter.[36] Throughout the New Testament period (which extends well into the second century), 'the elect' become the Church as the new Israel. Matthew is even more specific, because the elect represent the faithful few in the Church who accept the call to the higher righteousness and the doing of the will of God. In either case, these New Testament perspectives eliminate all ethnic or racial criteria for determining the elect.[37]

## SECULARIZATION IN THE NEW TESTAMENT

Ambiguities with regard to race in the New Testament do not appear within the context of what we have defined as sacralization. The New Testament disapproves of ethnic corporate election, or 'Israel according to the flesh.' In fact, the New Testament offers no grand genealogies to sacralize the myth of any ethnic or national superiority.

If one is to explore the subject of racialist tendencies in the New Testament, one may turn to a different phenomenon: the process of secularization. How did the expanding Church – in its attempt to survive without the temporary protection she derived from being confused with Judaism – begin to succumb to the dominant symbols and ideologies of the Greco-Roman world? We will see how the universalism of the New Testament diminishes as Athens and Rome subtitute for Jerusalem as the alleged new centers of God's redemptive activity.

The early Christian authors' understanding of the world barely included sub-Sahara Africa. They had no idea at all of the Americas or the Far East. These writers referred to Spain as 'the limits of the West' (1 Clem. 5.7, Rom. 15.28); they envisioned the perimeter of the world as the outer reaches of the Roman Empire.[38] For New Testament authors, Roman sociopolitical realities, as well as the language and culture of Hellenism, often determined how God was seen as acting in Jesus Christ. Just as Old Testament Jerusalem came to represent the preeminent holy city of the God of Israel (Zion), New Testament authors attached a preeminent status to Rome, the capital city of their world.[39]

It is no coincidence that Mark, the earliest composer of a passion narrative, goes to such great lengths to show that the confession of the Roman centurion brings his whole gospel narrative to its climax.[40] For his part, Luke expends considerable effort to specify the positive qualities of his various centurions.[41] There is even a sense in which their official titles symbolize Rome as the capital of the Gentile world, for their incipient acts of faith or confessions (according to Luke) find their denouement in the Acts 28 portrait of Paul, who relentlessly proclaims the kerygma in Rome. The immediate significance of this New Testament tendency to focus on Rome instead of Jerusalem is that the darker races outside the Roman orbit are for the most part overlooked by New Testament authors.

For lack of more descriptive terminology, this process may be called secularization. Here, sociopolitical realities tend to dilute the New Testament vision of racial inclusiveness and universalism. Early traditions are accordingly adapted at later stages in such a way as to expose an undue compromising of a religious vision and to show how secular sociopolitical realities cause religious texts to be slanted to the detriment of the darker races.

Perhaps one of the best illustrations of this process of secularization is Luke's narrative about the baptism and conversion of the Ethiopian official in Acts 8.26–40. On the surface, this is a highly problematic text. One wonders immediately if the Ethiopian finance minister is a

Jew or Gentile. One also wonders about the efficacy of his baptism and whether it constituted or led to a full conversion to Christianity. Probably the best survey of the problems posed by this story is that by Ernst Haenchen, who entitles the story 'Philip Converts a Chamberlain.'[42] According to Haenchen, Luke is intentionally ambiguous about the Ethiopian's identity as a Gentile or Jew. Luke merely appeals to this conversion story to suggest 'that with this new convert the mission has taken a step beyond the conversion of Jews and Samaritans.'[43] The story itself derives from Hellenistic circles and represents for Luke (in Haenchen's view) a parallel and rival to Luke's account of Cornelius, the first Gentile convert under the auspices of Peter.[44] Haenchen detects no particularly significant racial difficulties posed by Acts 8.26–40. For him, Luke merely edits this Hellenistic tradition to conform to his own theological design.

Certainly those who tend to exclude Black people from any role in Christian origins need to be reminded that a Nubian was possibly the first Gentile convert.[45] Nonetheless, Luke's awkward use of this story seems to have certain racial implications. Notice that in Acts 8.37, the Ethiopian says, 'See, here is water! What is to prevent my being baptized?' A variant reading immediately follows in some ancient versions of the text: 'And Phillip said, if you believe with all your heart, you may [be baptized]. And he [the Ethiopian] replied, I believe that Jesus Christ is the son of God.'[46] Whether or not one accepts this variant reading as an authentic part of the text, it is clear that the Ethiopian's baptism takes place in the water without reference to a prior or simultaneous descent of the Holy Spirit (compare John 3.5; I John 5.6–8).

By contrast, Luke provides an elaborate narrative about Cornelius' conversion and baptism (Acts 10.12–48), at the end of which, the Holy Spirit descends and the baptism by water follows. Furthermore, Peter's speech (Acts 10.34–43) indicates a new development in which Gentiles are unambiguously eligible for conversion and baptism. Given the importance of the Holy Spirit's role throughout Luke–Acts as a theological motif, Luke's narrative about Cornelius' baptism gives the distinct impression (perhaps unwittingly) that Cornelius' baptism is more legitimate than that of the Ethiopian.

This by no means suggests that Luke had a negative attitude about Black people. One need only consider the Antioch Church's leadership presented in Acts 13.1 to dispel such notions. There Luke mentions one 'Symeon who is called the Black man' (*Symeōn ho kaloumenos Niger*). The Latinism 'Niger' probably reinforces the idea that Symeon was a dark-skinned person, probably an African.[47] Luke's vision was one of racial pluralism in the leadership of the young Christian Church at Antioch (Acts 11.26). In no way is it important or useful to attempt to show, on the basis of any of the traditions in Acts of the Apostles, that the first Gentile convert was a Nubian rather than an Italian or member of any other ethnic group. This would be absurd, given the confessional nature of the entire Luke–Acts work, which does not come to us as objective history. But Luke's editorializing does result in a circumstantial deemphasis of a Nubian (African) in favor of an Italian (European) and thereby enables some Europeans to claim or imply that Acts demonstrates some divine preference for Europeans.

Luke is not innocent in all of this. His possible apologetics for the Roman official Theophilus, as well as the great significance he attaches to Rome as the center of the world, betrays the subtle way in which Luke's theology fell prey to secular ideological ideas.[48] In the last third of the first century, the Church generally struggled to survive in an increasingly hostile political environment. Luke, not unlike other New Testament writers of this period and after,[49] perhaps seeks to assuage Rome by allowing his theological framework to be determined by the assumption of a Roman-centered world.[50] In this process of secularization, the Lukan vision of universalism is undermined. Fortunately, this is not Luke's only message. We must remember that the New Testament's final vision of the holy remnant (Rev. 7.9) is consistent with Luke's notion of racial pluralism as reflected in the leadership of the church of Antioch (Acts 13.1). Both texts indicate that persons of all nations and races constitute part of the righteous remnant at the consummation of the ages.

Secularization in the New Testament needs much fuller exploration in terms of its racial dimensions. At one level, it highlights a certain ambiguity of race in the New Testament. At another level, it confronts us with a challenge to search for more adequate modes of hermeneutics by which the New Testament can be demonstrated as relevant to Blacks and other people of the Third World, even as it stands locked into the socioreligious framework of the Greco-Roman world. Of all the mandates confronting the Church today, the mandate of world community predicated on a renewed commitment to pluralism and the attendant acknowledgment of the integrity of all racial groups constitutes an urgent agenda for Bible scholars and laity alike. It is an agenda far too long neglected in the vast array of Eurocentric theological and ecclesial traditions that continue to marginalize people of color throughout the world today.

## NOTES

1  R. E. Clements, 'Goy', in G. J. Botterweck and H. Ringgren (eds), *Theological Dictionary of the Old Testament*, vol. 2 (Grand Rapids, Mich., W. B. Eerdman, 1974–84), pp. 426–9.

2  S. D. Goitein, *Jews and Arabs: Their Contacts Through the Ages* (New York, Schocken Books, 1964), pp. 19–21.

3  F. M. Snowden, Jr, *Blacks in Antiquity: Ethiopians in the Greco-Roman Experience* (Cambridge, Mass., Harvard University Press, 1970), pp. 118–19: '*Aithiops* ("burnt-face"): the most frequent translation of C U S H found in the LXX, designating usually Africans of dark pigmentation and Negroid features, used as early as Homer (*Odyssey* 19, pp. 246 ff). While *Aithiops* in ancient biblical and classical texts refers specifically to Ethiopians, the term also identifies Africans, regardless of race.'

4  G. A. Buttrick (ed.), 'Election', *Interpreter's Dictionary of the Bible*, vol. 2 (Nashville, Tenn., Abingdon Press, 1962), p. 77. G. E. Mendenhall employs the term *secularization* in this sense.

5  C. Westermann, *Genesis 1–11: A Commentary* (Minneapolis, Minn., Augsburg Publishing House, 1984 (1974)), p. 459.

6  ibid., p. 482.

7  ibid., p. 486.

8  G. Rice, 'The Curse That Never Was (Genesis 9.18–27)' (*The Journal of Religious Thought*, 29, 1972), p. 13.

9  Westermann, p. 47.

10  ibid., p. 54.

11  Rice, pp. 11–12; Westermann, pp. 488–9; E. Isaac, 'Genesis, Judaism and the "Sons of Ham"' (*Slavery and Abolition: A Journal of Comparative Studies*, 1, 1, May 1980), pp. 4–5.

12  Rice, pp. 7–8, suggests that the passage contains two parallel but different traditions – one universal (Gen. 9.18–19a; cf. 5.32; 6.10; 7.13; 10.1; 1 Chron. 1.4) and the other limited to Palestine and more parochial (Gen. 9.20–7, and seems presupposed in 10.21).

13  Westermann, p. 484.

14  Rice, pp. 17, 25.

15  See E. Isaac, ibid., p. 19.

16  Rice, p. 26, n. 116.

17  F. Jennings Dake, *Dake's Annotated Reference Bible* (Lawrenceville, Ga., Dake Bible Sales, 1981 (1961)), pp. 8, 9, 36, 40. One of my African seminarians, who had been given *Dake's Annotated* by fundamentalist American missionaries, innocently presented me with a gift copy for study and comment!

18  M. Noth, *A History of Pentateuchal Traditions*, trans. W. Anderson

Cain Hope Felder

(Chico, Calif., Scholars Press, 1981), pp. 21–3, 28 and the translator's supplement, pp. 262–3; Eissfeldt, *The Old Testament: An Introduction* (New York, Harper & Row, 1965), p. 184.

19 Buttrick, 'Sabeans', in *Interpreter's Dictionary*, vol. 4, p. 311.

20 The postexilic Priestly ('P') redaction accounts for the order Shem, Ham, Japheth (omitting Canaan) in Genesis 10.1 as well as for the inversion of this order in the subsequent verses, e.g. Genesis 10.2 the sons of Japheth, Genesis 10.6 the sons of Ham, and Genesis 10.21 'To Shem also, the father of all the children of Eber (Hebrew).'

21 Rice, p. 16.

22 Contra B. W. Anderson's note in *The New Oxford Annotated Bible* (RSV), p. 179: 'The term Cushite apparently [sic] includes Midianites and other Arabic peoples (Hab. 3.7).'

23 Isaac, pp. 3–17.

24 S. Hable Sellassie, *Ancient and Medieval Ethiopian History to 1270* (Addis Ababa, United Printers, 1972), p. 96; R. A. Morrisey, *Colored People and Bible History* (Hammond, Ind., W. B. Conkey Company, 1925); E. Ullendorff, *Ethiopia and the Bible* (London, Oxford University Press, 1968), pp. 6–8.

25 Snowden, pp. 115–17; C. Anta Diop, *African Origin of Civilization: Myth or Reality?*, trans. M. Cook (New York and Westport, Conn., Lawrence Hill, 1974 (1955)), pp. 220–1; Sir A. Gardiner, *Egypt of the Pharaohs* (New York, Oxford University Press, 1974 (1961)), p. 450.

26 C. B. Copher, '3,000 Years of Biblical Interpretation with Reference to Black Peoples' (*The Journal of the Interdenominational Theological Center*, 13, 2, spring 1986), pp. 225–46.

27 G. von Rad, *Old Testament Theology*, 2 vols, trans. D. M. G. Stalker (New York, Harper & Row, 1962), vol. 1, p. 7; vol. 2, p. 322.

28 ibid., vol. 1, pp. 118, 178; Botterweck and Ringgren (eds), 'Bāchar', *Theological Dictionary of the Old Testament*, vol. 2 p. 78; Buttrick, 'Election', *Interpreter's Dictionary*, vol. 2, p. 76.

29 Botterweck and Ringgren (eds), 'Bāchar', vol. 2, p. 82.

30 ibid., p. 83.

31 Buttrick (ed.), *Interpreter's Dictionary*, vol. 2, p. 79; G. F. Moore, *Judaism*, vol. 2 (Cambridge, Mass., Harvard University Press, 1932), p. 95; cf. Rashi's Commentary, *Deuteronomy*, pp. 56, 195.

32 von Rad, vol. I, pp. 178, 223.

33 Botterweck and Ringgren (eds), 'Bāchar', p. 78.

34 Moore, p. 95.

35 R. Bultmann, *Theology of the New Testament*, vol. 1 (London, SCM Press, 1965 (1952) and New York, Scribner's, 1952), p. 97.

36 (LXX) Isa. 43.20 *to genos mou to eklekton* = M.T. *'ammi běḥiri*.

37 W. Bauer, *'Eklektos,'* *A Greek-English Lexicon of the New Testament*, trans. and ed. W. E. Arndt and F. W. Gingrich (Chicago, University of Chicago Press, 1957), p. 242.

38 In 1 Clem. v.7, 'the limits of the west' (*epi to terma tēs duseōs*) designates Spain (of Rome). K. Lake (trans.), *Apostolic Fathers*, vol. I, Loeb Classical Library (Cambridge, Mass., Harvard University Press, 1975), p. 16. Cf. E.

Käsemann, *Commentary on Romans*, trans. and ed. G. W. Bromiley (Grand Rapids, Mich., W. B. Eerdman, 1980), p. 402.

39   Luke's Acts of the Apostles outlines this scheme quite decidedly: Jerusalem (Acts 2), Antioch (Acts 12), Athens (Acts 17), and Rome (Acts 28). See W. G. Kummel, *Introduction to the New Testament*, rev. English edn, trans. H. C. Kee (Nashville, Tenn., Abingdon Press, 1973), pp. 164 f.

40   V. Taylor, *The Gospel According to St Mark* (New York, St. Martin's Press, 1966), p. 598; W. H. Kelber (ed.), *The Passion in Mark* (Philadelphia, Pa., Fortress Press, 1976), pp. 120 n, 155, 166.

41   The good reputations of the centurion in Luke 7.2 ff and Cornelius the centurion in Acts 10.1, 22 are intentional designs by Luke. F. J. Foakes Jackson and K. Lake, *The Acts of the Apostles*, vol. 4 (Grand Rapids, Mich., Baker Book House, 1979), p. 112; E. Haenchen, *Acts of the Apostles: A Commentary* (Oxford, Basil Blackwell, 1971), pp. 346–9.

42   Haenchen, p. 309.

43   ibid., p. 314.

44   ibid., p. 315. Similarly, M. Hengel, *Acts and the Ancient History of Earliest Christianity* (Philadelphia, Pa., Fortress Press, 1980), p. 79.

45   Foakes Jackson and Lake, vol. 4, p. 98. Irenaeus (AD 120–202) reports that the Ethiopian became a missionary to 'the regions of Ethiopia'; Epiphanius (AD 315–403) says that he preached in Arabia Felix and on the coasts of the Red Sea. Unfortunately, there are no records of Ethiopian Christianity until the fourth century.

46   Irenaeus cites the text as if the variant reading is part of the text (*Adv. Haer.* iii.12.8). A. Roberts and J. Donaldson (eds), *The Ante-Nicene Fathers* (Grand Rapids, Mich., W. B. Eerdman, 1981), vol. 1, p. 433. See also *The Western Text, The Antiochian Text*, and *Textus Receptus*; the English AV includes v. 37. Jackson and Lake, *Acts*, vol. 4, p. 98, suggest that the principal significance of v. 37 is 'perhaps the earliest form of the baptismal creed. It is also remarkable that it is an expansion of the baptismal formula "in the name of Jesus Christ," not of the trinitarian formula.'

47   C. S. C. Williams, *The Acts of the Apostles* (New York, Harper & Row, 1957), p. 154. 'Simeon the "Black" may have come from Africa and may possibly be Simon of Cyrene.' Haenchen, *Acts of the Apostles*, p. 395, n. 2, reminds us that 1 Corinthians 12.28 ff lists first apostles, prophets, and teachers as persons endowed with *charismata*, and these constituted a charismatic office in Pauline churches.

48   Luke 1.3; Acts 1.1. See H. Conzelmann, *The Theology of St Luke*, trans. G. Buswell (New York, Harper & Row, 1960), pp. 138–41; R. J. Cassidy, *Jesus, Politics and Society* (Maryknoll, NY, Orbis Books, 1978), pp. 128–30.

49   Notably the pastorals and 1 Peter; cf. Romans 13.1–5.

50   It should be noted, however, that the extent of the political apologetic element in Luke–Acts continues to be at the storm center of New Testament debate. See Cassidy; R. Cassidy, *Society and Politics in the Acts of the Apostles* (Maryknoll, NY, Orbis Books, 1987); D. Juel, *Luke–Acts: The Promise of History* (Atlanta, Ga., John Knox Press, 1983); J. T. Sanders, *The Jews in Luke–Acts* (Philadelphia, Pa., Fortress Press, 1987).

# 13

# The David–Bathsheba Story and the Parable of Nathan

## ARCHIE C. C. LEE

In 1996 Hong Kong will be handed over to China. At a time when the country faces political and social uncertainties, a Chinese Old Testament scholar retrieves the role of the remonstrator in the Chinese tradition, comparable to that of the prophets in Judaism, as having a significant meaning in the context of the political theology of Hong Kong. This essay is another example of going beyond the traditional literary and grammatical methods, and how resources from one's own culture can be used to unravel the meaning of the biblical texts.

This essay was published in *East Asia Journal of Theology* (3, 2, 1985). This journal is now continued under a new title, *The Asia Journal of Theology*, and published bi-annually. The address is: The Editor, *The Asia Journal of Theology*, 324 Onan Road, Singapore 1542, Republic of Singapore.

Archie Lee is with the Department of Religion, Chinese University of Hong Kong, Hong Kong.

## I INTRODUCTION

Since the Second World War, with the recent rise of nationalism and its common recognition, many colonies have gained independence and self-government and become a nation of their own. This is something to be grateful for; as this indicates the right direction of a historical trend. However, behind all these glorious historical achievements we could find many tragedies: the people of these newly formed countries, while expecting peace, stability, freedom, democracy and law and order in society, find their dreams never being realized. Their present situation may not be anything better but maybe worse than before. There are many instances of a self-rule government inhibiting people's freedom, eliminating dissents and bullying the common people. Very often we can find dictators taking the place of colonial governments. When people are being used for political purposes, the value of life is being downgraded. Even when life loses its political and economic values, its existence is being threatened.

Hong Kong is now undergoing a transition. With the initialling of a Sino-British Declaration on 26th September, 1984, Hong Kong is set to revert to China in thirteen years' time. Hong Kong will no more be a British Colony or a British Dependent Territories but a Special Administrative Region; so it will be called. Facing the inevitable but somewhat obscure changes ahead, for there has not been such precedent in history; 'Hong Kong people ruling Hong Kong' is indeed the best model for the future. To achieve maximum autonomy is only regarded as a natural expectation for Hong Kong people.

Nevertheless, Hong Kong people have yet to prepare themselves for the 'autonomy' model. With the long-time lack of political and civic education, especially the concept of democracy, Hong Kong is handicapped in designing and implementing an appropriate political and administrative structure with sufficient efficiency and accountability to the people. What adds to the uncertainty is the drafting of the Basic Law whose outcome will surely affect the future administrative model of the Government of this Special Administrative Region. In view of the necessary preparations for the future, manpower and otherwise, the education system, especially the curriculum, need to be revised with a view to enhance political and civic education.

Besides positively participating in the social and political changes, are there other roles or functions the church can take up in such a time in Hong Kong? I'm sure there is; that is the prophetic role as seen in the Hebrew tradition and the role of remonstrator ( 諫議大夫 ) in the Chinese tradition. The roles of the two are not exactly the same, but it is their difference which is most important. From the ways these persons persuaded their political leaders, they are seen to take up the very important mission in their times. This paper studies the accusations of Prophet Nathan to King David and Wei Cheng's ( 魏徵 ) persuasions to Tang Tai Tsung ( 唐太宗 ), a Tang Emperor. With the comparison of these two court histories, we can see that those in political power cannot be free from the temptation of the abuse of power. This paper also aims at examining the stories of parables to see how they can be used as tools for doing theology in an Asian context, and also how the Old Testament expresses theological thoughts through stories and parables. The text chosen is the so-called Succession Narrative (2 Sam. 9–20; 1 Kings 1–2).

## II SELF-GIVING ABUSE OF POWER

In the spring of the year, the time when kings go forth to battle, David sent Joab, and his servants with him, and all Israel; and they ravaged the Ammonites, and besieged Rabbath. But David remained at Jerusalem.

It happened, late one afternoon, when David arose from his couch and was walking upon the roof of the King's house, that he saw from the roof a woman bathing; and the woman was very beautiful. And David sent and inquired about the woman. And one said, 'Is not this Bathsheba, the daughter of Eliam, the wife of Uriah the Hittite?' So David sent messengers, and took her; and she came to him, and he lay with her. . . . And the woman conceived; and she sent and told David, 'I am with child.' (2 Sam. 11.1–5)

The episode of David and Bathsheba (2 Sam. 11.1–12.25) is inserted in the context of war between Israel and Ammonites. If the whole episode is left out, the text can still be joined together very smoothly. 2 Samuel 12.25 continues what is told at the end of Chapter 10. The story is taken from the stock of folktales, not belonging originally to the present war context.

The story begins with Israel's external warfare, 'when kings go forth to battle'. Joab, as David's loyal general, was sent together with the army to fight with the Ammonites. The narrative then makes a striking contrast: 'But David remained at Jerusalem'. It seems to convey the idea that the king is not concerned very much with the well-being of the state and the soldiers who were risking their lives to protect the national interest. As the supreme ruler, David only idled about, enjoying himself. When he was in such a state, something disastrous happened: 'David exposes himself to the temptations of idleness'.

So 'it happened, late one afternoon, when David arose from his couch and was walking upon the roof of the king's house . . .' The king got up very late one afternoon. Nothing seemed to occupy himself. Walking upon the roof he saw a beautiful woman bathing. From then on things happened fast: lust, adultery and conception. The woman was the wife of Uriah the Hittite in the army of David, the commander-in-chief.

Here we need to stop for a while to appreciate the skill of narrative art that was used by the writer. The two characters involved, David and Bathsheba, are described objectively and soberly without any indications of the inner world of the hero and the heroine: David's leisure – the woman's beauty – her being married – her having purified herself.

The impersonal side of the human desire and passion is revealed. Bathsheba was taken only as an object of sexual desire. But this does not in any way lessen her responsibility in the crime. She was an accomplice.

When David heard the news that Bathsheba conceived a child he immediately sent for Uriah. He planned to have his sin covered up by sending Uriah home to his wife. In the following verses, the narrative makes use of dialogue to bring out the point David said to Uriah, 'Go down to your house' (v. 8). It is also repeatedly reported that Uriah 'did not go down to his house' (vv. 9, 10, 10, 13). For a reason probably unknown to Uriah, David sent him a gift.

The story contrasts the moral and ethical integrity of Uriah, a foreigner, with King David. When David asked Uriah why he did not go home after a long journey, Uriah said, 'The Ark and Israel and Judah dwell in booths, and my lord Joab and the servants of my lord are camping in the open field; shall I then go to my house, to eat and to drink, and to lie with my wife?' He swore that he would not do this thing. What a loyal servant with moral superiority, self-control and a high value of self-sacrifice!

When David failed to persuade Uriah to go home, he honoured him by inviting him to the king's table with the intention of making him drunk. But still Uriah, though with excess of alcohol, slept at the door of the king's house, showing great solidarity with his fellow men.

David's plan to conceal the evil was frustrated. He therefore sent Uriah back to the battlefield with a letter telling Joab to eliminate the letter-bringer: 'Get Uriah in the forefront of the hardest fighting, and then draw back from him, that he may be struck down, and die.' This was carried out as it was commanded. Joab did not question the justice of the operation. It was not easy to limit the casualties to Uriah alone. Some of the servants of David fell along with Uriah. This might have further increased the guilt of David. Joab apparently did not do all that David commanded, to station Uriah in a place of danger and to give a secret order to abandon him. He probably did the first part.

When Joab's messenger informed David of the matter, David's response is one of encouragement and comfort: 'Do not let this matter trouble you, for the sword devours now one and now another; strengthen your attack upon the city, and overthrow it' (2 Sam. 11.25). This rationalization does not help to release the guilt of a premeditated murder. In fact, David's guilt was intensified as some soldiers lost their lives with Uriah; they became victims of his selfish plan.

If we compare the dialogues in the story, we shall come to the conclusion that 'the writer means to direct our attention to the murder rather than to the sexual transgression as the essential crime'.[1] This conclusion is arrived at by the observation of Robert Alter that, generally speaking, the narrative writer lays stress on a narrative event by rendering it mainly through dialogue. In this case, the whole report of casualties was actually put in the form of dialogue.

## III NATHAN'S REPROOF OF DAVID

And the Lord sent Nathan to David. He came to him, and said to him, 'There were two men in a certain city, the one rich and the other poor. The rich man had very many flocks and herds; but the poor man had nothing but the little ewe lamb, which he had bought. And he brought it up, and it grew up with him and with his children; it used to eat of his morsel, and drink from his cup, and lie in his bosom, and it was like a daughter to him. Now there came a traveller to the rich man, and he was unwilling to take one of his own flock or herd to prepare for the wayfarer who had come to him, but he took the poor man's lamb, and prepared it for the man who had come to him.' Then David's anger was greatly kindled against the man; and he said to Nathan, 'As the Lord lives, the man who has done this deserves to die; and he shall restore the lamb fourfold because he did this thing, and because he had no pity.'

Nathan said to David, 'You are the man . . .' (2 Sam. 12.1–7a)

Nathan's parable presents the people's case, it is a story told from the side of the poor. David listens to the case as though he is the judge attending a court hearing.

The rich man and the poor man are both from the same city. But their fortune is quite different. The story makes great contrast between them: One is extremely rich in wealth; he has very many flocks and herds; but the poor man had nothing but one little lamb. The story, however, focuses our attention on the poor man's situation. Though he is poor he lives happily. The lamb he bought and brought in from outside became very much part of the family, like a daughter to the poor man. The rich man spares his own herds and flocks and does not show mercy to spare the lamb of the poor man. He, being a man of power and wealth, exploits the poor man. Nathan in the role of a story-teller intends to arouse David to the element of the ridiculous in the parable. This is why David reacts so strongly in great anger, 'the man who has done this deserves to die . . . because he had no pity'. What an incisive parable that produces the expected result!

Nathan went on courageously to confront this royal murderer with his own crime. 'Thou art the man'. This is so simple but so precise The parable successfully leads David to pass judgment on himself. Nathan then outlined David's crime: 'Why have you despised the word of the Lord, to do what is evil in his sight? You have smitten Uriah the Hittite with the sword, and have taken his wife to be your wife, and have slain him with the sword of the Ammonites' (2 Sam. 12.9). David has done violence to humanity in his act of murder. This deed is a 'violent desecration of community'. It is the same act that violates the God–man relationship, 'You have despised Yahweh' was therefore Nathan's prophetic condemnation of David. God might have withheld the dynastic promise in 2 Samuel 7; that he did not, was because David repented of his sin (2 Sam. 12.13).

There is no clear and definite point of contact between the David–Bathsheba–Uriah episode and the Nathan parable. If the rich man is David and the poor man is Uriah, then the poor man is not killed whereas Uriah was put to death. The parable is also no analogy to adultery at all. It is used to evoke pity not only for the poor man but also for the lamb which, though bought by the poor man, was treated as an intimate member of the family, being a 'daughter' of the household. There are two verdicts David pronounced in his role as a judge; one of which is that the rich man shall restore the lamb fourfold. This verdict is derived from the understanding that the rich man has committed theft or robbery. According to the law of theft, 'if a man steals an ox or a sheep, and kills it or sells it, he shall pay five oxen for an ox, and four sheep for a sheep' (Exod. 22.1; for theft of human beings, see Exod. 21.16; Deut. 24.7). David takes on a sense of righteousness and justice based on legal tradition. But more than this, he goes beyond the legal requirement in his first verdict. He is much concerned with the poor man's rights and the rich man's lack of compassion. That is why he takes an oath in his pronouncement of the death penalty: 'As the Lord lives, the man who has done this deserves to die' (2 Sam. 12.5).

## IV MONARCHY OF SERVICE OR GOVERNMENT OF EXPLOITATION

U. Simon rightly sums up the story of David and Bathsheba in the following lines: 'The king who had ceased to go forth as the head of his men yields to the temptation of exploiting his privilege position in order to satisfy his own lust and uses the royal machinery of government to cover up his crime.'[2]

The story of David, which is brilliantly written, can be a story of any ruler or government. Government that was meant to be a service to the people becomes the oppressor and self-serving. There are guidelines and principles laid down by the prophets for the king and his government officials. Jeremiah, addressing the king of Judah and his servants, clearly puts forward God's demand: 'Do justice and righteousness, and deliver from the hand of the oppressor him who has been robbed. And do no wrong or violence to the alien, the fatherless, and the widow, nor shed innocent blood' (Jer. 22.3; cf. Ps. 72). Put alongside this prophetic understanding of the function of kingship, it is clearly shown that David, the founder of the Davidic dynasty, badly violated God's commandment. He robbed and oppressed the poor and shed innocent blood.

In Nathan's judgment oracle there are two parts which correspond to the crime of murder and adultery. 'The sword shall never depart from your house' (v. 10) and 'I will take your wives before your eyes, and give them to your neighbour' (v. 11) are contents of the judgment which find fulfilment in the following chapters of the court history in 2 Samuel 13–20 and 1 Kings 1–2. David's sons became children of adultery and violence. Personal and family matters of a king produce a great effect on national and political affairs. David committed his crime secretly, but his sons did the same openly and in greater scale and intensity.

Whether a country can make good progress, maintain economic prosperity, keep good law and order and maintain a high standard of living, actually depends on a sound political structure and also a capable and virtuous leader. In ancient Chinese and Israelite societies, the supreme monarch possessed great authority and, because of the lack of an adequate system of check and balance of power, the monarch's moral well-being became the determining factor of a country's success. In order to put restraint on imperial power whenever a crisis situation came up, a critic has to avoid risking his life but to use tactics such as talking in fables, using symbolic acts to point out the monarch's mistakes, hoping that he could understand and learn the lesson.

The Israelite prophets were also taking on such responsibility. Ahab and Jezebel, the king and queen of Israel, thought that they could do whatever they wanted; they even went so far as to take possession of Naboth's vineyard, entered into accomplice with nobles and elders in tricking Naboth, paid two gangsters to accuse Naboth in court, laid charges against him, stoned him to death, and finally took possession of his vineyard. Elijah was brave enough to point out Ahab and Jezebel's mistakes (1 Kings 21). Israelite prophets very clearly showed us that the power of the king was not absolute and not challengeable. Power comes from God. For justice and the benefit of the people, the king's mistakes should be revealed and his power challenged.

Prophet Nathan is seen as taking up the responsibility of being the loyal opposition. When discussing the role of Prophet Nathan, David Petersen said, 'He lets David trap himself as he responds to the parable which Nathan proffers. The picture is of a prophet manoeuvering with consummate strategy, speaking with the deepest possible conviction and affecting not only the personal life of the king but issues of state as well.'[3]

In Chinese tradition, the Remonstrating Counsellors ( 諫議大夫 ) also took up similar roles. They were brave enough to confront and counsel the kings, thus changing many policies. The most famous one among them was Wei Cheng ( 魏徵 ) serving Tang Tai Tsung (唐太宗) in the Tang Dynasty. The book *Essentials of Government of Chen-kuan Period Chen-kuan Cheng-yao (CKCY)* ( 貞觀政要 ) affirms the contributions of Wei Cheng's remonstrations as being the important elements in the prosperity of the Tang Dynasty. The book idealizes the Chen-kuan period in the following passage:

> Officials were all of their own accord honest and cautious in their exercise of power. The families of the nobility and ranks of the great surnames and local elites all feared (the emperor's) awesome power and restrained themselves, not daring to encroach upon the common people. Merchants travelling in the wilderness were never again robbed by bandits. The prisons were always empty. Horses and cows roamed the open country. Doors were not locked. Repeatedly there were abundant harvests and the price of grain fell to three or four cash per tou. . . . There was nothing like this since antiquity.[4]

Wei Cheng was at great pains to uphold his belief in the rights and duties of civil officials to remonstrate to the emperor, head of government. At one time when Tang Tai Tsung was angry at a memorial of a local official in Honan, charging him of over-working the people with the construction of the Loyang Palace and also levying too high taxes, Wei Cheng advised him that:

From ancient times memorials which have been presented to the throne for the most part have been provocative. If they had not been provocative, then they would not have aroused the ruler. This type of provocation resembles slander; but there is a saying that 'a sage can select even the (good) words of a madman.' Your majesty should therefore select (his good words).

Because of Wei Cheng's advice, Tai Tsung did not accuse the official of slander but rewarded him of his memorial instead. Wei Cheng always made use of the overthrow of the previous dynasty to remind Tai Tsung of the need to keep the country stable and help the people to live a peaceful life. He regarded the ruler as a boat, and the people the sea water. The water could put the boat afloat but could also overturn it. If only politics could aim at improving the livelihood of the people, helping to heal the wounds left by the past political and economic upheavals, the people would then be loyal to their country. Tai Tsung learned much from the history of Sui Dynasty ( 隋朝 ) and Wei Cheng's remonstration about the philosophy of people-based political thinking.

Tang Tai Tsung realized at the beginning of this power the inter-dependency between the state and the people:

The ruler depends on the state and the state depends on the people. Oppressing the people to make them serve the ruler is like cutting one's flesh to fill one's stomach. The stomach is filled but the body is injured, the ruler is made wealthy but the state is destroyed. Therefore, when calamity strikes the ruler it comes not from outside but always from within himself.

However, at the end of the Cheng-Kuan period, Tai Tsung was not serious about the idea of remonstrance, paying lip service to it occasionally. He did not pay much regard to etiquette either; he always abused his power for self serving purposes. At one time, he became fond of a pretty, sixteen-year-old girl who had already been betrothed. When Tai Tsung was about to order his people to fetch the girl, Wei Cheng hurriedly went to see him:

Your Majesty is the parents of the people and you love the common folk as you do your own sons. You ought to worry about what worries them and be happy about what makes them happy. Since ancient time virtuous rulers have regarded the minds of the people as their own minds. Therefore, because the ruler lives in fine palaces he wants the people to have the security of roof beams. Because he eats rich fare he wants the people to be without the miseries of hunger and cold. Because he desires imperial concubines he wants the people to know the joys of family life. This is the normal way of rulers of men. Now for a long time the daughter of the Cheng Family has been betrothed to another, yet Your Majesty is taking her in disregard of this fact. If this be broadcast throughout the empire, would it be in accord with the morality of the parents of the people?[5]

The principles of Wei Cheng's remonstrances were to remind Tai Tsung of his role and responsibilities, to be the parents of his people, to show concern for them, to 'take their heart as his own' and work for their well-being. Wei Cheng also pointed out the possible results of his act – to have lost the morality of being the parent of his people. The episode of David bears a similar trend of humanism. Those in high power should beware of their life-style. Their ethical life affects their political life. All their decisions will have consequences which they have to be accountable for. The theological concepts in the episode of David have certain characteristics which are quite different from the pure humanistic ideas found in the Chinese Confucianism.

In the next section we will discuss in detail the theological ideas in the Succession Narrative.

## V STORIES AND THEOLOGICAL ASIDES

Scholars have the idea that both the Succession Narrative and the Joseph Narrative (Gen. 37, 39–50) originated from the same period, that is, the Early Monarchy Period. At that time the new situation required a new theological understanding and a new political structure. The aim of the Joseph Narrative was to demonstrate the struggles of an ideal courtier, and what qualities were needed for a person of the lowest level of society, namely a foreign slave, to become a person of the highest position in government. The Joseph Narrative is a didactic tale; setting up a model of the wise and effective official. The Succession Narrative shows that although David committed sin and yet was willing to accept the rebuke of the prophet, admit his sin, God's promise of an everlasting dynasty still stood. What's more, Solomon, not because of his own merit but merely the grace of God, inherited from David to be the King.

The previous section has already mentioned that in the David–Bathsheba episode, David abused his power and committed murder and adultery. W. Lee Humphreys rightly observes that the story is 'a subtle discourse on power, its acquisition and retention, its use and abuse'.[6] Since David, being king, father, husband and as man before

God, committed sin, his violence and abuse of authority recoiled on his family and the state as well: David's son, Amnon, raped his own sister, Tamar; Absalom avenged and murdered Amnon and then escaped from persecution. Later, Absalom rose in rebellion, the whole country fell in civil war and David had to flee for his life.

The Succession Narrative is not a systematic theological discourse. It represents the didactic tradition in the Wisdom Literature. Its message is expressed in the form of stories; very often long passages of comment are lacking. These stories are often taken from folklore and tales of the royal court and applied by the story-tellers or literary artists to new persons and situations.

The Succession Narrative was composed in the 'Solomonic Enlightenment' of the tenth century BC. When Judah was in a transition from pansacral understanding of reality to a secular perspective, man began to realize man's freedom to make decisions; but man has to be responsible for his acts and bear full accountability of his deeds. God is not a dictator; nor is He an incompassionate observer. He watches over man with great concern as an interested party. There is divine presence in human affairs. God communicates his word to man in and through story.

This is a profound way of looking at God's story with humanity. God's providence is conceived both in His governance of the world and the free will of man. This conception is expressed by the Succession Narrative through theological asides: 'But the thing that David had done displeased the Lord' (2 Sam. 11.27b), 'And the Lord sent Nathan to David' (2 Sam. 12.1).

God seems to be hidden, but he cares. He is the ultimate force operating in history. W. Lee Humphreys makes the following comment on the theological understanding in the story, 'it develops a striking vision of the controlling action of the deity in the course of human history'. A similar idea is also expressed in the Joseph Narrative: 'The divine action occurs behind the scenes, hidden from the human actors, and it neither annuls nor excuses their actions and intentions.'[7]

G. von Rad is of the opinion that both the Joseph Narrative and the Succession Narrative were a literary product of the period of Solomonic Enlightenment when the world-view of the authors became demythologized and profoundly secular. This was the period of the tenth century BC when the Yahwist was actively composing. Von Rad says that 'a radical change had come over the conception of Yahweh's action in history; for people were beginning to see that, in addition to activity by means of miracles, a dramatic, catastrophic event, Yahweh had another quite different field in which he worked, one which was much more hidden from men's view and lay rather in their daily lives'.[8] The author of the Succession Narrative uses a secular mode of presentation of historical matters. There was no more determinism understood in traditional terms. A new understanding or a new version of God and man was fostered during this 'theological revolution'.

Man is a trusted creature who has an option as well as the ability to choose. In every situation man has to make decisions wisely and responsibly. His decision will bring life or death and affect his own destiny. That means the future being open is 'largely determined by our present decisions'. God works in history through man and man is held accountable for the consequences of his own decision and choice.

A Chinese story from Chinese classics may illustrate this point clearly. It is taken from the Book of Lieh-tze ( 列子 ), 'On the way seeing a woman gathering mulberry' ( 道見桑婦 ):

> Wen-kung of Chin discussed invading Wei with his men. One of the officials laughed during that meeting. Wen-kung was very angry: 'How dare you?'
> 'I laughed not because of the discussion here but because of what I saw this morning.'
> 'Tell me.'
> 'My neighbour sent his wife back to her father's home this morning. On the way, he saw a beautiful woman gathering mulberries and he talked seductively to her. However, when he turned around, he also found that a young man was teasing his wife at the same time. It was a very funny situation.'
> Having heard this and understood the implicit meaning of this story, Wen-kung called off his plan of invading Wei and retreated homeward. Before arriving at Chin, there was news that his northern territory was being invaded.

Man has to bear the consequences of his acts. He has to be aware that whatever evil he does, the same may be done to him in due course. In Chinese tradition, the recoiling nature of evil deeds is commonly recognized. Retribution is sure to come; it is only a matter of timing.

The idea of man being trusted with freedom and responsibility, and also rightfully be held accountable for his acts, is not the whole picture presented by the Succession Narrative. The other side of the coin is that 'in spite of our plan, there is a miscountable mystery about our experience which we cannot master or manipulate'.[9] Unexpected things often happen to us which are beyond our calculation and rationalization.

In the David–Nathan story there are also two theological asides that communicate this mystery in life:

> And the Lord struck the child that Uriah's wife bore to David, and it became sick (2 Sam. 12.15b).

> Then David comforted his wife, Bathsheba, and went in to her, and lay with her, and she bore a son, and he called his name Solomon. And the Lord loved him, and sent a message by Nathan the prophet; so he called his name Jedidiah, because of the Lord (2 Sam. 12.24–5).

From the point of view of the Succession Narrative these two comments express two ideas: first, the disapproval of God on the adultery and that the son of the adulterous union has to die. Secondly, Solomon was born to Bathsheba, David's wife, and by reason unknown to us that Yahweh loved Solomon out of his own grace. Solomon then becomes the legitimate successor to the throne of David with God's approval.

But in addition to this, an extremely radical idea of God and human life is expressed in the story itself. When the child fell sick David locked himself up seven days, fasted, mourned, lay all night upon the ground and prayed to God earnestly for the sick child (2 Sam. 12.16–18). But when he knew that the child had died, he stopped his mourning and rose to live again. What an extraordinary reaction and indeed a violation of conventional practice (2 Sam. 12.19–21).

David's reaction to the death of his child ushers in his new understanding of the reality of death and hence the meaning of life. He realizes that there is a mystery in life which man as creature can never grasp. Life has limitations in the face of great possibilities. The author expresses his profound faith in God through David's words: 'While the child was still alive, I fasted and wept; for I said, "Who knows whether the Lord will be gracious to me, that the child may live?" But now he is dead; why should I fast? Can I bring him back again? I shall go to him, but he will not return to me,' (2 Sam. 12.22–3).

This trust in the creator, accepting the givenness of life and acknowledging the mystery of reality, are the basic elements of Wisdom Literature.

> A man's mind plans his way,
>   but the Lord directs his steps (Prov. 16.9).

A man's steps are ordered by the Lord
how then can man understand his way? (Prov. 20.24.)

The horse is made ready for the day of battle,
but the victory belongs to the Lord (Prov. 21.31).

These quotations from Proverbs explain the proper way of looking at life's possibilities and limitations, hopes and frustrations. There is always the presence of an element of mystery, the recognition of which can also be found in a popular Chinese folktale, 'A Skilled Horse-rider of the Frontier Losing His Horse' ('Sai Weng Shih Ma' 塞翁失馬):

Once there lived in the frontier an old skilled horse-rider whose favourite horse ran away and disappeared. The old man's friends felt sorry for him, but he shrugged it off and said: 'Well, maybe this will bring me good luck later.'

In a few days, the horse found its way back, not alone, but with another noble horse. Friends heard of it and came to congratulate him. The old man was not overjoyed at this good fortune and said: 'Yes, I have one more noble horse in my stable, but it might also bring me bad luck. Who knows?'

The man's son loved the new horse, and rode it often. One day, he fell off the horse and broke one of his legs. Friends came to console the old man for his son's mishap.

'Well', said the old man this time, 'My son's leg will eventually heal. The accident may be a blessing in disguise.'

Soon afterwards, war broke out between the two bordering countries. All the able bodied men were drafted into the army, and most of them died at the front. But the old man's son, owing to disability, was exempted from military service.

The skilled horseman was wise enough to perceive the inevitability of happenings in life and he was able to face all these happenings without losing his serenity.

## VI CONCLUSION

From the above presentation we may draw the conclusion that story has the unlimited power to capture our imagination and invite the readers to exert their own feeling and intention. It also inspires our thinking and communicates to us theological insights. The story of David gives new theological perspectives on the understanding of God and man as well as the role of government. It expresses the idea that God trusts in man and gives man freedom to become a responsible human being. But God remains a mystery beyond man's comprehension. There is a mysterious factor in life, the great Unknown. Man has to make responsible decisions in every situation, but must always 'keep himself open to the activity of God, an activity which completely escapes all calculation'.[10]

As to the role of government, the story of David inexplicitly warns government or monarchy to serve the people rather than abusing one's power for selfish desire. When government intends to cover up mistakes, greater wrongdoings would further be committed. Being the servant or spokesman of God the prophetic church should be brave enough to risk herself to remind the government that it has the power and responsibility to maintain the well-being and prosperity for the people. One of the major fears of the people is oppressive government. This is well told by a Chinese story: 'Oppressive government is more terrible than tigers' ( 苛政猛於虎 ):

In passing by the side of Mount Thai, Confucius came on a woman who was wailing bitterly by a grave. The Master bowed forward to the cross-bar, and hastened to her; and then sent Tze-lu to question her. 'Your wailing,' said he, 'is altogether like that of one who has suffered sorrow upon sorrow.' She replied, 'It is so, formerly, my husband's father was killed here by a tiger. My husband was also killed (by another), and now my son has died in the same way.' The Master said, 'Why do you not leave the place?' The answer was 'There is no oppressive government here.' The Master then said (to the disciples), 'Remember this, my little children, oppressive government is more terrible than tigers.'

There is every possibility that even a virtuous leader or government can gradually take on an oppressive role whenever the people in high positions misuse their power and engage themselves in the pursuit of personal gains instead of the well-being of their fellow men. Facing all possibilities ahead, during this transitional period, what worries Hong Kong people most is the fear of the unknown – whether the future government of Hong Kong can provide the people with the much anticipated democratic political structure under which people can enjoy their freedom and responsibilities as they have been doing in the past; though, up to the present, this is still very unsatisfactory and limited.

In view of the forthcoming changes and in order to avoid the occurrence of any possible oppressive government, Hong Kong people have positively to prepare themselves especially in the training of political leaders and manpower for various fields. We have to recognize the importance and urgency in promoting civic education among the grassroots, which is the most basic guarantee of creating a responsible and conscientious community. And, the Church has to realize the significant contribution of her role as a prophet in this time of great changes.

## NOTES

1  R. Atler, *The Art of Biblical Narrative* (New York, Basic Books, 1981), p. 182.

2  U. Simon, 'The Poor Man's Ewe-Lamb: An Example of a Juridical Parable' *(Biblica*, 48, 1967), p. 210.

3  D. L. Petersen, *The Roles of Israel's Prophets* (Sheffield, JSOT Press, 1981), p. 31.

4  Wu Ching, *Essentials of the Government of Chen Kuan Period*, p. 24. English translation taken from H. J. Wechsler, *Mirror to the Son of Heaven, Wei Cheng at the Court of Tang Tai-tsung* (New Haven, Yale University Press, 1974), p. 104.

5  Wechsler, p. 128.

6  W. Lee Humphreys, *Crisis and Story: Introduction to the Old Testament* (Palo Alto, Mayfield, 1979), p. 80.

7  ibid., p. 88.

8  G. von Rad, *Old Testament Theology*, vol. 1 (London, SCM Press, 1965), p. 51.

9  W. Brueggemann, *In Man We Trust: The Neglected Side of Biblical Faith* (Atlanta, John Knox Press, 1972), p. 60.

10  G. von Rad, *Wisdom in Israel* (London, SCM Press, 1972), p. 101.

# 14

# The Equality of Women: Form or Substance (1 Corinthians 11.2–16)

## CHRISTINE AMJAD-ALI

This essay is one of the first examples of women's exegetical reflection from Pakistan available in English. Christine Amjad-Ali's paper is among several presented at a 'Women in Reflection and Action' group meeting held in Multan, Pakistan, in April 1989. At this ecumenical gathering, Pakistani women concerned with the situation of women both within the Church and within their country, looked together at Paul's first letter to the Corinthians, especially the section on women's head covering, to help them focus on the issue of women and culture.

For Christine Amjad-Ali's piece and for other examples of hermeneutical reflections by the women of Pakistan on the contentious relationship between gospel and culture, see *Dare to Dream: Studies on Women and Culture with Reference to 1 Corinthians 11.2–16* by 'Women in Reflection and Action' ed. Christine Amjad-Ali. This monograph is available from Christian Study Centre, P O Box 529, Rawalpindi Cantt, Pakistan.

The passage from Paul's first letter to the Corinthians, 11.2–16, is a peculiarly appropriate starting point for a discussion on women and culture for at least two reasons. First, Paul's own arguments and the situation of the Corinthian Christians, already reflect – from their own context – the seemingly impenetrable mixture of tradition, religion and culture which seem to surround any discussion of women and culture. Second, this passage itself has become part of the religious tradition which often determines the culturally acceptable roles open to Christian women.

My paper basically tries to clarify what Paul says in this passage and to draw out some possible implications both for our discussions of 'women's issues' and for our behaviour as women.

# 1 CORINTHIANS 11.2–16[1]

2 I commend you because in all things you remember me and, just as I transmitted to you, you keep the traditions.

3 And (*de*) I want you to know that the head (*kephale*) of every man (*aner*) is Christ and (*de*) the head of a woman is (the) man and (*de*) the head of Christ is God.

4 Any man who prays or prophesies having [something] down over the head (*kephales*) shames his head.

5 but (*de*) any woman who prays or prophesies with the head uncovered (*akalypto*)[2] shames her head – because it is one and the same thing as it being shaved.

6 For if a woman does not cover [herself] (*katakalypto*), let her also cut off [her hair].

7 For, on the one hand, a man ought not to cover up his head since he comes into being (*hyparchon*)[3] as the image and glory of God; but the woman, on the other hand, is the glory of man.

8 For man is not out of woman but rather woman out of man. Because also man was not created for the sake of the woman, but rather woman for the sake of the man.

9 Because of this the woman ought to have authority (*exousia*)[4] upon the head for the sake of the angels.

10 However (*plen*) neither woman is without man, nor man is without woman in the Lord.

11 Since, just as the woman [was/is] from the man, so the man [was/is] for the sake of the woman. And all things [are/were] from God.

12 Judge for yourselves: Is it fitting for an uncovered woman to pray to God?

13 Does not nature herself teach you that on the one hand if a man wears long hair it is a dishonour for him; but on the other hand, if a woman wears long hair it is a glory for her,

14 because the hair is given instead of (*anti*) a covering (*peribolaion*).

15 But if any one seems to be obstinate we have not any other custom than this, and neither do the churches of God.

## INTRODUCTION

This passage in Paul is extremely difficult to understand for at least three reasons. First, the language is obscure. Paul uses at least five different ways of speaking about the head covering. In verse 4, in referring to men, he speaks in a roundabout way of something 'falling down over' the head. In verse 5, he talks of women who are 'uncovered' (*akalypto*), and verse 6, 'covered' (*kalyptra*), using slightly different words, both of which are related to the usual word for a woman's veil (*kalyptra*), but he never actually uses this term. In verse 9, he speaks of a woman having 'authority on the head', which presumably refers, in a symbolic way, to a head covering, but this is not the usual expression, and was probably coined by Paul. In verse 14, Paul speaks of a woman's hair acting as, or replacing, a covering (*peribolaion*), a very general term that could refer to any encircling material such as, for example, a fence (or a turban?). Verse 14 is very strange, in fact, because it seems almost to contradict what Paul has previously said. If a woman's hair is given as a covering, why does she need to cover (veil) her covering (hair)?

Second, it is not at all clear why Paul brings up the subject at all. What was going on in Corinth? A number of issues in 1 Corinthians are addressed by Paul in response to questions from the Corinthians; they are marked by the introductory phrase 'now concerning such and such' (e.g. 1 Corinthians 8.1, 'Now concerning food offered to idols . . .'). But 1 Corinthians 11.2–16 is not of these sections. The Corinthians did not address any question to Paul concerning the proper dress for women; Paul himself brought the issue up. Nor is it clear what was happening in Corinth that Paul objected to. Some commentators[5] have argued that Paul is not interested in *head coverings*, but rather *hair styles*. He objects to men and women having long unbound hair in worship. It is further suggested that the Corinthians adopted this hair style to show that they were Spirit-inspired prophets, who spoke in an ecstatic frenzy, in imitation of the devotees of pagan mystery cults. Paul, on this hypothesis, wants men to keep their hair short and women to keep theirs bound up. However, there is no evidence in 1 Corinthians 11 that this is the problem. Paul does not suggest the Corinthians are in danger of being mistaken for pagan initiates (contrast, for example, his discussion of eating sacrificed meat, where Paul is quite open about the possibility of the Christian being drawn into idol worship, or 'weaker' Christians thinking that this is what is happening). And while 'binding up the hair' could be what is referred to in two of Paul's references (v. 4 and v. 14), two of the other three clearly speak of 'covering' (the *kalypt* – root means 'covered' or 'hidden'; *apocalypse* is from the same root and means 'revealed' or 'un-covered'). Also, having 'authority on the head' suggests putting something on the head, not just binding up the hair.

Other commentators[6] suggest that the Corinthian women led worship with their head uncovered as a deliberate way of asserting their equality to men. Paul objected to this practice not because it affirmed women's equality with men (which Paul accepted), but because it obliterated the sexual distinctions between women and men (which Paul considered basic to human personality). That women led worship in Corinth with their heads uncovered does seem to me to be the point at issue. But I am doubtful that there was a specific, theological, conscious rationale behind this practice. Paul gives theological (and other) reasons for the counter-practice he wants to introduce, but he does not explicitly combat any alternative theology. Again, it is instructive to compare his discussion of eating food offered to idols. Here Paul clearly engages the Corinthian theological justification, that is, that 'all things are lawful' and 'idols have no real existence' (see 10.23, 8.4).

Thirdly, this passage is difficult to follow because we are not at all sure of what the customs of head covering generally were. High-class urban women seem to have worn elaborate hair styles, with the hair piled on top of the head and held there with pins, decorated with jewels and perhaps veils of some sort. Lower-class and working women, however, cannot have worn such styles, which were impractical except for the leisured class. One guesses that lower-class women probably plaited their hair, and perhaps wrapped the plait round the head. There is, however, no way of knowing – poor women are not the subjects of sculptures or paintings. Did urban women of any class cover their heads when they were out in public? One does not know. Urban men (especially those influenced by Rome) went short-haired and clean shaven. Greek and Roman men do not seem to have used head coverings. But Greek urban culture is not the only culture at issue. There is the question of Jewish practices, both the Jewish community in Palestine and the Jewish communities in the Greek cities. It is probable that Jewish practice allowed women less freedom than was customary in the Greek cities. Philo and Josephus (two famous Jewish writers from this period) both speak of the ideal situation as that where women are enclosed in the inner house and see no one but their immediate relatives. Again this may well be a class-specific ideal. As in Pakistan, *purdah* (veil) is the ideal mostly for the urban lower middle class – it is impractical for lower-class women who have to work, and it is often rejected by upper class women whose wealth allows them a greater freedom. It may also have been an urban phenomenon. However, the gospel stories, largely set in the country-side, suggest a greater interaction between men and women.

The question of Jewish male head coverings is even more interest-ing. Jewish practice now – like Muslim practice – is that men *should cover* their heads while praying. There is no reason at all to think this is a recent innovation. Further, long hair has not normally been con-sidered shameful in Jewish tradition (think of Samson), and one guesses that among Palestinian Jews – as among most eastern groups – men normally wore a head covering, for protection from the sun if for no other reason. Thus when Paul appeals to nature and custom, one has to ask which custom he is appealing to.

To sum up, not only is it difficult to work out what Paul is saying, we are not at all sure why he is saying it, what is going on at Corinth, and what the customary practices are. Nevertheless, this passage is very important because it has been used (and is still used) to supply a norm for both male and female dress in worship, and, because the way Paul argues, seems to be paradigmatic for the way 'women's questions' are discussed in the church.

## PAUL'S ARGUMENT

### 1 What he does not say

Before analysing what Paul says it is very important to see what he does not say, and to avoid reading things into the passage that are not there. In this passage Paul clearly assumes that women will lead in worship just as men lead in worship. He is not saying that women should not lead worship, only regulating what they should wear. This is important. In our Christian culture women are in the habit of covering their heads whenever someone (else) reads from the Bible, prays or preaches, and this is often justified on the basis of 1 Corinthians 11. Paul, however, is talking about what a women should do when *she* reads the scriptures, prays or preaches. He uses exactly the same words about men's activity as about women's ('if a man prays or prophesies . . . ; if a woman prays or prophesies . . .'). There are passages in the New Testament that say women should not lead in church, but *this passage takes for granted that women will lead worship services.*

### 2 The argument from religious tradition

Paul begins and ends his discussion with a reference to 'the traditions'

(v. 2) and Christian traditional practices (what the other Churches do, v. 16). He wants the Corinthians to follow his teaching in this matter because it is 'traditional'. The question is 'whose tradition?'

Head covering of women probably follows Jewish practice, and it may or may not match certain areas of Greek culture. It certainly goes against the Corinthian Church's local practice. (It is worth asking how Paul knew of the practice, in any case. My guess is some of the more conservative – perhaps Jewish – members complained privately. Again it may be that the Corinthian practice offended middle-class sensibilities.) Paul wishes to introduce Jewish culture for women and Greek culture for men, but he baptizes both in the name of religious tradition.

## 3 The argument from creation (vv. 3–12)

The theological justification for the practice Paul wants to introduce at Corinth comes from a hierarchical reading of the creation story found in Genesis 2. It is significant, in the first place, that Paul uses the Genesis 2 creation story. The Genesis 1 story speaks of the equality in creation of men and women ('God created man in his own image, male and female he created them'), and would not have served Paul's purpose here. The fact that Paul starts from Genesis 2 shows that Paul is justifying his practice through scripture – scripture is not the cause of his practice. In the Genesis 2 story God first creates the male (thus God is the 'source' or 'head'[7] of the man) who is thus the image and glory of God. The woman, however, 'comes out of' the man – being created from his rib. Thus her source is the man, and she is his glory. (Interestingly, Paul does not use the word 'image' in reference to women, perhaps because Genesis 1 clearly states that woman as well as man is the image of God. Paul cannot contradict this so he simply ignores it.)

This reading of Genesis 2 is first given by Paul in the hierarchical summary of verse 3. The implications are drawn, equally for men and women, in verses 4 and 5. (Why – even granting Paul's premise that a woman's head is the man – it should shame her head to be uncovered, I do not know. Nor do I know why it shames the man's head to be covered.) It is clear, however, that Paul is not equally concerned about men's and women's behaviour, since he rather irrelevantly brings in the question of women shaving their heads. What he seems to be saying is that women who do not cover their heads are no better than prostitutes.

From Genesis 2, Paul argues that women are not the same as men, they are subordinate to men, and therefore when they exercise leadership within the church they ought to show that they acknowledge this God-created differentiation by 'having authority on the head' (v. 10). Having 'authority on the head' is therefore either a symbol that, despite the God-given order of creation, within the Church women have a legitimate leadership role; or a symbol that, despite the fact they exercise leadership, women recognize their God-given subordination. They must do this also for the sake of the angels. Again this phrase is far from clear. It could mean that women should take care that the angels – who are the guardians of proper order – are not offended. Or it could be a reference to a Jewish tradition that blamed the fall on the mating of the angels (the sons of God) with the daughters of men (cf. Gen. 6.1 and 6.2). The women in this view must cover their heads so as not to tempt the angels to sin.

Finally, Paul draws back a little from the subordination he has been teaching. In verses 11 and 12 he argues that 'in the Lord', that is, in the Church, or the New Creation, women are not subordinate to men. Women and men are interdependent. However, in my view, the damage has already been done. Paul has argued that women are subordinate to men *from creation*. If he had argued that women's subordination was a result of the fall, then to say that women and men are equal in Christ, would be to affirm the restoration of God's creation which Christ's ministry effects. But Paul does not do this. He acknowledges the functional equality of men and women 'in the Lord', in terms of leading worship, but he also acknowledges the validity of traditional beliefs about the subordination of women, and justifies these beliefs theologically through an interpretation of Scripture. He, therefore, allows women to *function* as the equals of men, but even as they are doing this he wants them to *symbolically acknowledge* that they are in fact subordinate to men. Women may break the cultural stereotypes by being leaders in the Church, but they must not break the forms and symbols which give shape to these stereotypes.

## 4 The argument from 'nature'

Paul finally appeals to the Corinthian's own sense of what is 'natural' or proper. As always, in practice what is 'natural' is culturally defined, although the assumption is usually that it is a universal value. The question is again, which culture? There is nothing 'naturally' either good or bad about covering the head in worship. The problem with Paul's whole argument is that he has reified a cultural practice.

## IMPLICATIONS FOR OUR OWN CONTEXT

It seems to me that what Paul does in 1 Corinthians 11 is rather similar to what Benazir Bhutto does [in 1989]. The Prime Minister *functionally* disregards the traditional, cultural and religious understanding of the subordination of women, which is current in Pakistan, and is the leader of the country. On the other hand, in an effort to avoid criticism from conservative quarters, she *symbolically* acknowledges and validates the traditional view that women are subordinate. This is seen, for example, in her very visible deference to the dress code; she dresses far more conservatively than most women of her class – for example, Begum Nusrat Bhutto. The question is how long one can keep the symbols while transforming the substance. Jesus said that one cannot put new wine in old wine skins, because the wine will break the skins and *both* skins and wine will be lost. My fear is that the skins will remain, but the wine will go stale.

This is certainly what happened in the case of women's leadership in the Pauline churches. Paul acknowledged the equality of men and women 'in the Lord', but he wanted to preserve the cultural symbols of deference and subordination, presumably in order not to give offence. Within a few years, however, the theological argument from creation, which Paul used to enforce the covering of women's heads when they led in worship, had became the justification for shutting women out of all leadership roles. Women were to keep silent in church. Women could not teach or have authority over men. Women must be submissive to their husbands, calling them 'lord'.

My questions about women's dress in Pakistan – especially in the context of the Church – is what is the dress meant to symbolize? If it is simply a cultural expression of reverence for the holy, why don't our men also cover their heads (which would be culturally appropriate also). My fear, however, is that we are not just following Pakistani culture, we are also following western missionary culture, and that we cover our heads for the reasons Paul gave: to acknowledge our acceptance of our cultural position of subordination.

In my view, we cannot hope to manifest the *substance* of what it means to say we – as women – are created in God's image if we hold on to the *forms* which symbolize the belief that we are created as secondary beings, for the glory of man, and not in the image of God. The task for us is to find those forms which will express our human identity in ways which are culturally appropriate.

## NOTES

1    I have given below my own translation of this passage from the original Greek in order to bring out fully the problematic issues of this passage. I have therefore given the original Greek in parentheses in order to clarify the issues.

2    *Akalypto* means 'uncovered'; it is closely connected with *kalyptra* which means 'woman's veil' – or, more exactly, 'head covering'.

3    This is a slight overtranslation; *hyparchon* can simply mean 'is', but it is not the usual word for 'is'. Presumably Paul used it because it does have overtones of origination.

4    The word in Greek (*exousia*) means 'authority'; it is not an idiomatic expression for 'veil'. Presumably Paul means something like 'the woman ought to have a symbol of authority [i.e. a head covering] upon the head'.

5    Notably E. Schüssler Fiorenza, *In Memory of Her* (New York, Crossroad, 1983), p. 227.

6    See, for example, R. Scroggs, 'Paul and the Eschatological Women' (*Journal of the American Academy of Religion*, 41, 1972), pp. 283–303.

7    In Greek, 'head' can have the metaphorical meaning 'source' – as in 'the head of a river', but not the meaning 'ruler', which it has, for example, in English. However, concepts of origin can also lead to concepts of subordination.

# 15

# A Solomonic Model of Peace

## HELEN R. GRAHAM

This essay is an example of the use of socio-economic analysis to understand the biblical past in order to analyse the present. The Solomonic era is taken as a case study to illuminate the contemporary Filipino social, economic and political situation.

This piece appeared in R. Battung *et al.* (eds), *Religion and Society: Towards a Theology of Struggle Book I* (Manila, Forum for Interdisciplinary Endeavors and Studies (FIDES), 1988).

Helen R. Graham is Professor of Scriptures at Loyola School of Theology and Centre for Study of Religion and Culture, Ozamis City, Philippines.

---

The Hebrew word *shalom* is not easily translated into English; its meaning is broader and more complex than the English word 'peace.' *Shalom*, at root, means 'well-being' with a strong material emphasis. In many instances, *shalom* signifies bodily health and the related satisfactions. More commonly, *shalom* is referred to a collective; for example, a people enjoying prosperity.[1]

In a number of biblical passages, shalom describes a relationship rather than a state of being. We read for example that 'there was peace between Israel and the Amorites' (1 Sam. 7.14b) in the days of Samuel. And in the days of Solomon, there was also 'peace between Hiram and Solomon' (1 Kings 5.12). Linguistically, these statements are exactly the same with the exception of the proper nouns. But when these texts are taken in their socio-historical contexts, they convey two entirely different situations.

In the first case, the term 'Amorite' refers to the indigenous population of the Canaanite plains who had been in continual conflict with the proto-Israelites for approximately 200 years (1250–1050 BC). That there should suddenly be peace between these enemies requires an explanation that goes beyond merely a change of heart or reconciliation of differences.

A more penetrating analysis of the text shows that at this time, the Philistines, who had settled on the southwestern coast of Palestine, had gained considerable political and economic control from the major Canaanite cities in the great valleys. As a result, there was an appreciable decline in the prosperity of the Canaanite cities.

In addition, the Philistines' advanced military technology posed an immediate threat to the Israelite tribal groups that had settled in the southern and central Canaanite highlands.

The threat from the Philistines served as an impetus for 'peace' (i.e. a temporary truce) between the rival Israelites and the Canaanite kings. As Norman Gottwald notes: 'those who have a common enemy have common interests even if they maintain other very different and opposed interests as well. Canaanite city-states would have been indirect beneficiaries of Israelite successes in resisting or driving back the Philistines.'[2]

A convergence of anti-Philistine interests temporarily united Canaanites and Israelites against a common enemy. It was a pragmatic arrangement.

In the second case, we are told 'there was peace between Hiram (king of Tyre) and Solomon (king of Jerusalem)' such that 'the two made a covenant' (1 Kings 5.12). The covenant between Hiram and Solomon established mutually beneficial trade arrangements: 'Hiram supplied Solomon with all the timber of cedar and cypress that he desired, while Solomon gave Hiram 20,000 cors of wheat as food for his household, and 20,000 cors of beaten oil. Solomon gave this to Hiram year by year' (1 Kings 5.10–11, RSV).

It is to the analysis of the socio-historical context and implications of this 'peaceful' relationship that we now turn.

## THE SOCIO-HISTORICAL CONTEXT OF THE SOLOMONIC PEACE

The Israel of Solomon's time was on its way to becoming an advanced agrarian state. The 'peace between Hiram and Solomon' must be seen against this background.

The stage had been set for the rise of the Israelite monarchy by a combination of political and economic factors. Pre-monarchic Israel's egalitarian experiment in the hill country of Canaan was partially facilitated by a political power vacuum created by the general decline of the eastern Mediterranean monarchies.

In addition, a combination of technological innovations made it possible for a denser population to inhabit the hill country.[3] The important innovation of rock terracing made it possible to retain the thin soils and the vital seasonal rains of the highland ridge. The increased use of slaked lime plaster for water-proofing cisterns and possibly the introduction of reservoirs and small-scale irrigation works provided additional assistance.

The major development factor, however, appears to be the availability of iron tools which started with the decline of the Hittite Empire (1200 BC) and the consequent breaking of the Hittite monopoly of smelting techniques. Iron tools made it possible to clear and cultivate the hill country and to hew out many new cisterns that resulted in the large-scale increase in wheat and barley production in the highlands, previously possible only in the Canaanite plains.[4]

Increased grain production, however, gave the Philistines an incentive to conquer the highland ridge. Both incentive and means had been unavailable to the Canaanite kings of the plains. With superior weapons and military tactics, the Philistines attacked.

Israel's loosely organized tribal militia proved inadequate to defend the land from the Philistines (see 1 Sam. 23.1–5). The ensuing crisis led David to forge a monarchic state (2 Sam. 2.1–4; 5.1–5).

After a bitter dynastic fight (1 Kings 1–2), Solomon succeeded David to the throne and, using an iron fist, stabilized his control over Judah. Solomon also launched an ambitious program calculated to increase his kingdom's wealth.

He tightened his administration by subdividing his kingdom into twelve districts with officials appointed in each (1 Kings 4.1–19). Like the Europeans who carved up Africa in 1884, Solomon deliberately disregarded tribal boundaries to weaken tribal loyalties (1 Kings 4.7–19). Each district was obliged to furnish provisions for the court for one month (1 Kings 4.27).

> Solomon's provision for one day was 30 cors of fine flour and 60 cors of meal, 10 fat oxen and 20 pastured cattle, a hundred sheep, besides harts, gazelles, roebucks, and fatted fowl. For he had dominion over all the region west of the Euphrates; and he had peace on all sides around about him. And Judah and Israel dwelt in safety, from Dan even to Beersheba, every man under his vine and under his fig tree, all the days of Solomon. Solomon also

had 40,000 stalls of horses for his chariots, and 12,000 horsemen. And those officers supplied provisions for King Solomon, and for all who came to King Solomon's table, each one in his month; they let nothing be lacking. Barley also and straw for the horses and swift steeds they brought to the place where it was required, each according to his charge (see 1 Kings 4.22–8, 5.3–8.)

Agricultural surpluses, supplemented by income from trade, tolls and crafty commercial deals provided Solomon with his basic resources. To secure his growing economic empire, he engaged in huge building projects using the cedar and cyprus from Hiram – and forced labor.

Under Solomon, the levy of forced labor became a fully developed institution. A special minister for forced labor was appointed among the royal officials (1 Kings 4.6) and superintendents over the levies conscripted from the administrative districts (1 Kings 11.28, 4.7–19). Although it seems that much of the forced labor was conscripted from subject nations, it is certain that Israelites were also conscripted. According to the biblical text, Solomon's building projects involved some 30,000 men in 'a levy of forced labor' plus 70,000 burden-bearers and 80,000 hewers of stone in the hill country (1 Kings 5.13–15, RSV).

He secured his territory by fortifying and militarizing key cities: Jerusalem, Hazor, Megiddo, Gezer, Beth-horan, Baalath and Tamar (1 Kings 9.15–19). In Jerusalem, he built a temple of Tyrian-style architecture and a palace complex that took some thirteen years to complete (1 Kings 6–7). Solomon's program of forced economic development resulted in contradictory policies that weakened the empire. Gottwald describes these clashing positions:

> In order to create a privileged upper class of economic non-producers, he had to draw on expanding agricultural and commercial surpluses. He could only gather such forced wealth if he had a strong military establishment, which was itself exorbitantly costly, so that his resources were spread thinner and thinner. In order to build, Solomon needed timber and metals from abroad, for which he had mainly agricultural products to offer. In effect, the king commanded the laboring people to do tasks that contradicted one another: Stay on the land and produce more crops for export! Leave the land and serve in the army and build the cities![5]

The passage from the Davidic to the Solomonic administration was marked by a dramatic shift in the basic strategic concept of the national security forces.[6] While David's army was constructed around a small but highly mobile force of professional heavy infantry, Solomon's force included regular combat infantry as well as an elite personal foot guard of mercenaries, plus the chariot corps. (Although 1 Kings 4.26 places at 40,000 the number of stalls for the horses and 12,000 horsemen, 2 Chronicles 9.25 gives a more probable estimate of 4,000.)

Along with the chariot, which came to the fore during Solomon's time, elaborately fortified stronghold cities proliferated. The lowland fortress-cities such as Hazor, Meggido and Gezer were especially suitable for the deployment of chariots.

Hauer notes:

> The economic impact of the Solomic security establishment was heavy indeed. Some of its costs, such as the major fortifications, were one-time expenditures that would not have to be repeated for a long time, barring disaster.... The costs of Solomon's security establishment in its various aspects must have made a significant contribution to the exactions which contributed to disaffection and rebellion at his death.[7]

The style of Solomon's security establishment could be termed 'imperial.' Hauer describes it as 'grand in style and . . . was based on the great fortress cities that had once been subject to Thutmose III and Rameses II. In this way, if none other, Solomon was . . . an Israelite pharaoh.'[8]

## THE EFFECTS OF THE SOLOMONIC PEACE

The 'peace' between Hiram, king of Tyre, and Solomon, king of Israel, was maintained at great cost to the peasant population.

Angered by Solomon's taxation and corvee policies, the people arose in open revolt led by Jeroboam, to whom Solomon himself gave 'charge of all the forced labor in the house of Joseph' (1 Kings 11.29). (Eventually, the revolt of the northern tribes divided the monarchy. An independent northern Israel was subsequently created with Jeroboam as its first king.)

Clearly Solomon was successful in securing a luxuried and privileged life for a small upper class in government and trade. Economic advantage to the common people was marginal at best. Over the years, whatever improvements in productivity occurred were vulnerable to siphoning off for the benefit of the already-bloated rich. Insofar as this familiar model of the hierarchic city-state was totally contrary to the simplicities of previous Israelite social organization, it fueled intense resentment and grievance, and eroded the morale of the people. The overextended and unevenly 'modernized' Solomonic economy left the gaudy empire vulnerable to an eventual conqueror or, as proved first to be the case, to the rebellion of his own subjects.[9]

The numerous commercial ventures that brought great wealth to the state (1 Kings 9.26–8, 10.1–10, 28f), the ambitious building projects carried on in Jerusalem, along with the building and fortifying of key cities to secure the Solomonic state militarily, placed heavy economic and social burdens on the Israelite peasantry who were taxed and subjected to forced labor. The warning issued by the prophet Samuel to Israel's elders who had come to ask for a king who would govern them 'like all the nations' (1 Sam. 8.5), seems pertinent. Samuel said:

> These will be the ways of the king who will reign over you: he will take your sons and appoint them to his chariots and to be his horsemen, and to run before his chariots; and he will appoint for himself commanders of thousands and commanders of fifties, and some to plough his ground and to reap his harvest, and to make his implements of war and the equipment of his chariots. He will take your daughters to be perfumers and cooks and bakers. He will take the best of your fields and vineyards and olive orchards and give them to his servants. He will take the tenth of your grain and of your vineyards and give it to his officers and to his servants. He will take your menservants and maidservants, and the best of your cattle and your asses, and put them to his work. He will take the tenth of your flocks, and you shall be his slaves (1 Sam. 8.11–17).

For a people with a tradition of a successful struggle against slavery, the final summary statement – 'and you shall be his slaves' – was especially poignant. The fierce oppression of the advanced agrarian monarchic state eventually gave birth to the prophetic protest. One early record of such prophetic protest and critique is contained in the cycle of stories associated with the prophets Elijah and Elisha in the northern kingdom (1 Kings 17, 2 Kings 10), followed in the next century by Amos and Hosea. The prophetic protest continued in southern Judah with the strong words of Micah and Isaiah against the ruling elite of Jerusalem in the eighth century, and in the seventh century, we have the prophetic voices of Habbakuk and Jeremiah. The situation of injustice that resulted from the Solomonic-type 'peace' during the period of monarchic rule was termed 'violence' by the prophet Habakkuk in a complaint about the injustices in Judah:

> O Lord, how long shall I cry for help
> and you will not hear?
> Or cry to you 'Violence!'
> and you will not save?
> Why do you make me see wrongs
> and look upon trouble?
> Destruction and violence are before me;
> strife and contention arise.
> So the law is slacked
> and justice never goes forth.
> For the wicked surround the righteous,
> so justice goes forth perverted (1.2–4).

## SOLOMONIC PEACE – A MODEL OF STRUCTURAL VIOLENCE

In the language of contemporary peace research, the so-called Solomonic model of 'peace' is in reality a model of structural violence. If, with Norwegian peace researcher Johan Galtung, we define violence as 'any avoidable impediment to self-realization,' we may understand structural violence as, basically, an inter-relationship of dominance between two actors such that the net benefits or losses resulting from interactions between the two are inequitably distributed or shared. Where the actors are societies, an interaction relationship results in which the dominated are structurally impeded from realizing political, social, economic and cultural autonomy and growth.

In Solomonic Israel, the military–bureaucratic complex made it possible for a small elite to dominate and benefit with gross inequity, arising from interaction with the Israelite peasants and small artisans. The most significant characteristic of advanced agrarian societies of antiquity was the extreme social cleavage between the two main classes, the ruling elite and the peasantry. While there may have been 'peace' between Hiram and Solomon, there surely was anything but 'peace,' in the sense of *shalom*, for the peasantry.

The prophets of the pre-exilic period of the monarchy had already seen that the structures of interaction between the ruling elites of Samaria (the capital of northern Israel) and Jerusalem (the capital of southern Judah), and the vast majority of the common people who were peasants, was an interaction of violence. This is how the strongly worded, but seldom cited, oracle of the eighth-century prophet Micah describes it:

> And I said:
> 'Hear, you heads of Jacob
> and rulers of the house of Israel!
> Is it not for you to know justice? –
> you who hate the good and love the evil,
> who tear the skin from off my people,
> and their flesh from off their bones;
> who eat the flesh of my people
> and flay their skin from off them,
> and break their bones in pieces,
> and chop them up like meat in kettle,
> like flesh in a cauldron' (3.1–3).

Although less graphic, a similar sentiment is expressed by Isaiah of Jerusalem at the conclusion of the Song of the Vineyard (5.1–7):

> For the vineyard of the Lord of hosts
> is the house of Israel,
> and the men of Judah are his pleasant planting;
> and he looked for justice,
> but behold, bloodshed;
> for righteousness,
> but behold, a cry! (v. 7.)

The great prophets of the biblical period did not possess the refinements of contemporary social science methodology to engage in a structural analysis of their social situation. Nevertheless, based on the strongly egalitarian values inherited from early Yahwism to which they tenaciously adhered, the prophets judged the ruling elites of Samaria and Jerusalem. At a point of high prosperity in northern Israel, the prophet Amos announced:

> Thus says the Lord:
> 'For three transgressions of Israel and for four,
> I will not revoke the punishment;
> because they sell the righteous for silver,
> and the needy for a pair of sandals –
> they that trample the head of the poor into the dust of the earth,
> and turn aside the way of the afflicted (2.6–7a).

Likewise, against the ruling class of Jerusalem, Isaiah of Jerusalem lists seven woes (5.8–24 and 10.1–4) from which we draw the following example:

> Woe to those who decree iniquitous decrees,
> and the writers who keep writing oppression,
> To turn aside the needy from justice
> and to rob the poor of my people of their right,
> That widows may be their spoil,
> and that they may make the fatherless their prey,
> What will you do on the day of punishment,
> In the storm which will come from afar?
> To whom will you flee for help.
> and where will you leave your wealth?
> Nothing remains but to crouch among the prisoners
> or fall among the slain.
> For all this his anger is not turned away
> and his hand is stretched out still (10.1–4).

Thus were the prophets of Israel involved in the struggle for genuine *shalom* for the vast majority of the populations of Israel and Judah. The burden of the message of the great pre-exilic prophets was one of judgment, condemnation and destruction.

Since mutually beneficial trade arrangements such as those that existed between Hiram, king of Tyre, and Solomon, king of Israel, did not bring peace for the common people, such inequitable arrangements must, by the logic of Yahwistic religious faith, be destroyed. The interplay of destruction and construction is well articulated in the narrative of the prophet Jeremiah who seemed to know intuitively that the structure of peace could only be built when the structure of violence had been dismantled. He quotes Yahweh:

> See, I have set you this day
> over nations and over kingdoms
> to pluck up and to break down
> to destroy and to overthrow
> to build and to plant (1.10).

## SOLOMONIC PEACE – A CONTEMPORARY
## REFLECTION

As we have seen, the covenant of peace between Hiram and Solomon involved mutually beneficial bilateral trade relations resulting in severe oppression of the rural population of Israel.

Our brief study of the Solomonic model of peace, which we have described as a model of structural violence, leads us to reflect on our own situation. The world of Solomon was one in which technology, coupled with other innovations, contributed to the emergence of an advanced agrarian society in the ancient Near East. Characteristic of advanced agrarian societies is extreme social cleavage between the ruling elite and the peasantry. The primary means of subsistence is agriculture based on the use of the metal tipped plow, with tools and weapons made out of iron.[10]

The world in which the Filipino people struggle for life and that which is necessary to sustain and promote life is a world in which some nations have experienced an industrial revolution and currently enjoy its material benefits. In the context of the contemporary world, the Philippines is categorized as a hybrid, that is, as an industrializing agrarian society to which macro-sociologists assign certain typical characteristics:

1 a bewildering mixture of ancient and modern in terms of technology and productivity;

2 high birth rates coupled with a reduced death rate which strongly correlates with low rates of economic progress;

3 a dual economy comprising a traditional component and a modernizing sector;

4 a class structure much like that of agrarian societies of the past, though influenced by industrialization;

5 a governing class that is one of the greatest hindrances to change, which they fear and fight or exploit for their own private ends;

6 a society beset by a number of cleavages and conflicts.

Perhaps a major characteristic of the Philippines is its relationship with the United States, a bond celebrated on July 4th as 'Fil-Am Friendship Day.' When one examines the friendship (*shalom*) between the United States and the Philippines, it is clear that the interaction is inequitable or exploitative. It is a dominance–dependency relationship which political science refers to as 'imperialism.' Imperialism, as

Galtung points out, presupposes two collectivities. It is a type of relationship where one society dominates another. Imperialism, according to Galtung, is a general structure that may be filled with concrete economic, political, military, social, cultural and communicative content.[11]

The vertical interaction of this dominance system is the 'major source of the inequality of this world' and therefore of the world's peacelessness. Three mechanisms foster and maintain imperialism: (1) penetration, which is the opposite of autonomy, through which the Center penetrates 'under the skin' of the Periphery (2) fragmentation, the opposite of solidarity, the basic mechanism of which is separation, and (3) marginalization, which is the denial of the periphery of participation in decision-making.[12]

In short, Galtung concludes that imperialism is 'so paralyzing, so alienating a system' that it must be demolished before any serious development can take place.[13] Imperialism is anti-development and thus as long as it is in place, genuine peace is not possible.

As with the mutually beneficial bilateral trade relationship between Hiram and Solomon, the dominance–dependency relationship existing between the United States and the Philippines results in severe oppression and repression of the majority of Filipinos – those who labor in the fields, fish in the seas, work in the factories, etc.

Centuries of colonialism and economic dependency have left their mark on the Philippines. In a speech, Economic Planning Secretary Solita Collas-Monsod described the legacy of the Marcos regime as one 'that cannot begin to be described by mere statistics. An economy that had contracted by more than ten percent in real terms; per capita income levels that had fallen by 15 percent to levels of ten years previous, industry operating at less than half of capacity, and 59 percent of families with income below poverty levels, up from 49 percent in 1972' (*The Manila Chronicle*, September 28th, 1987).

But, for more than a decade, Marcos was kept in power by the United States government because Marcos was, in the words of Daniel Boone Schirmer, 'the best guarantor of the Philippine status quo' of cheap labor for US transnationals and military installations for the Pentagon.[14]

The Marcos legacy is, in a very real sense, the legacy of the dominance–dependency relationship between the USA and the Philippines.

Corazon C. Aquino became President after the February 1986

'People Power Revolution,' with a firm resolve to meet the Marcos legacy head-on. After some eighteen months in office, it is clear that she is succumbing to pressure to maintain the status quo. US military aid to the Philippines reached $104.7 million in 1986, more than double of that of 1985.

The Reagan administration has recently requested Congress for $112 million for 1987. The woman of peace who called for a ceasefire and peace negotiations with the National Democratic Front and the Moro National Liberation Front has 'unsheathed the sword of war,' saying that 'the answer to the terrorism of the Left and the Right . . . is not social and economic reform but police and military action.'

Meanwhile, a series of failed military coups has successfully brought about changes desired by the military. As columnist Renato Constantino wryly puts it, 'overt coups do not have to succeed to attain their objective' (*Malaya*, September 14th, 1987).

Boone Schirmer notes: 'the Philippine military has been the chief conduit of Washington's pressure on President Aquino'.[15]

Pressure from the Philippine military on President Aquino has taken the form of a squeeze play. Aquino has been caught in the middle of pressures coming from the various factions of the Philippine military.

It is undeniable that the US government has had access to one side of this squeeze play, that of Ramos and his military followers. It appears that the Reagan administration, through its overt unofficial body of operatives revealed in the Iran–Contra scandal, has connections as well with the other side, that of Enrile and the Marcos loyalists.[16]

The result of this double relationship with the two main factions of the Philippine military is the gradual sliding of President Aquino into the role designed for her by the US government (ibid.).

In short, the dominance–dependency interaction between Washington and Manila acts as an avoidable impediment to the self-realization of the Filipino people. It is therefore an incidence of structural violence that must be fought and eliminated if the Filipino people are to develop economically, socially, politically and culturally.

The 'peace' between Washington and Manila can only be described as a 'Solomonic peace,' that is, a situation of structural violence!

## NOTES

1   G. von Rad, *Old Testament Theology*, vol. II (Philadelphia, Westminster Press, 1968), pp. 402 f.

2   N. K. Gottwald, *The Tribes of Yahweh: A Sociology of the Religion of Liberated Israel, 1250–1050 BCE* (Maryknoll, NY, Orbis Books, 1979), p. 418.

3   ibid., pp. 655–63, and also M. L. Chaney, 'Ancient Palestinian Peasant Movements and the Formation of Premonarchic Israel' in D. N. Freedman and D. F. Graf (eds), *Palestine in Transition: The Emergence of Ancient Israel* (Sheffield, Almond Press, 1983), pp. 49–51.

4   Gottwald, p. 657.

5   N. K. Gottwald, *The Hebrew Bible: A Socio-Literary Introduction* (Philadelphia, Fortress Press, 1985), p. 322.

6   C. Hauer, Jr, 'The Economics of National Security in Solomonic Israel' (*Journal of the Study of the Old Testament*, 18, 1980), p. 63.

7   ibid., p. 67.

8   ibid., p. 68.

9   Gottwald, *The Hebrew Bible*, p. 323.

10   G. Lenski and J. Lenski, *Human Societies: An Introduction to Macrosociology*, 4th edn (New York, McGraw-Hill, 1982), pp. 180–212.

11   J. Galtung, *The True Worlds: A Transitional Perspective* (New York, Free Press, 1980), pp. 107–8.

12   ibid., pp. 113–24.

13   ibid., p. 127.

14   D. Boone Schirmer, 'Washington Presses Aquino for Militarization', *PIF Reprint* (Davao City, 1987), p. 2.

15   ibid.

16   ibid., p. 3.

# PART THREE

# *The Exodus: One Theme, Many Perspectives*

The statement 'The sun has set' can take on different shades of meaning, according to who hears it. To a person of religion it is time to say prayers, to a soldier to leave the battle-field, and to the lover to keep his tryst with his beloved.

(from an Indian oral discourse)

# 16

# A Latin American Perspective: The Option for the Poor in the Old Testament

## GEORGE V. PIXLEY

---

This piece is an attempt to situate the Exodus story in its historical setting and at the same time to draw out insights for contemporary concerns, namely that the liberating act has significance not only for the Hebrews, but for all the oppressed of the world.

Pixley teaches in Nicaragua. This is the opening chapter of his and Boff's book, *The Bible, The Church and the Poor* (Maryknoll, NY, Orbis Books, 1989; Tunbridge Wells, Burns & Oates, 1989).

For an extended and a fuller exposition on Exodus, see George V. Pixley, *On Exodus: A Liberation Perspective* (Maryknoll, NY, Orbis Books, 1987).

---

## 1 INTRODUCTION

This chapter seeks to establish just who the God of the Bible is. This might not seem necessary, as the question of who God is could seem to have been settled by the common understanding of our Western culture. God is the one perfect being, all-powerful and all-wise, creator of heaven and earth, whose goodness and justice never fail. But common understanding, in this as in so many other things, is deceptive. The long history of conflicts between Christians in Latin America has taught us that the common confession of one God hides different, and even opposing, ways of envisaging this all-powerful and all-wise creator God. The Bible takes great care to identify the God it speaks of, and does so using categories other than our common understanding. To simplify somewhat, but without distorting the matter in essentials, we can say that the God of the Bible is the God who led Israel out of Egypt and who raised Jesus Christ from the dead. This is the God who created heaven and earth, and this is the God whose perfection we have to postulate.

229

There is no reason to dispute the Western philosophical affirmation that for God's love to be perfect, it has to be universal. But this does need some qualification. The biblical narratives tell us that the concrete expression of this love favoured the slaves in Egypt and Palestine, and the poor of Galilee. God's love for Pharaoh was mediated through God's preferential love for the Israelite slaves. In the same way, God's love for the scribes and Pharisees was mediated through God's love for and solidarity with the fishermen and women of Galilee. And so the God whom the Bible calls creator of heaven and earth takes on specific characteristics.

So, having, we hope, established the importance of asking who the God of the Bible is, let us approach the question through the introduction to that admirable synthesis of law that we know as the Decalogue: 'I am Yahweh your God who brought you out of the land of Egypt, out of the house of slavery. You shall have no gods except me' (Exod. 20.2–3).[1]

The words are so familiar to us that we hardly pay attention to them, yet they contain affirmations that are far from obvious at first sight. In the first place, the God Yahweh displays a polemical tone with regard to other possible gods. The text neither denies nor affirms that there are other gods. Their existence or non-existence is not the case at issue. What is at issue is that *you,* Israelite, to whom the law is addressed, must base your justice on the prohibition to worship them or ask them for favours. In other words, any god who has not brought you out of the house of slavery cannot be your God.

All the commandments dealing with just conduct among people – 'honour your father and mother . . . you shall not kill . . . you shall not steal', etc. – are presented as the direct and personal commands of *this* God, who 'brought you out of the land of Egypt, out of the house of slavery'. There is nothing to show that it had to be this way; at least, there is nothing in the common understanding of Western culture that would indicate this. But let us look at the text a little more closely:

(a) 'I am *Yahweh* your God.' The proper name Yahweh serves to ensure that those gods who cannot or will not save Israel from the house of slavery in Egypt cannot hide under the generic term *god*. It is not possible to make definite assertions about the origin of the name Yahweh.[2] Nevertheless, the Elohist and priestly traditions, two of the three great narrative traditions in the Pentateuch, agree in placing the revelation of this divine name within the context of the exodus. In the Elohist tradition, Yahweh revealed his proper name to Moses in the desert at the time he was persuading him to undertake the liberation of his enslaved people (Exod. 3.14–15). In the priestly tradition, he revealed his name to Moses still in Egypt as a confirmation of his will to set the slaves free (Exod. 6.2–6). Both traditions coincide in having God already known to the patriarchs Abraham, Isaac and Jacob, though they did not know God's *name*. This was revealed only to the prophet who was to lead Israel in its liberation. So the name Yahweh asserts the singularity of God as liberator.

(b) 'I am Yahweh *your* God.' Because he brought Israel out of the land of Egypt, out of the house of slavery, Yahweh is the God of Israel. This liberation establishes a relationship of exclusive dependence on Yahweh. Yahweh cannot be adored except by those who confess themselves slaves liberated from the slavery in Egypt. To understand this, we have to be careful not to be confused by the patriarchal traditions. This *your* does not indicate a previous relationship independent of the liberation. The exodus formed the people of Yahweh. According to Exodus 12.38 (from the Yahwist tradition), 'people of various sorts' (*erev rav*) joined the Israelites on the march, showing that the unity of Israel had to be constituted on the basis of the exodus. What was ordained for the Passover shows how the nation was defined:

> No alien may take part in it. . . . Should a stranger be staying with you and wish to celebrate the Passover in honour of Yahweh, all the males of his household must be circumcised: he may then be admitted to the celebration, for he becomes as it were a native-born. But no uncircumcised person may take part (Exod. 12.43, 48).

In other words, for Yahweh to be *your* God, you have to unite yourself to those who are celebrating their liberation from slavery. And no one who shows solidarity with the liberated people, demonstrating it through the circumcision of his foreskin, will be excluded from the community that celebrates its liberation from Egypt. In Israel's later practice, things were not that simple, but this expresses an intention: Yahweh is *your* God.

(c) 'I am Yahweh your *God*.' Theology in the Old Testament is not organized round dogmatic themes. Strictly speaking, the Old Testament includes no Creed defining the nature of God. Its theology is narrative, and the great majority of the books that make up this collection of writings recognize the foundational character of the story of the exodus. Efforts at generalizing about the nature of God are based on this story:

Yahweh your God is God of gods and Lord of lords, the great God, triumphant and terrible, never partial, never to be bribed. It is he who sees justice done for the orphan and the widow, who loves the stranger and gives him food and clothing (Deut. 10.16–18)

The God of the exodus account is a God who heard the cries wrung from the slaves by the slave-drivers of Pharaoh and so came down to set them free and lead them to a land flowing with milk and honey. Moses, the man chosen to lead this project, had gained his credentials by risking his high social position by killing an Egyptian who was maltreating a Hebrew (Exod. 2.11–15). So the exodus account clearly shows that justice means taking sides with the oppressed. The Yahweh of the exodus takes the part of the oppressed. From this our text draws the theological principle that God's impartiality makes God love the orphan and the widow with preference. Curiously, but nevertheless logically, not making exception of persons means making a preferential option for the oppressed in a situation of oppression.

These initial observations show that Yahweh, the God of the Bible, is characterized by his preferential option for the oppressed. The remaining sections of this chapter will examine some of the principal witnesses of the Bible concerning the way in which they appropriated this Yahweh God of the exodus. We need to remind ourselves here that the Bible is not one continuous work, but a collection of writings originating at different periods. This diversity of origin is also shown in the different ways it takes up the basic themes of Israel's tradition. Yahweh's option for the oppressed, as an integral element in the exodus narrative, which has a foundational character for Israel, exercised a basic influence over virtually all the books of the Bible (the notable exception being Proverbs, which we shall examine in due course as an expression of the teaching of 'wise men'). Our examination will seek to bring out the different shades with which God's preferential option for the impoverished and oppressed is presented.

## 2 THE EXODUS REVEALS YAHWEH AS LIBERATOR GOD: THE TEXT AND THE SOCIAL CONTEXT IN WHICH IT WAS PRODUCED

In the account of the exodus from Egyptian slavery under the inspiration of Yahweh and the leadership of Moses, Israel narrates its origins as a people and confesses that it owes these to Yahweh and is, in consequence, the people of Yahweh. Although the events narrated are earlier than the formation of Israel as a nation with its own language and identity, the account presupposes the existence of this nation. It is an 'official' account; and, like the official accounts of any nation explaining its origins, it hides some elements while revealing others. We therefore need to have some idea of the social history of Israel, the context in which the account was produced. So in this section we begin by reconstructing the probable origins of Israel, and go on to examine the exodus narrative and what it tells us about Yahweh and his choice of a nation for himself, showing how the social changes that came about in Israel altered the way in which the foundational events were understood.

Israel first appeared on the historical scene around the end of the thirteenth century BC. The name features on the stele of Merneptah, king of Egypt, in the context of his campaign in Palestine in 1208 BC. Although this text tells us no more than the existence of Israel in Palestine at this date, later texts tell us that it originated in the central mountains of Palestine, which, till the thirteenth century, had been the least populated area of Palestine. There is an extensive correspondence between the Egyptian court and the kings of Canaan, dating from the fourteenth and thirteenth centuries. Letters from Tel-el-Amarna indicate that the centres of population were the coastal plain and the valley of Yezreel, which crosses the mountain range by Mount Carmel. These were precisely the areas Israel did not control at the time of its origins, which is significant. Another important fact derived from these letters is that Egypt was unable to maintain stable control in Palestine, owing to continuous wars among the kings of the cities.

According to its own traditions of the early period, as recounted in the Book of Judges, Israel consisted of various peasant groups scattered around the mountain areas. The valleys and plains were controlled by hostile tribes, whose material culture was superior to that of the Israelites (they possessed horses and carts).

Around 1200 BC, archaeology shows a vital transitional point in the material culture of Palestine, the introduction of iron tools. This must be the major factor leading at just this period to the clearing of mountain areas previously unserviceable for agriculture, producing the population shift that brought together groups who were to make up the nation of Israel.

All these facts are explained by the thesis that Israel arose in the thirteenth century BC from a process of internal migration in Palestine.

Families and clans that had previously lived on the plain and in the valleys fled from the endless wars to seek a new life in country that had become cultivatable through the introduction of iron tools. This movement is illustrated in the biblical tradition of the migration of the tribe of Dan from the cities of Zorah and Eshtaol to the extreme Northeast of Galilee (Judg. 17–18). These migrations also had a social effect. Those who migrated were peasants; not only did they escape the political conflicts; they also escaped the tributes they had previously paid to the lords of the cities. In their new hill areas they did not build cities because they were not city people. Archaeological excavations have produced cases of cities destroyed at this period and rebuilt on a smaller scale, with humbler materials. This diminution of urban life can be explained by the incursion of peasant groups coming up from the plain. If this is the demographic origin of the clans that were to make up the nation of Israel, then one can talk of a movement of migration/uprising.³

These peasant groups were joined around 1200 BC by a group that came from Egypt, where it had carried out an uprising and an exodus into the desert under the leadership of Moses, a prophet of the God Yahweh. Their rebellion had been provoked by King Rameses II (1290–1224 BC), whose construction projects had placed an intolerable burden on the peasant population of Egypt. The social system obtaining in Egypt is described in Genesis 47.13–26: the people lived in their own villages and with their own families, but all the land belonged to the state and its produce was subject to a tax imposed by the Pharaoh. This was the same 'Asiatic' system as in Palestine, aggravated by the fact that the Egyptian state was far more powerful. The Hebrews who came out of Egypt understood that their success had been due to Yahweh, their God, being with them. The coincidence of this experience with that of the clans of Israel was noteworthy, and the clans gradually came to accept Yahweh as their God. The exodus of the Hebrews came to be the founding history of Israel.⁴

So the material basis of confession of faith in Yahweh was the diffuse peasant movement arising from the particular conditions in Palestine in the fourteenth and thirteenth centuries BC. Israelite society was made up of small villages organized by ties of blood relationship into families, clans and tribes. At the beginning, they had neither cities nor kings. The arrival of the Hebrew group gave the movement a political and social consciousness, the axis of which was confession of Yahweh as their only king.⁵ The laws given on Sinai lent coherence to the movement and a consciousness of the group's difference from the 'Canaanites' who dwelt in the cities, subject to human kings and worshipping Baal. The Israelites spoke the language of Canaan (see Isa. 19.18), from where they had come. The telling of the exodus and their confession of faith in Yahweh gave weight to their consciousness of being different from the inhabitants of the valleys and the cities. They were the people of Yahweh and had no kings 'like the other nations' (1 Sam. 8.5).

Reflecting on the importance of their movement, the tribes of Israel gradually came to see its universal significance, and to recognize Yahweh as God *tout court*, not simply as the God of Israel. One tradition held that Yahweh had promised Abraham: 'All the tribes of the earth shall bless themselves by you' (Gen. 12.3). Deutero-Isaiah (sixth century) proclaimed that Israel, the servant of Yahweh, would be a 'light to the nations' (Isa. 49.6). So some biblical texts give universal value to the Israelite experience that God is a saviour of the oppressed. Logically, Israel also came to confess Yahweh as creator of heaven and earth. It also saw in Yahweh a companion to those who wander the face of the earth without a home, a God who gave them land in which to settle.[6] And so the people of Israel came to understand that the Yahweh of the exodus was the one God who governs all nations. This is the historical thesis we follow here.

After this brief reconstruction of the origin of Israel, let us turn to its founding text, the account of the exodus. The book of Exodus, like the whole of the Pentateuch of which it forms part, was not finally completed till the fifth century BC, eight hundred years after the events it recounts. During these eight centuries, several major changes took place in the life of Israel:

(i) For two hundred years, Israel existed as a loose grouping of clans and tribes of peasants, surrounded by cities under monarchical regimes, generally hostile to Israel (with some exceptions, such as Gibeon and Shechem).

(ii) Around the year 1000 BC, the attacks from the cities forced Israel to create its own monarchical state, which lasted some four hundred years.

(iii) After the destruction of the capital (587 BC), the Jewish people organized themselves as a religious nation led by a priestly caste, under the tolerant suzereignty of the Persian empire.

As the account of the exodus is the founding document of Israel, it was naturally revised in each of these three epochs. The final text of the book of Exodus contains elements from each of these revisions. So it is a text made up of superimposed layers, with differing interpretations of those events in Egypt in the thirteenth century BC.

The earliest stage of the account, probably exclusively oral, calls the people of the exodus 'Hebrews'. This term did not originally denote a race, but was a designation given to various groups in several localities from Egypt to Mesopotamia. Such people were mercenaries, nomads, rebels; the name denoted the fact that they were not integrated into the broader framework of society, were outside the general rule of law.[7] When the exodus narrative was the foundational text of the Israelite tribes, the experience in Egypt was read as that of a group of peasants who had rebelled and placed themselves outside Egyptian law. Those who heeded the call of Yahweh and Moses to undertake a struggle that would set them free from slavery in Egypt were, therefore, 'Hebrews', 'people of various sorts' who decided to break with the Egyptian legal system, under which they had to hold their flocks, lands and bodies at the king's disposition.

The central feature of the account for the tribes of Israel was the part played by Yahweh in their liberation. They did not read the exodus as a secular revolutionary movement. Yahweh was on their side and guided the movement through his prophet Moses. The fact that they succeeded in escaping from their enforced serfdom despite the powerful Egyptian army showed that God, who took the side of the poor in Egypt, was the true God.

With the establishment of the monarchical state in Israel, the exodus narrative was taken up by the official scribes and converted into a national epic, together with the ancient traditions concerning the patriarchs Abraham, Isaac and Jacob. This process of adapting the Israelite traditions for the ends of the new monarchy probably took place at the court of Solomon. This produced the written version of the traditions that exegetes call the Yahwist version (known as J), the earliest writings that survive as part of the Pentateuch.

At this period, when the state was seeking to create a consciousness of national identity built up round the Davidic dynasty, it had to re-read the exodus as a national liberation struggle. The children of Israel, according to this re-reading, had been enslaved in Egypt after settling there to escape the famine in their own land of Canaan. A perverse king took advantage of their presence as guests, and the struggle that followed was between Egyptians and Israelites. The Israelites conceived the plan of 'returning' to the land of Canaan. In this way the account ceased to describe a social movement within Egyptian society and replaced it with a struggle between peoples, in which Yahweh took the side of Israel. Israel was an exploited people, but more importantly, it was the people of Yahweh, and this from before the time of its exploitation in Egypt. This is the emphasis in the Yahwist version:

> Go and gather the elders of Israel together and tell them, 'Yahweh, the God of your fathers, has appeared to me – the God of Abraham, of Isaac, and of Jacob; and he has said to me: I have visited you and seen all that the Egyptians are doing to you' (Exod. 3.16).

The children of Israel are shown as having a relationship with Yahweh going back to the time of their ancestors who lived in Canaan. They are his people and this is the reason Yahweh intervened to rescue them from their slavery. In this way the exodus lost a large part of its challenging content and could become useful for the monarchical aim of creating a national consciousness.

On the basis of this re-reading of the exodus, a theological reflection on the election of Israel as the special people of God was developed in the late monarchical period (seventh century BC):

> If Yahweh set his heart on you and chose you, it was not because you outnumbered other peoples: you were the least of all peoples. It was for love of you and to keep the oath that he swore to your fathers that Yahweh brought you out with his mighty hand and redeemed you from the house of slavery, from the power of Pharaoh king of Egypt (Deut. 7.7–8).

The exodus changes from Yahweh's option for the oppressed to being an inscrutable favour conferred by Yahweh in fulfilment of his promises to the patriarchs. This does not mean that the memory of the favour enjoyed by the poor in Yahweh's eyes was lost, but it was carried on as part of a thought-process that enhanced Yahweh's special relationship with his people dating from commitments entered into with the patriarchs.

The final re-reading of the exodus further overlaid the revelation of Yahweh as the liberator God who showed his preference for the oppressed. This is the reading made by the priests in the sixth century BC, when Judah existed as a national group within the Persian empire, internally led by the priestly caste. This re-reading could not quite efface the privilege of the poor, but it changed the emphasis so as to exalt the greatness of Yahweh. The following is an example:

Yahweh said to Moses, 'See, I make you as a god for Pharaoh, and Aaron your brother is to be your prophet. You yourself must tell him all I command you, and Aaron your brother will tell Pharaoh to let the sons of Israel leave his land. I myself will make Pharaoh's heart stubborn, and perform many a sign and wonder in the land of Egypt. Pharaoh will not listen to you, and so I will lay my hand on Egypt and with strokes of power lead out my armies, my people, the sons of Israel, from the land of Egypt. And all the Egyptians shall come to know that I am Yahweh when I stretch out my hand against Egypt and bring out the sons of Israel from their midst' (Exod. 7.1–5).

In the earlier layers of the account, the blows delivered against Pharaoh were to force him to let the Hebrews go. Every time Pharaoh hardened his heart, Yahweh visited a fresh plague on him so as to soften it. In the priestly re-reading, the marvels have another purpose: to demonstrate the greatness of Yahweh. This is why Yahweh himself hardens Pharaoh's heart so as to give himself new opportunities of showing his greatness.

In this priestly re-reading of the exodus, the desire to show the greatness of Yahweh has grown to such an extent that it obscures – though it cannot completely erase – Yahweh's predilection for the poor and oppressed. So Yahweh's option for the slaves and their liberation, the inspiration of pre-monarchical Israel, was gradually weakened in later re-readings. The original vision was kept in prophetic circles.

## 3 COULD ISRAEL HAVE KNOWN CLASS CONSCIOUSNESS?

Discussion of the origins of Israel as coming about through an uprising/migration and repudiation of the structures of domination personalized in the kings of the surrounding peoples raises a doubt: are we not imposing on these early years a level of social consciousness that could not have existed two thousand years before Christ? This is a legitimate concern, and needs examination.

Obviously, there were no 'social sciences' either in Canaan or in Egypt in the thirteenth century BC. So there was no possibility of making a 'scientific' analysis of the structure of society and the dynamics of its reproduction. Hence if we raise the above question with reference to a kind of social consciousness grounded in social–scientific analysis, the reply has to be affirmative.

So let us put the question differently. Was it possible for groups of peasants in Canaan to arrive at a realization that their interests as peasant groups were being threatened by their subjection to the king of their cities – Dor, Megiddo, Bethshean? In a stable society, even though the king sequestered a large portion of agricultural produce and required significant labour quotas for state works, it is highly unlikely that a peasant class which had never known any other way of life would have hankered after alternative lifestyles. Furthermore, the king was not regarded as a man, but as a god, on whom they were dependent for such essentials as sun and rain.

Nevertheless, Canaan in the fourteenth and thirteenth centuries BC was going through a critical phase in the Egyptian domination, reflected in the continual wars among the kings of its cities. Such a situation would lead to each village undergoing changes of overlord, besides interruptions to its crop production. One god/king would take the place of another as 'benefactor' responsible for giving life to the people of one place, without any internal change taking place within the people themselves. These changes would create the possibility of thinking of alternatives to the system of domination by kings. The peasants, well organized in large families on the local level, could come to realize that their interests were not identical with those of the city which demanded a quota of their produce. The presence of nearby virgin land, even if not as fertile as that of the plain, would have completed the process of 'conscientization' concerning the possibility of an alternative to their traditional subjection.

In Egypt, conditions that could have led to an alternative consciousness among the peasants were different. Here there was only one state, and it was a very strong state, with a very convincing religious underpinning. Conditions for a consciousness of oppression were created by the excessive exploitation of the peasant base of society for funerary constructions. It was natural to attribute these excesses of exploitation to abuses by the king's henchmen, which the king would correct if he knew the wrong being done his servants. That is, exploitation in itself would not have produced an alternative consciousness. As long as everyone continued to believe in the supreme god, whose goodness was shown in the richness of the country, irrigated every year by the flood waters of the great river Nile, the social structure was very secure. There was no alternative cultivatable land in the region. No one suggested the possibility of an alternative, and the wrongs suffered by a particular group of workers were a very localized incident compared to the overall riches of a land blessed by heaven.

239

Here, consciousness of an alternative must have come principally from an outside element introduced, undoubtedly, from the East, in the form of the God Yahweh, who appeared on the holy mountain. Yahweh had presented himself as a God of the poor, promising their liberation. It seems certain that very few peasants in the land of Egypt were prepared to receive such a message, though the conditions of exceptional oppression produced by the construction works of Rameses II would have led some to this extreme. So a small group of 'Hebrews' gathered round Moses, determined to understand their withdrawal from society as a repudiation of the oppression they now associated with Pharaoh, demystified for them by their acceptance of the God who had appeared to Moses with the promise of another land flowing with milk and honey.

## NOTES

1  Biblical quotations are taken from the Jerusalem Bible, adapted occasionally in accordance with the authors' own references to the original Hebrew and Greek.

2  J. Severino Croatto, 'Yavé, el Dios de la "presencia" salvífica: Exod. 3:14 en su contexto literario y querigmático' (*Revista Bíblica*, 43, 1981), pp. 153–63.

3  Though there are antecedents on the insurrectional theory of the origins of Israel, the definitive work is N. K. Gottwald, *The Tribes of Yahweh: A Sociology of the Religion of Liberated Israel 1250–1050 BCE* (Maryknoll, NY, Orbis Books 1979).

4  For a detailed examination of the texts, see J. V. Pixley, *On Exodus: A Liberation Perspective* (Maryknoll, NY, Orbis Books, 1987).

5  See Judges 8.22–3, and for an interpretation, J. V. Pixley, *God's Kingdom: A Guide for Biblical Study* (Maryknoll, NY, Orbis Books, 1981).

6  A good reading of the Pentateuch in the light of lack of land for Israel can be found in J. Severino Croatto, 'Una promesa aún no cumplida. La estructura literaria del Pentateuco' (*Revista Bíblica*, 44, 1982), pp. 193–206.

7  Much has been written on Hebrews/'apiru. See G. E. Mendenhall, 'The 'Apiru Movements in the Late Bronze Age' in *The Tenth Generation: The Origins of the Biblical Tradition* (Baltimore, John Hopkins University Press, 1973), pp. 122–41; M. L. Chaney, 'Ancient Palestinian Peasant Movements and the Formation of Premonarchic Israel' in D. N. Freedman and D. F. Graf (eds), *Palestine in Transition: The Emergence of Ancient Israel* (Sheffield, Almond Press, 1983), pp. 39–90.

# 17

# A Korean Minjung Perspective: The Hebrews and the Exodus

## CYRIS H. S. MOON

A biblical scholar from Korea sees parallels between the social history of the Korean minjung and the Hebrews.

This chapter is reprinted from the author's book, *A Korean Minjung Theology: An Old Testament Perspective* (Maryknoll, NY, Orbis Books, 1985).

Cyris H. S. Moon is a professor of Old Testament studies and has published papers on political history and the sociology of hermeneutics.

At the outset, we should note that the Old Testament is a collection of writings by scribes, priests, and other learned people from a society dominated by a patriarchy. The *minjung* of the Old Testament did not participate in writing these documents. Therefore, these writings portray the world from the perspective of men and royalty. From the vantage point of the rulers, they describe events and activities engaged in primarily by men (such as war, cult, and government). However, the Old Testament is also filled with stories of liberation. So although the *minjung* of the Old Testament could not and did not write their own aspirations and biographies of suffering and oppression, there is ample evidence of the liberation movement of the *minjung* in the Old Testament.

The first such movement that comes instantly to mind is that of the Exodus, which took place in the thirteenth century BC. The Hebrews, during the reign of Rameses II,[1] were being forced to serve as slaves under the repressive rule of the Egyptians. Moses emerged as the liberator of the Hebrews and brought about the confrontation between himself and the Pharaoh that eventually led to the Hebrews' liberation. In order to appreciate the enormousness of this achievement, we must first focus our attention on the object of Moses' concern: the Hebrew slaves, the despised, the powerless, the outcasts, and those who had no rights at all. Indeed, Moses' greatness lies in his identifying himself with these people in order to liberate them.

The word *habiru* (which is often equated with the word 'Hebrew' and is also spelled *apiru* or *habiru*) is a term that can be traced to records in the second millennium BC in Egypt, Babylonia, Syria, and Palestine; it appears frequently also in the oldest extant tablets and written records. The nature and identity of the *habiru* have been the subject of considerable literature, for the term provides a clue to who the *minjung* of that time were. The 1976 supplementary volume of *The Interpreter's Dictionary of the Bible* describes the *habiru* as mercenary soldiers, people under treaty, and prisoners of war.[2] Other sources suggest that they were outlaws, outcasts, and those who stood outside the dominant social system. At any rate, they most certainly were rebels standing in defiance of the prevailing social or power structure.[3] The *habiru*, therefore, were part of the *minjung* of their time, driven by their *han* (grudge or resentment)[4] to act against what they felt to be injustices imposed on them by those in power.

The social system in Egypt was a strict bureaucracy within which the functions of the various classes were strictly regulated. The structure of the state was largely dependent on four influential factors: the king, his civil servants, the army, and the priests. These were the dominating groups which exerted their power over everyone else, particularly the Hebrews.

Apart from the individuals who were closely connected with some of the basic institutions of the country, there were two more groups of people. The first group consisted of the free citizens, that is, the peasants and tillers of the land. These individuals, though free in the technical sense of the word, were actually bound to the soil they worked, often living on a starvation level. And then, apart from the free population, there was a large group of slaves spread throughout the land.

There were three types of slaves: those who worked as the personal property of individuals, those who worked as state-owned property on public works or military projects, and those who were temple slaves. How they were treated varied according to times and circumstances, but if the members of the lower class of free citizens were referred to as 'children of nobodies,' one can well imagine in what regard a slave was held. In short, the slaves were the lowest class of people, and under the oppressive Egyptian system, they suffered total and brutal exploitation.

Despite the fact that the Hebrews suffered this complete loss of their rights and freedom, Moses had difficulty in persuading them to act toward achieving their liberty. According to Exodus 3.1–14, he had to make them realize that they had to escape from Egypt in order to be a liberated people. This is important, for one would think that because the Hebrews had suffered an oppressed life, they would realize that the only way to liberation was to trust God and Moses and act accordingly. However, it seems that they did not have this kind of trust. As a result of such a long and cruel oppression by the Egyptians, the Hebrews had developed the mentality of slaves. This is one way rulers can prevent rebellion before it begins: they break the spirit of their slaves by driving them more severely and depriving them of tolerable living conditions. As the people are deprived of their humanity, they are subordinated. It is not difficult to see why a completely dominated people, who are reduced to being concerned only with eating the food distributed regularly by the ruler, would not want to risk escape from the protection of the ruler and make a long journey to a virtual wasteland.

In this way, the Exodus narrative points out an important fact: Yahweh cannot be the sole actor in the movement for liberation. Rather, humanity is invited to act as a partner with God. People are to assist in the restoration of their own rights which have been infringed upon, a concept which differs from the idea that the fulfillment of all human history is carried out under God's sovereignty alone. The writers of Exodus stress that if oppressed people are to obtain liberation, they must – with God's aid – confront the pharaohs of the world: in order for the Hebrews to participate in the struggle for their human rights, they had first to realize that it was Pharaoh who had infringed upon their rights and that their struggle had to begin with a direct confrontation with Pharaoh. Thus, the third chapter of Exodus says that Moses was ordered to confront Pharaoh in order to help the Hebrews escape from slavery.

At the same time, the writers of Exodus did not presume to say that the Hebrews deserved to receive God's protection and the restoration of the human rights. Rather, their liberation was the result of God's gracious action. Thus Exodus reveals what anyone who participates in the struggle for liberation comes eventually to realize: God is on the side of the oppressed and downtrodden and will always give encouragement and protection to them. In fact, some of the first words with which God is introduced to Moses in the Exodus narrative indicate that God is concerned with the *minjung*. In Exodus 3.7 God states: 'I have seen indeed the affliction of my people which are in

Egypt.' God relates not just in a general way as the creator of human beings, but as concerned with a specific oppressed people to whom Moses stands in a special relationship.

In the Hebrew text of Exodus 3.7 the verbal construction of the form 'I have seen' makes the 'seeing' an emphatic process. Furthermore, the little phrase 'which are in Egypt,' instead of the simpler 'in Egypt,' seems to show an incongruent situation: God's *minjung* are in Egypt when they should be in the promised land. At this point it should be remembered that the Hebrews must have regarded the promised land as a kind of never-never land, and to the question 'Whose people are you?' they would very likely have answered: 'Do you not see that we are Pharaoh's people?' Thus, it is significant that even while the people did not call themselves Yahweh's people, Yahweh immediately thinks of them as 'my people.' In other words, God owns them long before they own God.

Moreover, when in Exodus 3.6 the encounter between God and Moses is linked to the patriarchs, the faithfulness and reliability of God are emphasized. God is not one to change God's mind or to forget; God stands true to God's promise. In Exodus 3 God is revealed as a liberator first, as one who would liberate God's *minjung* from bondage and settle them in a land of their own. This liberation is also connected with a religious purpose which is clearly stated in Exodus 3.12: 'God said, "But I will be with you; and this shall be the sign for you, that I have sent you; when you have brought forth the people out of Egypt, you shall serve God upon this mountain."'

Apart from the revelation of God in this personal and historical sense, we have at this encounter between God and Moses a further statement (Exod. 3.14) concerning God's personal self, a statement which stands unique even in the pages of the Old Testament. It furnishes us with the only explanation of the name Yahweh, a name which is used more than six thousand times in the Old Testament. When we consider the meaning of the name Yahweh as given to Moses in the striking phrase 'I am who I am,' two factors seem to emerge clearly. On the one hand, the words strike us as mysterious, enigmatic; they seem to conceal more than to reveal; on the other hand, considering the situation in which they were spoken, they are meant to reassure, to make real the presence of God.

'I am who I am' tells us indeed that we are face to face with a God whose being is beyond comprehension, beyond human intellect which would seek to define God within certain categories of thought. The essential Being of God cannot be understood by reference to human beings or nature, for God stands outside time and space and God's Being is beyond cause and effect. The infinite and eternal, that which transcends our realm altogether, is implied in the statement 'I am who I am.' Yet this Being of God is not expressed in a form which could make God synonymous with the idea of the infinite or eternal, for Being is linked here to the personal 'I.' God is not to be understood as an impersonal force behind the universe; rather God is revealed as a personal Being. As the eternal 'I am' (the phrase could also be rendered 'I shall be who I shall be'), God makes history indeed, for this transcendent God is revealed as being actively present within the realm of human experience. The phrase 'I am who I am' stresses the truth of both the transcendence and the immanence of God. God's Being is not only 'throned afar,' but God is also the God of justice and compassion who is a very helpful presence in time of oppression and trouble. And it is obvious that the revelation of the name of God given to Moses has the purpose of assuring him and the Hebrews of the very real presence of God who will act justly for the liberation of the *minjung.* 'I am who I am' should be understood in the sense of 'you can take my presence as a guarantee for action on your behalf for the cause of justice and compassion.' Thus, with the assurance of Yahweh, the Hebrews began to make their freedom march, crossing the Red Sea and the wilderness. And after many years of wandering, they finally found themselves in Canaan, the promised land.

As the contextual situation of this Exodus motif is reconstructed, parallels between it and Korea come to light. For instance, Koreans, like the Hebrews, suffered for years under the domination of ruthless governments and foreign oppressors. In order to see these parallels more clearly, let us now turn briefly to a short history of the Korean people.

According to tradition, Korean history dates back to 2333 BC when Tangun, the son of a bear, founded Korea. In early history it appears that tribal communities developed and matured into three states: Koguryo in the North, and Silla and Paekche in the South. It was during this era, the Three Kingdom Period (57 BC–AD 668), that Korean recorded history began. It was also during this period that Buddhism was first introduced into Korea by the Chinese.

By 668, with the help of the T'ang Dynasty in China, the state of Silla had unified Korea. However, in the latter part of the ninth century, the power of the Silla Dynasty began to weaken steadily.

There were several reasons for this decline. The hereditary nature of the government positions had resulted in a ruling elite which was restricted to members from a few clans. These family factions were constantly vying for power and influence; this weakened the central government.

Out of all this political chaos a new leadership finally emerged. In 918 Wan Kon defeated his opponents and founded the Koryo Dynasty. He immediately instituted several new ordinances and changes. One such change was in the system of land ownership. It was declared that all property was to belong to the government, the high officials, and the Buddhist priesthood. During this period, Buddhism reached its height of power. This was due to the fact that the aristocracy supported Buddhism, as it promised happiness for the ruling class and Buddha's protection for the king. The priests gradually became powerful landowners, and their influence on political decisions greatly increased. Toward the end of the fourteenth century, Buddhist priests controlled much of the national economy and became *de facto* rulers in many areas.

From 1219 to 1392 the country was in deep trouble. In 1219, the new Mongolian leadership in China invaded Korea and Koryo became a tributary state. In the midst of this political turmoil, many of the ruling elite and Buddhist priesthood began to exercise their power ruthlessly. This led to excessive exploitation of the *minjung*, especially the peasantry, which in turn resulted in rebellion and unrest.

Because of these problems, the government desperately tried to institute several reform programs. These programs had a two-fold purpose: one, the revitalization of the nation after almost a century of Mongol domination and, two, the elimination of the social and political abuses of the *minjung* for which the Buddhist priesthood was held responsible. The persons initiating the reforms were the Confucian scholar-officials, those who had obtained their positions by passing the civil service examinations.

In 1392, Yi Songgye, the newly risen military leader, overthrew the Koryo Dynasty, thus founding the Yi Dynasty. Yi immediately turned the new administration over to the classical scholars, who then instituted numerous reform programs. All of the estates were confiscated and redistributed to those who had been loyal to Yi Songgye. In addition, Buddhism was deemed unacceptable as the official religion; Confucianism, or more accurately Neo-Confucianism, was substituted for it. There were several reasons for this change. Toward the end of the Koryo period there was a definite deterioration in the moral and spiritual leadership of the Buddhist priests. As they grew wealthier and more powerful, they also became more corrupt. Thus, in order for the new dynasty to retain its position and increase its power, it was imperative that the Buddhists lose their influence and power. The administration confiscated all temple property and forbade all Buddhist activities. Not surprisingly, this change received wide support. An anti-Buddhist movement had already started in the late Koryo years as a result of the resentment generated by the priests' manipulation of power and wealth. Thus the switch from Buddhism to Neo-Confucianism was, for most of the *minjung*, a welcome change. However, as it turned out, this shift to Neo-Confucianism was not beneficial to the *minjung*, for basically two social strata emerged. They were the *yang ban* (the ruling class people) and the *xiang rom* (the slaves, the landless peasants, the powerless, and the lower-class people).

The Korean Confucian scholars believed that the universe was comprised of two forces which were manifested in light and darkness, heaven and earth, male and female. These forces were called *Yang* and *Yin*. According to the scholars, *Yang*, which symbolized heaven, was superior to *Yin*, symbolizing earth. As long as this natural hierarchy was obeyed, the human world and the cosmic order would be in balance, and society would be in harmony and peace. If this hierarchical system was disrupted, a state of barbarism and chaos in which human desires would be uncontrolled would result. Thus, according to the Confucianists, a harmonious and orderly society could exist only when the *minjung* had served their superiors, the *yang ban*. The Confucianists also taught that the female was created especially for the purposes of procreation and of giving pleasure to the male. Thus, they insisted upon the inferiority of women, placing them in the same class as slaves.[5] *Xiang rom* and women were the *minjung* of the time.

During the reign of King Sungjong (1469–94), the classical scholars emerged as a new force, and the number of the ruling class increased. This was followed by the reign of King Kusanghaegun (1608–23), during which many independent middle-class farmers and wholesale dealers also became part of the ruling class. Yet the two distinct classes remained evident until the end of the Yi Dynasty in 1910. In this kind of socio-economico-political context Protestant Christianity was introduced to Korea in the year 1884.

Dr Horace N. Allen was the first Protestant missionary (co-worker) to come to Korea. A member of the Presbyterian Mission Board, he brought courage, vision, and devotion with him in his desire to be a partner with the Koreans to work for the extension of God's kingdom. However, one of the policies of the Yi Dynasty toward the West at that time was *choksa chongwi* ('expel the wrong and defend the right'). This policy was evident in a series of persecutions of the Catholics (who came to Korea in 1784) and in an uncompromising closed door policy toward the Western powers.[6] Therefore, Dr Allen arrived in Korea through the 'back door' of the American legation, which appointed him the legation doctor. With his Western medical skills he gradually gained the favor of the royal family and laid a foundation for future mission work. On April 5, 1885, Rev M. G. Underwood, a Presbyterian missionary, and Henry Apenzeller, a Methodist missionary, and his wife joined Dr Allen. As time passed, the missionary community grew and carried out a considerable amount of medical work.[7]

A landmark occasion for the American Protestant mission was the opening of a school for girls in 1885. The opportunities that the missionaries made available through education were both for girls (who were still considered to be inferior creatures) as well as boys of the *minjung*. The sons of the *yang ban* were not attracted to the schools.[8]

Meanwhile, because Christian evangelism was still banned, the work of the American mission had to be done among the *minjung*, and it had to be secret and underground work. The early missionaries tried to gain the favor of the government, being cautious and patient in doing their work to gain the confidence of the government and the people. They were very busy, for, on the one hand, the missionaries were using the good offices of the American legation while, on the other hand, they were slowly penetrating the lower class, that is, the *minjung*, of the Korean society.[9]

During this period the missionaries made a major breakthrough. Discovering that *Hangul*, the Korean vernacular script, was being despised and neglected, they picked it to study and to use to communicate to the *minjung* of Korea. Thus the medium through which they worked was the language of the *minjung*, while Chinese was the official written language of the Korean officialdom and the *yang ban* class. Using this medium encouraged the facilitated the contact of the Christian message and of its missionary bearers with the *minjung* in Korea. This was the beginning of the process of rehabilitating the language of the Korean *minjung*.[10]

Next, the Bible was translated into *Hangul*. The translation of the

New Testament began in 1887, and by 1900 the entire Bible was translated into the Korean vernacular. Other books and tracts were also published; the circulation of these and of the Bible became the most effective strategy of the missionaries in spreading the gospel of Jesus Christ.

In January 1893, the early Protestant missionaries adopted a very significant mission policy, which was called the 'Nevius Method.' The four articles of the policy were outlined as follows:

1 It is better to aim at the conversion of the working classes than that of the higher classes.

2 The conversion of women and the training of Christian girls should be a special aim, since mothers exercise so important an influence over future generations.

3 The Word of God converts where humankind is without resources; therefore it is most important that we make every effort to place a clear translation of the Bible before the people as soon as possible.

4 The mass of Koreans must be led to Christ by their own fellow countrymen; therefore we shall thoroughly train a few as evangelists rather than preach to a multitude ourselves.[11]

During the latter years of the Yi Dynasty there were also many important political events that took place. Much social unrest and many political revolts by the *minjung* against the ruling class occurred. Among them, one event deserves special attention. That is the *Tonghak* Rebellion. Among the *yang ban* class the buying and selling of government positions was a common practice. Then, anyone who purchased an official position could generally reimburse himself through extortion. Taxes and levies were increased by local and national governments until they reached three or four times the legal rate. Extravagance, licentiousness, and debauchery were the order of the day at the court. The suffering *minjung* could no longer remain silent. In 1895, the *Tonghaks*, a group mostly comprised of poor peasants, rose in rebellion in the South.[12] This *Tonghak* Rebellion had both religious and political significance. In many ways, it represented the first indigenous, organized *minjung* movement in Korea. Through struggle against the feudal social system in Korea and armed with the ideology 'humanity is heaven,' the oppressed *minjung* began to define themselves as subjects, rather than objects, of history and destiny.

Also during the Yi Dynasty, bands of armed peasants called

*Hwalbindang* rose up in every part of the country. The social ideal that they possessed came from a story written by Ho-Kyun about Hong Kil Dong. Ho-Kyun was a *chungin* (member of the social class between the ruling *yang ban* class and the commoners). He wrote this popular story in the *Hangul* so that the *minjung* could read it easily. The story was told and retold and was most popular during the Yi Dynasty, when the ruling powers were making the *minjung* suffer most.[13]

The story of Hong Kil Dong is as follows: An alienated social hero named Hong Kil Dong leaves home and joins a group of bandits because he cannot fulfill his life's ambitions and goals in the existing society. Collecting a gang around him he names it *Hwalbindang* (party to liberate the poor and oppressed). The hero of the story attacks the rich and distributes wealth to the poor *minjung*. This creates great social disturbances. Finally, the hero is persuaded by his father to leave the country, and he goes off to an island called Yuldo, which is his paradise. It is characterized by the absence of social and class divisions.

With its picture of a messianic kingdom, the novel prompted a new social vision among the people. Just like the hero in the story, the *Hwalbindang* in Korea were concerned with national rights and equality of all. Driven by the desire to eliminate the gap between the rich and the poor, they too robbed the rich in order to help the poor.[14]

Meanwhile, after the crushing of the *Tonghak* Rebellion (1895) by the government, the countryside was wide open for missionary penetration. Missionaries went deep into the countryside and made contacts with the *minjung* who were associated with *Tonghak* movement. Christianity was then accepted by the *minjung* as a tool for fighting for justice, equality, and human rights. Christianity became a politically oriented faith and a religion of hope and power for the oppressed and suffering *minjung*.

During this period the major emphasis of Korean Christianity was to achieve equality of human beings and to assure human rights and social justice for the Korean people. The *minjung* became enlightened and inspired, and they were stirred up against the administration and illegal acts of government officials. An important part of the Korean Christian movement was the 'common meeting,' at which a cross section of the *minjung* voiced their common concerns.[15] The common meetings also engendered a new *minjung* leadership. For instance, after attending the meetings a butcher (whose occupation was classified as *xiang rom*) named Park Song-chun became a Christian and later went on to lead the Butchers' Liberation Movement from 1895 to

1898 and to become one of the founding members of the Seungdong Presbyterian church in Seoul.[16] These common meetings spread throughout the countryside. Since the missionaries had to travel to reach the *minjung*, they had to train more Korean Christian leaders who could go with them. Thus Dr Samuel A. Moffett founded a theological institution (which is now the Presbyterian College and Seminary) in 1901.

The missionaries gradually ceased to be pioneers and to preach directly to the *minjung*. They became organizers or managers, directing and supervising the Korean Christians' evangelical enterprise. They would make occasional trips into the countryside, visiting newly established churches and administering sacraments. The Korean churches used the *Hangul* Bible widely as a very important tool for evangelizing Korea. The Bible became the greatest factor in evangelization. The Korean churches derived their power, spirituality, great faith in prayer, and liberality from the fact that all the churches were saturated with a knowledge of the Bible. Bible study and training classes constituted the most unique and most important factor in the growth of the Korean churches.[17]

The *minjung* in Korea responded to the Christian message. The motives and reasons for the response, in great measure, were to improve their social and political condition. This was true particularly after 1895. Certainly the Christian message gave some hope to the *minjung*, the outcasts. Political oppression was another cause of the increase in believers. The *minjung* felt that they had reached the summit of misery.

The year 1905 was a fateful year for the Korean people. That year Korea lost its independence and became a protectorate of Japan. The treaty of the protectorship robbed the kingdom of Korea of its diplomatic rights to deal with foreign powers, for the Japanese established the office of governor general under the Korean king to control the Korean government. For the Korean people this meant that their historical situation now provided a new external focus. Independence and the expulsion of Japanese power from Korea became the main concern of the Korean people.[18]

In the political arena, Korean Christians were not exempt from a sense of national crisis and national humiliation, and they harbored an intense anti-Japanese feeling. The missionaries also felt keenly the estrangement between the Koreans and the Japanese which seemed to presage a general uprising. However, they not only understood the hopelessness of fighting against the Japanese imperial army, but also foresaw the danger of making the young Korean churches a political agency. It seems that missionaries were successful in depoliticizing the Korean Christians through mass revival meetings. The main features of the several Protestant revival meetings held in 1907 were the confession of sins after a sermon convincing the people of their sins, loud prayers, and various forms of collective emotional expressions. These revival meetings brought a deep sense of fellowship among Christian communities and a moral transformation of individual lives. However, the Christian message was no longer geared to the social and national crisis of the Korean *minjung*, but was limited to the rigid and narrow definition of salvation of the soul. The Korean Christians' aspiration for national liberation was completely ignored, and the missionaries' tight control of the Korean Christian communities stifled the dynamism of the autonomous communities which could have responded better to the historical predicament.

August 29, 1910, was a day of national humiliation for the Korean people. This was the day that Korea was formally annexed to Japan. The Korean people lost their country and became enslaved *minjung* subjected to the Japanese military rule. The Yi Dynasty formally ended and the right of government was transferred to the Japanese emperor.

The Japanese government strongly infused the policy of Japanese ultranationalism into Korea. According to that policy, all values and institutions came under the imperial authority of the emperor. Hence, the government, the military, business, and all truth, beauty, and morality were linked to the institution of emperor. The infamous Education Rescript was an open declaration of the fact that the Japanese state, being a religious, spiritual, and moral entity, claimed the right to determine all values. This was the spirit of Japanese national policy. It was combined with the doctrine of the divinity of the emperor, a belief championed by the Japanese military, which was the holy army of the emperor and which had launched the mission of bringing the 'light of the emperor' to Korea.[19]

For the Korean Christians, political neutrality was not possible whether they were in the churches or outside of them. The oppression, exploitation, and alienation by the Japanese government of the Koreans became extraordinarily cruel. Physical tortures and imprisonments were common practices. Living under the oppressive Japanese rule meant inevitable suffering for powerless Koreans, the *minjung* of the time.

Under the extreme conditions of political oppression, economic exploitation, social alienation by a foreign regime, and internal control by the missionaries, the Korean Christians had no positive outlet to express their feelings and aspirations other than in dreams, but dreams were powerful forces for the people's historical self-understanding. In their dreams, Korean Christians found the God of the Exodus most meaningful for their historical condition. For example, a preface to a Sunday school lesson from this period states:

> The Book of Exodus is written about the powerful God, who liberated the people of Israel [which would have been interpreted as meaning the Korean people] from suffering and enslavement and made them the people who enjoyed glorious freedom; God appeared as Yahweh before Israel, and as the whole and just God. God exists by himself and of himself, God has sympathy, and God is the Saviour. Exodus is the book of the miracle of God's liberation of the people of Israel from the power of Pharaoh [the Japanese emperor] with God's power. God has saved Israel first and established it as holy. This book is a foreshadowing of the redemptive love of Jesus in the Gospels and of God's power that cleanses; that is, the miracle of the grace shown forth.[20]

The struggles of the Korean Christians for independence and social justice were persistent despite the regulation concerning meetings (1910) and that concerning guns and explosives (1912). The continuing efforts of the Korean Christians became the spiritual backbone of the March First Independence Movement of 1919. From 1896 to 1898 many intellectuals, merchants, and industrialists had organized the Independence Association. With the help of the *minjung* who participated in the *Tonghak* Rebellion in 1895, the Independence Association formed a society which later provided two main leaders of the March First Independence Movement. These people had the consciousness of the struggle of the *minjung* for liberation. Perhaps this movement was the broadest in scope of the *minjung* liberation movement. Of the people who constituted the movement, 48 percent were peasants, 22 percent were Christians, and 30 percent were ordinary men and women in their twenties. Christians provided much of the leadership of this movement. Unfortunately, the March First Independence Movement was crushed by the Japanese imperial army.

The missionaries in this period were products of early twentieth-century fundamentalism, and their only concern was the 'salvation of souls.' Also, in order to do their mission work, they found it necessary to collaborate with the Japanese authorities. However, these relationships changed as World War II approached and began, and toward the end of World War II, the missionaries were expelled from Korea, leaving the Korean churches to carry on their mission by themselves. We may characterize the Korean church between 1920 and 1945 in the following manner: (1) It lacked a historical consciousness. (2) It yielded to the enforcement of worship at the Japanese shrine (Shintoism). (3) It was under the sway of fundamentalistic dogma and imported theology. (4) It became a captive to those who were striving for ecclesiastical authority. This was the period of the 'Egyptian Captivity' of the Korean church's history.

The Koreans did not see their liberation until the end of World War II in 1945. It was at this time that they finally were liberated from the rule of the Japanese emperor who, like Pharaoh, had exploited them to the utmost. Thus, the Exodus Model parallels the Korean experience in many ways. The *minjung* of Korea, like the Hebrews, had to assume responsibility and strengthen their awareness of the depths of their bondage in order to rise up against the system in rebellion. In other words, the *minjung* in Korea were actively participating in the process of their own liberation, fully aware that God stood with them and for them.

Furthermore, in the context of the Exodus event, the *minjung* can be clearly understood as a force that stands in opposition to the powerful. The *minjung* are the oppressed who have their rights infringed upon by rulers. They are 'uprooted people' who have no national identity or legal protection and who are considered to be slaves. In Korea, the pattern of slavery, like that experienced by the Hebrews in Egypt, was not questioned and was considered reasonable by those who benefited from the social system. A slave society had long been accepted as the natural and unchangeable order of things. In both Egypt and Korea, while the government leaders regarded the subjected people as a most important element in their economy, they never considered giving them fair compensation for their work. Finally, the Hebrews, being the objects of God's liberation, cried out to God for liberation from the oppressive and unjust Egyptian society. These cries reflected the same aspirations as those of the *han*-ridden *minjung* in Korea.

## NOTES

1   There is no agreement among the scholars who take the view that the Exodus took place in the thirteenth century BC as to who the actual Pharaoh was when Moses liberated his people from Egypt. Some believe that Rameses II was the pharaoh of the oppression as well as that of the Exodus, and there are those who date the Exodus as being during the time of Maniptah, the son of Rameses II. The problem lies in the Old Testament reference to the death of the Pharaoh from whom Moses had fled. If we assume that it was Sethi I who initiated the oppression, then we would have some difficulty in accounting for Moses' stay of forty years in Egypt and an equal stay in Midian before returning to liberate his people near the end of Rameses II's reign. Of course, it has been suggested with some plausibility that the period of forty years is often taken as a round figure to describe a generation, and that the actual figure would be much lower, say twenty-five years. Even though we are not able to solve the chronological problem satisfactorily, the reign of Rameses II seems to be at the time of Moses' challenge to Pharaoh.

2   M. C. Astour, 'Habiru, Hapiru', in *The Interpreter's Dictionary of the Bible*, supplementary volume (Nashville, Abingdon Press, 1976), pp. 382–5.

3   M. L. Chaney, 'Ancient Palestinian Peasant Movements and the Formation of Premonarchic Israel,' in D. N. Freedman and D. F. Graf (eds), *Palestine in Transition: The Emergence of Ancient Israel* (Sheffield, Almond Press, 1983).

4   For a more detailed study on *han*, see S. Nam-dong, 'Towards a Theology of *Han*', in *Minjung Theology*, ed. CTC-CCA (Maryknoll, NY, Orbis Books, 1983), pp. 55 ff.

5   R. Young-jin Moon, 'A Study of the Change in Status of the Korean Woman from Ancient Times through the Yi Period' (dissertation, Emory University, Atlanta, 1982), pp. 4–16.

6   K. Yong-bock, 'Korean Christianity as a Messianic Movement of the People', in *Minjung Theology*, p. 81.

7   ibid.

8   ibid.

9   ibid.

10   ibid., p. 82.

11   ibid., p. 83.

12   C. Chai-yong, 'A Brief Sketch of Korean Christian History from the Minjung Perspective', in *Minjung Theology*, p. 75.

13   K. Yong-bock, 'Messiah and Minjung', in *Minjung Theology*, p. 188.

14   ibid.

15   C. Chai-yong, p. 76.

16   ibid.

17   K. Yong-bock, 'Korean Christianity', p. 86.

18   ibid., p. 88.

19   ibid., p. 95.

20   W. L. Swallen, Preface to *Sunday School Lessons on the Book of Exodus* (Seoul, Religious Tract Society, 1907).

# 18

# A Black African Perspective: An African Reading of Exodus

## JEAN-MARC ELA

To read the Exodus in Africa means to enter into solidarity with individuals and groups who are refused the dignity of being human, to denounce the abuses of established systems, and to intervene to protect the weak, as Moses did.

This chapter is taken from the author's book, *African Cry* (Maryknoll, NY, Orbis Books, 1986).

Jean Marc Ela is a Cameroonian and worked among the Kirdis in North Cameroon. He is on the staff of the Department of Sociology, University of Yaoundé, Cameroon.

What is the message of the Book of Exodus today for so many millions of Africans in their religious, cultural, political and socioeconomic situations? What can men and women in black Africa who seek deliverance from political and economic oppression look for in a reading of Exodus? This is a towering question facing us. I shall examine it here.

It is not difficult to see the import of this question. Our faith in the God of revelation cannot be lived and understood abstractly, in some atemporal fashion. It can only be lived through the warp and woof of the events that make up history. Faith will grapple with the tensions and conflicts of global society. It runs into the crucial questions and urgent aspirations of all women and men. The praxis of the Christians struggling in situations of injustice must be reckoned with in any effort to understand the living faith. We must reflect on this activity, bring it into confrontation with the gospel, and make explicit the theological intent it expresses.

Ultimately, the sense of revelation will need to be understood in history through the situations and experiences by which the word of God makes itself heard. After all, theology is nothing but a reflection fashioned of the stuff of living experience. One extracts the current meaning of God's word from a point of departure in the historical understanding that human beings have of themselves and the world. Theology is a labor of deciphering the sense of revelation in the historical context in which we become aware of ourselves and our situation in the world. We must respect this hermeneutic function of theology, remembering that the enterprise it supposes is that of the Bible itself. The Bible in the life of God's people never was anything but a reflection on, a resumption of, the basic meaning of the biblical message and the promise of salvation at the heart of the happenings and the history being lived out by the people of God.

We are called today to understand ourselves in the light of a living revelation, to understand the profound sense of the situations and events that we experience, to read the word of God in the world. History, then, including the history of the life of the church, must be the locus par excellence of theological research and reflection. And so we must renounce any discourse on the exodus that we might generate *in absoluto* without taking into consideration our own concrete, vital context. In other words, from a point of departure in the center of vital interest and in view of the historical experiences and questioning that mark the life of our peoples, we must overcome the temporal distance between us and the exodus and lay hold of the meaning that God seeks to impart to us by means of this key event in salvation history.

And so the questions arise: In the colonial or neocolonial situation that has marked Christianity in Africa, is Exodus not a book terribly absent to us? And is the reason for this absence not that the message it delivers calls into question not only a certain theology but also an ecclesiastical praxis, a worship, and a spirituality?

The God of missionary preaching was a God so distant, so foreign to the history of the colonized peoples. Exploited and oppressed, they find it difficult to identify this God with the God of Exodus, who becomes aware of the situation of oppression and servitude in which the people find themselves. The primary role of the Bible, and of the Old Testament in a special way, in African religious movements is to express the reaction and revolt of African Christians within the institutional churches in which the despised, humiliated human being lives a relationship to God under the rubric of absence.

The God of the Old Testament, the God of the Promise, continually shows human beings a future of hope, which enables them to criticize the existing situation. God summons up from within the hoping consciousness of the human being a nonconformity with reality. In short, God carries human beings forward, toward a future characterized by a new reality. But in the official churches, God's divinity has been posited in a changelessness, an immutability, an impassibility such that the history of human beings is effectively abandoned to its own devices, deprived of the capacity to appear as the locus of manifestation of God's action. If the God of preaching, when all is said and done, is simply the God of the theodicies, that is, of Greek metaphysics, then God is nothing but a supreme, eternal idea, having no connection with anything that happens on earth, where human beings live their lives. Devoid of any openness to the world, God cannot become involved in the human drama, for God cannot compromise the divine purity in any historical becoming.

My point is this: The God proclaimed to the African human being in the precise context of the colonial situation is a God who is a stranger to the times, indifferent to political, social, economic, and cultural occurrences, having no prospect of involvement such as would necessarily be implied in the Promise. At most, the God of the Christian churches in the times of colonization commanded adaptation and submission to the existing order of things. At the First Vatican Council, did not a group of missionary bishops beseech Pope Pius IX to release the black race from the curse of Ham? A like request is not only perfectly logical in a theology of established disorder; it implies a praxis that accepts a ready-made world, accepts the status imposed on the colonized peoples and justified by a popular theology that interprets the condition of the black race as a punishment from God.

It is scarcely surprising, then, that the missionaries did not seek to spell out the biblical notion of the salvation they claimed to be bringing to the African. In the mind of most African converts, being saved meant going to heaven. Missionaries failed to point out that in the Bible the notion of salvation is shot through with that of liberation, and that salvation (or liberation) is expressed at once as present and future. Salvation is indeed the object of hope, but it has a present dimension as well. To be saved means to be delivered now, to be liberated already, from the forces of alienation that enslave persons.

By contrast, the church, by its silence or by hiding behind an apolitical disguise, reinforces and legitimates dependency. It fails to enunciate the sociohistorical dimensions of salvation and hope. In thrall to a religious anthropology that sees the human being only as a soul to be saved, the church has consolidated a state of misery by teaching the colonized peoples contempt for earthly values. A prayer frequently recited in Christian assemblies, in village and town, went as follows: 'I ask thee not for earthly riches and happiness. I ask thee but for one thing: Give me thy grace and I shall learn to condemn the joys of this world.' The notion of religion as the opium of the people, one might conclude, is not devoid of foundation here.

In the colonial situation that has marked imported Christianity, mission has undergone a systematic distortion. Globally the Christian message has been cut off from its political extensions, which give it its human, concrete meaning. Where world and society are concerned, missionaries have not generally sought to raise up rousers and doers, leaders of men and women, liberators, but have trained passive Christians, persons to be treated as minors. It would have been difficult for missioners emerging from the colonial seminary to teach anything calculated to impugn the situation of colonial dependence. In the missions the privatization of Christianity reached its zenith. The colonized peoples never had a complete view of Christianity. Bereft of a historical, critical sensitivity that would relate the salvation message to the particular context of colonial domination, the church kept Africans in line with taboos and sanctions instead of launching them into the historical adventure of liberation – where, precisely, the living God is revealed.

If the exodus has any meaning for us, it will be first and foremost in its capacity to illuminate the living relationship between revelation and history. The central event through which God is revealed by intervening in people's history is the exodus. God utters the divine being definitively in the action by which God snatches the people from the servitude of Egypt, and leads them, with mighty hand and outstretched arm, to the very land of Canaan, the land of the promise Abraham has received: 'When Israel was a child I loved him, and out of Egypt I called my son' (Hos. 11.1). Deuteronomy capsulizes Israel's religion thus: 'We were once slaves of Pharaoh in Egypt, but the Lord brought us out of Egypt with his strong hand' (Deut. 6.21).

Israel's liturgy is shot through from beginning to end with the memory of the exodus. The core, as we know, is the Feast of Passover – no longer a feast of returning spring, such as neighboring peoples celebrated – but a commemoration of the flight from Egypt (see Exod. 12.12–14). The Jewish religion is steeped in the memory of the Passover. The whole psalter seems driven by Miriam's refrain after the passage through the sea (Exod. 15.21–2). There is no psalm without an echo of *In exitu Israel de Egypto* . . . (see Pss. 105, 66, 78). Indeed, for

Israel the entire Bible is simply a rereading of the exodus, when the people of the covenant became aware of the crucial moment when God genuinely created them as a people.

Thus the exodus theme is a commonplace in prophetical preaching. Hosea speaks of leading Israel back to the desert to 'speak to her heart' (see Hos. 2.16–17). Ezekiel transforms his memory of the espousal of the exodus to a promise of a wedding (Ezek. 16). The Song of Songs, so rich with reminiscences of the exodus, is a foretaste of the end of the ages, when Jesus of Nazareth will assume the divine name of the exodus to manifest that in him all revelation is accomplished (John 8.28). The Christ appears in some way as the burning bush, out of which the name of God is communicated to human beings (see John 17.26). This appearance of Christ, wherein the story of the burning bush receives its fuller sense, sheds light on the meaning of the exodus. In the logic of revelation, the word of God develops by a projection into a future that had been awaited throughout the past. In the first great deeds of God, a messianic hope will discern the proclamation of the crowning action to consummate God's revelation in history.

Thus the state of things toward which history is moving is something that mythic time or cosmic cycles could never produce: the full and real accomplishment of divine promises is only partially realized at a given moment in history. In this perspective, the exodus, in which God, in a first moment, has created a people by the first convenant, will be a presage and presentiment of a future event that will be a second exodus. Thanks to the prophets, Israel comes to realize that the liberation from Egypt does not exhaust God's promise. Second Isaiah proclaims to the exiles a liberation that will be as a new exodus (Isa. 43.16–21; 52.4–6; 41.17–20). Cyrus restores freedom to God's people, but this liberation does not yet fulfill expectations. All of these partial realizations, far from quenching hope, only sharpen it. In other words, the capital event, in which God – in a conflict where God triumphs over the forces of slavery and death, symbolized by Egypt and its Pharaoh – bestows on Israel existence as a free people (Ezek. 16.3–9), is not the fulfillment of the promise, but a partial accomplishment and reiteration of the promise.

Such an event refers to a future of God in history, then. More precisely, it refers not to the God who is, but to the God who comes, and whose promise is never exhausted by its historical realizations. Ultimately the basic meaning of the exodus is bestowed by the revelation of a God who personally 'owns' the future. Revelation is not mainly a doctrine, but a promise, which remains to be verified in its realization in the future of the world. Thus it unceasingly opens out upon the future of a new creation, a new exodus. God's revelation in history always comports a horizon of the future, in which the divine design will be accomplished in its fullness. Out beyond events having the value of a sign, a more distant perspective appears, that of the end of the ages. Israel thus appears ever the people to whom God addresses the divine word, to be sure; but Israel is also created by this word, which endlessly bears this people toward a future – inasmuch as the promise of salvation in its plenitude constitutes the essential kernel of God's word, the thing that awakens hope in the human being.

We must seek the meaning of the God of the exodus in light of the fact that the fulfillment of the promises is the locus of intelligibility of revelation as a whole. When we interpret the divine name of the exodus in a dynamic perspective, we understand that, in giving the divine name, God is not content with showing that the divinity is not a being turned inward upon itself. God is actually turned toward human beings, the subject of personal relationships, to the precise extent that it is God's intervention in history that will say that God is God. But God does not designate the divinity as 'I am' in order to say that the divine being abides and subsists in the midst of events (Isa. 40.6–8); rather, God's word is immutable and was, is, and will be *revealed* in history. Through the exodus event, God is revealed in the history of the promise. Deliverance from servitude in Egypt is an event that illuminates the language of the promise: it is an act of fidelity on the part of God. In a word: In the exodus, God is revealed under the formality of promise.

God's revelation is still bound up with history, through the happenings in which Israel's faith deciphers the intervention of the hand of God, through events that are the vessels of the future by reason of God's promises with which they are intertwined. Just so, we see, the divine name of the exodus not only unveils the mystery of God's personhood, but is at the same time a name to be used on a journey, a name revealing God in the direction of the future, a name of promise to show forth, in the darkness of an unknown future, what it is that can be relied upon. It is in an event to be awaited, and not only in reference to an earlier event already known, that God is made known. As Moltmann says so well:

The God of the exodus [is] a God of promise and of leaving the present to face the future, a God whose freedom is the source of new things that are to come. . . . His name is a wayfaring name, a promise that discloses a new future, a name whose truth is experienced in history inasmuch as his promise discloses its future possibilities.[1]

The God who reveals the divine name shows thereby that God is not a force of nature whose epiphany signifies the eternal processes of life and death. God is a God concerned to orient the human being not toward the perpetual recommencement of the cosmic cycle, but toward a future constituting the goal of all of the human being's history. When all is said and done, the God who reveals the divine name is the God of hope in the future of an irreversible movement and a radical novelty. The exodus is the event par excellence reread by the people of God and commemorated by them in precise function of its revelation to them of who God is. In referring the human being to a future of God, the divine name of the exodus becomes a call of hope.

In a perspective in which the history of human beings is of value for God, who gets involved in that history and fulfills the divine promise there, we cannot posit the happiness of human beings, justice and freedom, reconciliation and peace, in a beyond having no connection with the realities and situations of the present world.

It is impossible to speak of hope without recalling that social and temporal reality is the locus of God's interventions and revelation alike. There God proposes to human beings a collective project of communion and oneness. Hence not only are liberation movements, mobilizing the collective aspirations, the locus where we are to read the history of the promise, but we must know, too, that God's revelation, in ongoing fashion, calls for the transformation of the world. Charged with a message of hope, God's revelation protests the present in order to actualize the future. God's revelation gives birth to a people who are witnesses to the promise. Their corresponding task is to do something new in history. Ultimately, revelation stirs up a community in exodus, whose mission is not only to live in expectation of the fulfillment of the promise, but also to promote the historical transformation of the world and of life.

Of necessity, the revelation of the God of the exodus enables us to renounce the temptation to short-circuit time and history. It enables us to rediscover the importance of the future and the depth of the present moment. It constrains us to assume historicity and thus to rethink the divine message in the space where the economy of solidarity characterizing God's designs on men and women and their world is being realized. In obedience to God's promise, we are to discern and prepare the roadways to the future. A grasp of the mystery proper to the God of the exodus arouses us to react against a flight to the future that would disregard the historical now. The God of the promise invites us to make history the locus of the progressive fulfillment of the promises.

Thus God's revelation not only has the purpose of illuminating and interpreting the existing reality of the world and of human beings; it also introduces a contradiction into present reality and thus initiates a dynamism whose thrust is toward the definitive fulfillment of the promise. In the perspective of divine revelation, the world itself is on a journey. It is impossible to speak of the promise, of its radical openness to the future, and at the same time to consider the world a self-enclosed system, a perfect order, or a ready-made reality. The fact is that history's end is not yet here. History is the tension between promise and fulfillment. Accordingly, knowledge of God is always provisional – and impossible without a transformation of the world. In other words, if the world is not yet a theophany, if reality is still open to the future, our true situation is still ahead of us. Thus we are at once on the way toward the God who comes and on the way toward a world as it ought to be, in conformity with the final fulfillment of the promise. Revelation in its plenitude coincides with the end of the process of transformation of the world. In short, the expectation of another world calls for another kind of world.

For millions of Africans, the signs of a world in quest of freedom and justice are too evident not to attract the attention of churches that boast the Judaeo-Christian revelation or claim that the message of the exodus occupies a central place. How many illiterate people are paralyzed today by their ancestral (and modern) fears in societies in which the accumulation of new knowledge operates according to the model of an elitist culture? Ignorance is not limited here to an inability to read and write. It extends to the functioning of political institutions, to the mechanisms of economics, to the laws of society. In the face of the manifold harassments and blind bullying of which they are the victims, the illiterate African rural masses are ignorant of the very law designed to protect them. Their very fear of defending themselves, even when they know they are in the right, itself constitutes a stumbling block, one from which many human groups need to be liberated.

In any breach with situations of servitude, a first step will be to promote a mentality of active solidarity. Of course no such mentality can exist without an inventory of the factors or mechanisms of oppression. No change is possible without an awareness of injustices such as will render them intolerable in the mind of the people. Ultimately, in raising up leaders for a determinate community who will perform the function of prophets in that community, the group will receive a 'word' from which it can draw the strength to forge ahead. There must be individuals to take up the questions and traumas of a group and awaken the group to injustices from within and injustices from without. Certain individuals must decide to speak, in the conviction that many in the group are aware of their suffering.

In any community, village or city neighborhood, the prime interest in reading the Book of Exodus is to rescue the majority of African Christians from ignorance of the history of liberation. After all, this text is about nothing else. Moses is not sent to Egypt to preach a spiritual conversion, but to lead Israel 'out of the house of slavery.' In this escape God is revealed as the unique, matchless God. In today's world changes do result from liberation movements, and Africans must not be kept from knowing that, in our age, living communities are struggling for respect for their rights.

A knowledge of the history of today's liberation movements will spur on communities held down by fatalism and resignation. It will be crucial to remember that through this history God's spirit is at work, toiling internally for the transformation of the world, in view of the fact that injustice and domination, with contempt for men and women and the violence all these things engender, constitute a key aspect of the sin of the world.

Accordingly, a reading of the Book of Exodus in Africa today demands that the Christian churches attempt to solve the problem of the interrelationship between the proclamation and education of faith and projects that will permit local communities to move from servitude to freedom. More radically, in a cultural context marked by the theme of withdrawal or estrangement from God as recorded in most African mythic traditions, how will it be possible to create any space for a desire of the living God apart from liberation experiences? What can supply a starting point for the proclamation of the word of God to human beings in a cultural universe in which, as for the Kirdi of North Cameroon, God has been killed, abandoning men and women to misery, suffering, and death? In the African churches where, all too frequently, a moralizing instruction has influenced generations of Christians, a reading of Exodus can help recall that God utters the divine being in history. It is precisely the place of Exodus in the Bible that obliges us to question ourselves concerning our forms of celebration of salvation in connection with all of the enterprises of human promotion. In other words, how may God's benevolent interventions in human history be recalled from within an experience of life, of joy and freedom, of sharing and communion – all concretely signified in the life of local communities? Must faith and salvation, and the church itself, be imprisoned in purely religious matters? Salvation comes from God, to be sure; but must one experience it outside the concrete history of a people? Or should we rather receive it in the context in which people live, taking account of their creative effort to construct a future that will be different from their past, a past so cruelly marked by slavery and domination? In Africa, where these situations form an integral part of the collective memory, one cannot shut Christianity up within the limits of a religion of the beyond.

If the church's mission is before all else a supernatural one, it can scarcely proclaim the One who fulfills the revelation of the cloud-wrapped God of the exodus without including, in its perceptions and its awareness, the concrete life of human beings, institutions and structures, social categories and ideologies – because these can all promote or paralyze the ascent of the daughters and sons of God. In this view, should the churches not confront today's Pharaohs and demand that they allow the people of God speech, decision, and freedom? Will it be enough to continue to run schools and hospitals, dispensaries and orphanages, all manner of charitable activities, or rather will it be in order to prioritize the assumption of the new aspirations of all of the disinherited by bringing the problems of women and men crushed by injustice into religious education, religious formation, and prayer?

In short: By entering into solidarity with the individuals and groups who are refused the dignity of being human, are the churches not called upon, on the one hand, to rediscover the function of Moses and the prophets as the spokespersons of the oppressed and collectively denounce the most crying abuses of the established systems, and, on the other hand, to intervene at all levels of the social system to protect the weak and the little from the arbitrary will of the great? The churches of black Africa ought to distinguish themselves in this role by the quality of their reflection and ought to be able to count on a laity committed to the process of transformation and change of society.

Beyond the shadow of a doubt, a reading of the exodus is a must in the Christian communities of Africa today. As the oppressed of all times have turned to this primordial event, thence to draw hope, we shall never come to any self-understanding without ourselves taking up that same history and discovering there that God intervenes in the human adventure of servitude and death to free the human being. The exodus event is the grid permitting the deciphering of human history and the discovery of its deeper sense – that of an intervention of God revealing the divine power and love.[2]

## NOTES

1   J. Moltmann, *Theology of Hope: On the Ground and the Implications of a Christian Eschatology* (New York and Evanston, Harper & Row, 1967), p. 30.

2   As his public life opens (see Luke 4.16–21), Jesus quotes a text of Isaiah (ch. 61), the latter being what is called an 'actualisation de l'Exode' – a recovery of the exodus event for the present. Jesus was steeped in the tradition of the exodus and the prophets. This tradition permeates the Old Testament from beginning to end. For the witnesses of revelation, the exodus was the prototype both of God's action and of the action God expected of the people.

# 19

# An Asian Feminist Perspective: The Exodus Story (Exodus 1.8–22, 2.1–10)

## AN ASIAN GROUP WORK

This piece is refreshingly different from the other essays in Part Three. For one thing, it is not a formal discourse on the narrative, but a skit centred around some lesser-known characters of the Exodus; for another, it is not written by an individual, but by a group of women.

In the hermeneutical tradition of the West, the biblical documents are studied in silence and it is assumed that only the printed word can communicate the authentic meaning. What this feminist reflection goes on to show is that hermeneutics can use not only philosophical tools, but also the medium of performing arts to unlock the biblical narratives. It further reiterates the point that interpretation can be a meaningful communal activity.

This skit was produced by a group of Indian women – Cresy John, Susan Joseph, Pearl Derego, Sister Pauline, Mary Lobo, Sister Margaret and a Korean, Lee Sun Ai, at the Human Liberation Workshop held in Bombay, May 1988, and is reprinted from *In God's Image* (September 1988). *In God's Image* is a feminist quarterly and it is available from The Editor, *In God's Image*, Kiu Kin Mansion, 568 Nathan Road, Kowloon, Hong Kong.

## SCENE I

*The house of Moses's mother. A Hebrew home – not lavish in any way.*
*Time: Afternoon 1–3 p.m.*
*Cast:  Moses's mother Jochebed*
   *Miriam*
   *Susannah (another mother)*
   *Hannah*
   *Shiprah (midwife)*
   *Puah (midwife)*

JOCHEBED:   Shalom, sisters, Shalom. There is much to thank our God. Yahweh has protected us and our leaders out of difficulties in this land of slavery.

HANNAH:   To think that we came as a privileged minority in the time of our father Joseph and now we are slaves bereft of our herds and cattle and lands.

JOCHEBED:   We have been strong through it all. Our days have not been easy, but God has been faithful. We are not in any easier times. But God has given us wisdom. It has grown through the experience of pain and as women we can unite and have courage. In solidarity is our wisdom. We must preserve ourselves and have faith. In this way we praise Jehovah our God, the source of our life, wisdom and hope. Let us share our stories . . .

SUSANNAH:   Our stories are not sweet. Wherever I turn my eyes and ears there is only pain and suffering. Yesterday Judah came home from the building site, bruised badly having been beaten by the foreman. He was in such pain while I cleaned his cuts with wine and oil. I have never seen Judah so close to cursing God. (*She sighs*) This morning he could barely stand, but he had to go back to work. Amos was with him. But before leaving, Judah told me to keep the water boiling when he returns because he expects to be injured further. The foreman, he said, seems more interested in killing the wounded than getting bricks made. It seems almost as though it doesn't matter that the city of Rameses should be built. What matters to our Egyptian lords is that we should all be finished.

JOCHEBED:   But Susannah, why did this foreman do this to Judah again?

SUSANNAH:   For no good reason. Judah made beautiful bricks without straw. Pharaoh's new scheme is merely to disable and demoralize our men in their place of work. But our men are producing miracles. Our people have a power from God, from above.

HANNAH:   It is not just our men who are facing tribulations. Our women and children are also going through difficulties. My Egyptian mistress orders me around, always finding more work when I finish my share at the end of the day. I come home when it is dark. Sometimes she sends me to her husband who uses me and then spits in my face and I have to return home totally unable to help mother in the housework – knowing always that one of our men will never take me as I am. I am afraid to leave – because it will mean public flogging. Death seems easier.

SUSANNAH: (*Putting her arm around Hannah*) How our children suffer!

JOCHEBED: (*Deep sigh*) Yes. Their suffering breaks my heart more than anything. Our husbands work in the building site; we work in their homes as servants and yet our income is not enough for our livelihood. My Aaron . . .

SUSANNAH: Yes, I heard about what happened to him. How is he today?

HANNAH: What happened to Aaron?

SUSANNAH: He also went to the work site. Towards the end of the day, a couple of days ago, while carrying bricks, he stumbled and the bricks fell on his feet. How is he today?

JOCHEBED: He had to go to work this morning. He is still limping.

(*Two midwives enter*)

PUAH: Sisters, there's bad news, bad news.

SHIPRAH: Bad news for our people.

JOCHEBED: Sit, Puah. Sit, Shiprah. Tell us what the trouble is.

PUAH: We were both summoned to Pharaoh's Palace this morning.

SHIPRAH: Pharaoh has ordered us to kill all the Hebrew male children at birth.

JOCHEBED: Oh my God, my God. Would that God will help us.

SUSANNAH: Why did you bring her this news like this? Lie down. Don't panic. You need to keep from worrying. When is your baby due?

JOCHEBED: Any time now, really. And I am sure this will be a boy. The way he kicks! This child is very different from Miriam. We must plan a strategy to get out of this. Puah and Shiprah, have you any ideas? What did you do? Were there any babies born this morning?

PUAH: Yes, two male Israeli babies – such strapping young ones and five Egyptians.

HANNAH:   Tell us, what did you do?

SHIPRAH:   Puah and I took the Israeli births.

JOCHEBED:   Did you kill the babies?

SHIPRAH:   No. God have mercy. We did not.

SUSANNAH:   God bless you. Does Pharaoh know?

SHIPRAH:   Yes, while I was coming home, Pharaoh summoned me. And I told him that the babies were born before we reached the women. But we thought we should come and inform you. We felt you sisters should know Pharaoh's plan.

PUAH:   We can only fulfil our role in giving life and helping it live, not in killing it.

SUSANNAH:   But why does Pharaoh want to kill our boys and not our girls?

PUAH:   They are afraid that the numbers of our men are increasing. They are afraid that if our men increase and become strong, they may rebel and go to war.

SHIPRAH:   Our girls, of course, can become their concubines, domestic servants and salves.

JOCHEBED:   By killing our men they will slowly destroy the only trade we have now – of brick-making. They will finish the line of our mothers Sarah and Rebecca and of our Father Abraham. They will annihilate us as a people. We will have no identity.

SUSANNAH and HANNAH:   Oh God, have mercy on us all!

PUAH:   We must go. Pharaoh may have set spies on us.

SHIPRAH:   Yes, we must go.

HANNAH:   Be strong, sisters. Peace to you and us.

SUSANNAH:   I must go too. (*Draws Miriam to herself and strokes her head*) Take care of your mother, girl. If there is any need, come and tell me. (*Embraces Jochebed*) Shalom. Be at rest.


## SCENE II

*The market place. Jochebed and Susannah and Leah are walking down. Puah and Shiprah walk hastily to them.*
*Cast: Jochebed*

Susannah
Leah
Shiprah
Puah
Soldiers

PUAH:   (*Drawing Jochebed aside*) Let us go home. We have more news for you.

*Shiprah talks to the other women and they draw their skirts and veils and scuttle away to Jochebed's house.*

(*Jochebed sits resting with her feet up. Miriam brings a bowl of water and towel for each of them to wash their feet*)

PUAH:   Pharaoh summoned us again.

SUSANNAH:   Again?

JOCHEBED:   Why? When?

SHIPRAH:   This morning. He was angry because he got a report that we did not kill three male Jewish babies.

SUSANNAH:   What did you say?

SHIPRAH:   We told Pharaoh that the Hebrew women are so strong that they delivered their babies before we arrived to assist.

JOCHEBED:   Praise God for giving you wisdom.

SUSANNAH:   You were not treated badly, were you?

PUAH:   Pharaoh's men kicked us and threatened to kill us if we would not follow Pharaoh's command.

JOCHEBED:   The power of Yahweh be with you and protect you.

SHIPRAH:   Don't worry about us. But we must make plans. We think we should train some more Hebrew women who can act as midwives so that we do not come to each delivery. But that will take time. Before that we must plan about you, our dear Jochebed. We must find a way to save your baby if it is a boy.

(*Sound of banging on the door. The door opens ajar. Soldiers enter*)

SOLDIER:   So Puah and Shiprah, you are on another lifesaving mission, are you?

SHIPRAH:   No. We were here to dine.

JOCHEBED:   Jehovah is mightier than Pharaoh. He is the defence of the weak.

SOLDIER:   There is a new decree then, women, for Yahweh to work with. The great Pharaoh says that all the newly born baby boys must be thrown into the river Nile. (*Points to Jochebed with a stick*) Anyone who disobeys will bring death to the entire household. (*Steps out grinning*) May your gods have wisdom to meet the wisdom of the Pharaoh of Egypt.

(*Out in the street. The gong is sounded and the decree announced while the women listen. Miriam is clinging to the skirt of her mother*)

JOCHEBED:   (*Taking Miriam in her arms*) It is a death sentence to my baby. The death sentence is on me and my family, on all Hebrew babies and families. God have mercy. Have mercy.

SUSANNAH and PUAH:   (*Going up to Jochebed and holding her*) Be brave, Jochebed. Be strong. Let us think of ways to save the baby – to save you and your family.

PUAH:   You are the last of the Hebrew women that are to have babies this season. For some weeks now there aren't others.

SUSANNAH:   Yes, we must do what we can.

PUAH:   Leah, you have been very silent. You haven't said a word. What have you been thinking?

LEAH:   I was thinking about the Princess. How different she is from her father.

SHIPRAH:   Yes, I heard she is very kind and very good to her Hebrew slaves. I also heard rumors in the palace that she isn't pleased with Pharaoh's decree.

LEAH:   Yes, that's true.

PUAH:   I have an idea. The Princess comes to the river to bathe every Thursday, does she not?

LEAH:   Yes.

PUAH:   You are also very close to her, Leah. She loves you because you have been her nurse since she was young. You can influence her, can't you?

LEAH:   Into what?

PUAH:   Into saving Jochebed's baby if he is a boy.

LEAH:   I can try.

SHIPRAH:   Jochebed, don't go out of the house any more so that the day of the birth is not known. Either Puah or I will be with you all the time. After the baby comes, if Leah has found favour with the Princess, we will hide the baby in the bulrushes in a basket and have Miriam hide to watch. If the Princess finds favour towards the baby, who knows what can happen.

LEAH:   Yes, we can try.

JOCHEBED:   All this seems like a dream. It all sounds too good to be true. May Yahweh have mercy on me and on this child. If my baby is a son and he is spared, Yahweh must have a purpose for him. If he lives I live. If he dies I die.

SUSANNAH:   He will live.

JOCHEBED:   The Princess may find him and may even kill him.

LEAH:   Jochebed, be strong. You have charged us to be strong through many things. Trust God and remember his faithfulness to Sarah when he returned Isaac alive and honoured her womb.

SUSANNAH:   Yes, Sister, be strong. We will meet again and plan further, but Leah go and do all you can.

## SCENE III

*The palace. The Princess getting ready for a walk by the river. Leah and the Princess are talking while she dresses the Princess.*
*Cast: Princess Zephartiti*
       *Leah*
       *Maidens*

PRINCESS:   Leah, you have been very quiet and sad these past few days. What is disturbing you?

LEAH:   Your majesty, I am grieving with my people.

PRINCESS:   It has shaken me to see how my father has passed these commands. But Leah, tell me, Puah and Shiprah are not following those insane commands of my father.

LEAH:   In most cases the babies have lived and been born before the nurses got there. But things are getting more and more difficult for them.

PRINCESS:    In my case I have longed for a child and it hasn't been possible, and there is no heir to the throne. So my father has now chosen to build a city in his name with the blood of others for posterity to remember him.

LEAH:    The Pharaoh is wise. In so many ways he has been good, but when he sees a Hebrew something happens to him. We became slaves in the days of his father. So why should he persecute us now?

PRINCESS:    He is afraid, more afraid of your God. Your cattle grew stronger than ours and multiplied so well. So he was forced to take them over, and now that they belong to us they are no longer virile. The same thing with your fields: when you gave up your tenancy, the fields became fallow. It is mysterious. But perhaps my father doesn't realise that it is important to work with you and to win fame with love rather than with hate.

LEAH:    True, your highness. But now shouldn't you go to the river for your walk? The sun will be setting soon and then it may be too late.

PRINCESS:    Leah, you have been a mother to me, speak your heart to me when you need to. Do not ever be afraid. (*Pats Leah lovingly*) Let us go.


## SCENE IV

*Walking beside the river – the Princess and her entourage. The maidens walking beside the princess, fanning her, and some of them clean the river of bulrushes and prepare a place for her to sit.*
*Cast: Princess*
    *Leah*
    *Maids – 5*
    *Miriam*
    *Baby in a basket*
    *3 soldiers*

PRINCESS:    The evening is beautiful. Leah, it is a better day to bathe than to walk. Prepare for it, Leah; have the sentries posted further.

LEAH: Yes, your majesty. (*She instructs the soldiers and the maidens. The Princess begins to undress. Just then a baby cries. Princess stops*)

PRINCESS: Who's that, Leah? (*Baby cries*) It is a baby, Leah. Where is it? Look for it, women.

(*They begin looking through the bulrushes with the Princess. She comes across the basket and the baby*)

PRINCESS: Leah, it is a Hebrew baby boy! He is beautiful! Just so beautiful! And only a few days old.

LEAH: Yes, your highness. It must be somebody's child, hidden for the fear of Pharaoh.

PRINCESS: Draw him here.

(*They draw out the crying baby and hand him over to the Princess. The baby is comforted*)

LEAH: He chooses you, Princess.

PRINCESS: I choose him too. He will be saved from my father's wrath. But he must be nursed. Is there a wet nurse among the Hebrews?

A MAID: Your highness, there is a little Hebrew girl that's peeping out of the bulrushes.

PRINCESS: Bring her to me. Leah, she must belong to this baby.

LEAH: Perhaps.

(*Maid comes with Miriam. Miriam is very frightened*)

PRINCESS: Come here, girl. Don't be afraid. (*Draws Miriam to herself*) Do you know of a wet nurse among your Hebrew women?

MIRIAM: Yes, your highness.

PRINCESS: Then go and bring her here at once.

MIRIAM: Yes, your highness. (*She runs out*)

PRINCESS: I am sure she is his sister. (*She is rocking the baby in her arms*) I will call him Moses because I drew him out of the water. The gods must be his protector for him to find favour with the Princess of Egypt. He must be a special baby. Leah, how I have longed for a child! I feel so fortunate to receive this gift.

(*Miriam comes running and stares aghast while the Princess kisses the baby. Jochebed follows her. Her eyes open wide in surprise. Jochebed falls at the Princess's feet*)

JOCHEBED:     Your highness – you called for me.

PRINCESS:     Woman, can you nurse my child?

JOCHEBED:     Yes, your highness. (*Eyes filling with tears*)

PRINCESS:     Take this child. His name shall be Moses. Nurse him for a
while. Bring him to me each day and let no harm come to him.
Leah, give this woman all she needs from my kitchen – fruits and
milk and good food. Let her not lack in any way. Woman, he is
mine. Yours, only to care for now. Remember he is to be prince.

JOCHEBED:     Yes, your highness.

PRINCESS:     (*Kisses the baby. Removes her ring and chain and puts it around
the baby. Gives him to Jochebed*) Be wise, woman. Be very careful.
Go now.

JOCHEBED:     (*Bows*) Yes, your highness.

(*Jochebed leaves with Moses close to her bosom and Miriam trailing
behind*)

PRINCESS:     There could not be a better caretaker or nurse than his
own mother.

(*Leah is silent but surprised*)


## SCENE V

*Pharaoh's palace. Sentries are around him. Pharaoh is pacing.*
*Cast: Pharaoh*
*        Sentries*
*        Princess*


PHARAOH:     What news of the Hebrews?

SOLDIER:     All's well at the building sites. They are flogged and they
are working hard.

PHARAOH:     Sure. Sure – but have the Hebrew babies been killed?

SOLDIER:     Your Majesty, in that regard, there is some confusion in the
land.

PHARAOH:     Confusion – what confusion?

SOLDIER:     I hesitate, your Majesty.

PHARAOH:  Your hesitation will cost you your life. Speak of what you know.

SOLDIER:  Surely you will not be angry with the Princess.

PHARAOH:  The princess? What has she done?

SOLDIER:  Your majesty, she has saved a Hebrew baby out of the water.

PHARAOH:  What?

SOLDIER:  It is true. While she was bathing in the river. I was her guard. I saw this happen. It has created quite a stir in the Hebrew camp.

PHARAOH:  Send for her immediately.

(*Soldier bows and leaves*)
(*Princess enters*)

PHARAOH:  Zephartiti, you have defied the orders of the Pharaoh of Egypt?

PRINCESS:  What have I done?

PHARAOH:  You have saved a Hebrew boy when you should have ordered to have him killed –

PRINCESS:  Oh, so you do have your spies on me, do you?

PHARAOH:  What you do is told me by the gods.

PRINCESS:  Strange gods these, that give us opposite commands.

PHARAOH:  Find a better reason for your sin.

PRINCESS:  The gods have not deemed to give me a child in spite of all the feasts and sacrifices I have offered.

PHARAOH:  That is because of your rebellious nature. Is that why you have defied the justice of Pharaoh?

PRINCESS:  Do you call the killing of babies – the shedding of innocent blood destroying life, the very gift of the gods – Justice?

PHARAOH:  How can you justify yourself? You have prevented my orders from being carried out.

PRINCESS:  Father, your orders were to throw the babies into the water to die. That order was carried out. But your decree did not say that the babies could not be rescued.

PHARAOH:   Foolish woman. These are the follies of a female mind. Bring me the baby and I will have him killed.

PRINCESS:   Then you go against your own decree. As well as against my protection for the baby. He wears my insignia – he is my heir.

PHARAOH:   (*Pacing restlessly*) Damn the gods!

PRINCESS:   Father, have you ever thought what would happen if you let this baby grow in the palace and be educated as a king? He is strong and beautiful. Think of what will happen when they see a Hebrew worshipping our gods chief of whom is Pharaoh. Their God will be insulted.

PHARAOH:   (*Pondering*) You propose to have a friend in the enemy's camp. You plan to have a Hebrew Pharaoh – worshipping me. (*Laughs*) Ha Ha.

PRINCESS:   I will enforce that he grows up in the wisdom of Egypt.

PHARAOH:   Yes, I think it will be a new and stronger bondage in their slavery. You can have the child.

PRINCESS:   So I will keep him. I will not forget your wishes.

PHARAOH:   I see that, occasionally, the wisdom of the line of Pharaohs shines through your natural darkness as a woman. Go with my blessing. (*To the sentry*) Revert the decree. There is no need to kill the babies any more.

(*Princess leaves after kissing the Pharaoh's ring. Sentry also goes out*)

## SCENE VI

*The Princess walks into her palace. Leah is pacing restlessly. She stops short as she hears the Princess entering.*
Cast: *Princess*
  *Leah*
  *Maids*

PRINCESS:   Leah.

LEAH:   Your majesty.

PRINCESS:   Leah, your God must be powerful – he saved my baby. The Pharaoh has already changed his mind and the decree has gone out that your children may live – sons and daughters. Go immediately – bring my baby to me with his mother. She can stay here; he will grow up in this palace just like the Pharaohs.

LEAH:   Really, your majesty?

PRINCESS:   Hasten, Leah. Don't waste time – today before the sun sets he should be here.

## CONCLUSION

*This is an episode in history of a people whose women refuse to accept the verdict of the male oppressor – in this event the Pharaoh. Instead, women gather in solidarity to save and protect life. The role of the princess, Pharaoh's daughter, is that of a woman, who, irrespective of her nationality and class, saves a child from the water. Linked together as women, Pharaoh's daughter joins the ranks of women in the triumph of life over death. The conspiracy of the midwives and Leah in saving the male babies and not adhering to Pharaoh's edict is a heroic witness to the strength of women. Every woman is close to life and loves her child. Woman is Life and Love. The killing of the male baby is ironic of the two-edged sword that patriarchy has in itself, namely, in male power is also death!*

# 20

# A Palestinian Perspective: The Bible and Liberation

## NAIM STIFAN ATEEK

---

This essay is a reminder that a biblical paradigm that is liberative in one context may be enslaving in another. This Palestinian example shows the unsuitability of the Exodus for that context.

This is from the author's book, *Justice, and Only Justice: A Palestinian Theology of Liberation* (Maryknoll, NY, Orbis Books, 1989).

Naim Stifan Ateek describes himself as an Arab, a Palestinian Christian, and a citizen of the state of Israel; he is a canon of St George's Cathedral, Jerusalem.

---

The Spirit of the Lord is upon me, because he has anointed me to preach good news to the poor. He has sent me to proclaim release to the captives and recovering of sight to the blind, to set at liberty those who are oppressed, to proclaim the acceptable year of the Lord (Luke 4.18–19).

The purpose of this chapter is to explicate the major thrust of a Palestinian theology of liberation. Since nothing of its kind has been done before, I will attempt to lay the cornerstone for such a theology. It will not exhaust the subject; but I will try to raise the main theological issues as I have come to see them as a Palestinian Christian through my interaction with parishioners, colleagues, and other Christians during the last twenty years of my ministry.

## THE TWO MAJOR ISSUES

The first major issue, which stands above all others and lies at the heart of the Palestinian problem, is justice. Since 1948 and the creation of the State of Israel, Palestinians everywhere have been talking about the injustice done to them – to young and old, educated and uneducated, rich and poor, male and female, religious and secular, Muslim and

Christian – all talk about the problem of justice. All of them remember what happened in 1948 and 1967, and they relate both the story of the loss of Palestine and their own stories of personal loss.

I have heard some Jews in Israel say that there is a great difference between the Palestinian and the Jewish claim to the land. The Palestinian's concern is focused on the loss of his house, his home, his business, and maybe his village. Injustice to him has to do with the fact that he was deprived of his own private property. The Jew's concern is said to be with the whole of the land, not with a particular spot.

My experience shows that such a distinction is a specious attempt on the part of some Jews to give a greater weight to their claim, a rationalization that only the ignorant or the prejudiced would accept. When Palestinians talk about injustice, they are talking about the tragedy of Palestine. When they tell their own story, it is told in order to illustrate vividly and to substantiate the extent of the injustice and the dehumanization to which the people of Palestine have been subjected; when Jews do not tell personal stories of how they lost their homes or villages in Palestine, it is because they did not have them.

Any theology of liberation must of necessity address the issue of justice. It is, after all, the major issue for Palestinians regardless of their religious affiliation.

For Palestinian Christians there is a second major issue that needs to be tackled in a theology of liberation: the Bible. The Bible is usually viewed as a source of strength, offering solutions and leading people to faith and salvation. Strangely – shockingly – however, the Bible has been used by some Western Christians and Jews in a way that has supported *in*justice rather than justice. Liberation theologians have seen the Bible as a dynamic source for their understanding of liberation, but if some parts of it are applied literally to our situation today the Bible appears to offer to the Palestinians slavery rather than freedom, injustice rather than justice, and death to their national and political life. Many good-hearted Christians have been confused or misled by certain biblical words and images that are normally used in public worship; words that have acquired new connotations since the establishment of the State of Israel. For example, when Christians recite the *Benedictus*, with its opening lines 'Blessed be the Lord God of Israel, for he has visited and redeemed his people,' what does it mean for them today? Which Israel are they thinking of? What redemption? The eminent historian Arnold J. Toynbee comments:

Within my lifetime the mental associations of the name 'Israel' have changed for those religious communities, the Jews and the Christians, in whose liturgies this name so often recurs. When, as a child, I used to take part, in church, in the singing of the Psalms, the name 'Israel' did not signify, for me, any existing state on the face of the globe. No state of that name was in existence then. Neither did the name signify the ancient Kingdom of Israel that was liquidated in 722 BC by the Assyrians. The history of Ancient Israel was familiar to me. But the name, when I recited it in the liturgy, meant a religious community of devout worshippers of Ancient Israel's God – the One True God in the belief of present-day Jews, Christians, and Muslims. 'Israel' signified 'God's people,' and we worshippers of God were living members of Israel, but members only conditionally. Our membership was conditional on our obeying God's commands and following His precepts as these had been declared by Him through the mouths of His Prophets.

This traditional spiritual connotation of the name 'Israel' has been supplanted today by a political and military connotation. Today, if I go to church and try to join in the singing of the Psalms, I am pulled up short, with a jar, when the name 'Israel' comes on to my lips. The name conjures up today a picture of a small, middle-Europe type state, with bickering political parties like all such states, with a rigid – and unsuccessful – foreign policy with respect to its neighbours and with constant appeal to the Jews of the world either to send them money or to come themselves. This picture has now effaced that one in our minds. It has effaced it, whoever we are: Jews or Christians, diaspora Jews or Israelis, believers or agnostics. The present-day political Israel has, for all of us, obliterated or, at least, adumbrated, the spiritual Israel of the Judeo-Christian tradition. This is surely a tragedy.[1]

If this has been true among Western Christians, it has been more painfully true of Palestinian and other Christians in the Middle East. The establishment of the State of Israel was a seismic tremor of enormous magnitude that has shaken the very foundation of their beliefs. Since then, no Palestinian Christian theology can avoid tackling the issue of the Bible: How can the Bible, which has apparently become a part of the problem in the Arab–Israeli conflict, become a part of its solution? How can the Bible, which has been used to bring a curse to the national aspirations of a whole people, again offer them a blessing? How can the Bible, through which many have been led to salvation, be itself saved and redeemed?

These two concerns – justice and the Bible – will occupy most of our attention. Most of the other issues for a theology of liberation for Palestinian Christians, as we shall see, are derived from them. In fact, the two issues are very much interrelated. I will treat them in reverse order, beginning with the issue of the Bible; then in the next chapter, move to the issue of justice; and finally, consider the victims of injustice and the challenges that face them.

## THE BIBLE: PROBLEM OR SOLUTION?

### The political abuse of the Bible

For most Palestinian Christians, as for many other Arab Christians, their view of the Bible, especially the Hebrew Scriptures, or Old Testament, has been adversely affected by the creation of the State of Israel. Many previously hidden problems suddenly surfaced. The God of the Bible, hitherto the God who saves and liberates, has come to be viewed by Palestinians as partial and discriminating. Before the creation of the State, the Old Testament was considered to be an essential part of Christian Scripture, pointing and witnessing to Jesus. Since the creation of the State, some Jewish and Christian interpreters have read the Old Testament largely as a Zionist text to such an extent that it has become almost repugnant to Palestinian Christians. As a result, the Old Testament has generally fallen into disuse among both clergy and laity, and the Church has been unable to come to terms with its ambiguities, questions, and paradoxes – especially with its direct application to the twentieth-century events in Palestine. The fundamental question of many Christians, whether uttered or not, is: How can the Old Testament be the Word of God in light of the Palestinian Christians' experience with its use to support Zionism?

Closely involved in the question of the Hebrew Scriptures in our concept of God. With the exception of relatively few people within the Christian communities in the Middle East, the existence of God is not in doubt. What has been seriously questioned is the nature and character of God. What is God really like? What is God's relation to the new State of Israel? Is God partial only to the Jews? Is this a God of justice and peace? Such questions may appear on the surface trite and their answers may seem obvious. Nevertheless, they are part of a battery of questions that many Christians, both in Israel–Palestine and outside of it, are still debating. The focus of these questions is the very person of God. God's character is at stake. God's integrity has been questioned.

Generally speaking, the Church in Israel–Palestine has stood impotent and helpless before these questions. It is no wonder then that there is widespread apathy among many Christians toward the Church. The pervasive and crucial question for its leadership has been, and still is: How can the Church, without rejecting any part of the Bible, adequately relate the core of the biblical message – its concept of God – to Palestinians? The answer lies largely in the doing of theology. The only bridge between the Bible and people is theology. It must be a theology that is biblically sound; a theology that liberates; a theology that will contextualize and interpret while remaining faithful to the heart of the biblical message. Unless such a theology is achieved, the human tendency will be to ignore and neglect the undesired parts of the Bible.

Some Christians, clergy included, have found a way to deal with the text through allegorization. Others use what I call spiritualization. Although these and other methods can be helpful, they do not meet the challenge of the political abuse of the Bible. One observes, too, that especially in this century in the West, biblical scholarship has made real strides in the application of critical methods to the study of the Bible. These scientific tools can clarify many ambiguities and help the student to get as close as possible to the original text – its author, date, source, context, and so on. Unless these methods are guided and informed by a larger theological understanding, however, they tend to leave the text dissected and to confuse rather than clarify matters of faith.

Generally speaking, all these methods do not throw light on whether or not the text is the Word of *God*. For Palestinian Christians, the core question that takes priority over all others is whether what is being read in the Bible is the Word of *God* to them and whether it reflects the nature, will, and purpose of *God* for them. In other words, is what is being read an authentic insight from God about who God is? Is it an authentic insight from God about persons or relationships or about human nature and history? Conversely, is what is being heard a reflection of authentic human understanding about God at that stage of development? Is it an authentic statement of humans about other human beings or about human nature at that stage of development? Or, to put it bluntly, is it basically a statement from humans put into the mouth of God, that has become confused as an authentic message from God to people? Do the words reflect an authentic and valid message from God to us today? What is eternally true in the Bible and what is conditioned? What is lasting and what is temporal? These are important questions for Palestinian Christians, whose answers will ultimately determine what God is or is not saying to them in the Bible.

## The central biblical hermeneutic

Palestinian Christians are looking for a hermeneutic that will help them to identify the authentic Word of *God* in the Bible and to discern the true meaning of those biblical texts that Jewish Zionists and Christian fundamentalists cite to substantiate their subjective claims and prejudices.

The criterion that Palestinians are looking for must be both biblically and theologically sound, lest it in turn becomes a mere instrument to oppose Jewish and Christian Zionists and support subjective Palestinian claims and prejudices. The hermeneutic must ring true of a God whom we have come to know – unchanging in nature and character, dynamically constant rather than fickle and variable, responding to but not conditioned by time, space, or cirsumstances.

The canon of this hermeneutic for the Palestinian Christian is nothing less than Jesus Christ himself. For in Christ and through Christ and because of Christ, Christians have been given a revealed insight into God's nature and character. For the Christian, to talk about the knowledge of God is to talk about knowing God through Christ: this is the best source of the knowledge of God; this is the concept of God that has matured through the period of biblical history. For the Christian, it has found its fulfillment in Jesus Christ's understanding of the nature and character of God. This understanding of God was vindicated for us in the life, death, and resurrection of Jesus, whom we acclaim as the Christ, God incarnate. Jesus the Christ thus becomes – in himself and in his teaching – the true hermeneutic, the key to the understanding of the Bible, and beyond the Bible to the understanding of the action of God throughout history. In other words, the *Word* of God incarnate in Jesus the Christ interprets for us the *word* of God in the Bible.

To understand God, therefore, the Palestinian Christian, like every other Christian, begins with Christ and goes backward to the Old Testament and forward to the New Testament and beyond them. This becomes the major premise for the Christian.

Due to the human predicament of evil, however, one discovers that the use of this hermeneutic does not mean that all of our theological problems are solved automatically; but one can discover that the new hermeneutic (which after all is not new at all in the Church) is really liberating. The Bible for Palestinian Christians, then, can be retained in its entirety, while its contents would be judged by this hermeneutic and scrutinized by the mind of Christ. To let the mind of Christ bear on situations and events is very important theologically. As C. H. Dodd explains:

Perhaps one of the most striking features of the early Christian movement was the re-appearance of a confidence that man can know God immediately. . . . Jesus Christ, with a confidence that to the timid traditionalism of His time appeared blasphemous, asserted that He knew the Father and was prepared to let others into that knowledge. He did so, not by handing down a new tradition about God, but by making others shares in His own attitude to God. This is what Paul means by 'having the mind of Christ.' Having that mind, we do know God. It was this clear, unquestioning conviction that gave Paul his power as a missionary: but he expected it also in his converts. To them, too, 'the word of knowledge' came 'by the same Spirit.' He prayed that God would give them a spirit of wisdom and revelation in the knowledge of Him. Such knowledge is, as Paul freely grants, only partial, but it is real, personal, undeniable knowledge. In friendship between men there is a mutual knowledge which is never complete or free from mystery: yet you can know with a certainty nothing could shake that your friend is 'not the man to do such a thing,' or that such and such a thing that you have heard is 'just like him.' You have a real knowledge which gives you a criterion. Such is the knowledge the Christian has of his Father.[2]

This criterion gives Christians great confidence, and informs their approach to the various problems that they encounter.

## NOTES

1  E. Berger, *Prophecy, Zionism and the State of Israel*, Introduction by A. J. Toynbee (New York, American Alternative to Zionism, n.d.).
2  C. H. Dodd, *The Meaning of Paul for Today* (New York, Meridian, 1957), pp. 131–2.

# 21

# A Native American Perspective: Canaanites, Cowboys, and Indians

## ROBERT ALLEN WARRIOR

Like the last essay, this exegetical discourse throws a different light on the Exodus story and points out its inappropriateness as a model for liberation for all contexts and all people. Here is an attempt by a member of the Osage Nation of American Indians, who reads the Exodus from the perspective of the Canaanites and discerns parallels between the humiliated people of biblical times and his own people in the history of America, and draws out implications for hermeneutical reflection and political action.

This essay appeared in *Christianity and Crisis* (49, 12, 1989). *Christianity and Crisis* is an American journal of Christian opinion. The address is: 537 W. 121 St, New York 10027.

Robert Allen Warrior is a New York correspondent for the *Lakota Times*, published in Rapid City.

Native American theology of liberation has a nice ring to it. Politically active Christians in the US have been bandying about the idea of such a theology for several years now, encouraging Indians to develop it. There are theologies of liberation for African Americans, Hispanic Americans, women, Asian Americans, even Jews. Why not Native Americans? Christians recognize that American injustice on this continent began nearly 500 years ago with the oppression of its indigenous people and that justice for American Indians is a fundamental part of broader social struggle. The churches' complicity in much of the violence perpetrated on Indians makes this realization even clearer. So, there are a lot of well-intentioned Christians looking for some way to include Native Americans in their political action.

For Native Americans involved in political struggle, the participation of church people is often an attractive proposition. Churches have financial, political, and institutional resources that many Indian activists would dearly love to have at their disposal. Since American Indians have a relatively small population base and few financial

287

resources, assistance from churches can be of great help in gaining the attention of the public, the media, and the government.

It sounds like the perfect marriage – Christians with the desire to include Native Americans in their struggle for justice and Indian activists in need of resources and support from non-Indians. Well, speaking as the product of a marriage between an Indian and a white, I can tell you that it is not as easy as it sounds. The inclusion of Native Americans in Christian political praxis is difficult – even dangerous. Christians have a different way of going about the struggle for justice than most Native Americans: different models of leadership, different ways of making decisions, different ways of viewing the relationship between politics and religion. These differences have gone all but unnoticed in the history of church involvement in American Indian affairs. Liberals and conservatives alike have too often surveyed the conditions of Native Americans and decided to come to the rescue, always using *their* methods, *their* ideas, and *their* programs. The idea that Indians might know best how to address their own problems is seemingly lost on these well-meaning folks.

Still, the time does seem ripe to find a new way for Indians and Christians (and Native American Christians) to be partners in the struggle against injustice and economic and racial oppression. This is a new era for both the church and for Native Americans. Christians are breaking away from their liberal moorings and looking for more effective means of social and political engagement. Indians, in this era of 'self-determination,' have verified for themselves and the government that they are the people best able to address Indian problems as long as they are given the necessary resources and if they can hold the US government accountable to the policy. But an enormous stumbling block immediately presents itself. Most of the liberation theologies that have emerged in the last twenty years are preoccupied with the Exodus story, using it as the fundamental model for liberation. I believe that the story of the Exodus is an inappropriate way for Native Americans to think about liberation.

No doubt, the story is one that has inspired many people in many contexts to struggle against injustice. Israel, in the Exile, then Diaspora, would remember the story and be reminded of God's faithfulness. Enslaved African Americans, given Bibles to read by their masters and mistresses, would begin at the beginning of the book and find in the pages of the Pentateuch a god who was obviously on their side, even if that god was the god of their oppressors. People in Latin

American base communities read the story and have been inspired to struggle against injustice. The Exodus, with its picture of a god who takes the side of the oppressed and powerless, has been a beacon of hope for many in despair.

## GOD THE CONQUEROR

Yet, the liberationist picture of Yahweh is not complete. A delivered people is not a free people, nor is it a nation. People who have survived the nightmare of subjugation dream of escape. Once the victims have been delivered, they seek a new dream, a new goal, usually a place of safety away from the oppressors, a place that can be defended against future subjugation. Israel's new dream became the land of Canaan. And Yahweh was still with them: Yahweh promised to go before the people and give them Canaan, with its flowing milk and honey. The land, Yahweh decided, belonged to these former slaves from Egypt and Yahweh planned on giving it to them – using the same power used against the enslaving Egyptians to defeat the indigenous inhabitants of Canaan. Yahweh the deliverer became Yahweh the conqueror.

The obvious characters in the story for Native Americans to identify with are the Canaanites, the people who already lived in the promised land. As a member of the Osage Nation of American Indians who stands in solidarity with other tribal people around the world, I read the Exodus stories with Canaanite eyes. And, it is the Canaanite side of the story that has been overlooked by those seeking to articulate theologies of liberation. Especially ignored are those parts of the story that describe Yahweh's command to mercilessly annihilate the indigenous population.

To be sure, most scholars, of a variety of political and theological stripes, agree that the actual events of Israel's early history are much different than what was commanded in the narrative. The Canaanites were not systematically annihilated, nor were they completely driven from the land. In fact, they made up, to a large extent, the people of the new nation of Israel. Perhaps it was a process of gradual immigration of people from many places and religions who came together to form a new nation. Or maybe, as Norman Gottwald and others have argued, the peasants of Canaan revolted against their feudal masters, a revolt instigated and aided by a vanguard of escaped slaves from Egypt who believed in the liberating god, Yahweh. Whatever happened, scholars agree that the people of Canaan had a lot to do with it.

Nonetheless, scholarly agreement should not allow us to breathe a sigh of relief. For historical knowledge does not change the status of the indigenes in the *narrative* and the theology that grows out of it. The research of Old Testament scholars, however much it provides an answer to the historical question – the contribution of the indigenous people of Canaan to the formation and emergence of Israel as a nation – does not resolve the narrative problem. People who read the narratives read them as they are, not as scholars and experts would *like* them to be read and interpreted. History is no longer with us. The narrative remains.

Though the Exodus and Conquest stories are familiar to most readers, I want to highlight some sections that are commonly ignored. The covenant begins when Yahweh comes to Abram saying, 'Know of a surety that your descendants will be sojourners in a land that is not theirs, and they will be slaves there, and they will be oppressed for four hundred years; but I will bring judgment on the nation they serve and they shall come out' (Gen. 15.13,14). Then, Yahweh adds: 'To your descendants I give this land, the land of the Kenites, the Kenizzites, the Kadmonites, the Hittites, the Perizzites, the Rephaim, the Amorites, the Canaanites, and the Jebusites' (15.18–21). The next important moment is the commissioning of Moses. Yahweh says to him, 'I promise I will bring you out of the affliction of Egypt, to the land of the Canaanites, the Hittites, the Amorites, the Perizzites, the Hivites, and the Jebusites, a land flowing with milk and honey' (Exod. 3.17). The covenant, in other words, has two parts: deliverance and conquest.

After the people have escaped and are headed to the promised land, the covenant is made more complicated, but it still has two parts. If the delivered people remain faithful to Yahweh, they will be blessed in the land Yahweh will conquer for them (Exod. 20–3 and Deut. 7–9). The god who delivered Israel from slavery will lead the people into the land and keep them there as long as they live up to the terms of the covenant. 'You shall not wrong a stranger or oppress him [*sic*], for you were strangers in the land of Egypt. You shall not afflict any widow or orphan. If you do afflict them, and they cry out to me, I will surely hear their cry; and my wrath will burn, and I will kill you with the sword, and your wives shall become widows and your children fatherless' (Exod. 22.21).

*intend scrip it indigenous eye
why not?
"make Indians are not
in their land"*

# WHOSE NARRATIVE?

Israel's reward for keeping Yahweh's commandments – for building a society where the evils done to them have no place – is the continuation of life in the land. But one of the most important of Yahweh's commands is the prohibition on social relations with Canaanites or participation in their religion. 'I will deliver the inhabitants of the land into your hand, and you shall drive them out before you. You shall make no covenant with them or with their gods. They shall not dwell in your land, lest they make you sin against me; for if you serve their gods it will surely be a snare to you' (Exod. 23.31b–33).

In fact, the indigenes are to be destroyed:

> When the Lord your God brings you into the land which you are entering to take possession of it, and clears away many nations before you, the Hittites, the Girgashites, the Amorites, the Canaanites, the Perizzites, the Hivites, and the Jebusites, seven nations greater and mightier than yourselves, and when the Lord your God gives them over to you and you defeat them; then you must utterly destroy them; you shall make no covenant with them, and show no mercy to them (Deut. 7.1,2).

These words are spoken to the people of Israel as they are preparing to go into Canaan. The promises made to Abraham and Moses are ready to be fulfilled. All that remains is for the people to enter into the land and dispossess those who already live there.

Joshua gives an account of the conquest. After ten chapters of stories about Israel's successes and failures to obey Yahweh's commands, the writer states, 'So Joshua defeated the whole land, the hill country and the Negeb and the lowland and the slopes, and all their kings, he left none remaining, but utterly destroyed all that breathed, as the Lord God of Israel commanded.' In Judges, the writer disagrees with this account of what happened, but the Canaanites are held in no higher esteem. The angel of the Lord says, 'I will not drive out [the indigenous *cf* people] before you; but they shall become adversaries to you, and their gods shall be a snare to you.'

Thus, the narrative tells us that the Canaanites have status only as the people Yahweh removes from the land in order to bring the chosen people in. They are not to be trusted, nor are they to be allowed to enter into social relationships with the people of Israel. They are wicked, and their religion is to be avoided at all costs. The laws put forth regarding strangers and sojourners may have stopped the people of Yahweh from wanton oppression, but presumably only after the land was safely in the hands of Israel. The covenant of Yahweh depends on this.

The Exodus narrative is where discussion about Christian involvement in Native American activism must begin. It is these stories of deliverance and conquest that are ready to be picked up and believed by anyone wondering what to do about the people who already live in their promised land. They provide an example of what can happen when powerless people come to power. Historical scholarship may tell a different story; but even if the annihilation did not take place, the narratives tell what happened to those indigenous people who put their hope and faith in ideas and gods that were foreign to their culture. The Canaanites trusted in the god of outsiders and their story of oppression and exploitation was lost. Interreligious praxis became betrayal and the surviving narrative tells us nothing about it.

Confronting the conquest stories as a narrative rather than a historical problem is especially important given the tenor of contemporary theology and criticism. After 200 years of preoccupation with historical questions, scholars and theologians across a broad spectrum of political and ideological positions have recognized the function of narrative in the development of religious communities. Along with the work of US scholars like Brevard Childs, Stanley Hauerwas, and George Lindbeck, the radical liberation theologies of Latin America are based on empowering believing communities to read scriptural narratives for themselves and make their reading central to theology and political action. The danger is that these communities will read the narratives, not the history behind them.

And, of course, the text itself will never be altered by interpretations of it, though its reception may be. It is part of the canon for both Jews and Christians. It is part of the heritage and thus the consciousness of people in the United States. Whatever dangers we identify in the text and the god represented there will remain as long as the text remains. These dangers only grow as the emphasis upon catechetical (Lindbeck), narrative (Hauerwas), canonical (Childs), and Bible-centered Christian base communities (Gutierrez) grows. The peasants of Solentiname bring a wisdom and experience previously unknown to Christian theology, but I do not see what mechanism guarantees that they – or any other people who seek to be shaped and molded by reading the text – will differentiate between the liberating god and the god of conquest.

Robert Allen Warrior

# IS THERE A SPIRIT?

What is to be done? First, the Canaanites should be at the center of Christian theological reflection and political action. They are the last remaining ignored voice in the text, except perhaps for the land itself. The conquest stories, with all their violence and injustice, must be taken seriously by those who believe in the god of the Old Testament. Commentaries and critical works rarely mention these texts. When they do, they express little concern for the status of the indigenes and their rights as human beings and as nations. The same blindness is evident in theologies that use the Exodus motif as their basis for political action. The leading into the land becomes just one more redemptive moment rather than a violation of innocent peoples' rights to land and self-determination.

Keeping the Canaanites at the center makes it more likely that those who read the Bible will read *all* of it, not just the part that inspires and justifies them. And should anyone be surprised by the brutality, the terror of these texts? It was, after all, a Jewish victim of the Holocaust, Walter Benjamin, who said, 'There is no document of civilization which is not at the same time a document of barbarism.' People whose theology involves the Bible need to take this insight seriously. It is those who know these texts who must speak the truth about what they contain. It is to those who believe in these texts that the barbarism belongs. It is those who act on the basis of these texts who must take responsibility for the terror and violence they can and have engendered.

Second, we need to be more aware of the way ideas such as those in the conquest narratives have made their way into Americans' consciousness and ideology. And only when we understand this process can those of us who have suffered from it know how to fight back. Many Puritan preachers were fond of referring to Native Americans as Amelkites and Canaanites – in other words, people who, if they would not be converted, were worthy of annihilation. By examining such instances in theological and political writings, in sermons, and elsewhere, we can understand how America's self-image as a 'chosen people' has provided a rhetoric to mystify domination.

Finally, we need to decide if we want to accept the model of leadership and social change presented by the entire Exodus story. Is it appropriate to the needs of indigenous people seeking justice and deliverance? If indeed the Canaanites were integral to Israel's early

293

history, the Exodus narratives reflect a situation in which indigenous people put their hope in a god from outside, were liberated from their oppressors, and then saw their story of oppression revised out of the new nation's history of salvation. They were assimilated into another people's identity and the history of their ancestors came to be regarded as suspect and a danger to the safety of Israel. In short, they were betrayed.

Do Native Americans and other indigenous people dare trust the same god in their struggle for justice? I am not asking an easy question and I in no way mean that people who are both Native Americans and Christians cannot work toward justice in the context of their faith in Jesus Christ. Such people have a lot of theological reflection to do, however, to avoid the dangers I have pointed to in the conquest narratives. Christians, whether Native American or not, if they are to be involved, must learn how to participate in the struggle without making their story the whole story. Otherwise the sins of the past will be visited upon us again.

No matter what we do, the conquest narratives will remain. As long as people believe in the Yahweh of deliverance, the world will not be safe from Yahweh the conqueror. But perhaps, if they are true to their struggle, people will be able to achieve what Yahweh's chosen people in the past have not: a society of people delivered from oppression who are not so afraid of becoming victims again that they become oppressors themselves, a society where the original inhabitants can become something other than subjects to be converted to a better way of life or adversaries who provide cannon fodder for a nation's militaristic pride.

With what voice will we, the Canaanites of the world, say, 'Let my people go and leave my people alone?' And, with what ears will followers of alien gods who have wooed us (Christians, Jews, Marxists, capitalists), listen to us? The indigenous people of this hemisphere have endured a subjugation now 100 years longer than the sojourn of Israel in Egypt. Is there a god, a spirit, who will hear us and stand with us in the Amazon, Osage County, and Wounded Knee? Is there a god, a spirit, able to move among the pain and anger of Nablus, Gaza, and Soweto? Perhaps. But we, the wretched of the earth, may be well advised this time not to listen to outsiders with their promises of liberation and deliverance. We will perhaps do better to look elsewhere for our vision of justice, peace, and political sanity – a vision through which we escape not only our oppressors, but our oppression as well. Maybe, for once, we will just have to listen to ourselves, leaving the gods of this continent's real strangers to do battle among themselves.

# PART FOUR

# *One Reality, Many Texts: Examples of Multi-faith Hermeneutics*

When will people understand that it is useless for a man to
read his Bible unless he also reads everybody else's?

(Father Brown in G. K. Chesterton
*The Sign of the Broken Sword*)

# 22

# Discovering the Bible in the Non-biblical World

## KWOK PUI LAN

For many centuries the Christian Scripture has been taken as the norm to judge other, non-biblical cultures. Seldom do biblical scholars and others feel the need to rediscover the Bible through the issues raised by people whose lives are not shaped by the biblical vision. Kwok Pui Lan, a Chinese biblical scholar, questions the rigidity of the biblical canon and its universal truth-claims, and offers a proposal for interpreting the Christian Scripture in a religiously plural world and from a woman's perspective.

Kwok Pui Lan is one of the prominent Asian theologians and has written numerous articles in various journals. This article is reprinted from *Semeia* (47, 1989).

Kwok Pui Lan is a member of the faculty at Chung Chi College, Chinese University of Hong Kong, Hong Kong.

'To the African, God speaks as if He [*sic*] were an African; to the Chinese, God speaks as if He [*sic*] were a Chinese. To all men and women, the Word goes out over against their particular existing environment and their several cultural settings.' Thus spoke T. C. Chao, a Protestant theologian from China.[1] The central *Problematik* of biblical hermeneutics for Christians living in the 'non-Christian' world is how to hear God speaking in a different voice – one other than Hebrew, Greek, German or English.

Christianity has been brought into interaction with Chinese culture for many centuries, but the Christian population in China never exceeded 1 percent. Since the nineteenth century, the Christian missionary enterprise has often been criticized as being intricately linked to western domination and cultural imperialism. Chinese Christians have been struggling with the question of how to interpret the biblical message to our fellow Chinese, the majority of whom do not share our belief.

In fact, this should not only be a serious concern to the Chinese, but a challenge to all Christians with a global awareness, and to biblical scholars in particular. For two-thirds of our world is made up of non-Christians and most of these people are under the yoke of exploitation by the privileged one-third of our world. The interpretation of the Bible is not just a religious matter within the Christian community, but a matter with significant political implications for other peoples as well. The Bible can be used as an instrument of domination, but it can also be interpreted to work for our liberation.

This paper attempts to discuss some of the crucial issues raised by the interaction of the Bible with the non-biblical world. My observation will be chiefly based on the Chinese situation, with which I am most familiar, drawing also upon insights from other Asian theologians. I shall first discuss biblical interpretation in the context of the political economy of truth. The second part will focus on biblical interpretation as dialogical imagination based on contemporary reappropriation of the Bible by Asian Christians. Finally, I shall offer my own understanding of the Bible from a Chinese woman's perspective.

## BIBLICAL INTERPRETATION AND THE POLITICS OF TRUTH

Biblical interpretation is never simply a religious matter, for the processes of formation, canonization and transmission of the Bible have been imbued with the issues of authority and power. The French philosopher Michel Foucault helps us to see the complex relationship of truth to power by studying the power mechanisms which govern the production and the repression of truth. He calls this the 'political economy' of truth:

> Each society has its regime of truth, its 'general politics' of truth: that is, the types of discourse which it accepts and makes function as true; the mechanisms and instances which enable one to distinguish true and false statements, the means by which each is sanctioned; the techniques and procedures accorded value in the acquisition of truth; the status of those who are charged with saying what counts as true.[2]

Foucault's analysis leads me to examine the power dynamics underlying such questions as: What is truth? Who owns it? Who has the authority to interpret it? This is particularly illuminating when we try to investigate how the Bible is used in a cross-cultural setting.

*Who owns the truth?* In the heyday of the missionary movement of the late nineteenth century, John R. Mott, the chief engineer of what was called the campaign of the 'evangelization of the world in this generation', cried out:

> The need of the non-Christian world is indescribably great. Hundreds of millions are today living in ignorance and darkness, steeped in idolatry, superstition, degradation and corruption. . . . The Scriptures clearly teach that if men are to be saved they must be saved through Christ. He alone can deliver them from the power of sin and its penalty. His death made salvation possible. The Word of God sets forth the conditions of salvation.[3]

Mott and others saw the Bible as the revealed Word of God which had to be made known to all 'heathens' who were living in idolatry and superstition. The Bible was to be the 'signifier' of a basic deficiency in the 'heathen' culture. This is a western construction superimposed on other cultures, to show that western culture is the norm and it is superior. It might be compared to the function of the 'phallus' as a signifier of the fundamental lack of female superimposed on women by men in the male psychological discourse.[4] It is not mere coincidence that missionary literatures describe Christian mission as 'aggressive work' and western expansion as 'intrusion' and 'penetration.'

The introduction of the Bible into Asia has been marked by difficulty and resistance mainly because Asian countries have their own religious and cultural systems. The issue of communicating the 'Christian message in a Non-Christian World' was the primary concern of the World Missionary Conference in 1938. Hendrik Kraemer, the key figure in the Conference, acknowledged that non-Christian religions are more than a set of speculative ideas, but are 'all-inclusive systems and theories of life, rooted in a religious basis, and therefore at the same time embrace a system of culture and civilizaton and a definite structure of society and state.'[5] But his biblical realism, influenced much by Karl Barth's theology, maintains that the Christian Gospel is the special revelation of God, which implies a discontinuity with all cultures and judges all religions.

This narrow interpretation of truth has disturbed many Christians coming from other cultural contexts. T. C. Chao, for example, presented a paper on 'Revelation' which stated: 'There has been no time, in other words, when God has not been breaking into our human world; nor is there a place where men have been that He [*sic*] has not entered and ruled.'[6] Citing the long line of sages, moral teachers of

China, such as Confucius, Mencius and Moti, he questioned, 'Who can say that these sages have not been truly inspired by the spirit of our God, the God of our Lord Jesus Christ? Who can judge that the Almighty has not appeared to them in His [*sic*] Holy, loving essence and that they have not been among the pure heart of whom Jesus speaks?'[7]

In this battle for truth, many Chinese Christians reject the assumption that the Bible contains all the truth and that the biblical canon is rigidly closed. Po Ch'en Kuang argued in 1927 that many Chinese classics, such as Analects, Mencius, the Book of Songs and Rites are comparable to the prophets, the Psalms, and the Book of Deuteronomy of the Old Testament.[8] Since the Bible contains the important classics of the Jewish people which preceded Jesus, he could see no reason why the Chinese would not include their own. Others such as Hsieh Fu Ya[9] and Hu Tsan Yün[10] argue that the Chinese Bible should consist of parts of the Hebrew Bible, the Christian Bible, Confucian classics, and even Taoist and Buddhist texts! For a long time, Chinese Christians have been saying that western people do not own the truth simply because they bring the Bible to us, for truth is found in other cultures and religions as well.

*Who interprets the truth?* Another important issue in the political economy of truth concerns who has the power to interpret it. In the great century of missionary expansion, many missionaries acted as though they alone knew what the Bible meant, believing they were closer to truth. The Gospel message was invariably interpreted as being the personal salvation of the soul from human sinfulness. This interpretation reflects an understanding of human nature and destiny steeped in western dualistic thinking. Other cultures, having a different linguistic system and thought form, may not share similar concerns. As Y. T. Wu, a Chinese theologian, notes, 'Such terms as original sin, atonement, salvation, the Trinity, the Godhead, the incarnation, may have rich meanings for those who understand their origins and implications, but they are just so much superstition and speculation for the average Chinese.'[11]

More importantly, this simplistic version of the Gospel functions to alienate the Christians in the Third World from the struggle against material poverty and other oppressions in their society. But in the name of a 'universal gospel,' this thin-sliced biblical understanding was pre-packaged and shipped all over the world. The basic problem of the so-called 'universal Gospel' is that it not only claims to provide the answer but defines the question too! The American historian William R. Hutchison rightly observes that: American missionary ideologies at the turn of the century shared the belief that 'Christianity as it existed in the West had a "right" not only to conquer the world, but to define reality for the peoples of the world.'[12] If other people can only define truth according to the western perspective, then Christianization really means westernization! Chinese Christians began a conscious effort to re-define what the Gospel meant for them in the 1920s, as a response to the anti-Christian movement which criticized Christianity as 'the running dog of imperialism.' Chinese Christians became collectively aware that they had to be accountable to their fellow Chinese in their biblical interpretations, not just to the tiny Christian minority. They tried to show that biblical concepts such as 'agape' were compatible to 'benevolence' in Chinese classics and that the moral teachings of Jesus were comparable to the teachings of the Confucian tradition. As foreign invasion became imminent, the central concern of all Chinese was national salvation and the gospel message, too, became politicized.[13] Y. T. Wu, for example, reinterpreted Jesus as 'a revolutionary, the upholder of justice and the challenger of the rights of the oppressed'[14] in the mid-1930s, anticipating the kind of liberation theology that developed decades later. These attempts of indigenization clearly show that biblical truth cannot be pre-packaged, but that it must be found in the actual interaction between text and context in the concrete historical situation.

*What constitutes truth?* The last point I want to consider briefly concerns the norm by which we judge something as truth. Here again, Chinese philosophical tradition is very different from the west in that it is not primarily interested in metaphysical and epistemological questions. On the contrary, it is more concerned with the moral and ethical visions of a good society. The Neo-Confucian tradition in particular has emphasized the integral relationship between knowing and doing. Truth is not merely something to be grasped cognitively, but to be practised and acted out in the self-cultivation of moral beings.

For most Chinese, the truth claim of the Bible cannot be based on its being the supposed revealed Word of God, for 99 percent of the people do not believe in this faith statement. They can only judge the meaningfulness of the biblical tradition by looking at how it is acted out in the Christian community. Some of the burning questions of Chinese students at the time of foreign encroachment were: 'Can Christianity save China?', 'Why does not God restrain the stronger nations from oppressing the weaker ones?', 'Why are the Christian nations of the west so aggressive and cruel?'[15] These probing questions can be compared to what Katie G. Cannon, an Afro-American ethicist, has also asked: 'Where was the Church and the Christian believers when Black women and Black men, Black boys and Black girls, were being raped, sexually abused, lynched, assassinated, castrated and physically oppressed? What kind of Christianity allowed white Christians to deny basic human rights and simple dignity to Blacks, these same rights which had been given to others without question?'

The politics of truth is not fought on the epistemological level. People in the Third World are not interested in whether or not the Bible contains some metaphysical or revelational truth. The authority of the Bible can no more hide behind the unchallenged belief that it is the Word of God, nor by an appeal to a church tradition which has been defined by white, male, clerical power. The poor, women, and other marginalized people are asking whether the Bible can be of help in the global struggle for liberation.

## BIBLICAL INTERPRETATION AS DIALOGICAL IMAGINATION

To interpret the Bible for a world historically not shaped by the biblical vision, there is need to conjure up a new image for the process of biblical interpretation itself. I have coined the term 'dialogical imagination' based on my observation of what Asian theologians are doing. I will explain what this term means and illustrate it with some examples of the contemporary use of the Bible in Asia.

Dialogue in Chinese means talking with each other. It implies mutuality, active listening, and openness to what the other has to say. Asian Christians are heirs to both the biblical story and to our own story as Asian people, and we are concerned to bring the two in dialogue with one another. Kosuke Koyama, a Japanese theologian, has tried to explain this metaphorically in the title of his latest book, *Mount Fuji and Mount Sinai*. He affirms the need to do theology in the context of a dialogue between Mount Fuji and Mount Sinai, between Asian spirituality and biblical spirituality.[16] Biblical interpretation in Asia, too, must create a two-way traffic between our own tradition and that of the Bible.

There is, however, another level of dialogue we are engaged in because of our multi-religious cultural setting. Our fellow Asians who have other faiths must not be considered our missiological objects, but as dialogical partners in our ongoing search for truth. This can only be done when each one of us takes seriously the Asian reality, the suffering and aspirations of the Asian people, so that we can share our religious insights to build a better society.

Biblical interpretation in Asia must involve a powerful act of imagination. Sharon Parks[17] shows that the process of imagination involves the following stages: a consciousness of conflict (something as not fitting), a pause, the finding of a new image, the repatterning of reality, and interpretation. Asian Christians have recognized the dissonance between the kind of biblical interpretation we inherited and the Asian reality we are facing. We have to find new images for our reality and to make new connections between the Bible and our lives.

The act of imagination involves a dialectical process. On the one hand, we have to imagine how the biblical tradition which was formulated in another time and culture can address our burning questions today. On the other hand, based on our present circumstances, we have to re-imagine what the biblical world was like, thus opening up new horizons hitherto hidden from us. Especially since the Bible was written from an androcentric perspective, we women have to imagine ourselves as if we were the audience of the biblical message at that time. As Susan Brooks Thistlethwaite suggested, we have to critically judge both the text and the experience underlying it.[18]

I have coined the term 'dialogical imagination' to describe the process of creative hermeneutics in Asia. It attempts to capture the complexities, the multi-dimensional linkages, the different levels of meaning in our present task of relating the Bible to Asia. It is dialogical, for it involves a constant conversation between different religious and cultural traditions. It is highly imaginative, for it looks at both the Bible and our Asian reality anew, challenging the established 'order of things.' The German word for imagination is *Einbildungskraft*, which means the power of shaping into one.[19] Dialogical imagination attempts to bridge the gap of time and space, to create new horizons, and to connect the disparate elements of our lives in a meaningful whole.

I shall illustrate the meaning of dialogical imagination by discussing how Asian theologians have combined the insights of biblical themes with Asian resources. We can discern two trends in this process today.

The first is the use of Asian myths, legends and stories in biblical reflection. The second is the use of the social biography of the people as a hermeneutical key to understand both our reality and the message of the Bible.

For some years now, C. S. Song, a theologian from Taiwan, has urged his Asian Colleagues to stretch their theological minds and to use Asian resources to understand the depths of Asian humanity and God's action in the world. He says: 'Resources in Asia for doing theology are unlimited. What is limited is our theological imagination. Powerful is the voice crying out of the abyss of the Asian heart, but powerless is the power of our theological imaging.'[20] To be able to touch the Hindu heart, Buddhist heart, the Confucian heart, we have to strengthen the power of theological imaging.

C. S. Song demonstrates what this means in his book, *The Tears of Lady Meng*[21], which was originally delivered in an Assembly of the Christian Conference of Asia. Song uses a well-known legend from China, the story of Lady Meng, weaving it together with the biblical themes of Jesus' death and resurrection. In one of his recent books, *Tell Us Our Names*, Song shows how fairy tales, folk stories and legends, shared from generation to generation among the common people, have the power to illuminate many biblical stories and other theological motifs. Song reminds us that Jesus was a master storyteller who transformed common stories into parables concerning God's Kingdom and human life.[22]

The use of Asian resources has stimulated many exciting and creative ways of re-reading the scriptures. A biblical scholar from Thailand, Maen Pongudom, uses the creation folktales of the Northern Thai to contrast with the creation story in Genesis, arguing that people of other faiths and traditions share certain essential ideas of creation found in the biblical story.[23] Archie Lee, an Old Testament scholar from Hong Kong, uses the role of the remonstrator in the Chinese tradition to interpret the parable of Nathan in the context of political theology in Hong Kong. His creative re-reading of the stories from two traditions shows that 'story has the unlimited power to capture our imagination and invite the readers to exert their own feeling and intention.'[24]

Asian women theologians are discovering the liberating elements of the Asian traditions as powerful resources to re-image the biblical story. Padma Gallup reinterprets the image of God in Genesis 1.27–8 in terms of the popular Arthanareesvara image in the Hindu tradition which is an expression of male/female deity. She argues that 'if the Godhead created humans in its image, then the Godhead must be a male/female, side-by-side, non-dualistic whole.'[25] I myself have used Asian poems, a lullaby, and a letter of women prisoners to interpret the meaning of suffering and hope.[26] I have also used the story of the boat people in Southeast Asia to reappropriate the theme of the diaspora.[27]

In her observations concerning the growing use of Asian resources in theologizing, Nantawan Boonprasat Lewis, a Thai woman theologian, makes the following perceptive remarks:

> The use of one's cultural and religious tradition indicates the respect and pride of one's heritage which is the root of one's being to be authentic enough to draw as a source for theologizing. On the other hand, it demonstrates a determination of hope for possibilities beyond one's faith tradition, possibilities which can overcome barriers of human expression, including language, vision, and imagination.[28]

The dialogical imagination operates not only in using the cultural and religious traditions of Asia, but also in the radical appropriation of our own history. We begin to view the history of our people with utmost seriousness in order to discern the signs of the time and of God's redeeming action in that history. We have tried to define the historical reality in our own terms and we find it filled with theological insights.

In Korean *minjung* theology, Korean history is reinterpreted from the *minjung* perspective. *Minjung* is a Korean word which means the mass of people, or the mass who were subjugated or being ruled. *Minjung* is a very dynamic concept: it can refer to women who are politically dominated by men, or to an ethnic group ruled by another group, or to a race when it is ruled by another powerful race.[29] The history of the *minjung* was often neglected in traditional historical writing. They were treated as either docile or as mere spectators of the rise and fall of kingdoms and dynasties. *Minjung* theology, however, reclaims *minjung* as protagonists in the historical drama, for they are the subject of history.

Korean theologians stress the need for understanding the corporate spirit – the consciousness and the aspirations of the *minjung* – through their social biography. According to Kim Yong Bock: 'The social biography is not merely social or cultural history: it is political in the sense that it is comprehensively related to the reality of power and to the "polis," namely the community. . . . Social biography functions to integrate and interrelate the dimensions and components of the people's social and cultural experiences, especially in terms of the dramatic scenario of the people as the historical protagonists.'[30] The social biography of the *minjung* has helped Korean Christians to discover the meaning of the Bible in a new way. Cyris H. S. Moon reinterprets the Hebrew Bible story through the social biography of the *minjung* in Korea. He demonstrates how the story of the Korean people, for example, the constant threat of big surrounding nations, and the loss of national identity under Japanese colonialization, can help to amplify our understanding of the Old Testament. On the other hand, he also shows how the social biography of the Hebrew people has illuminated the meaning of the Korean *minjung* story. Through powerful theological imagination, Moon has brought the two social biographies into dialogue with one another.[31]

The hermeneutical framework of the *minjung*'s social biography also helps us to see in a new way the relationship between Jesus and the *minjung*. According to Ahn Byung Mu, the *minjung* are the *ochlos* rather than the *laos*. In Jesus' time, they were the ones who gathered around Jesus – the so-called sinners and outcasts of society. They might not have been the direct followers of Jesus and were differentiated from the disciples. They were the people who were opposed to the rulers in Jerusalem.[32] Concerning the question of how Jesus is related to these *minjung*, theologian Suk Nam Dong says, in a radical voice, '[T]he subject matter of *minjung* theology is not Jesus but *minjung*. Jesus is the means for understanding the *minjung* correctly, rather than the concept of '*minjung*' being the instrument for understanding Jesus.'[33] For him, 'Jesus was truly *a part of* the *minjung*, not just *for* the *minjung*. Therefore, Jesus was the personification of the minjung and their symbol.'[34]

Social biography can also be used to characterize the hopes and aspirations of the women, as Lee Sung Hee has demonstrated.[35] The question of whether Jesus can be taken as a symbol for the women among the *minjung* has yet to be fully clarified. Social biography is a promising hermeneutical tool because it reads history from the underside, and therefore invites us to read the Bible from the underside as well. Korean *minjung* theology represents one imaginative attempt to bring the social biography of *minjung* in Korea into dialogue with the *minjung* of Israel and the *minjung* in the world of Jesus. It shows how dialogical imagination operates in the attempt to reclaim the *minjung* as the center of both our Asian reality and the biblical drama.

Kwok Pui Lan

# LIBERATING THE BIBLE: MANY VOICES
# AND MANY TRUTHS

After this brief survey of the history of the politics of truth in the Chinese Christian community and a discussion of dialogical imagination as a new image for biblical reflection, I would like to briefly discuss my own understanding of the Bible. I shall focus on three issues:
(1) the sacrality of the text, (2) the issue of canon and (3) the norm of interpretation.

*Sacrality of the text.* The authority of the Bible derives from the claim that it is the Scripture, a written text of the Word of God. However, it must be recognized that the notion of 'scripture' is culturally conditioned and cannot be found in some other religious and cultural traditions, such as Hinduism and Confucianism. This may partly account for the relative fluidity of these traditions, which can often assimilate other visions and traditions. These traditions also do not have a crusading spirit to convert the whole world.

Why has the Bible, seen as sacred text, shaped western consciousness for so long? Jacques Derrida's deconstruction theory, particularly his criticism of the 'transcendent presence' in the text and the logocentrism of the whole western metaphysical tradition offers important insights. In an earlier volume of *Semeia* which focuses on 'Derrida and Biblical Studies,' the editor Robert Detweiler summarizes Derrida's challenge to biblical scholarship:

> The main characteristic of sacred texts has been their evocation and recollection of sacred presence – to the extent that the texts themselves, the very figures of writing, are said to be imbued with that divine immanence. But Derrida argues that such a notion of presence in writing is based on the false assumption of a prior and more unmediated presence in the spoken word; this spoken word in the religious context is taken to be none other than the utterance of deity, which utterance is then reduced to holy inscription in and as the text. For Derrida, however, written language is not derivative in this sense; it does not find its legitimacy as a sign of a 'greater' presence, and the sacred text is not rendered sacred as an embodiment of an absolute presence but rather as the interplay of language signs to designate 'sacred'.[36]

The notion of the 'presence' of God speaking through the text drives us to discover what the 'one voice' is, and logocentrism leads us to posit some ultimate truth or absolute meaning which is the foundation of all other meanings. But once we recognize the Bible is one system of language to designate the 'sacred,' we should be able to see that the whole biblical text represents one form of human construction to talk about God. Other systems of language, for example, the hieroglyphic Chinese which is so different from the Indo-European languages, might have a radically different way to present the 'sacred.' Moreover, once we liberate ourselves from viewing the biblical text as sacred, we can then feel free to test and reappropriate it in other contexts. We will see more clearly the meaning of the text is very closely related to the context and we will expect a multiplicity of interpretations of the Bible, as Jonathan Culler says, 'meaning is context-bound but context is boundless.'[37]

*The issue of canon.* Canonization is the historical process which designates some texts as sacred and thus authoritative or binding for the religious community. This whole process must be analyzed in the context of religio-political struggles for power. For example, scholars have pointed out that the formation of the canon of the Hebrew Bible was imbued with the power-play between the prophets and priests. The New Testament canon was formed in the struggle for 'orthodoxy' against such heresies as Marcionism and Gnosticism. Recently, feminist scholarship has also shown how the Biblical canon has excluded Goddess worship in the Ancient Near East and that the New Testament canon was slowly taking shape in the process of the growing patriarchalization of the early church.

The formation of the canon is clearly a matter of power. As Robert Detweiler so aptly puts it: 'A Text becomes sacred when a segment of the community is able to establish it as such in order to gain control and set order over the whole community.'[38] This was true both inside the religious group as well as outside of it. Inside the religious community, women, the marginalized and the poor (in other words, the *minjung*), did not have the power to decide what would be the truth for them. Later, when Christianity was brought to other cultures, the biblical canon was considered to be closed, excluding all other cultural manifestations.

As a woman from a non-biblical culture, I have found the notion of canon doubly problematic. As my fellow Chinese theologians have long argued, Chinese Christians cannot simply accept a canon which relegates their great cultural teachings and traditions to the secondary. As a woman, I share much of what Carol Christ has said, 'women's experiences have not shaped the spoken language of cultural myths and sacred stories.'[39] Women need to tell our own stories, which give meaning to our experience. As Christ continues, 'We must seek, discover, and create the symbols, metaphors, and plots of our own experience.'[40]

I have begun to question whether the concept 'canon' is still useful, for what claims to safeguard truth on the one hand can also lead to the repression of truth on the other. A closed canon excludes the many voices of the *minjung* and freezes our imagination. It is not surprising that feminist scholars of religion are involved in the rediscovery of alternate truths or the formulation of new ones. Rosemary R. Ruether's recent book, *Womanguides*, is a selection of readings from both historical sources and modern reformulations that are liberating for women.[41] Elisabeth Schüssler Fiorenza's reconstruction of the early Christian origins borrows insights from non-canonical sources.[42] Carol Christ describes women's spiritual experiences from women's stories and novels.[43] Black women scholars such as Katie G. Cannon[44] and Delores Williams[45] have also emphasized black women's literature as resources for doing theology and ethics. These stories of the liberation of women as well as other stories from different cultural contexts must be regarded as being as 'sacred' as the biblical stories. There is always the element of holiness in the people's struggle for humanhood, and their stories are authenticated by their own lives and not the divine voice of God.

*The norm for interpretation.* Since I reject both the sacrality of the text and the canon as a guarantee of truth, I also do not think that the Bible provides the norm for interpretation in itself. For a long time, such 'mystified' doctrine has taken away the power from women, the poor and the powerless, for it helps to sustain the notion that the 'divine presence' is located somewhere else and not in ourselves. Today, we must claim back the power to look at the Bible with our own eyes and to stress that divine immanence is within us, not in something sealed off and handed down from almost two thousand years ago.

Because I do not believe that the Bible is to be taken as a norm for itself, I also reject that we can find one critical principle in the Bible to provide an Archimedian point for interpretation. Rosemary Ruether has argued that the 'biblical critical principle is that of the prophetic–messianic tradition,' which seems to her to 'constitute the distinctive expression of biblical faith'. This is highly problematic for three reasons: (1) The richness of the Bible cannot be boiled down to one critical principle. Ruether often makes comments like 'God speaks through the prophet or prophetess . . . the spokesperson of God . . .'[46] as if the utterance of God is the guarantee of the one principle. Here again we discern the need for 'absoluteness' and 'oneness' which Derrida questions. The *minjung* need many voices, not one critical principle. (2) The attempt to find something 'distinctive' in the biblical tradition may have dangerous implications that it is again held up against other traditions. (3) Her suggestion that this critical principle of the Bible can be correlated with women's experiences assumes that the prophetic principle can be lifted from the original context and transplanted elsewhere. She fails to see that the method of correlation as proposed by Tillich and Tracy presupposes the Christian answer to all human situations, an assumption which needs to be critically challenged in the light of the Third World situation today.

Conversely, I support Elisabeth Schüssler Fiorenza's suggestion that a feminist interpretation of the Bible must 'sort through particular biblical texts and test out in a process of critical analysis and evaluation how much their content and function perpetuates and legitimates patriarchal structures, not only in their original historical contexts but also in our contemporary situation.'[47] The critical principle lies not in the Bible itself, but in the community of women and men who read the Bible and who, through their dialogical imagination, appropriate it for their own liberation.

The communities of *minjung* differ from each other. There is no one norm for interpretation that can be applied cross-culturally. Different communities raise critical questions to the Bible and find diverse segments of it as addressing their situations. Our dialogical imagination has infinite potential to generate more truths, opening up hidden corners we have failed to see. While each community of *minjung* must work out their own critical norm for interpretation, it is important that we hold ourselves accountable to each other. Our truth claims must be tested in public discourse, in constant dialogue with other communities. Good news for the Christians might be bad news for the Buddhists or Confucianists.

The Bible offers us insights for our survival. Historically, it has not just been used as a tool for oppression, because the *minjung* themselves have also appropriated it for their liberation. It represents one story of the slaves' struggle for justice in Egypt, the fight for survival of refugees in Babylon, the continual struggles of anxious prophets, sinners, prostitutes and tax-collectors. Today, many women's communities and Christian base communities in the Third World are claiming the power of this heritage for their liberation. These groups, which used to be peripheral in the Christian Church, are revitalizing the Church at the center. It is the commitment of these people which justifies the biblical story to be heard and shared in our dialogue to search for a collective new religious imagination.

In the end, we must liberate ourselves from a hierarchical model of truth which assumes there is one truth above many. This biased belief leads to the coercion of others into sameness, oneness, and homogeneity which excludes multiplicity and plurality. Instead, I suggest a dialogical model for truth where each has a part to share and to contribute to the whole. In the so-called 'non-Christian' world, we tell our sisters and brothers the biblical story that gives us inspiration for hope and liberation. But it must be told as an open invitation: what treasures have you to share?

(I am grateful to Kesaya Noda for editing the manuscript and to the Asian Women Theologians, US Group, for mutual support and challenge.)

## NOTES

1   T. C. Chao, 'The Articulate Word and the Problem of Communication' (*International Review of Mission*, 36, 1947), p. 482.

2   M. Foucault, *Power/Knowledge: Selected Interviews and Other Writings 1972–1977*, ed. C. Gordon (New York, Pantheon, 1980), p. 131.

3   J. R. Mott, *The Evangelization of The World in This Generation* (New York, Arno, 1972), pp. 17–18 (reprinted from the original 1900 edition).

4   J. Lacan and the 'echoe Freuidinne, *Feminine Sexuality*, ed. J. Mitchell and J. Rose (New York, W. W. Norton, 1982), pp. 74–85.

5   H. Kraemer, *The Christian Message in a Non-Christian World* (Grand Rapids, Michigan, Kregel, 1956), p. 102.

6   Chao, p. 42.

7   ibid., p. 43.

8   Po Ch'en Kuang, '*Chung-Kuo ti chiu-yüeh*' (Chinese Old Testament) (*Chen-li yu Sheng-ming* (*Truth and Life*), 2, 1927), pp. 240–4.

9   Hsieh Fu Ya, '*Kuan-hu chung-hua Chi-tu-chiao Sheng-ching ti pien-ting wen-ti*' ('On the issues of editing the Chinese Christian Bible'), in *Chung-hua chi-tu-chiao shen-hsueh lun-chi* (*Chinese Christian Theology Anthology*) (Hong Kong, Chinese Christians Book Giving Society, 1974), pp. 39–40.

10   Hu Tsan Yün, '*Liang-pu chiu-yüeh*' ('Two Old Testaments'), in *Chung-hua chi-tu-chiao shen-hsueh lun-chi*, pp. 67–71.

11   Y. T. Wu, 'The Orient Reconsiders Christianity' (*Christianity and Crisis*, 54, 1937), p. 836.

12   W. R. Hutchison, 'A Moral Equivalent for Imperialism: Americans and the Promotion of Christian Civilization, 1880–1910', in *Missionary Ideologies in the Imperialist Era: 1880–1920*, ed. T. Christensen and W. R. Hutchinson (Aarhus, Aros, 1982), p. 174.

13   Ng Lee Ming, 'The Promise and Limitations of Chinese Protestant Theologians, 1920–50' (*Ching Feng*, 21 and 22, 4 and 1, 1978–9), pp. 178–9.

14   Wu, p. 837.

15   ibid., p. 836.

16   K. Koyama, *Mount Fuji and Mount Sinai: A Critique of Idols* (Maryknoll, NY, Orbis Books, 1984), pp. 7, 8; London, SCM Press, 1984).

17   S. Parks, *The Critical Years: The Young Adult Search for a Faith to Live By* (San Francisco, Harper & Row, 1986), p. 117.

18   S. Brooks Thistlethwaite, 'Every Two Minutes: Battered Women and Feminist Interpretation of the Bible', in *Feminist Interpretation of the Bible*, ed. L. M. Russell (Philadelphia, Westminster Press; Oxford, Basil Blackwell, 1985), p. 98.

19   Parks, p. 113.

20   C. S. Song, *Theology from the Womb of Asia* (Maryknoll, NY, Orbis Books, 1986), p. 16.

21   C. S. Song, *The Tears of Lady Meng* (Geneva, WCC, 1981).

22   C. S. Song, *Tell Us Our Names: Story Theology From An Asian Perspective*, (Maryknoll, NY, Orbis Books, 1984), p. x.

23   M. Pongudom, 'Creation of Man: Theological Reflections based on Northern Thai Folktales' (*East Asia Journal of Theology*, 3, 2, 1985), pp. 222–7. See Part Four of this volume.

24   A. C. C. Lee, 'Doing Theology in the Chinese Context: The David–Bathsheba Story and the Parable of Nathan' (*East Asia Journal of Theology*, 3, 2, 1985), pp. 243–57. See Part Two of this volume.

25   P. Gallup, 'Doing Theology – An Asian Feminist Perspective', in *Commission on Theological Concerns Bulletin* (Christian Conference in Asia, 4, 1983), p. 22.

26   P. lan Kwok, 'God Weeps with Our Pain' (*East Asia Journal of Theology*, 2, 2, 1984), pp. 228–32.

27   P. lan Kwok, 'A Chinese Perspective', in *Theology by the People: Reflections on Doing Theology in Community*, ed. S. Amirtham and J. S. Pobee (Geneva, WCC, 1986), pp. 78–83.

28   N. Boonprasat Lewis, 'Asian Women's Theology: 'A Historical and Theological Analysis' (*East Asia Journal of Theology*, 4, 2, 1986), p. 21.

29   Y. Bock Kim, 'Messiah and Minjung: Discerning Messianic Politics over against Political Messianism', in *Minjung Theology: People as the Subjects of History*, ed. by the Commission on Theological Concerns of the Christian Conference of Asia (Maryknoll, NY, Orbis Books, 1983; London, Zed Press, 1983), p. 186.

30   Y. Bock Kim, 'Minjung Social Biography and Theology' (*Ching Feng*, 28, 4, 1985), p. 224.

31   See C. H. S. Moon, *A Korean Minjung Theology: An Old Testament Perspective* (Maryknoll, NY, Orbis Books, 1985).

32   A. Byung Mu, 'Jesus and the Minjung in the Gospel of Mark', in

*Minjung Theology: the Subjects of History*, pp. 140–1. See Part Two of this volume.

33   S. Nam Dong, 'Historical References for a Theology of Minjung', in *Minjung Theology: People as the Subjects of History*, p. 160.

34   ibid., p. 159.

35   S. Hee Lee, 'Women's Liberation as the Foundation for Asian Theology' (*East Asia Journal of Theology*, 4, 2, 1986), pp. 2–13.

36   R. Detweiler, 'Introduction' (*Semeia*, 23, 1982), p. 1.

37   J. Culler, *On Deconstruction: Theory and Criticism After Structuralism* (Ithaca, New York, Cornell University Press, 1982), p. 128.

38   R. Detweiler, 'What is a Sacred Text?' (*Semeia*, 31, 1985), p. 217.

39   C. P. Christ, 'Spiritual Quest and Women's Experience', in *Womanspirit Rising: A Feminist Reader in Religion*, ed. C. P. Christ and J. Plaskow (San Francisco, Harper & Row, 1979), p. 230.

40   ibid., p. 231.

41   R. R. Ruether, *Womanguides: Readings Towards a Feminist Theology* (Boston, Beacon Press, 1985).

42   E. Schüssler Fiorenza, *In Memory of Her: A Feminist Theological Reconstruction of Christian Origins* (New York, Crossroad, 1983; London, SCM Press, 1983).

43   C. P. Christ, *Diving Deep and Surfacing: Women's Writers on Spiritual Quest* (Boston, Beacon Press, 1980).

44   K. Geneva Canon, 'Resources for a Constructive Ethic in the Life and Work of Zora Neale Hurston' (*Journal of Feminist Studies in Religion*, 1, 1985), pp. 37–51.

45   D. Williams, 'Black Women's Literature and the Task of Feminist Theology', in *Immaculate and Powerful: The Female in Sacred Image and Social Reality*, ed. C. W. Atkinson, C. H. Buchanan and M. R. Miles (Boston, Beacon Press, 1985).

46   R. R. Ruether, 'Feminist Interpretation: A Method of Correlation', in *Feminist Interpretation of the Bible*, p. 117.

47   E. Schüssler Fiorenza, 'The Will to Choose or to Reject: Continuing Our Critical Work', in *Feminist Interpretation of the Bible*, p. 131.

# 23

# The Bible in Self-renewal and Church-renewal for Service to Society

## D. S. AMALORPAVADASS

Christian people who are engaged in liberation struggles, especially in Asia, are discovering that the Word of God is found in scriptures and traditions of other religions as well as their own. This experience poses many challenges, and the author provides a new criterion to read the Christian Scripture in the context of the Indian religious and cultural traditions.

This article is reprinted from *Voices from the Third World* (10, 2, 1987). *Voices from the Third World* is the journal of the Ecumenical Association of Third World Theologians (EATWOT). The address: The Editor, *Voices from the Third World*, Asian Theology Centre, 281 Deans Road, Colombo 10, Sri Lanka.

D. S. Amalorpavadass is a Catholic, the Head of the Department of Christianity, University of Mysore, India. He has written extensively on inter-faith issues and Indian spirituality.

*From the Bible*:

> In the beginning was the Word
> The Word was with God
> and the word was God
> Everything was made through him.
> The word was made flesh and dwelt among us.
> We saw his glory, full of grace and truth
> out of his fulness we have all received
> truth and grace (John 1.1,3,14,16).

*From the Upanishad*:

> Fulness there fulness here
> from fulness fulness proceeds
> once fulness has proceeded from fulness
> fulness remains
> Peace! Peace! Peace!

D. S. Amalorpavadass

# RENEWAL BY ENCOUNTER BETWEEN THE WORD AND THE PEOPLE

Most people – and to some extent all of us – lead a *meaningless and purposeless life*. We do not always know the meaning of what happens at present, the purpose of human existence and the direction for the future. One could just be drifting, subject to various forces, like a boat on the sea or lake at the mercy of the winds; or one could be just carried by mere routine, moving in a rut; or one could be caught up in a vicious circle not knowing, and helpless to come out of it; and one could also be a part of a machine leading a mechanical life.

Further, one could also be leading a very peripheral and superficial life on the margin of self and on the margin of society. Which is worse is one could also be, consciously or unconsciously, in a state of holiness and isolation, left to oneself and centred on self, with all doors and horizons closed, related with neither the Other nor the others, the only reality being self. To have none but oneself is a *state of non-existence and non-person*. It is also a state of chaos and void: '*Tohu bohu*'.

It is then that the Spirit of the Lord hovers over it. It is then that *the Word of God manifests itself with dynamism*. It becomes a fresh a creative and transforming Word; order and harmony come into existence; light begins to shine; an opening is made on the horizon; something happens at the core of oneself. Call it intervention of God or irruption of the Spirit, call it the explosive manifestation of the immanent word or the opening out to the dimension of transcendence. A vision of the goal appears and it sheds light on everything and gives meaning to everything.

Genuine human life or serious religious life begins when one poses basic questions of human existence and looks for satisfactory answers in the ultimate, absolute, supreme and transcendent, and when one discovers some *meaning and purpose in life*. In the measure in which one has discovered the ultimate goal and deepest significance and moves towards it, one's life becomes meaningful and purposeful and hence fruitful and worthwhile. Likewise one becomes a person and one's life becomes meaningful when one begins to break open one's self, to move out of it and transcend it, and to relate onself with others in the reality of life.

How does one get this meaning and purpose in life? What is the occasion in which this vision of the whole appears and sheds light on life so that some meaning may emerge? How does one get related and become a person? Here we are not dealing with a mere psychological experience alone, but also with a theological reality of God's manifestation in one's life. This process is what is called *revelation and faith, a personal and effective manifestation of God's Word.* It is how the Bible is considered as the record of the experience of God's Word in the life of individuals, communities and peoples, after its first manifestation in creation and history.

Revelation of the Word in the Bible is concerned primarily with persons. It is a *communication and relation among persons* and what happens to them. This is an inter-personal relationship between God and man in openness and acceptance, reverence and trust, love and self-sacrifice. It is God taking the initiative freely; opening himself out, unveiling the mystery of his person and manifesting his designs in an act of self-donation, self-communication and self-gift, inviting us to response and communion. Thus at that very moment revelation is personalized and personalizing.

This process of personalization is also the beginning of a new existence as persons and communities. *This relationship is dynamic, this communication is interacting and the Word is indeed powerful.* Hence it brings about a change in persons and communities, and transformation of society and the world. It is impossible to meet persons really – all the more the person of God – without being transformed; and inversely, in order to be transformed, one must have met persons and communicated with others, all the more so, with God.

## SELF-RENEWAL, CHURCH-RENEWAL AND SOCIETAL CHANGE

### Person – self-renewal

*Self-renewal* is the whole gamut of transformation which a person undergoes when he comes into a vital encounter with God's Word, especially in crucial events and decisive moments of one's life when one poses basic questions of human existence. Hence an encounter at such moments brings about a change of heart (change of attitudes which is a change in the position of the heart), a change of vision, a change of values and priorities, a change in relationships and therefore a change in behaviour and comportment (a change in the position of the body); in short, a change of life and a change of life-style.

The Bible is full of examples of such personal renewal. Today the

Bible with God's Word is effecting such a renewal in numerous persons. And I, as a minister of the Word, have been witness to numerous marvels of such a transformation in the lives of individuals, over the length and breadth of our country and beyond.

## Community: Church renewal

Persons suppose relationship and community. A community is possible only with persons, it is in a community that persons can emerge and become! Inversely it is genuine persons who make a community.

Every communication is communitarian in that the Word is addressed to a living people, to a community of persons, not merely to individuals. God relates himself to people in communication and communion as members of a living community in their interrelatedness so that the inter-personal relationship between God and people may be the source and basis, climax and summit, pattern and model of the interpersonal relationship among people, so that the human community in which revelation takes place may gradually be built up and transformed into a community of sisters and brothers, a genuine human community, a community of faith, a community of sharing and love, witness and service, a pledge and hope for the future, a community of salvation. Communication calls for community or relationship as condition and it also brings about and leads to community as a consequence.

Such a communication (divine revelation to man) takes place when one comes into contact with the Word of God, and when the Bible is proclaimed and listened to. A community is necessary to enter into communication with God, to accept his message in faith and to share it with others by the proclamation of the Word. Inversely, the very proclamation of the Word in the Bible brings about and gathers a community. The power of the Word which is creative and transforming is manifested here as a new relationship among persons in community and as a new order of things in society.

The communitarian dimension of the Word is highlighted in the Bible. The Word of God in the Bible forms community by making individuals move out of isolation, to listen to the Lord and to others, and to respond together with others to the common life-situations experienced by them and to the Lord who is present in that reality/ event/situation. It is personalized from within and therefore experienced by them. The Word thus makes the community of persons, a community of the Word and a community of response (faith). The community of persons is first awakened to become the community of the Word: namely, to listen to God speaking in the community and through the situation as the Bible is read. The Church is not a talking community, but primarily a listening community. Then every member of this community is enabled to share oneself, all that one is and all that one has, one's experience and one's relationship with others to be a sharing community. This is manifested when the members share the message that each one has received from the proclamation of the Word. The rays of the Biblical Word pass through the prism of our own life-situations and experiences and are refracted in all colours and shapes, namely in a variety of messages. Every word is a call for dialogue, it is equally true for God. Every message expects from us a response to the Word; we become a community of response, and so become more of a community! Finally, we become a caring, sharing and serving community, to become a sign and instrument of the ever widening community of women and men. In this process of listening, sharing and responding both with men and women and with God, the Word comes alive. It manifests itself in all the vitality and dynamism, bringing with it enrichment and transformation. The formative power of the Word is unleashed and experienced and the community is formed. The whole process makes it a witnessing community.

To sum up, the Bible is a record of the experience of the Word in the life of individuals and peoples. It is a human response to the Word of God in concrete life-situations by persons belonging to a community and involved in the reality. Now as the *paradigm of challenge and response*, God's will as grace and human response in freedom, in the concrete reality of people's lives, it is a model and process of metanoia! *The Bible for self-renewal* means that an individual person grows into the community of metanoia. *The Bible for Church-renewal* means that the word brings into a new existence a community, facilitating the fellowship of its members and transforming them in spirit and heart, in vision and relationships, in structures and activities.

## The Bible in service to society

This revelation or communication takes place *in the concrete reality of our existence and through the events and trends of our history.* Therefore this communication is existential, historical, experiential and concrete. The word is never addressed to anybody in a vacuum, nor does it fall like a bolt from the blue. It is always addressed to a people living in concrete situations. Rather it emerges from within the life of the people and therefore it is an integral part of their life. It is immanent to their existence and therefore nothing can be farther from the reality/ from themselves and from their being, all the more the Word of God. Hence it is making itself meaningful and relevant. It also challenges people to be personally involved and committed. It initiates a process of transformation both in persons and within every reality which we call society.

The awareness of the Word is brought about by a wider understanding of the Word, the Word-event in concrete situations (the reality), in all aspects and areas of human life (totality) and of all peoples and all periods of history (universality). The Bible enables the community and individual persons to discern God's presence in life-situations and to interpret the concrete realities of life, especially the signs of the times, the events, the needs and aspirations of the people, the voices of our age, and to respond to them, if necessary by commitment to change the reality, to change society.

Now this interpretation is a very delicate and challenging task. A concentration on the Word of God in our lives and at a particular moment of history, while making it relevant, can also lead us to subjectivism and therefore subject us to all the ambiguities of finding our own selves and our own ideas and wishes. On the other hand, having recourse to the past of God's people and their faith-experiences as recorded in the Bible and tradition in an historico-critical process and going beyond us, could take us far away from the present reality in which we are involved. Consequently there will be no connection between the actual reality and the Word. The Word cannot be merely past-oriented, for our commitment is to the present. If at all we refer to the past it is precisely to find a source and light as part of it; and as one pole of the dialectic of interpretation. For an authentic and relevant interpretation it is imperative to be really involved in the actual, existential and living word of the present reality where we are committed. At the same time it is necessary to illuminate that word by all the other forms and expressions of God's Word which have been already lived and incarnated, which down the periods of human history have been guiding the life of the faith-communities, and which thus have become for us the normative word – *norma non normanda*. The historical–critical method should be combined with the empirical–critical method.

The present Word in the actual reality has to be enlightened and dialectically interpreted by a *sevenfold Word*:

(a)  the Word manifested in creation;

(b)  the Word active throughout human history as a whole;

(c)  the Word at work in the history of every nation;

(d)  the Word especially in the history of Israel and the Word become flesh in the person of Jesus Christ, the human existence of the Word and the experience of the early community of Christ's disciples, witnesses to that event, therefore the Word in the Bible (OT and NT);

(e)  the Word ever since present in the Church through his Spirit through twenty centuries of the Church's history and in its life-witness today;

(f)  the Word in the Church's worship (Liturgy);

(g)  the Word in common faith and understanding of the people of God today (*sensus fidelium*) but articulated through the official teaching and preaching of leaders (*magisterium*).

When this sevenfold Word of God which has become normative illuminates the Word of God in our concrete existential situation, then the ambiguity disappears to give place to clarity and unequivocity; what is complex becomes simple, what is hidden gets surfaced, and what is opaque becomes transparent. *The Bible* is recognized as a light that illuminates the reality of life which is often opaque, ambiguous and complex. The opacity, ambiguity and complexity is transformed into transparency, clarity and simplicity.

It is then that we are able to discern the real presence of the Lord in the word of life and in the present community. It is then that it becomes possible for us to discover and experience God in each situation of our life, to understand his designs for our times, to interpret correctly the plan of God for our situation and to respond to him by our personal life, and commitment to social change. The Bible enables the community and individual persons *to interpret the concrete situation* (hermeneutical) and makes them aware of their *mission*, to interpret prophetically and to enable an interpretation of and response to the concrete word.

Hence what is being done and achieved through this process is an authentic interpretation of the concrete situation in which the unambiguous Word of God becomes clear (namely welfare for all and justice in every reality) in the light of God's Word in the Bible. It enables individuals and communities to respond to that will by becoming afresh a denouncing word and announcing word, in the total language of word and deed.

This is a process of discernment and interpretation which should be included in every form of ministry. This hermeneutical service is implied in all forms of evangelization, catechesis, preaching and liturgical celebrations and prayer in all other forms of pastoral service, and in all socio-political commitments. In short, this is what is meant by *the renewal of the ministry of the Word in the Church.* This is the all-pervading prophetic ministry which should animate and *guide all the other ministries of the Church.*

One such ministry of the Church and hence service to society is its response to a situation of oppression and exploitation, domination and enslavement, injustice and dehumanization. In this context, self-renewal and Church-renewal become a *service to society* in that they become *commitment to social change, to the creation of a human world, a just society and a fraternal community.*

Hundreds and thousands of groups emerging all over the world, especially in Asian countries, have something in common, namely they have *recourse to the Bible to find their source of nourishment and inspiration,* to discover in God's Word an enlightenment and guidance for their social commitment. These 'grassroots-level action groups', struggling against injustice and domination, are committed to the integral human development and allround liberation of persons and communities at various levels. The whole problem is, *what happens to these groups when they come into contact with the Bible?* Or why are these groups which have difficulties with authorities, structures, situations and the establishments of Church and society comfortable with the Bible itself and are even fascinated by it? There is something attractive about the Bible which immediately gives it a place within the dynamic of their community life and of their commitment to social change.

## Re-reading (interpretation) of the Bible

Whether it is self-renewal or Church-renewal, whether it is service to society in the form of social change and creation of a new society, it calls for a re-reading of the Bible.

One could speak of a neutral reading or an ideological reading of the Bible. First of all, there can be no neutral reading of the Bible nor an exclusively objective interpretation of the Bible by any community. Consequently there cannot be a neutral ministry of the Word in this context nor is it sufficient to have a critical study of the text only; one cannot stop with a mere exegesis without moving on to hermeneutics to make the Word really relevant by its analysis and interpretation of the reality, by its denunciation and announcement. Further, neutrality is not only non-involvement and lack of response to the Word, but also aligning ourselves with the forces opposed to God's Word.

The prophetic Word is uttered to promote and challenge, to interpellate and evoke a response, whatever it be. The Bible has become an integral part of faith-reflection, faith-interpretation and faith-response. In this regard, there have been attempts all over the world in various action groups and basic communities to read and re-read the Scriptures 'from the underside of history', as we state in our Third World Theology, in order to respond to situations of injustice and oppression. It is well known that the poor and the oppressed all over the world are today re-reading the Bible and finding in it the source of inspiration and strength for their struggle against injustice and resistance to oppression. It offers them hope of new life and vision of a new society. For instance, the *magnificat*, Mary's song of praise, which many people sing in a moment of self-satisfaction, is read in the Third World as a song celebrating God's promise of liberation to the oppressed. This re-reading of the Bible is really inspired by the Bible itself. We find there the paradigm of all the major aspects of our own human existence and main events of history with all the originality and newness proper to our life and our period of history (*Kairos*). When re-read in the context of oppression, the Bible is considered as a subversive element by many defenders of the *status quo* and by those who control the systems that are to their advantage.

But we also know that the Bible has been used many a time as a weapon of domination and instrument of oppression in other places. An *ideological use of the Bible* has been frequent, and the Prophetic Word has been made to legitimate and justify unjust structures. How often have some theologians and a few Church leaders betrayed God by the way they have used the Scriptures, particularly in situations of conflict, injustice and oppression! Not only has the Bible been misquoted by the devil, but it also has been used by some theologians, Church leaders, governments and simple Christians to justify authoritarianism or to defend their own positions. The feminists affirm that the Bible has been used to justify sexism and to legitimate the oppression of women. In South Africa the Bible is being used to legitimate apartheid. Today in many parts of Latin America, the Bible is used for justifying domination and oppression, to cover torture and death, and to under-cut the legitimate struggle of the people for their own liberation. In the past a distorted theology legitimated even the destruction of traditional religious and indigenous cultures of people colonized in Asia, Africa and America.

However, when the Bible is re-read by the oppressed and enslaved people as a call to liberation, some critics consider this method of interpreting the Bible as *subjective*. According to the broad principles of hermeneutics, we can say that the religious text is based on an event, the praxis of a specific group, for example, the Exodus. It is not simply a praxis that has become a theopraxis. The text, however, does not exhaust the meaning of an event. Every reading is done from the perspective or mindset of the reader, as well as in a specific context and experience. Even the technical scholar reads out of his particular perspective.

The people of the Third World engaged in struggles, especially in Asia, are discovering the Word of God not only in the Bible, but also in the Scriptures and traditions of other religions, such as Hinduism, Buddhism, Shintoism and Islam, the primal religions of Africa and the spirituality of indigenous peoples of South America. These experiences pose as many challenges to the traditional ways of understanding the Bible.

The contradictory and sometimes ambiguous use of the Bible necessitates and makes it a crucial task to clarify the criteria for reading and re-reading the Bible!

## WITHIN INDIAN RELIGIOUS AND CULTURAL TRADITIONS, AS AN INTEGRAL PART OF INDIAN CHRISTIAN SPIRITUALITY

All that I said above can be expressed in a different way in the *context of Indian spirituality*.

One of the characteristic elements of Indian spirituality is *wholeness*. This wholeness consists in gathering one's whole self at the focal point of one's being, namely, gathering our broken pieces from the surface level of existence in noise, exteriority and alienation and integrating them into one by unifying them from within. This implies interioriz-ation, concentration and convergence of everything in self towards the centre of ourself, with one-pointedness and single focus. This whole-ness has to be realized on three levels as personal integrity, community fellowship and cosmic harmony. These three correspond to what we have said above; first of all, the Bible in self-renewal, corresponding to personal integrity; secondly, the Bible in Church-renewal, corre-sponding to community fellowship; thirdly, the Bible in service to society corresponding to social order, cosmic harmony, humanity and the whole problem of ecology and environment. When one has realized this three-level wholeness, one is fully himself or herself. These three are not isolated realities, but are dynamically interconnected and all three make a single whole. Cosmic harmony should be reflected in the social order and the social order (or justice) is a sign of community fellowship; and community becomes possible because of the whole-ness realized by every person who is integral. It reflects the totality of the person, the whole gamut of community life and the total society, and the whole creation.

Now this renewal is not something exterior. Totality can be realized only from within. This brings me to the second characteristic of Indian spirituality: *interiority*. Since we do not want any form of domination or control from outside by others, and since our aim is to realize wholeness in freedom, this can only be done by gathering ourselves from within. The principle of our unity has to be an inner principle and not an external structure, power, authority or law. In that sense when one is at the superficial level, one is enslaved. Instead one becomes more interior when one goes deeper and deeper, and reaches the level of the mystery of being. There one finds not only one's total self, but reaches the ground of oneself. In the mystery of being of oneself, one discovers and identifies the mystery of others, the mystery of the Other (of God), the mystery of all realities.

Once we have wholeness and interiority then we have the *dialectic of our immanence and transcendence*. This movement of interiority can be misunderstood by some as introversion. This introversion is not the ultimate goal, as this movement towards the core of self culminates in discovering at the deepest level the total reality and opening out to a transcendence, transcendence understood as discovering other dimensions of self, namely, God, others and the whole world. The word in this experience is both immanence and transcendence, intro-version and openness, an indwelling presence and all-pervading presence! All these are interrelated, interacting and integrated. The biblical word then is no more a word from outside, nor exclusively a word from inside either, but it is both: a word that goes from outside and finds a home in us, as Christ tells us. It is also a word which emerges from within, from the ground of being, from the abyss from which it emerges, vibrates, resounds, utters and manifests itself as sound. It is in this sense that the Word of God resounds through the universe, resounds in our ears, and resounds in our hearts.

The moment that we accept that the Word can emerge from within, then we have to conclude that the Word of God is not a *flatus vocis*, a noise, but a sound that emerges from *total silence*. Silence is the total language, the perfect communication, sign of plenitude and therefore the basis of fellowship. In Indian tradition, every sound emerges from silence. God who is unutterable utters himself. The unutterable is silence; what is uttered is sound, music, therefore it is called primordial sound: Adi Sabdha and Nada Brahman.

In this sense the Word of God is to be experienced not only in the reading of the Bible, but in everything which resounds with it. Every time the Bible is read it finds an echo in *other forms of God's Word*, or it becomes the articulation of our experience of other forms of God's Word. In this way there is coherence between study and spirituality, action and contemplation, reality and Word. Various forms of God's word echo in our hearts as a symphony and polyphony. We can find their articulation when the Word of God is read from the Bible or from the Scriptures of other religions.

The Bible is not to be taken in isolation only as a book. It is a record of what has been experienced. So today the Bible can bring about an experience as it emerges from an experience and leads us to an experience, and as this, *experience becomes an outreach understood as evangelization*, as sharing of God-experience in Jesus Christ with people of other religions and ideologies, all engaged in a common pilgrimage with a common origin and common goal. It is in response to the sharing of God-experience by people of other religions and thus each experience evokes another experience. Each experience of the partner articulates and gives a new expression to what he has experienced. Thus we meet not at the level of academic dialogue, nor simply at the level of oral and verbal sharing; but it is a surfacing of what is deep down, like the current of water at the deepest level of our being.

We also experience the Word in every form *of dialogue* with people of other religions. Dialogue implies not only discussion but a dialogue of life and all-round collaboration in all the common concerns of the human community. We have also to share in all that nourishes and inspires their religious life, chiefly their scriptures (not exclusively), also their sacraments (samskaras), their temple worship, their home religious life, their festivals, etc. The prayerful reading of their scriptures become an integral part of Indian Christian spirituality.

Each Indian Christian experiences within himself *two streams flowing and merging into one*: the stream of Judeo-Christian experience communicated through the biblical Word and continued through twenty centuries of Christian experiences and then the stream of 4,000 years of Indian religious life articulated by Indian Scriptures. These two streams do not flow in parallel lines as two separate streams, but both merge at the depth of our being as a single river and become an ocean of single experience. Christians benefit from the Indian Scriptures for a deeper understanding of the biblical word and the Hindus benefit by the biblical word to re-interpret their scriptures and to discover the unknown riches and facets. In Mahatma Gandhi we have a beautiful example of one who made not only an intellectual synthesis of Bhagavadgita and the Gospel (especially Sermon on the Mount) but also an inspirational synthesis for social reform, religious renewal and struggle for political independence on the rock of authenticity of personal renewal and holiness!

## CONCLUSION

My overall experience is one of *universality, totality and unity* in wholeness and integrity, depth and silence. (In the beginning was the Word, The Word was made flesh and dwelt among us. From him we have received grace and truth in fullness. One who is at the bosom of the Father has taken us back to him.) The Bible today has become more universal not only because it is used by many people, but also because it has gone to the depth of one's being in the totality of the person. The Bible has become more universal also because it is read, interpreted, experienced and shared in communities. Every community open to other communities shares with them their enriching experience and thus creates a wider human community. Further, the Bible has become universal because it resounds with the Word of God in the Scriptures of other religions. The Bible has become universal because it interacts with peoples of all religions and ideologies. It permeates all actions for justice and peace; it makes a critique of all ideologies denouncing and announcing. The Biblical Word has become universal because it is most interiorized at the core of the being and also it is resounding in the entire universe. Universality and totality are not at the cerebral level, but at the level of vision and experience.

The best way to conclude my experience of the Biblical Word is through silence! Where there is fullness and wholeness there is stillness and silence! Where there is silence there is peace. It is out of peace (*santi*) that an authentic joy (*ananda*) can emerge; it is this joy and this peace that shine on our faces as glory (*jyoti*).

| | |
|---|---|
| Antar jyoti bahir jyoti | Inner lustre, outer lustre, |
| Pratyagjyoti paratparah | The one lustre, greater than the great. |
| Jyoti jyoti svayamjyoti | Lustre of lustre, self-effulgent lustre |
| Atmajyoti sivoasmyaham | Self-effulgence, auspicious One I am |
| Antar jyoti bahir jyoti | Inner lustre, outer lustre, |
| Pratyagjyoti paratparah | The one lustre, greater than the great |
| Om santi, santi, santi! | Peace, Peace, Peace! |

# 24

# 'I' in the Words of Jesus

## SEIICHI YAGI

This essay examines the 'I am' sayings of Jesus from a Buddhist perspective, but draws on biblical scholarship and presents a reinterpretation of it. Yagi demonstrates how one tradition might use the lens of another to see the truth in a new way. He enables Christians to move beyond both inclusive and exclusive understandings of Jesus, while at the same time not denying the uniqueness of either Jesus or Buddha.

This article is reprinted from J. Hick and P. Knitter (eds), *The Myth of Christian Uniqueness* (Maryknoll, NY, Orbis Books, 1987; London, SCM Press, 1988).

Seiichi Yagi is from Japan, and is considered one of the prominent leaders in Buddhist–Christian dialogue in his country. His books in Japanese on dialogue issues have sold widely.

## I

In the contemporary theological scene of Japan, if we ask how Christians can and should understand Buddhism, we would do well to look to the thought of Takizawa Katsumi (1909–1984).[1] He distinguished between what he termed the primary and the secondary contacts of God with the human self. The first contact is the unconditional fact that God is with each one of us, no matter what we are or what we have done, even though we are usually ignorant of this unity lying at the very ground of the self. Despite this ignorance, it can happen, by virtue of the primary contact of God with the self, that we are awakened to this fact. Then it becomes possible for the self to live in conscious accord with the will of God. Takizawa named this awakening the secondary contact of God with the self.

According to Takizawa, Jesus was a man who was awakened to the primary fact – that is, he attained the secondary contact, and he did this so thoroughly and completely that he became the model for other selves. This does not mean, however, that before the coming of Jesus, the primary contact of God with the human self did not exist; for Takizawa, the 'event of Jesus' alone is not the exclusive ground of our salvation. Rather, Jesus was the person who in Hebrew tradition played the same role as did Gautama Buddha in the Indian tradition. The ground of salvation is the primary contact of God with the self, and this is the common ground of both Buddhism and Christianity.

I am in full agreement with Takizawa's perspective (though there are other aspects of his thought that I would question).[2] With his distinction between the two contacts and with his understanding of Jesus, he offers Christians possibilities of genuine dialogue with Buddhism that would go beyond Protestant superficial admiration of the depths of Buddhist faith, as well as beyond Catholic efforts to use the method of Zen meditation without having to leave their sanctuary of Christian exclusivism.

In this essay I shall, for the most part, offer an explanation and interpretation of Takizawa's thought (without laying out his full understanding of the common ground between Christianity and Buddhism) as the basis for coming to a clearer understanding of the distinction between the self and the ego. This understanding will enable us, then, to grasp both the 'person' of Jesus and the resurrection[3], in such a way that the significance and uniqueness of Jesus will be both more existentially meaningful and at the same time more dialogically open to other religious traditions. In a sense, this essay is an example of how a dialogue with Buddhism might aid Christians in formulating a more *pluralistic* christology and theology of religions.

Let me begin with an examination of 'I' in the New Testament.

## II

In the light of 'form criticism,' accepted as the general approach to investigating the synoptic traditions, most scholars would respond negatively to the question whether Jesus had a 'messianic consciousness.' During the 'new quest of the historical Jesus' of the 1950s and 1960s, scholars explored the 'self-consciousness' of Jesus from a new angle; many of them concluded that although Jesus did not understand himself as 'messiah' or 'son of man,' the fact that he spoke and acted with an unparalleled authority, which surpassed even that of Moses, constituted the root of subsequent christology.[4] But unless I am mistaken, none of these scholars inquired deeply into the meaning of

'I' in such statements of Jesus as 'But I say to you . . .' This 'I' has many levels of meaning. We can ask, then, just what the 'I' in the words of Jesus really means.

To answer that question, we can begin by considering certain analogies or parallels in Paul's writings. What is the 'I,' or the subject, in the words of the Apostle Paul? He states: 'For through the law I died to the law – to live for God. I have been crucified with Christ. It is no longer I who live; Christ lives in me. And the life I live now in the flesh I live by faith in the Son of God, who loved me and sacrificed himself for me' (Gal. 2.19 f).

The 'I' in Paul has a double structure. When Paul was 'crucified with Christ,' a change of subject took place so that Christ became Paul's ultimate subject. This does not mean, however, that the 'ego' of Paul disappeared.[5] On the contrary, it was Paul's ego that believed in Christ, or more correctly, it was his ego that, aware of the reality of Christ in him, proclaimed that he believed in the Son of God who was, in this case, the object of his faith. In the words of Paul quoted above, Christ is both Paul's ultimate subject as well as the object of his faith referred to in the third person. So we can say that for Paul, Christ as the object of faith and Christ as the ultimate subject of the believer are, paradoxically, identical.

This corresponds to Paul's understanding of the person as consisting of the ultimate subject and the ego. As we shall see below, for Paul the ultimate subject and the ego are both one and two at the same time. They are one, for Paul states: 'For I will not dare to speak that which Christ did not wrought *through me* to make the Gentiles obedient, by word and deed' (Rom. 15.18). Paul's mission is his own work – none other than what he himself was doing. And yet it was also the deed of Christ who was working through him. We can say that Christ acted *as Paul* because Christ can work in history only through those who are aware of the reality of Christ. In this way, the ultimate subject and the ego of Paul are one.[6]

This same structure is implied in such passages as: 'If any man think himself to be a prophet, or spiritual, let him acknowledge that the things I write to you are the commandments of the Lord. If he does not recognize this, he himself is not recognized' (1 Cor. 14.37 f; cf. 2 Cor. 5.20). Or: 'Since you seek a proof of Christ speaking in me . . .' (2 Cor. 13.3). Note how the subject changes in the following words: 'And to the married I command, not I, but the Lord, a wife must not separate herself from her husband. . . . To the rest I say, not the Lord: If any brother has a wife who has no faith, and she is willing to live with him, he must not deliver her' (1 Cor. 7.10–12). In verse 12, Paul's ego is clearly distinguished from the Lord. In verse 10, the relationship between the ego and the Lord is more complicated: 'I command, not I, but the Lord.' We might, of course, assume that Paul is here referring to some synoptic tradition (e.g. Mark 10.9). Yet if we consider that Paul generally does not depend on synoptic traditions but directly on the heavenly Lord (see Gal. 1.1; 1 Cor. 14.37f), and especially if we attend to the remarkable statement 'I command, not I, but the Lord,' then it seems clear that we are dealing here with a unity between the Lord and Paul. The statement 'I command, not I, but the Lord' means that Christ commands through him. Keeping in mind that Jesus Christ was Paul's Lord and that Paul was his servant, we see the double structure in Paul's self (or subjectivity). On the one hand, Christ is the ultimate subject of Paul, Paul's very self; on the other hand, the ego of Paul is clearly distinguished from the Lord. The two realities are both one and two.

In what follows, I used the word 'self' in this sense: 'Christ in me' – that is, the paradoxical identity of the divine and the human. Paul was aware that all his life-activities were the works of Christ (Phil. 1.21: 'To me, to live is Christ'). Human life is at the same time divine. This is the case with the 'self' – 'Christ in me' – but not with the empirical ego. The ego is the locus where the self becomes manifest.

We can comprehend how important this expression, 'Christ in me,' was for Paul from the way it appears at decisive passages in his letters. It occurs in the account of his conversion: '[But when it pleased God] to reveal his Son *in me* that I might proclaim him in the Gentiles.' The Greek *en emoi* should be translated 'in me.' Some contemporary theologians consider this revelation to be an interpersonal encounter between Christ and Paul, and not a moment of 'enlightenment' (cf. 2 Cor. 4.6), and so they prefer to render *en emoi* as 'to me.'[7] But the same expression appears again in the very next chapter: 'Christ lives *in me*' (Gal. 2.20). Both these expressions are closely related; it makes good sense that the Christ who was once revealed 'in me' now 'lives in me.' Paul uses this expression in passages that express that which grounds his entire being.

Romans 7.17 offers a third example of Paul's use of 'in me.' Here he describes how the ego in general, including his own ego, is captive to the power of sin by standing under the law and not coming to faith. 'It is no longer I who perform it, but sin that dwells *in me.*' This passage stands as a kind of negative counterpart to Galatians 2.20: 'It is no longer I who live, but Christ lives in me.' So Paul's expression, 'in me,' merits serious attention; most contemporary scholars, however, prefer to focus their attention on the more 'mystical' expression: 'in Christ.'

Paul's understanding of being 'in Christ' reflects his notion of the person. As is well known, 'in Christ' signifies the grace of Christ. God's gracious gifts are presented 'in Christ' (1 Cor. 1.4).[8] Whoever is in Christ is a new creature (2 Cor. 5.17). Christians find themselves, so to speak, in the field of Christ's power, so that they can receive the gifts of Christ's grace. The beings in the field, like music formed in the heart, reflect the field. Or, the field expresses itself as the beings in it – as, for example, the church as the Body of Christ (1 Cor. 12). In this 'expresses itself as' we see the unity of the human and the divine. This is the case, as we saw above, with the Christian life. When Paul says, 'By the grace of God I am what I am' (1 Cor. 15.10), he is affirming that the grace of God given 'in Christ' forms the ground of what he is – the ground of his being. We are dealing here with another paradoxical identity: Christ as the ultimate subject (Christ in) and Christ as the ground of being (in Christ) are identical. And so Paul can say, 'I am what I am.' In this case, 'I' means first of all the ego that has become aware of the reality of Christ in him. Yet 'I' signifies the whole person who is in the field of the gracious power of Christ, and at the same time the whole person whose ultimate subject is Christ working 'in' and 'through me.' Christ and 'I' are one in such a way that 'I' am at the same time a servant of Christ in whom 'I' believe.

Figure 1 may throw some light on what I have been talking about.

*Figure 1*

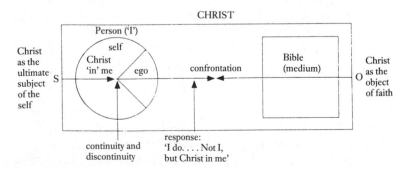

Seiichi Yagi

The person is in the field where Christ is at work ('I' in Christ), but at the same time, Christ lives 'in me.' Christ as the ground of my being is Christ as my ultimate subject. So now, Christ grounds all my life-activities ('To me to live is Christ': Phil. 1.21). In this way, then, Christ and the person are one. My living, though a purely human activity, is the work of Christ; or more precisely, the human is the human based on the activity of Christ, not separated from it. So the activity of the ego is based on Christ working in me – that is, the self (God working in the person produces both willing and performing: Phil. 2.13). On the other hand, Paul could make a clear distinction between 'I' and Christ. Indeed, believers can always abandon their faith (Gal. 1.6). This is why Paul (we too) makes the distinction between his ultimate self ('Christ in me') and his ego. Between 'Christ in me' and the ego there is both continuity and discontinuity. This is why we are still responsible for our decisions.

All of this makes for a rather complicated reality. Christ speaks to me, for instance, through the Bible. He encounters me personally. And so Christ is the object of my faith and I respond to him. But the response is based on the working of the Holy Spirit (1 Cor. 12.3). This response, this decision of faith, is a dual reality (I . . . not I, but the grace of God). This duality reflects the structural duality according to which Christ in me constitutes my life activities.[9]

We find the same kind of relationship in the fourth Gospel, only here it is more clearly present in the relationship between Father and Son. 'And thou, Father, art in me and I am in thee' (John 17.21, and *passim*). But because the relationship between the Father and the Son in the fourth Gospel is analogous to that between Christ and Christians, we can say that the relationship between Christ and his believers reflects the relationship between Father and Son (e.g. John 10.14–15; 15.13; 17.21–3). 'Do you not believe that I am in the Father and the Father in me? The words I speak to you I do not speak of myself; but the Father who dwells in me does his works' (John 14.10).

When the Jesus of the fourth Gospel speaks, it is, fundamentally, the Father speaking through him. Once again, therefore, 'in me' indicates the ultimate subject of the Son. Yet although the Father and Son are considered to be one, there is also a distinction between them. The Son obeys the Father when Jesus says: 'For I have not spoken of myself; but the father who sent me gave me a commandment, what I should say, and what I should speak' (John 12.49). In John 14.10, Father and Son can be seen as two concentric circles in which the two centers coincide, whereas in John 12.49, Father and Son appear as two centers in an ellipse, the latter obeying the former. It is not likely that one relationship is based on the other, for that would oversimplify the matter. If we think that Christ and God are in all respects two different realities, so that what Christ does coincides with what God does only insofar as Christ obeys God, we lose the essential unity of Father with Son – the unity expressed in the words: 'Anyone who has seen me has seen the Father' (John 14.9). Christ is the Son of God insofar as the ultimate subject of the Son is the Father, but also insofar as the Father and Son are distinguished from each other. They are paradoxically one. As verse 10 indicates, those who have encountered Christ and have seen who speaks through him have seen the Father. Because of this unity, the Son reveals the Father. So we cannot categorize one kind of relationship as primary and the other as secondary.

Both types of relationship between Father and Son – concentric and elliptic – remind us of the two kinds of christology in the ancient church: the Antiochean and the Alexandrian. The Antiocheans maintained that there were two centers in the person of Jesus, the divine and the human, and that the human obeyed the divine; the Alexandrians held that both centers coincided. The ancient church, therefore, maintained that both christologies were true when, in the Council of Chalcedon, it declared that the divinity and humanity of Christ were distinguishable but not separable.

Also in Paul's understanding of his relationship with Christ we find the same two concentric and elliptic models. This illustrates how closely christology and anthropology are related. When Paul declares that he is dead and that Christ lives in him, the relationship between them is concentric. On the other hand, he states that it is he who speaks, not Christ. This does not mean that Paul is entirely separated from Christ and much less that he has been cut off from Christ. But it does show how Paul distinguished himself from Christ. We know further that Paul understood himself as the servant of Christ who is the paradoxical identity of the ultimate self and the object of faith. In this servant relationship, the elliptical model is at least implied – that is, the ego of Paul is subordinated to Christ in him, to Christ as the ultimate subject of Paul. So the relationship between the ego of Paul and Christ in him is not only concentric but also elliptic. Indeed, we find this implied in formulas such as 'to be led by the Spirit' (Rom. 8.4 ff, and *passim*), by the Spirit – that is, in whom Christ is present (Rom. 8.9 f).

If this understanding of Paul's relationship with Christ is correct, then the christological models – Antiochean/elliptic and Alexandrian/ concentric – reflect the structure of the person in which Christ and the believer are neither one nor two[10] – that is, the subjectivity of believers is composed not only of their own ego but also of 'Christ in them' as the ultimate subject in them. This is again analogous to Johannine Christology in which the Son, who obeys the Father, is at the same time united as one with God, who is present in the Son as the ultimate subject of the Son. In the fourth Gospel, Christ can speak out of and as his ultimate subject when he says 'I speak,' so that his words are at the same time the words of the Father who speaks through him. And so it can be said that whoever has seen the Son has seen the Father. This is why I said at the beginning of this chapter that it is important to examine closely what 'I' means and who, in the last analysis, speaks when one uses the form, 'I say to you.' As we shall see more closely below, Jesus himself could speak out of and as his ultimate subject when he said 'I say to you.' The 'I' in these words can be the 'divine in him,' which spoke through the empirical ego of Jesus. This does not contradict the fact that Jesus was just as much a human being as any of us. For all human beings are so constituted, in their very natures, that the divine and the human are at the same time one and two.[11] It is just that most persons have not yet awakened to this reality.

## III

We can carry on this same discussion from the perspective of Zen Buddhism. Hisamatsu Shin-ichi (1889–1980), a great Zen Master who was also professor of philosophy of religion at Kyoto University, was a well known 'atheist.' This does not mean that he denied the existence of God when affirming the existence of the world and of humanity. Hisamatsu directed his atheism against 'theism.' For him, God was not something 'out there'; he denied God as *das ganz Andere*. In his study entitled 'Atheism' (1949),[12] he asserted a paradoxical identity: 'the Formless' (ultimate reality) is not something outside, or merely *das ganz Andere*. To those who would insist that the ultimate must in some way be *das ganz Andere*, Hisamatsu responded that at the same time the ultimate is the self insofar as it is the human being's ultimate subject. *Das ganz Andere*, therefore, is also the ultimate self; this means that absolute heteronomy and absolute autonomy are, paradoxically, identical. According to Hisamatsu, 'I do' means, at the ground of the human being, 'the Formless does.' So he could even say, 'I do not die.'[13]

But is this not the apotheosis of the human being? Some critics made just this accusation against Hisamatsu. To understand what he meant, we have to look beyond the literal sense of his words. When he and I were once having a philosophical discussion, he said to me, 'Since I am so old, I may die at any moment. If I die, please carry on a conversation with me who am in you.' What he was trying to make clear to me, I think, is just whom I was talking with at that moment.[14] Yet, from what he was saying, it was clear that he was well aware of his own mortality. So for him, 'I' had a double structure: it was composed of the ego and the ultimate self (or, the Formless). Both selves for him are essentially concentric. Indeed, from the figure he drew, we see that when the self is awakened, the infinite (Formless) self contains the finite self (ego) within its circle.[15]

The Formless is also at work in the arts where it finds a visible form. (Hisamatsu was a famous calligrapher.) I asked him, 'How can one be sure that the Formless expresses itself as a work of art?' He answered, 'The Formless itself in the artist sees it.' 'But how can spectators see it?' I countered. 'If spectators are aware of the Formless within themselves, or if the Formless is awakened to itself in the spectators, they can see the expression of the Formless in a work of art.' So for Hisamatsu the Formless produces a work of art through the artist and then sees its own expression as and in a spectator, 'for it transcends the empirical ego infinitely.' This also explains why artists can also fail to express the Formless in themselves.[16]

Although Hisamatsu maintained that the Formless was the self and the self was the Formless, he also held that 'to be I' possessed structure and articulation.[17] He could speak directly from the Formless within him. When he said 'I do,' it meant that the Formless acted *through* his empirical ego, but at the same time *as* his empirical ego, for the Formless expresses itself only through the empirical ego – that is, the ego that is awakened to the Formless. And because the Formless is immortal, he could say 'I do not die.'

All this became clear to me in a conversation with him. When he said that the Formless was the self and the self was the Formless, I asked him whether there were *bonnos* (the sinful cares of the unenlightened ego when it acts only for itself) in the Formless Self. On the one hand, no human being is free from *bonnos*; on the other, it is impossible for the Formless to produce *bonnos* in the human being. Now if the human self and the Formless are identical, how can there be *bonnos?* He answered me, 'I have no *bonnos.*' When I pointed out that all human beings have *bonnos*, he answered, 'That's true. But suffering is for me the suffering of that which is free from suffering.'[18] However one understands what Hisamatsu was trying to say, one does have a sense of what was speaking through him. Hisamatsu was a person who could speak directly from and as the Formless within him. That this is often the case with Zen Buddhists is something we can keep in mind as we turn to our analysis of what Jesus meant when he said 'I.'

# IV

Usually, any attempt to understand the 'self-consciousness of Jesus' begins with an examination of what he had to say about 'the son of man.' As is well known, Jesus in the synoptic gospels speaks about the son of man as an eschatological figure – the son of God (Mark 8.38) who would appear from the heavens at the end of the world and, by destroying the enemies of God, would save God's people. Therefore, it is argued by those involved in 'the quest for the messianic consciousness of Jesus,' if Jesus called himself the son of man, he was aware of himself as a divine being.

Since the studies of Jackson-Lake,[19] the synoptic passages on the son of man have been classified into three groups: (1) the son of man to come (2) the son of man who would suffer and be resurrected, and (3) the son of man active on this earth. Rudolf Bultmann, in basic agreement with this classification, argued:

> The third group arose only because of a misunderstanding of the translation into Greek. In Aramaic, 'the son of man' was not a messianic title at all, but signified 'man' or 'I.' The second group comprises *vaticinia ex eventu* [prophecies after the fact], which are not found in Q. Only the first group contains the oldest tradition. In this group the expression the son of man is used in the third person.[20]

It is not necessary to enter into the history of scholarly debate on this issue. After Philipp Vielhauer had negated the authenticity of all the son of man sayings,[21] other New Testament scholars argued for the authenticity of the first groups of sayings.[22] The views of T. W. Manson are especially interesting: he understood the figure of the son of man as a 'collective personality.'[23]

We have seen that according to Paul, Christ was paradoxically both the ultimate subject and the object of faith. In Hisamatsu, the *das ganz Andere* was paradoxically his ultimate self, so that although he spoke of the Formless in the third person, he could also speak out of and as the Formless within him. Might we not say the same about Jesus? In Mark 8.38 he states, 'If anyone is ashamed of me and my words in this wicked and godless age, the son of man will be ashamed of him, when he comes in the glory of his Father and of the holy angels.' Although Jesus here refers to the son of man in the third person, he himself is at the same time the representative of the son of man on earth. In this way we can say that Jesus and the son of man are one, despite the qualitative differences between them. We could say that Jesus is here speaking out of and as the son of man. This means that we do not need the theory of a mistake in the Greek translation to interpret the third group of son of man sayings. Rather, we can say that Jesus announced that in his words and actions it was the son of man acting and speaking in and through him, even though from the outside it seemed that his empirical ego was the agent.

For Jesus, therefore, the son of man was both *das ganz Andere* and his own ultimate subject (in a paradoxical unity). Just as only those who are awakened to the Formless in them can see how the Formless expresses itself in a work of art, so only those who are awakened to the reign of God in them can see that the son of man – that is, the son of God – is at work in, through, and as Jesus, in whom the reign of God has been revealed as 'the lightning flash that lights up the earth from end to end' (Luke 17.24).[24]

I think we can best understand the unity between the son of man and the reign of God when we assume that the figure of the son of man as used in the words of Jesus is the personification of the reign of God, just as Amida Buddha in Pure Land Buddhism is the personification of the saving activity of the transcendent Amida, who comes from the Formless and reveals it to his believers.[25] This helps us understand the words of Mark 2.27 ff: 'The Sabbath was made for the sake of the person and not the person for the sake of the Sabbath: therefore the Son of man is sovereign over the Sabbath.' The law is the form that the reign of God (the will of God) assumes on earth in order to show itself, to make itself known to human beings. In this sense, the law is made for the sake of the person. The law itself is not the ultimate, but is a visible form of the invisible reign, will, of God. The law is based on the reign of God, which is personified in the son of man. *Therefore* the son of man is sovereign over the law.[26] This means that a human being through whom the son of man acts – as is the case with Jesus – can break the law if the law is estranged from the reign of God and so binds a person in a heteronomous way. For according to the original nature of every person, the 'son of man' (reign of God) is the person's ultimate subject (concentricity), while the empirical ego obeys with inner understanding, so that when one is 'enlightened' one understands the law as the expression of ultimate reality. But if the law ceases to be the medium of the reign of God, it can be broken. Therefore Jesus could invalidate the entire ritual system of ancient purification and say: 'Nothing that goes into a person from the outside can defile the person. No, it is the things that come out of a person that defile a person' (Mark 7.15).

So the title 'son of man' is not a mere self-identification of Jesus. Therefore we can say that the sayings of the third group are for the most part authentic, with the exception of the sayings in which 'the son of man' is clearly used only as a way of identifying Jesus or in which the understanding of Jesus in primitive Christianity is clearly reflected (e.g. Mark 8.31; 10.45). With the sayings of the third group, therefore, Jesus declared his work and words to be those of the son of man in him. As we said, the son of man is for Jesus both *das ganz Andere* and his ultimate self. But to those who were not awakened to the reality of the reign of God in them, it seemed that Jesus as an empirical person held himself to be divine and so able to forgive sins (Mark 2.10) and also to break the law (Mark 2.23 ff). So although many of 'the Jews' were scandalized at such blasphemy, Jesus' followers went on simply to identify him with the divine, without any distinction between the ultimate subject and the empirical ego of Jesus. But for Jesus himself, it was the son of man who had the right to forgive sins and break the law, not Jesus as an empirical ego. Once again: for him the son of man was both *das ganz Andere* and his ultimate subject. This was Jesus' self-understanding. He did not apotheosize himself, for as an empirical man, he did not hold himself to be divine (Mark 10.18); but he was aware that his actions were those of the son of man in him. Though it was no self-apotheosis, such an awareness could be reached only by someone who 'has died' entirely, so that 'the son of man' could live in him (cf. Gal. 2.20).

In this context, we can take up the so-called antitheses in the Sermon on the Mount[27] (Matt. 5.21–44) and ask who is actually speaking when we hear 'But I say to you':

You have learned that our forefathers were told, 'Do you commit murder; those who commit murder must be brought to judgment.' But I say to you: Those who nurse anger against their brother or sister must be brought to judgment (vv. 21 f). . . . You have learned that they were told, 'Do not commit adultery.' But I say to you: If a man looks on a woman with a lustful eye, he has already committed adultery with her in his heart (vv. 27 f). . . . You have learned that they were told, 'Do not break your oath,' and 'Oaths sworn to the Lord must be kept.' But I say to you: you are not to swear at all (vv. 33 f). . . . You have learned that they were told, 'An eye for an eye, and a tooth for a tooth.' But I say to you; Do not set yourself against the person who wrongs you. If someone slaps you on the right cheek, turn and offer him your left (vv. 38 f). . . . You have learned that they were told, 'Love your neighbor, hate your enemy.' But I say to you: Love your enemies (vv. 43 f).

With such words, Jesus clearly surpassed the authority of Moses. But whoever is superior to Moses, must be divine. So if Jesus spoke this way, he must have considered himself to be divine. Many did indeed think the same thing about him, and in their confessions, the christology of primitive Christianity can be found.[28] According to this christology, Jesus is a divine being of heavenly origin, the Lord, the son of God who is equal with God. This christology was much discussed in the 'quest of the historical Jesus,' and many scholars still hold to its views. But such an interpretation does not take into sufficient account that the 'I' of Jesus had two centers, the ultimate subject and the empirical ego, and that these centers related to each other concentrically as well as elliptically. Still, we have to ask what is the 'I' in the antithetical sayings. If it is the empirical ego of Jesus, he is suspect of self-apotheosis. His enemies could accuse him of being a blasphemer of God, whereas his followers thought this empirical man was divine.

I can suggest a different perspective. In the antitheses – really, in the words of Jesus in general – something divine (the reign of God or the son of man as its personification) spoke through the mouth of his empirical person. This was possible because the divine was for him both *daz ganz Andere* and his own ultimate subject. To grasp more fully what is really contained in such talk of the divine, one would have to make a further distinction between God, the reign of God (the son of man who is in nature the son of God), and the Spirit of God (cf. Matt. 12.28). At the moment, however, I limit myself to investigating the 'I' in Jesus. Jesus was speaking directly from and as the divine when he said, 'But I say to you' – that is, he was speaking from his 'ultimate subject,' which was at one with his humanity (divine-human). The 'reign of God' was so clearly revealed in him (to his ego) that he could tell others what it brought forth in the human heart (cf. Phil. 2.13). It called forth love of one's enemy, exemplified in the figure of the good Samaritan; there is an immediacy of love that is so natural and yet so paradoxical that its roots go deeper than the ego, for its roots are the activity of 'the reign of God.' So Jesus spoke as the divine: the son of God, for the son of God is real in our historical reality only in and through empirical human beings who are aware of the son – just as 'Christ' did his work through Paul (Rom. 15.18).

In the depth of the human *self*, the divine and the human are one. We call this reality the incarnate Logos. If my interpretation is correct, Jesus lived *as* the incarnate Logos. An authentic human existence is so structured that the incarnate Logos becomes real in our history in, through, and as the authentic human existence that is aware of its own depths. Yet Jesus also called God *Abba* ('papa'). As an empirical person (the ego), Jesus understood himself to be subordinated to God (cf. Mark 10.18), though, of course, in an intimate union with God.

If this interpretation is correct, we can more clearly understand the antitheses of Jesus; they are by no means only 'the highest moral attainment' of humanity. They are not mere morality or ethics, for ethics makes up a moral program valid for the ego. Ethics constitutes social norms for the ego, or the norms for the sociality of the ego. The antitheses in Jesus' sayings are not a matter of the ego; they do not provide social norms for the ego. Rather, they show what is there in the *self* under the reign of God, for they are the words of this reign. Just as the Formless does not produce any *bonnos* in the human heart, so under the reign of God – that is, insofar as it is revealed to the ego and thus works in the human being – there is no anger, nor lustful desire, nor vengeance, nor hatred in the human self. When the reign of God in the person is so revealed that it becomes reflected in the ego, then it constitutes the will of the ego (cf. Phil. 2.13); then what is realized is 'I will,' not 'you should.'

Of course, to speak as Jesus did is not easy. But it is possible, I think, for all of us insofar as it is based on the activity of God who is at the same time both *das ganz Andere* and the ultimate subject of every human being. If God is merely *das ganz Andere*, the absolutely transcendent that is named only in the third person, then God is something absolutely objective and heteronomous. If this is so, then human beings could know God only through special, supernatural revelation; and such a unique revelation would be the ground for the exclusivity of

Christianity. If, on the other hand, God is merely the ultimate subject of the human being, something that speaks and acts only in the first person, then suspicion of the self-apotheosis of the relative is likely. So the understanding of the transcendent as the paradoxical identity of *das ganz Andere* and the ultimate subject of every human being is indispensable not only for our understanding of Jesus, but also for our theological thinking today.

## V

1  In the first part of this chapter, I mentioned Takizawa's distinction between the primary and the secondary contacts of God with the self. In light of my study of Paul and Jesus, I might interpret that distinction to mean that every human being, a priori, is in the field of God's grace (*in Christo*). The unconditional given of our existence is that God is with each one of us (the primary contact of God with us). This is comparable to the fundamental notion of Mahayana Buddhism that every living thing has a 'Buddha-nature.' But this reality is found at the depth level of our being (the self as divine-humanity), a level we are generally not aware of; and because we are not aware of it, this reality is not activated in our hearts. And so we do not know God at all.

The primary contact of God with us – the fact that at the ground of our existence we are in the field of God's grace so that our being reflects this field – constitutes and conditions the very existence of each of us. In this sense, the divine and the human are structurally and a priori one. But it is a dialectical oneness. Insofar as the divine does not reveal itself to the ego – that is, insofar as we are not aware of it – this reality is virtually nonexistent and in this sense we are not united with the divine. Or to put it in a Buddhist expression: 'There is in the living things no Buddha-nature.'[29] But when this reality reveals itself in and to the ego, when the ego becomes aware of it, then the divine begins to act through, in, and as the empirical human being so that the 'self' is discovered to be divine-human. The divine realizes itself in our historical reality. This is the second contact of God with the human being according to Takizawa. It is an event. And then we can say that we have become aware of it because it was already there, a priori.

But can we really say that this divine-human oneness is activated or actualized when we become aware of it? And how do we become aware of it? By a decision of faith? Yes. Through enlightenment? That too is possible. In any case, because the reality of the primary contact of God with the human being is virtually nonexistent insofar as the ego is ignorant of it, its 'revelation' in the ego is an event that is discontinuous with the ego's past. It has no real grounding in the past. This 'revelation' is not a necessary result of the primary contact; it does not have to happen. And so one is justified in speaking of the 'Holy Spirit' who gives the gift of faith (1 Cor. 12.3) or brings us to the Truth (John 14.17; 16.13), just as in Jodo-Buddhism the power of Amida Buddha brings forth faith in the person. In such descriptions, the ego is realizing its groundedness in that which transcends it.

If all this is so, we can make a distinction between the self and the ego – that is, between the primary contact at the depths of the self and the secondary contact as an event taking place in the ego. Earlier I distinguished between the self and the ego because of the continuity and the discontinuity between them. Here I am making this distinction for another reason.[30] I am using Takizawa's distinction, but with a necessary adjustment, for it seems to me that Takizawa leaves no room for the role of the Holy Spirit – or, that he does not fully see the meaning of enlightenment.

2  We can extend our analysis to provide an explanation as to how faith in the resurrection of Jesus arose: that which primitive Christianity called the 'risen, pneumatic Christ,' or 'the heavenly Lord,' or 'the son of God,' was none other than that which spoke through the mouth of Jesus of Nazareth when he said 'But I say to you . . .' 'The Risen Christ' is what Jesus called 'the reign of God' or 'the son of man.' The disciples of Jesus did not understand Jesus when he was with them. After his death on the cross, 'the reign of God' was revealed in them in the same way it was revealed to Paul: 'The son of God was revealed to me' (Gal. 1.16). This is the event of religious enlightenment, in which the divine reveals itself in the structure of paradoxical identity between *das ganz Andere* and the person's ultimate subject, and in the oneness of the divine and the human. But the disciples took this experience for the appearance of Jesus who had been resurrected from the dead. For in the activity of that which they had become aware of and that which was realized in and as the depth of themselves, they acknowledged the very same reality that had spoken and acted *as* Jesus when he lived with them.

Furthermore, at that time, 'resurrection' would have been the way they interpreted such an event. After the death of John the Baptist, for instance, when Jesus appeared center stage and took the place of his teacher (the Baptist), some said that the Baptist was resurrected and that his power acted in Jesus (Mark 6.14ff). In the same way, the disciples of Jesus interpreted the event of their enlightenment and believed that Jesus who had been killed on the cross was resurrected and that the power of Jesus was now at work in them, for they had now become 'new creatures' (2 Cor. 5.17), agents of Jesus. In other words, the disciples did not distinguish between Jesus' depth and his empirical ego (that is, between the primary and secondary contacts in Jesus, as Takizawa put it), so that they held that Jesus as a historical person was resurrected. In this way, the 'event of Jesus' (his death and resurrection) came to be considered the absolute ground of human salvation.

But what they named 'the risen Christ' was really what Takizawa would call the primary contact of God with the human being – that is, divine-humanity, Logos incarnate, oneness of the divine and the human at the depth of every human being (self). Therefore Paul could say that 'Christ' lived in him when 'the son of God' was revealed to him (Gal. 1.16; 2.20). In Takizawa's terms again, primitive Christianity did not distinguish between the primary and secondary contacts of God with the person of Jesus. And so they thought that the primary contact itself – the divine-human oneness – was brought about by Jesus who was resurrected in order to remain with them in the flesh. But the divine-human oneness is not confined to Jesus alone; it is a reality in the depth of every human self, a reality in the church as the Body of Christ in which Christ is truly present (1 Cor. 12), as well as in each believer (Rom. 8.10). In its depth, the divine is one with the human in every human self as well as in humanity as a whole. Here 'Christ' remains divinity with flesh, which becomes manifest as well as real in the event of enlightenment, the secondary contact of God with the person. But in its nature, it is prior to enlightenment as the ground common to Buddhism and Christianity.

This is my interpretation and explanation of Takizawa's views, in relation to contemporary New Testament studies. Of course, the results of New Testament studies are not certain; at most, they are probable. Still, it is important that religious pluralism not contradict the results of New Testament studies, just as our investigation of the New Testament is given new stimulus and light from dialogue with other world religions.

*Seiichi Yagi*

## NOTES

1 See the discussion of his lectures in 'The First Conference of Tōzai Shūkyō Kōryū Gakkai' (*Buddhist–Christian Studies*, 3, 1983), pp. 123–56. In the same volume (pp. 63–97), Tokīyukī Nobuhara compares Takizawa with John Cobb, Jr: 'Principles for Interpreting Christ/Buddha: Katsumi Takizawa and John B. Cobb, Jr'.

2 See my own critical comments on his views, in ibid., pp. 137–41, 152–3. I should like to add here that even if one accepts Takizawa's distinction, together with his understanding of Jesus, one could in a sense still say with the fourth evangelist that 'truth came through Jesus Christ' (John 1.17). Paul is an example; by the grace of God he had been separated from his mother's womb to be a missionary to the Gentiles, and yet he was ignorant of all this before the revelation of the son of God in him so that he persecuted Christians (Gal. 1.15–16; cf. 2 Cor. 4.6). But after Christ was revealed in him, he could say 'Christ lives in me' (Gal. 1.20), so that from then on, he proclaimed Christ among the Gentiles as Christ worked through him (Rom. 15.18). Therefore, in so far as the self is ignorant of the primary contact of God with the self, this contact is not real; it does not work in and through the self. It is virtually nonexistent. The fundamental importance, therefore, of 'awakening' or 'enlightenment' lies in the fact that 'Truth' (*dharma*) is activated in the self through enlightenment; it works in the self when the self is awakened to it. In this sense, we can say that 'Truth' was virtually nonexistent in history before Jesus (or, in the East, before Buddha) came – or, more exactly, before Jesus was awakened to it. It is true that the reason why one can be awakened to the primary contact of God with the self is that it is there prior to the awakening. But it is also true that the primary contact becomes real and is activated in the self only when the self is awakened to it. The same paradox is contained in the well-known statement, 'Those who are given to Christ by God believe in him' (John 6.37). And yet, 'those who believe in Christ become the children of God' (John 1.12).

3 Takizawa's views contain implications concerning the manner in which the disciples of Jesus came to believe in his resurrection. He holds that after the death of Jesus, the eyes of his disciples were opened to see the primary contact of God with the self – that is, 'Christ,' 'the son of God,' which is at the ground of each self. See Takizawa, *Seishono Kiristoto Gendaino Shi'i* (*Biblical Christ and Modern Thinking*) (Tokyo, Shinkyō Shuppansha, 1965), pp. 51–3. This viewpoint agrees substantially with my study of biblical faith in the resurrection of Jesus: *Shin'yaku Shisōno Seiritsu* (*Formation of New Testament Thoughts*) (Tokyo, Shinkyō Shuppansha, 1963); *Kiristoto Iesu* (*Christ and Jesus*) (Tokyo, Kōdansha Gendai Shinsho, 1969). In the context of the 'new quest of the historical Jesus,' I made a careful comparison of Jesus with Paul, and came to the conclusion that 'the reign of God' according to Jesus and 'the risen pneumatic Christ' according to primitive Christianity are different names for the same reality. I present this claim in the last section of this chapter, though in a different and abbreviated form. Concerning the thesis that Christianity and Buddhism are based on a common ground, see Seiichi Yagi, *Bukkyōto*

*Kōristokyōno Setten* (*The Point of Contact between Buddhism and Christianity*) (Kyoto, Hōzōkan, 1975). My article, 'Paul and Shinran: Jesus and Zen', in *Buddhist–Christian Dialogue – Mutual Renewal and Transformation*, ed. P. O. Ingram and F. J. Streng (Honolulu, University of Hawaii Press, 1986) is a resumé of my book with the same title: *Paulo-Shinran; Iesu-Zen* (Kyoto, Hōzōkan, 1983).

4 E. Käsemann, 'Das Problem des historischen Jesu', in *Exegetische Versuche und Besinnungen*, vol. 1 (Göttingen, Vandenhoeck & Ruprecht, 1960, 1st ed). Rudolf Bultmann had argued earlier that Jesus' call for a decision on the part of his hearers already implied a Christology; see 'Die Christologie des Neuen Testaments', in *Glauben und Verstehen*, vol. 1 (Tübingen, J. C. B. Mohr, 4th edn, 1961), p. 266.

5 Ego is the subject of feeling, thinking, and doing – the I, insofar as I am conscious that I feel, think, and do something. When dreaming, I am not conscious that I am producing the dream. The dream is therefore not a product of the ego, but of the unconscious. It is important to bear in mind that 'enlightenment' means that the ego becomes aware of the reality of *dharma* which bears the whole existence of the person. If this is so, we have to make a clear distinction between the 'ultimate subject' and the 'ego.' As we shall see below, the ego makes decisions, but it has deeper roots.

6 In affirming this twofold unity of ultimate subject and ego, I think I am in agreement with the views of D. M. Baillie in *God Was in Christ* (New York, Scribner's, 1948). Baillie finds the mystery of the incarnation reflected in the structure contained in 'not I . . . but the grace of God' (1 Cor. 15.10). I agree with this interpretation of the incarnation, but I cannot understand why Baillie, throughout his book, insists on a qualitative difference between Jesus and other believers (for instance, p. 145). 'I do . . . not I, but the transcendent' – these words indicate the very structure of incarnation. Logos incarnate, therefore, is not confined to Jesus; it is a reality in the church as 'the body of Christ' (1 Cor. 12) insofar as in this body there is the unity described above. Indeed, Paul can in a sense identify the body of Christ with Christ himself (v. 12). But this unity is not always found in the empirical church or in its members. So we must examine more closely the structure of the person: the relationship between the ultimate self and the ego. Between them, there is both continuity and discontinuity. See below.

7 A. Satake, *Galatea Sho* (*Galatians*) (Tokyo, Shinkyō Shuppansha, 1974), pp. 94–5. I agree with this interpretation as long as 'to me' means that the ego becomes aware of the reality of Christ 'in me.' 'Christ was revealed in me' and 'Christ was revealed to me' do not really contradict each other, for, as I said above (note 2), 'Christ in me' becomes real when 'Christ is revealed to me.'

8 H. Conzelmann, *Grundriss der Theologie des Neuen Testaments* (Munich, Kaiser, 1968), pp. 232 ff.

9 P. L. Berger (ed.), *The Other Side of God: A Polarity in World Religions* (New York, Anchor Press, 1981) examines the typology of religious experience proposed by Berger (confrontation and interiority) and finds that many religious personages – Paul, Francis of Assisi, Shinran, for example – evince both a confrontation model and an interiority model in their understanding of the person's relationship with God. According to Figure 1 in my text, the

transcendent both 'confronts' and 'reveals' itself 'in' the person. From the standpoint of the religious ego responding to the call of the transcendent, the transcendent is dominantly *das ganz Andere* that confronts it through some medium (e.g. the Bible); but in the experience of inward unity ('Christ in me' constituting my life-activity), the unity of the transcendent and the self is dominant. Here we touch on the roots of mysticism. But I find the *structural* unity in the self, not in the ego.

10    Again, this issue is quite complicated. (1) Christ and the self are one in the depths of the self: 'Christ in me' constitutes 'my' life-activity. This relationship transcends my consciousness, though it is activated through consciousness. (2) But in the activity of the ego, there is also a twofoldness, insofar as its activity is based on inward unity. There is then a continuity between 'Christ in me' and the activity of the ego (concentricity). On the other hand, there is structural discontinuity between the two. In this sense, we can say that the ego obeys Christ, for it responds to the call of Christ in encounter, and it acts through its own decision, though its activity is based on the activity of Christ 'in' the person (ellipticity).

11    If 'Christ in me' constitutes 'my' life-activity, the divine and the human are neither one nor two, or at the same time, one and two. There are many instances in which A constitutes non-A as part or condition of the latter (I call this 'front-structure'). So a word from another person, when changed into my own word, constitutes a part of my own thinking. In such mental activity the person and I are at the same time one and two. Or in the case of music, the human heart and physical sounds are neither one nor two. Music is human-physical as the self is divine-human. They are different realities, but insofar as the human heart expresses itself *as* music, they are one. M. Honda sees in the structure 'not one, not two' the essence of religious thinking. See his 'The Encounter of Christianity with the Buddhist Logic of Soku', in *Buddhist–Christian Dialogue*, pp. 217–30.

12    *Zettai Shutai Dō* (*The Way of the Absolute Subject*), Collected Works of Hisamatsu Shin-ichi, vol. 2 (Tokyo, Risōsha, 1972), pp. 53–93.

13    *Shinnin Hisamatsu Shin-ichi* (*Hisamatsu Shin-ichi as True Man*) (Tokyo, Shunjūsha, 1985), p. 168. Here one of Hisamatsu's leading disciples, Ryūtarō Kitahara, reports what the master said to him: 'I do not die though my fleshly body dies. I am always with you.'

14    This dialogue between Hisamatsu and Yagi was published as *Kakuno Shūkyo* (*Religion of Awakening*) (Tokyo, Shunjūsha, 1980).

15    'Ningenno Bukkyōteki Kōzō' ('The Buddhist Structure of the Human Being'), in *Zettai Shutai Dō*, p. 253.

16    *Kakuno Shūkyo*, pp. 129–31.

17    I understand Hisamatsu in this way: though he maintained the identity of the Formless with the self, he said that the Formless transcends the empirical ego infinitely. So for Hisamatsu, the subject is composed of the self, which is one with the Formless, and of the ego, which is continuous–discontinuous with the self.

18    *Kakuno Shūkyo*, pp. 5–7.

19    *The Beginnings of Christianity*, pt 1 (Grand Rapids, Baker Book House, 1979), pp. 368 ff (originally published in 1920).

20 *Theologie des Neuen Testaments* (Tübingen, J. C. B. Mohr, 2nd edn, 1954), p. 31. Translation by Yagi.

21 'Gottesreich und Menschensohn in der Verkündigung Jesu', in *Festschrift für G. Dehn* (Neukirchen, Neukirchener Verlag, 1957), pp. 51 ff.

22 F. Hahn, *Christologische Hoheitstitel* (Göttingen, Vandenhoeck & Ruprecht, 1966), pp. 32 ff; Kenzō Tagawa, *Maruko Fukuinsho (The Gospel according to Mark)* (Tokyo, Shinkyō Shuppansha, 1972), pp. 190–1.

23 For my understanding and criticism of the son of man sayings I am indebted to N. Perrin, *The Kingdom of God in the Teachings of Jesus* (London, SCM Press, 1963), ch. 7. Shinran, too, affirms the collective figure of Amida Buddha; Amida, the great Light, consists of infinite little lights that are also considered to be Amidas (*Genseiriyaku Wasan 12*, in *Jōdo Wasan*). This reminds us of Christ in Paul: Christ is present in the church as his body (1 Cor. 12) as well as in each member of it (Rom. 8.10).

24 It may not be too bold a conjecture to see in this saying a reflection of the enlightenment of the heart, for cosmological reality is at the same time reality in this world. See Luke 17.21b.

25 'The Kingdom of God' and 'the Pure Land', or, more correctly, 'the son of man with the kingdom of God' and 'Amida Buddha with his Pure Land' are at least comparable. See T. Tamaru, 'Jōdoto Kamino Kuni' ('The Pure Land and the Kingdom of God'), in *Jōdokōyto Kiristokyō (Jodo-Buddhism and Christianity)* (Tokyo, Sankibō, 1977). The following parallels are noteworthy: God and Christ in Paul, the relationship between God and 'the son of man' (i.e. the son of God, Mark 8.37) in Jesus, and the relationship between the Formless (*Dharma-kāya*) and Amida Buddha (*Sambhoga-kāya*) in Jōdo Buddhism. In other words, 'the son of man' in Jesus and 'Christ' in Paul correspond to 'Amida Buddha' in Shinran. They all come from the ultimate reality (God or *Dharma-kāya*) and represent it, in the role of 'savior' (in the case of 'the son of man' and Christ, also in the role of judge). It is also noteworthy that both the son of man in our understanding and Amida Buddha are transcendent-incarnate: they are at work in and as human beings. As incarnate divine-human, they are reminiscent of traditional claims of christology. Amida Buddha who is at work in the believer corresponds to 'Christ in me' in Paul.

26 In this passage, 'the son of man' can also mean true human nature, as Tagawa argues; he also considers this saying to be genuine. See *Maruko Fukeuinsho*, p. 190. This interpretation does not call into question the point I have been making, for 'true human nature' consists in the fact that: I live, not I, but 'Christ' in me, or in the case of Jesus, that Jesus lives, not Jesus, but the son of man in him. This is comparable to the 'True Person' in Rinzai (Chinese: *Lin-chi I-hsüam*) who is at work in every life activity of the enlightened (*Rinzairoku*, Jōdō, 3: Jishū, 1).

27 J. Jeremias, *Die Bergpredigt* (Stuttgart, Calver Verlag, 1959); this little pamphlet offers a fine summary of contemporary understandings of the Sermon on the Mount in Germany. A short history of how the Sermon on the Mount has been understood is given in U. Luz, *Das Evangelium nach Matthäus* (Evangelisch-katholischer Kommentar zum Neuen Testament, vol. 1/1) (Zürich, Benziger Verlag/ Neukirchen-Vluyn, Neukirchener Verlag, 1985),

pp. 191 ff. Here I am not trying to interpret the Sermon on the Mount but only asking 'christological' questions.

28 See note 4 above.

29 So Dōgen, *Shōbō-Genzo*, 3 (on the Buddha-nature). Dōgen holds that (1) there is Buddha-nature in every living thing (2) there is no Buddha-nature in every living thing (3) Buddha-nature realizes itself when human beings become aware of it (enlightenment).

30 This distinction is perhaps similar to C. G. Jung's distinction between the self and the ego. See *Die Beziehung zwischen dem Ich und dem Unbewussten* (Zürich, 1933). I read this book in translation (translated by Akria Noda, Tokyo, Jinbunshoin, 1982. Jung even refers to Galatians 2.20 (p. 164 of the Japanese translation) and holds the true self to be something divine in us (p. 120 of the translation). Yet Jung's notion of the self is not the same as our 'ultimate subject,' for in Jung the true self is hidden and does not necessarily show itself in its fulness to those who are aware of it. See his dialogue with S. Hisamatsu in *Tōyōteki Mu* (*Nothingness in the Far East*) in the collected works of Hisamatsu Shin-ichi, vol. 1, 1970, p. 389.

# 25

# Inter-faith Hermeneutics: An Example and Some Implications

## R. S. SUGIRTHARAJAH

This essay addresses the question of using the Christian Scripture in a multi-faith context, and the need for biblical scholars to be sensitive to the people of other faiths in their interpretative task. Conversion is one of the key theological issues in a religiously pluralistic world, and among other things it causes cultural and religious dislocation and resocialization. Taking a cue from Latin American liberation hermeneutics, the texts that are associated with what is commonly known as Paul's conversion experience are looked at from a multi-faith point of view. The essay also points out the implications and new possibilities offered by such a re-reading, and sets out some ground rules for multi-faith hermeneutics.

This essay was first presented at the British New Testament Conference, Bristol, 1989, and was subsequently published in *Misson Studies* (VII-1, 1990) – a journal of the International Association for Mission Studies, available from Dr Joachim Wietzke, IAMS Secretariat, EMW, Mittelweg 143, D-2000 Hamburg, West Germany.

The fact that we in Britain live in a multi-faith context is an existential reality of our times. This has been increasingly recognized by the media, politicians and church people. But the key question is how seriously have biblical interpreters taken into account the people of other faiths in their exegetical cogitations.

Biblical interpretation in a multi-faith context should be aware of at least two things. One, it must be sensitive to the scriptural texts of other faith communities and the spiritual sustenance they provide for many of their adherents. Mahatma Gandhi, so sympathetic to the person and teaching of Christ, nevertheless regarded the *Bhagavad Gita* as 'the supreme book for the knowledge of Truth' affording him invaluable help 'in times of distress'.[1] He also held the view that 'many things in the Bible have to be reinterpreted in the light of discoveries – not of modern science – but in the spiritual world in the shape of direct experiences common to all faiths'.[2]

Secondly, Christian scriptural interpreters should be conscious that their literary output is likely to reach a wide audience which is not necessarily exclusively Christian. Wilfred Cantwell Smith has been warning Christian interpreters that in their theologizing they should not only take note of Hindu, Buddhist and Muslim scholars who are 'equally intelligent', 'equally devout' and 'equally moral', but also be conscious of a prospective readership which is likely to include Buddhists, or those who have Muslim husbands or Hindu colleagues.[3]

The task then for a biblical interpreter is not only to discover how to live as a member of a multi-faith society, but also how to interpret the scriptural texts taking note of the presence and the spiritual intuitions of people of other faiths.

One way of facing the situation is to take a cue from the Latin American liberation theologians and re-read some of the biblical materials in the light of the multi-faith context. Recently the Latin American liberation theologians have been vigorously arguing for a re-reading of the biblical texts from the perspective of the poor. In doing so they have given a new meaning to the phrase 're-read'. It means more than to read again or to re-interpret. It means to take a fresh look at the data and read anew and reformulate the message. It means investing the text with new meanings and nuances.

There are a number of passages that one could subject to such a re-reading. I would like to have a re-look at the narratives which are commonly used to understand Paul's change of mind, traditionally known as his conversion.

Before that, we need to look briefly at the matter of religious conversions and the deep theological and sociological questions they raise.

In the religiously pluralistic context of India, religious conversion means a shift from one religion to another, but also more importantly, from one community to another. Therefore conversion to Christianity means not only experiencing, relating to and realizing the ultimate reality in a totally different way, but also stepping into an utterly strange social and religious milieu. It is a change of outlook and an orienting of one's life to a different focal point, but it also means leaving one's own cultural heritage and joining a Christian community whose style of worship and church structure follows western cultural patterns. Therefore conversion raises many theological issues. Among them are: (a) Is one religion superior to the other? (b) What aspects of culture and social life should a convert be encouraged to preserve? (c) In what ways should he or she be helped to make use of his or her rich tradition to interpret the new faith? and (d) Should one leave one's own cultural social tradition entirely in accepting another faith? The words of T. K. Tiwari, a Brahmin convert who became a Christian, echo these questions:

> When I decided to be baptized, I did not think that I was 'leaving' Hindu society. I thought I was adding something anew, something glorious to my Hindu heritage. I wanted to continue to live with my parents, to co-operate with other Hindus in social service work, to visit the temple etc. I was like the early Christians who met daily at Solomon's porch in the temple. Soon I discovered that this was not possible.[4]

## PAUL'S EXPERIENCE: TWO APPROACHES

Paul's spiritual experience on the Damascus highway – Acts 9.1–9, 22.4–16 and 26.9–19, and his assumed reference to it in Galatians 1.11–17 – have been exegeted in many ways. Scholarly energies have been spent looking at these texts historically, philologically, psychologically, and of course, theologically. Basically there are two approaches to these texts and they can be summed up as the Conquest approach and the Reorientation approach.

### The Conquest approach

The Conquest approach sees Paul's experience in terms of conversion and commissioning him to preach Christ to the Gentiles. He is conquered by Christ and he is sent to conquer others for Christ. This approach neatly bifurcates Paul's life – Saul, the fanatical Pharisee bent on persecuting the followers of the Jesus movement, and Paul the Christian, equally fanatical about preaching his new-found saviour to the Gentiles. F. F. Bruce captures the essence of this approach:

> With astonishing suddenness the persecutor of the church became the apostle of Jesus Christ. He was in mid-course as a zealot for the law, bent on checking a plague which threatened the life of Israel, when, in his own words, he was 'apprehended by Christ Jesus' (Philippins 3.12) and constrained to turn right round and became a champion of the cause which, up to that moment, he had been endeavouring to exterminate, dedicated henceforth to building up what he had been doing his best to demolish.[5]

The Conquest approach functions at two levels. Theologically, it tends to project a Paul who is deeply dissatisfied with the arid spirituality of his own faith. His own tradition, the Judaism of his day, is seen as outmoded and legalistic. Romans 7 is taken to be Paul's autobiographical reflection on his inability to fulfil the requirements of the Jewish law. Missiologically, this approach sees his conversion as a warrant to take the Christian message to all parts of the world. In essence, the Conquest approach sees Paul's conversion from the Christian church's apologetical and propagandistic point of view.

## The Reorientation approach

This approach tries to rehabilitate Paul within Judaism and sees his turning point not as conversion, but as call – a call to a specific task, in the fashion of the Hebrew prophets. Krister Stendahl is the main exponent of this position.[6] This view does not see Paul as changing from one religion to another, but as changing from one of the Jewish sects to another. Therefore Paul's earlier life is not perceived as one of dejection and spiritual impoverishment. Instead, he is seen as a person who was proud of his traditions, his people and their calling. Put differently, Paul's life is not the case of a person without faith finding his way to God, nor of a person who is dissatisfied with his own faith, but rather of a person who gets a new understanding of his task.

This approach emphasizes two things. Firstly, it stresses Paul's call as a call to a particular assignment, and secondly, it detects prophetic character in his call. K. Stendahl's words sum up these concerns:

> If, then, we use the term 'conversion' for Paul's experience, we would also have to use it of such prophets as Jeremiah and Isaiah. Yet we do not speak of their conversion, but rather of their call. Paul's experience is also that of a call – to a specific vocation – to be God's appointed apostle to the Gentile.[7]

From a multi-faith perspective both these approaches are insensitive to the people of other faiths. Both see Paul's so-called conversion from a mission and proselytization point of view. The difficulty with such an exegetical approach is that it envisages confrontation with the people of other faiths. It sees its task in terms of conversion of people who are not within the Christian-fold. While one plans for an open aggressive propaganda of the Christian gospel, the other opts for a soft, covert operation. Under this second approach, the prophetic vocation is seen in terms of purifying and castigating evil elements in other faiths.

## A third way: Dialogical approach

In the multi-faith context, there is another way of exegeting the data that is linked with Paul's experience. That is, the Dialogical approach – an approach which acknowledges the validity of the varied and diverse religious experiences of all people and rules out any exclusive claim to the truth by one religious tradition. In this approach, every religion is worthy of love and respect. All religions contain liberative as well as oppressive elements and the hermeneutical task is to enlist the liberative aspects to bring harmony and social change to all people. It is from this perspective I invite you to look at the biblical datum.

Traditionally, scholars have used two sources – Luke's account and Paul's own meagre recollections. It is from the accounts of Acts that one gets the popular images of Paul's conversion – supernatural voice, blindness, companions, etc. Paul's letters are virtually silent about these and it would be difficult to construct a conversion scenario from them. Moreover, one has to cull it from his letters which are in fact essentially concerned with other matters, his apostolic status and authority, his integrity, the practical problems of his communities and the non-arrival of the End.

Paul's letters namely, the ones accepted by the majority of scholars – 1 Thessalonians, Galatians, 1 and 2 Corinthians, Philemon, Philippians and Romans – do not suggest that he agonized over his past or that he rejected his own tradition. Rather, they claim that he was blameless (Phil. 3.6); he was proud of his Jewish calling and in religious fervour he was well ahead of people of his time (Gal. 1.14).

Interestingly, Paul does not use the traditional vocabulary that is normally associated with the process of conversion. He does not use the noun form of 'conversion' (*epistrophe*) or 'forgiveness' (*aphesis*) or the verb *aphienai*. There are three places where he uses 'repentance' (*metanoia*) or 'repenting' (*metanoun*), but on all these occasions they refer not to his own experience but to that of others who have already accepted Christ (Rom. 2.4, 2 Cor. 7.9–10, 12.21).

If one were to look for a word that epitomizes Paul's change of perspective, it is Transformation – *metamorphosis*. In his letter to the Romans he wrote, 'Do not be conformed to the world, but be transformed by the renewal of your mind' (12.2). The vocabulary and the imagery of transformation is evident in his letter to the Philippians as well. In chapter 3 he speaks about his transformation and re-formation into the body of Christ – 'becoming him in his death', *symmorphosis*, verse 10. One of the exciting pictures Paul paints of becoming a child of God is that of transforming from the state of slavery into the state of sonship (Rom. 8.15–17). His hope for the Roman Christians is that they, too, will be conformed (*symmorphosis*) to the image of the Son (8.29).

Naturally, the question then arises as to what caused this radical transformation in Paul's life. Paul, in his letter to the Galatians, says that the gospel he preaches comes from 'the revelation of Jesus Christ' (1.12). In the next verse he goes on to say that this disclosure caused him to change from his 'former life in Judaism'. It was this revelation that opened up new horizons for Paul. But Paul nowhere tells what the content or the nature of this revelation was. It is here where one has to deal with conjectures.

What then was 'the revelation of Jesus Christ' which transformed Paul? The meaning of the genitive 'of Jesus Christ' is very ambiguous. It could mean either that Jesus was the agent through whom Paul received the revelation, or that Jesus was the content of the revelation, namely, that he was the Messiah. The majority of scholars tend to concur with this latter reading. But I would like to agree with George MacRae that Jesus as the Messiah was not central to Paul's gospel.[8] Incidentally, Paul does not use Messiah in the sense of a title.

I would like to opt for the other reading which points to the revealing aspect of Jesus Christ, which may give us a clue to unravel the reason for Paul's radically rethinking his 'former life in Judaism'. Paul by his own admission was a Pharisee, and as such he was brought up in the understanding that God was holy. This notion of God as a holy One emerged in Judaism as a strategy during the exile and continued to dominate Jewish thinking till the time of Jesus. The Torah, too, was interpreted from the perspective of holiness. Marcus Borg writes:

> 'Holiness' became the paradigm by which the Torah was interpreted. The portions of the law which emphasized the separateness of the Jewish people from other peoples, and which stressed separation from everything impure within Israel, became dominant. Holiness became the *Zeitgeist*, the 'spirit of the age', shaping the development of the Jewish social world in the centuries leading up to the time of Jesus, providing the particular content of the Jewish ethos or way of life.[9]

Marcus Borg goes on to show that Jesus on the other hand advocated a different kind of holiness:

> Instead, he proposed an alternative path grounded in the nature of God as merciful, gathered a community based on that paradigm, and sought to lead

his people in the way of peace, a way that flowed intrinsically from the paradigm of inclusive mercy.[10]

Jesus, as an initiator of a revitalization movement within Judaism, opened up another aspect of the God of Israel – God as merciful and compassionate. Jesus was not handing down a new tradition. He was simply reiterating a forgotten aspect of God – that he was merciful and gracious (Exod. 34.6) – and as a consequence Jesus was urging his contemporaries to show solidarity and compassion towards one another. 'Be merciful, even as your Father is merciful' (Luke 6.36). Jesus' healing miracles, his acceptance of the marginalized of the time – the sinners, tax-collectors and the women – was an indication that (a) God's mercy was available to the very people who were cut off by the pharisaic interpretation of the law, and (b) that this was available without any intermediaries such as the law or the temple. It is not unreasonable to surmise that it was Jesus' retrieval of the availability of God to people without any mediating agencies which caused Paul to rethink his 'former life in Judaism'. It was Jesus' announcement of God's generosity to the people who are not normally within the pharisaic pale that contributed to his death. It is this death which becomes Paul's gospel, because in this death God demonstrated that he had abolished the impediments and the powers that dominate human life. It was Jesus' words and actions that prompted Paul to re-trieve neglected elements in the tradition and transformed his think-ing so that he preached a gospel of salvation which is available to all.

This Dialogical approach, which sees Paul's experience as trans-formation, offers new possibilities in a multi-faith context.

Firstly, it changes the understanding of what conversion is. Paul's experience shows that conversion can take place within a religious tradition itself. Conversion does not necessarily mean changing from one religion to another. It can mean a conversion to a new dimension of one own's faith. One can be rooted in one's tradition and yet learn more and be open to its forgotten aspects. Peter is another case in point. When we talk about the Cornelius–Peter episode, we always refer to the conversion of Cornelius. What we often overlook is that Peter too was converted. It was a rude shock to him, as it was to Jonah before him, that God's grace knows no bounds and extends to outsiders who are not normally recipients of such love.

Secondly, this approach views the people of other faiths differently. It does not see them in terms of mission and conversion, but accepts them unconditionally without the requirement of ritual purity. One of the key issues that Peter, Paul and those who met at Jerusalem faced was not inculcation of Christian ideas into Gentile minds but incorporation of them into the fellowship. It was to this end that Paul became the apostle to the Gentiles – to accommodate them as God's people.

Thirdly, it points to the fact that any spiritually transforming experience is not something that is private, subjective and emotional. But it involves praxis and engagement. Paul's experience underlines not only the solidarity of the believer with Christ, but his/her ethical obligation to walk in the newness of life (Rom. 6.4). This means imitating Paul by sharing maximum solidarity with people who are theologically, socially and economically marginalized.

## SOME IMPLICATIONS AND SOME LESSONS

### General

1  There is no universal interpretation of a text. All interpretations are contextual and tentative. A text becomes authoritative and sacred when it has contextual quality.

2  Biblical texts are not static or final. They possess a reservoir of meanings and nuances. When one particular meaning fails to meet the need of a community, one can always choose other meanings or other texts that can speak to the situation meaningfully and imaginatively. It is here one can learn from the hermeneutical principles of Hindus and especially how they handle the story of Rama. The story of Rama is told in the epic called Ramayana. But this story is told in a variety of ways within India and also in South Asia. Harry M. Buck has shown how different nationalities (Indians, Sri Lankans, Malaysians, Indonesians) and various sectors of community (women, students, non-brahminical castes) reject the bits that fail to meet their needs and project narratives that continue to excite and speak to their situation.[11] In other words, the community chooses to re-tell the episodes that empower them to meet new demands.

3  There is no value-free exegesis. All interpretations are biased. Bultmann himself has said that there is no pre-suppositionless exegesis. The Form-critical school has always insisted on the *sitz im leben* of a text. The Latin American liberation theologians point out the importance not only of the context of the text but also the *sitz im leben* of the interpreter. All interpreters bring their own academic, ideological

and religious biases into their interpretation. Karl Barth in his preface to the English edition of the commentary on Romans wrote, 'No one can, of course, bring out the meaning of a text (*auslegen*) without at the same time adding something to it (*einlegen*).'[12]

4  How then do we overcome our own prejudices? One way is to engage in communitarian exegesis. It is an exercise in which the community of the faithful – lay and professional, male and female, oppressed and oppressor, adults and children, Blacks and Whites – read the text in a dialectical relationship, each questioning, correcting and enabling the other. This way the pre-suppositions of one community are mutually challenged and critiqued by the other. It is an enterprise in which the questions posed by one section of community preoccupied with their context are read along with the critical reflections on the text with a view to seeking the truth together. In this way biblical scholars are compelled to come to grips with the problems of the ordinary people. Biblical scholars tend to withdraw from the harsh realities of social problems by taking refuge in the biblical past or, to use the words of J. C. Beker, they tend to wander into the hinterland of archaeology. A good example of communitarian exegesis is the hermeneutical engagement of the peasants of Solentiname with Ernesto Cardenal.[13]

## SOME GROUND RULES FOR MULTI-FAITH HERMENEUTICS

### 1  Calling names

Christians traditionally divide their scripture into two sections and call the first thirty-nine books the Old Testament, and the last twenty-seven the New Testament. What Christians regard as the Old Testament is held by the Jews to be their sacred scripture. The popular assumption among Christians is that the Old Testament is spiritually and morally somewhat inferior and obsolete, whereas the New Testament is superior and theologically up-to-date. But such a view, as history shows, reflects the very hostile, anti-Jewish stance that we commonly find among Christians.

The customary understanding that the new covenant of the Christians (NT) supersedes the old covenant (OT) is no longer tenable. The books of the new covenant have their own share of theologically and spiritually dubious elements – for example subjugation of women and complacency about slavery. The Jews do not like their sacred scripture to be treated as old. The two adjectives 'Old' and 'New' give the impression that one is outdated, archaic and no longer applicable, and the other is recent, interesting and relevant. As historical writings, both are ancient, belong to the distant past, and are products of an alien culture.

Therefore, when using sacred writings in an inter-faith context, one cannot speak of them in a way that exalts one and denigrates the other, but must allow each to be unique and speak on its own terms. In order to value the integrity of these scriptures, we might call the first thirty-nine books, the Jewish Scriptures, or the Canonical Scripture of Israel or the Sacred Scripture of Israel, and the last twenty-seven books could be referred to as the Canonical Literature of the Jesus Movement, or the Sacred Writings of the Early Followers of Jesus or the Canonical Writings of the Jesus Movement.

## 2 Place of other scriptures

Christians can no longer claim with Tertullian that 'I possess the Scripture and I am the only one to possess it'. In the present hermeneutical task Christian interpreters cannot ignore the religious texts of other faith communities. In the past, biblical concepts were taken as a yardstick to evaluate other scriptural traditions. For example, the Johannine understanding of Incarnation was viewed against the *Gita's* concept of *Avatar*, and the latter was judged inadequate and limited. Or the biblical notion of Grace is compared with Saiva Siddhanta's view of *Arul* (Grace) and it is critiqued for its impersonal nature. Similarly, other scriptural traditions are judged defective for their lack of a salvation history model.

A proper hermeneutics should go beyond these tendencies and look for what these religious texts are trying to convey, and understand them on their own terms rather than pre-judge them. All scriptures seek to tell in their own way the story of how they understand the mercies of God and the mysteries of life. Of course there is a radical diversity in the form and content of their stories. Traditionally Christians have insisted that their story is superior and more valid than the others. Christians may tell their story differently, but they cannot claim that theirs is the only story. In fact, these stories belong to all humankind. The fact that the Tamil classic *Tirukural* is claimed by different religions prove the point of its catholic nature. *The Tirukural* – a book of wisdom sayings – and speaks about God, righteousness, right praxis, etc. – is used by Saivites, Jains and Buddhists and it is called *Pothumarai* – Common Scripture. In one of the Father Brown stories, 'The Sign of the Broken Sword', Father Brown remarks, 'When will people understand that it is useless for a man to read his Bible unless he also reads everybody else's?'

## 3 Wisdom tradition

Probably one way to initiate multi-faith hermeneutics is to retrieve the Wisdom tradition. The strength of the Wisdom tradition is that it is universal. It is not confined to one culture or a nation. This tradition acknowledges that if wisdom is spirit, it is not restricted to Israel alone but embraces the whole world (Wisd. 1.17) and finds expression in all peoples and all lands. 'In the waves of the sea, in the whole earth, and in every people and nation I have gotten a possession' (Sir. 24.6).

The other positive feature of the Wisdom tradition is its ability to borrow freely and modify materials from other cultures and sources. The Synoptic Gospels record at least 100 proverbial and aphoristic sayings of Jesus. C. E. Carlston has shown that not all of them were from rural Palestine and that one can detect the influence of wider Hellenistic culture.[14] The undue concentration on the distinctive features of Jesus' teaching not only diverted attention from the aphoristic elements in his sayings, but also encouraged a dim view of other cultures. The bracketing of Jesus' message with that of other sages is not to minimize his importance, but to point to the creative possibilities of the commonly held universal elements in his message. These common elements should provide starting points to engage in multi-faith hermeneutics in a way that the traditional missionary view that Christians have the superior truth, does not. An African proverb says that it is through other people's wisdom that we learn ourselves, and no single person's understanding amounts to nothing. While acknowledging the distinctiveness of each tradition, the role of the interpreter is to bring out the common elements in them. Three recent examples of such an attempt are Ishanand Vempeny's work on *The Bhagavad Gita* and the New Testament;[15] A. C. Amore's exegetical study of the Buddhist scriptures and their influence on the message of Jesus,[16] and John Eaton's comparative reading of the Wisdom spirituality of the Hebrew scriptures in the context of world religion.[17]

Finally, the task of interpretation is not merely description but engagement. The goal of biblical interpretation is not only understanding of the biblical text, but ultimately enacting it. The meaning of a text is discovered not only through reflection upon it, but also in concrete social action based upon it. The primary concern of an interpreter lies not only in transforming social inequalities, as the Latin American liberation theologians are vigorously reminding us, but also in bringing racial and religious harmony among peoples of different faiths.

## NOTES

1  C. F. Andrews (ed.), *Mahatma Gandhi: His Own Story* (London, George Allen & Unwin, 1930), p. 31.

2  M. K. Gandhi, *Christian Missions: Their Place in India* (Ahamedabad, Navjivan Press, 1941), p. 159.

3  W. C. Smith, *Religious Diversity*, ed. W. G. Oxtoby (New York, Harper & Row, 1976), p. 9.

4  Y. D. Tiwari, 'From Vedic Dharma to the Christian Faith' (*Religion and Society*, 10, 3, 1963), pp. 117–18.

5  F. F. Bruce, *Paul: Apostle of the Free Spirit* (Exeter, Paternoster Press, 1980, rev. edn), p. 74.

6  See his *Paul Among Jews and Gentiles* (London, SCM Press, 1977), pp. 7–23.

7  ibid., p. 10.

8  G. MacRae, 'Messiah and Gospel', in *Judaisms and their Messiahs at the turn of the Christian era*, ed. J. Neusner *et al.* (Cambridge, Cambridge University Press, 1987), p. 171 f.

9  M. Borg, *Jesus a New Vision: Spirit, Culture and the Life of Discipleship* (San Francisco, Harper & Row, 1987), p. 87.

10  M. Borg, *Conflict, Holiness and Politics in the Teaching of Jesus* (New York, The Edwin Mellen Press, 1984), p. 199.

11  H. M. Buck, 'Rama and the Asian World' (*World Faiths Insights*, 9, Summer 1984), pp. 27–36.

12  K. Barth, *The Epistle to the Romans* (London, Oxford University Press, 1933), p. ix.

13  E. Cardenal, *Gospel in Solentiname*, vols 1–4 (Maryknoll, NY, Orbis Books, 1982).

14  C. E. Carlston, 'Proverbs, Maxims, and the Historical Jesus' (*Journal of Biblical Literature*, 99, 1, 1980), pp. 87–105.

15  I. Vempeny, *Krsna and Christ: In the light of Some of the Fundamental Themes and Concepts of the Bhagavad Gita and the New Testament* (Pune, Ishvani Kendra, 1988).

16  A. C. Amore, *Two Masters: One Message: The Lives and Teachings of Gautama and Jesus* (Nashville, Abingdon Press, 1978).

17  J. Eaton, *The Contemplative Face of the Old Testament in the Context of World Religions* (London, SCM Press, 1989).

# 26

# Creation of Man: Theological Reflections Based on Northern Thai Folktales

## MAEN PONGUDOM

This essay is an example of how Christian theologians of Asia are drawing on common religio-cultural sources to illuminate the biblical narratives, for the mutual enrichment and enablement of different faith communities.

This essay appeared in *East Asia Journal of Theology* (3, 2, October 1985). This issue contains other examples of cross-religious hermeneutics.

Maen Pongudom is the Dean of the Faculty of Theology, Payap University, Chiang Mai, Thailand.

## THE NORTHERN FOLKTALE, LIU TRADITION: GENESIS

In the beginning came fire and floods on earth. The fire consumed all things, including the mountains. Then the floods came to extinguish the fire. The surface of the earth was perfectly flat, without mountains and hills. Poo Sang See and Ya Sang Sai, a couple who gave existence to mankind, came from above. They wished to meet other beings with whom they could have conversation, but no one was on earth. They made human beings from clay, female and male. They consecrated them with magical power, therefore these two objects became living beings. This couple had sexual relations and gave birth to their children. They multiplied quite rapidly.

Poo Sang See and Ya Sang Sai also made animals. They began with rats, followed by cows and on up to twelve kinds of animals.

It has been told that hills and mountains, after fire and flood, were the heaps of clay by the ploughshares of a giant couple named Poo Liu Herng and Ya Liu Herng. Their bodies were tremendously huge. They used elephants as bait for fishing. It has been told that one day they fished at Muan Nan (Nan province in the North) and used an elephant as bait. Poo Liu Herng stirred up the water with his penis and Ya Liu Herng opened up her vagina to trap the fish.

The rivers were the products of ploughshare tracts. All trees were planted by Poo Liu Herng and Ya Liu Herng without knowing the real origin of trees. But grass was made by Poo Sang See and Ya Sang Sai.

No one really knows the origin of the wind and rains. However, some animals ate other animals for food because they were made so by Poo Sang See and Ya Sang Sai. It was their design to control the growth of animals.

## THE NORTHERN FOLKTALE, NORTHERN THAI TRADITION: GENESIS

The story of world-consuming fire is an ancient, oral tradition. It is not written anywhere. First of all the earth was on fire. Nothing was left. Then came rains and floods. Nothing else appeared except water and sky. The streams of water swept the pebbles, sand and dirt into heaps in certain places. Thus mountains came into existence. The rains on burned soil made a good smell which evaporated, ascending to the kingdom of giants above. They descended and ate the burned soil. As a result they were unable to fly back.

Once more the heavy rains came and washed away some parts of the mountains from which small hills came into existence.

The burned soil eaten, the naked giants scattered all over and survived. After the floods receded and the earth became dry, these naked giants found a variety of trees, vegetables, and fruits including rice, which they collected. These things came into existence by themselves. No one made them. The naked giants had them for food. Other things that came into existence after the floods were canals and rivers, seas and oceans. The naked giants lived a husband and wife way of life. They dug the earth, making holes as their houses. They used the leaves to cover their bodies before they made clothes from the tree barks. They gave birth to their children. Gradually they learned to develop their way of living and built communities, towns and cities.

## THE NORTHERN FOLKTALE, THAI YAI
## TRADITION: GENESIS

In the beginning the earth was burned by fire, including rocky mountains. The fire kept burning for millions of years, and was followed by heavy rains for millions of years. When the rains stopped, the fragrance of the burned soil evaporated, ascending to heaven. It reached the head of heaven, named Khun Sig Cha, and proceeded to the realm of celestial beings. The celestial beings smelled the fragrance of the burned soil. Eight of these beings, four male and four female, went to Khun Sig Cha and made a plea to go down to earth.

Khung Sig Cha gave permission, but with a serious warning: 'You may go down to earth, but I warn you: absolutely do not eat the cream of the soil. If you eat it, you will lose your might and will not be able to return to your realm.' They promised to strictly obey his warning.

They came down to earth and roamed around. They walked on the creamy soil, felt its softness, and smelled its fragrance. They could not resist the temptation. One of them ate and was impressed with its sweetness. Others were also persuaded to eat the creamy soil. After they had eaten it, they wanted to return to heaven, but could not fly back. So ever since they have stayed on earth.

All eight celestial beings married. Time passed and they had nothing to eat. Khun Sig Cha came down and, knowing they lacked food, he gave them eight pumpkins. They ate, but kept the seeds for future reproduction. The four couples had children. They multiplied rapidly to a total of eight million within a short time. They were crowded and scattered to the four corners of the earth. Every group grew rapidly.

In the beginning there were three kinds of trees and one kind of grass brought by the celestial beings. Animals in the forest heard about the human beings and came to see for themselves. They saw, and decided to stay with the human beings.

## PREFACE

Justin Martyr believed that everyone is a spermatic logoi of the Logos. Or, in other words, there is a divine element in every human being. Thus, the partial logos in man is a bridge connecting man and God, the Logos. At this point the revelation of the Logos before the event of

'Jesus of Nazareth' was only partially received. Justin Martyr realized and accepted the premise that there is partial divine truth in the system of Greek philosophy. That is to say, God the Logos has revealed Himself of Greeks through Greek philosophy. Put the other way round, God has revealed Himself to Greek people from which Greek philosophy came into existence. In short, God has revealed Himself through other religions and philosophical systems besides the Jewish system. God loved and loves other people besides the Jews. He has never forsaken any tribe of human beings at any moment. Justin Martyr's bold statement that 'Socrates is Christian before Christ', has encouraged many to accept the fact that there are divine truths in non-Jewish–Christian religious traditions. From this basis one would like to explore some of the Northern Thai folktales in the area of the creation of man.

## THE SOCIO-ECONOMIC BACKGROUND OF PEOPLE IN NORTHERN THAILAND

The Northern people have had their own spoken and written language for centuries. When Christian missionaries came to Chiang Mai in the middle of the nineteenth century and introduced the Western type of education, the Northern language was used in school both for speaking and writing. Later, early in the twentieth century the central Siamese government adopted the policy of Siamization or unification by which the Northern dialect was prohibited in the classroom. Fortunately, Northern Thai people were not forced to eliminate it from speaking. The tone of the Northern dialect is very similar to that of the Northeastern people, the Laos. And their customs are also similar. For centuries the people of the North were known as Laos. (In those days the people of the central plateau called the Northern people 'Laos', with a sense of looking down upon them.)

Besides the Northern people in general or the low-landers in the North, there are several hilltribe peoples who live in the mountains.

Each tribe has its own dialect and customs. Both lowlanders and highlanders are in general agriculturalists – peasants and farmers. They are families who plant paddy rice, deal with clay and 'creamy' soil, burn the woods to clear and prepare the land for farming. They all have the experience of smelling the burned soil with the first touch of the rains. Many pregnant mothers have experienced eating 'creamy soil' when they had morning sickness.

## COMPARATIVE STUDY

Three traditions or versions of genesis from North Thailand have been selected for study, including: the Northern Thai tradition, the Thai Yai tradition, and the Liu tradition.

All these three traditions have a common basic vision: First, that the earth was on fire, and flood came to extinguish the holocaust. Nothing was left in existence.

As farmers, the Northerners are familiar with the cycle of fire and rains. They have experienced the 'consuming or destroying power of fire. The forests are burned into a heap of ashes before their eyes.' Fire has regularly played the role of 'cleansing and preparing'. And their farming is very much dependent on the rains. They have experienced how powerful the rains are, not merely in extinguishing fire, but in softening and enriching the soil as well.

With regard to the creation of man, Northern Thai and Thai Yai traditions are similar. Originally human beings came from heaven. They were fallen angels, formerly celestial beings. They were tempted by the enticing fragrance of the burned soil. When they ate the soil, however, they lost their might and power.

It is interesting that the mothers-to-be experiencing morning sickness still engage in eating 'creamy soil' from the paddy fields, down to the present day.

At this point the Thai Yai folktale has more interesting details. There are ideas of 'the head of heaven and earth', 'temptation', 'command', 'promise', and of 'disobedience', Khun Sig Cha knew that 'burned creamy soil' was dangerous. He commands the heavenly beings not to eat it. 'Whenever you eat it you will lose your might and power and be unable to return!' Nevertheless, one ate it anyway, and starting with that one it was passed on to the others. Finally, all had broken the promise and disobeyed.

Both traditions hold the same view that temptation leads to disobedience, and disobedience leads to 'the loss of primal status'.

In the Northern Thai tradition the disobedient celestial beings are naked and scattered all over the place. They had to forage for food and use leaves and bark for clothing. They married and gave birth to children.

In the Thai Yai tradition there is concern from the 'head of heaven and earth,' Khun Sig Cha. He came down to visit them and supplied them with food. They built up families and grew up rapidly.

The Liu tradition has a different story after the fundamental vision of the consuming fire and the extinguishing floods. It tells of a couple from above named Poo Sang See and Ya Sang Sai. They needed companions and they made them from clay. They gave them (or rather spelled on them) power to be living beings. It is understandable that their vision of the creation of mountains and hills, rivers and canals, came through the experience of 'ploughshare tracts'. It is also interesting that Poo Sang See and Ya Sang Sai made animals with a design to prevent unnecessary growth.

## THEOLOGICAL REFLECTIONS

Several theological reflections are in order, based on a comparison of these Northern Thai traditions with the Biblical account of the Genesis-creation of man in particular.

### 1 'As in the beginning'

Even though the Northern Thai folktales have not mentioned 'in the beginning' as clearly as the Biblical account, they also give a definite impression of the 'formlessness' of the earth. There was a real chaotic situation before the existence of permanent mountains and hills, oceans, rivers and canals, before the existence of human beings, animals and other life-forms. The folktales include a vision of 'real creation' after fire and floods.

### 2 The dual nature of human beings

Human beings have basically two natures. They have a celestial nature with divine elements, either through the process of once being angels themselves, or of being given a celestial nature by a couple from heaven.

And they have earthly natures, either through the process of eating 'the burned creamy soil' or from being made from clay.

In Biblical Genesis we find the truth that 'man is made of dust and of divine breath' (Gen. 2.7).

## 3 Temptation

Temptation is placed before man. The Biblical story tells that there was an irresistibly charming fruit on the tree of knowledge. It was right before their eyes! In the Northern Thai folktales the temptation was even wafting up into their 'room' above.

Both the Biblical story and the Northern Thai folktales contain the idea that temptation is not superficial, but is a crucial matter dealing with the essential nature of human life.

## 4 Disobedience

Man yielded to temptation and disobeyed the commandment.

In the Biblical story the Creator knew the strength of the 'tempting fruit', whereas in the Thai Yai tradition Khun Sig Cha realized the powerful fragrance of 'burned and creamy soil'. Man had been warned. Both Khun Sig Cha and the Biblical creator gave the warning in the form of a 'command'. Man, both in the Biblical account of Genesis and in the Thai Yai folktale, was too weak to resist, and consequently has disobeyed. In both traditions there is the idea of disobedience.

## 5 Fallen man

Both the Thai Yai and Northern Thai traditions have a concept of man as 'fallen angel', as compared to the Biblical concept of man as fallen, but not fallen from a celestial state. However, there is no real conflict between the two cultures if we consider that Adam and Eve before the Fall were perfect beings.

The more important thing is that these different traditions share the idea of 'Fall' and of a rather desperate 'status after the Fall'.

Once Adam and Eve yielded to temptation and disobeyed the divine command, they 'were lost', their strength and confidence to stand before God was lost. They hid themselves when they heard God walking in the Garden. They suffered.

Once the celestial beings yielded to temptation and ate the burned creamy soil they too 'lost their might and power' and were not able to return to their 'original status'. They suffered.

## 6 Divine concern

In Biblical Genesis the Creator showed his concern by coming down and seeking the fallen man, Adam and Eve.

In the Thai Yai tradition Khun Sig Cha also came down from heaven and gave help to the fallen angels. In both traditions we can see the truth of the 'unceasing relationship between divine and human'.

## 7 Inclusiveness

In the tradition of the Liu and in the Biblical story as well, we see the idea of 'we' or 'us' in the creation of man. In the Liu tradition, Poo Sang See and Ya Sang Sai 'made man from clay and gave them power to live'.

In Biblical Genesis there is this expression: 'Then God said, "Let us make man in our image, after our likeness"' (Gen. 1.26).

Briefly, if we look carefully with an unbiased mind into the folktales as mentioned above, we will see that men of other faiths and tradition share certain essential ideas of the creation of man, which are found in the Biblical story. Moreover, our religious experiences and religious interpretations could be enriched, and its theologians and ministers or teachers would be enabled to do more contextualized and indigenized theological reflection, which would be more understandable and acceptable to their audiences, in particular in communities with a common religio-cultural root.

# 27

# Liberation in Indian Scriptures

## JACOB KATTACKAL

Liberation is not the monopoly of Christian Scriptures. This essay is an example of how the Hindu Sacred Texts view the concept of liberation in their own terms.

This article is reprinted from *Bible Bhashayam* (9, 1, 1983).

Jacob Kattackal is Professor of Indology at the Pontifical Oriental Institute of Religious Studies, Kottayam, India.

## INTRODUCTION

*Moksha* or *mukti* or liberation is a leading theme in all the religious philosophies of India. Hinduism, Buddhism and Jainism, in all their different schools of thought, have discussed 'liberation' and offered various means of attaining it. Here we shall expound briefly the Indian doctrines of liberation with special reference to Hinduism.

## THE CONCEPT OF LIBERATION

The familiar English term 'liberation' approximately translates the rich variety of Sanskrit terms such as *mukti, moksha, kaivalya, apavarga, aikantya, nirvana, nirvriti, sakshatkara, sayujya, samadhi*, etc. used by various religious schools of thought of India. Liberation is a term that implies a relation, for liberation is liberation *from* something: the term 'liberation' evokes the question: 'Liberation from what?' And naturally, the Indian answer is, 'From bondage': from the bondage of the rounds of rebirths and redeaths; from earthly existence that is essentially a 'bondage'. And the next question with practical implications would be: 'And what are the means of, or what are the paths to, liberation?' The different Indian religions and their various schools of thought point out many paths of *moksha* or *mukti* or liberation. Such is the general method of treatment of the subject of *moksha* in the Indian context.

# I IN THE VEDAS

In the ancient hymns of the Vedas (*c.* fifteenth century BC) the problem of liberation is not much discussed. Still, a happy life in Heaven (*Svarga*, the Eternal Paradise) was conceived as liberation from the woes of earthly existence. Sin, the wilful violation of the moral order established by God Varuna, was admitted to be the bondage or chain that prevents the entry into the blissful Heaven. See the following verses from the *Rig-veda*:

> Loose me from sin as from a band (knot) that binds me (2.28.5).
>
> Whatever sin is found in me, whatever evil I have wrought, if I have lied or if I have falsely sworn, Waters (Gods), remove it far from me (1.23.22).

## (A) A *Vasistha*-hymn of the *Rig-veda* 7

So humble was the worshipper in Varuna's presence, so conscious of weakness, guilt and shortcoming, that on reading the hymns to Varuna one is inevitably reminded of the penitential psalms of the Old Testament. It has been suggested that Varuna owes much of his character to Semitic influence – certainly not to the Jews, for the penitential psalms were composed long after the hymns to Varuna, and as far as we know the early Hebrews never came in contact with the Aryans, but perhaps to the Babylonians, who often approached their gods in a similar penitential spirit'.[1] The following are the prayers of a man afflicted with an acute sense of sin (*Rig-veda* 7.86.2–7):

> I am searching my heart and wondering: When may I be united with Varuna. Will he, without displeasure, accept my oblation; when shall I, I, rejoicing in mind, behold him gracious to me?
> Fain to know my guilt I have questioned the wise; the sages verily have said the same thing to me, 'This Varuna is displeased with thee'.
>
> What has that great wickedness been, O Varuna, that thou wouldst slay the friend who sings thy praises? Thou, insuperable Lord, declare it to me, so that, freed from sin, I may quickly approach thee with my homage.
>
> Free us from sins committed by our fathers, and from those wherein we have ourselves offended . . . Not our own will betrayed us, O Varuna, but intoxication, wrath, gambling, ignorance, The old is near to lead astray the younger.

Even sleep removes not all evil-doing.
Slave-like may I do service to the Bounteous; serve, free from sin, the God inclined to anger.

The following is a prayer for forgiveness by a man afflicted with dropsy (*Rig-veda* 7.89):

Let me not go to the House of Clay, O Varuna!
Forgive, O gracious Lord, forgive.
When I go tottering, like a blown-up bladder,
Forgive, O gracious Lord, forgive.
Holy One, in want of wisdom I have opposed you.
Forgive, O gracious Lord, forgive.
Though in the midst of waters, thirst has seized your worshipper,
Forgive, O gracious Lord, forgive.
What sins we mortals have committed against the people of the gods. If, foolish, we have thwarted your decrees, O God do not destroy in your anger.

In the Vedic hymns, God Indra or the twin Gods 'Indra–Varuna' are praised as the Promulgator and Custodian of Eternal Law, and whoever violates this Eternal Law, forges a chain for himself. And God Varuna or Indra alone can liberate from the bondage of sin. The following lines are from Griffith's translation of the *Rig-veda* (10.89):

8 Wise art thou, Punisher of guilt, O Indra. The sword lops limbs, thou smitest down the sinner,
The men who injure, as it were a comrade, the lofty Law of Varuna and Mitra,
9 Men who lead evil lives, who break agreements, and injure Varuna, Aryaman and Mitra –
Against these foes, O mighty Indra, sharpen, as furious death, thy Bull of fiery colour.

God Varuna is the Guardian of Cosmic as well as Moral Order (*Rta*). Any breach of the Moral Order on the part of man might result in Cosmic Disorder too. Besides, the breacher of the Moral Order will be enchained by his own immoral act (*Rig-veda* 4.23):

8 Eternal Law hath varied food that strengthens; thought of Eternal Law removes transgressions; the praise-hymn of Eternal Law, arousing, glowing, hath opened the deaf ears of the living.
9 Firm-seated are Eternal Law's foundations; in its fair form are many splendid beauties . . .
10 Fixing Eternal Law, he (Indra), too, upholds it; swift moves the might of Law and wins the booty. (Griffith's translation)[2]

## (B) Varuna, the custodian of the law, moral and cosmic

1 To make this Varuna come forth, sing thou a song unto the band of Maruts wiser than thyself –

This Varuna who guardeth well the thoughts of men like herds of kine. Let all the others die away.

3 The night he hath encompassed, and established the morns with magic art: visible over all is he.

His dear ones, following his law, have prospered the three dawns for him.

5 He who supports the worlds of life, he who well knows the hidden names, mysteries of the morning beams;

He cherishes much wisdom, sage, as heaven brings forth each varied form.

6 In whom all wisdom centres, as the nave is set within the wheel. Haste ye to honour Trita (Varuna) as kine hast to gather in the fold, even as they muster steeds to yoke.

He is an ocean far-removed, yet through the heaven to him ascends the worship which these realms possess.

With his right foot he overthrew their magic, and went up to heaven.

The Twin Gods of Dyaus and Prthivi (Dyava-Prthivi) are often invoked for divine blessings and internal liberation (*Rig-veda* 1.185):

3 I invoke the 'gift of Aditi' ['sinlessness'?], the gift free from hatred, inviolable, heavenly, invulnerable, worshipful. This, O Worlds, beget for the singer. May Heaven and Earth protect us from fearful evil. (Thomas's translation)[3]

Sometimes we hear the Vedic sage extolling the Divine Wisdom (*Vak*), or Sophia, with the desire of possessing her for a blessed life (*Rig-veda* 10.125):

1 I travel with the Rudras [Tempest Gods] and the Vasus [another class of Gods], with the Adityas and all-gods I wander. I hold aloft both Varuna and Mitra, Indra and Agni, and the Pair of Asvins.

2 I cherish and sustain high-swelling Soma, and Tvashtr; I support Pūshan [Sun-god] and *Bhaga* [a deity who bestows wealth and presides over love and marriage].

I load with wealth the zealous sacrificer who pours the juice and offers his oblation.

3 I am the queen, the gatherer-up of treasures, most thoughtful, first of those who merit worship. Thus Gods have established me in many places with many homes to enter and abide in.

5 I, verily, myself announce and utter the word that Gods and men alike shall welcome. I make the man I love exceedingly mighty, make him a sage, *Rishi*, Brahmin.

This longing for the Saving Wisdom is expressed also in the hymns to the *Viśvedevas* or *Pantheon* (*Rig-veda* 1.164):

> 6 I ask, unknowing, those who know, the sages, as one all ignorant for the sake of knowledge:
> What was that One who in the unborn's image hath established and fixed firm these worlds' six regions
> 46 They call him Indra, Mitra, Varuna, Agni and he is heavenly nobly-winged Garutman.
> To what is One, sages give many a title; they call it Agni, Yama and Matarsvan (Griffith's translation).

Freedom from material want, and acquisition of wealth rather than spiritual and eternal liberation, are often prayed for.

### (C)  (Hymn to the Unknown God (*Rig-veda* 10.12):

> 2 He who gives breath, who gives strength, whose command all the Gods wait upon, whose shadow is immortality, is death – what God with our oblation shall we worship?
> 5 Through whom the mighty heaven and the earth have been fixed, through whom the sun has been established, through whom the firmament; who in the middle sky measures out the air – what God with our oblation shall we worship?
> 9 May he not injure us, who is the generator of the earth, he of true ordinances, who produced the heaven, who produced the shining mighty waters.
> 10 O Prajapati, none other than thou hast encompassed all these created things. May that for which we desiring, have invoked thee be ours. May we become lords of wealth (Thomas's translation).

Liberation from the bondage of guilt and sin is again conceived of as genuine liberation; the poet asks for it (*Rig-veda* 189.1):

> May our spirit [life-breath] enter into the Eternal Spirit [God, Paramatman] ... O Fiery God, lead us along the right path to the (supernatural) riches (*raye*); Lord, you know all our (past) deeds; kindly remove from us (liberate us from) the wicked sin. I will offer you praises in plenty (Isopanishad, 18).

## II LIBERATION IN THE *BRAHMANAS*

*Moksha* or *mukti* in the *Brahmanas* is depicted as blissful life in the Eternal Heaven in company with Hiranyagarbha (created God, Demiurgue) and communion with other gods. At the dissolution or 'pralaya-period', the souls fully satiated will enter into the Highest Abode together with Brahma. Some of the older Upanishads referred to above speak of liberation as co-residence with Brahma, i.e. the *karya-brahma* or Hiranyagarbha. Sankara thinks all such passages refer to '*kramamukti*', or gradual liberation (see later).

In line with the Brahmana-theology, some of the older Upanishads (Brhadanyka, Chandogya, Katha etc.) describe the life of the *muktas* in Heaven and *Brahma-loka*; these Upanishads describe the *muktas'* pleasure trips to the *Brahma-loka* through the abodes of Gods and Fathers, or through the Sun and Moon. The Chandogyaupanishad (7.6.6) says: 'One of the hundred and one arteries of heart leads up to the crown of head. Going upward through that, one – the dying person – becomes immortal; through the other arteries, he goes in various other directions.' In the Kathopanishad (1.3.16) we read: 'He who hears and recounts the Naciketas-episode, will live gloriously in the *Brahma-loka-Brahma-loke mahiyaie*.' Again, 'knowing this, one will reign in the world of Brahma' (1.2.17). The belief expressed in these Upanishads is that those '*muktas*', or liberated ones, who reach the *Brahma-loka* live there with Brahma, the Creator, for a whole '*kalpa*', which is calculated to be four thousand, three hundred, and thirty million years.

## III IN THE UPANISHADS

In the Upanishads, however, the dominant and persistent theme is man's liberation through 'apotheosis' or deification through mystic ecstasy or rapture. For this reason those Upanishadic statements that emphatically proclaim man's divinity or identity with Brahman that is attainable in mystic rapture are venerated as the 'Great Sayings' (*maha vakyas*): 'That thou art', 'I am *Brahman*', 'This *Atman* (of mine) is *Brahman*', '*Brahman* is Bliss'. Celebrated indeed are also the Upanishadic passages such as 'The *Brahman*-knower becomes very *Brahman*'. 'Knowing *Brahman* all else is known'. 'Seeing the Supreme *Brahman*, all the knots of the heart are severed'. So, then, this deification through God-experience (mystic ecstasy) is proposed by the Upanishads as *mukti* or *moksha* or liberation.

### (A) The higher wisdom
The deifying mystic experience, often qualified as the 'unity-vision'

(*ekatva-drasanam*), is extolled by the Upanishads as 'wisdom par excellence', the 'superior knowledge' or '*para vidya*'; on the contrary, all empirical knowledge, conceptual knowledge, knowledge of mundane realities – knowledge derived from empirical sciences – came to be called '*apara vidya*', or lower wisdom or inferior knowledge; often enough this *apara vidya* was depreciated as 'avidya,' or ignorance, or nescience. Thus, for instance, the Kathopanishad sings: 'The worldly wise, thinking themselves to be wise, but actually remaining in the midst of ignorance, go round and like the blind led by the blind without ever reaching the goal.' For the Upanishadic mystics, this 'experiential knowledge through which *Brahman* is attained' is the real knowledge. And the Upanishads constantly remind us that this saving wisdom (*para vidya*, or mystic wisdom or vision) cannot be attained by human skill or intellectual acumen; divine grace and human effort are indispensable for this higher saving knowledge; the aspirant should assiduously practise all moral virtues and scrupulously abstain from all sorts of evil.

*Mukti*, for the Upanishads, is not a post-mortem affair, but is something that can be tasted here and now, though its culmination is with 'the fall of the body' (*deha-pata*), that is, death.

So in the Upanishads, *mukti* seems to be a kind of '*jivanmukti*' (i.e. *mukti* attainable while a person is still alive) that culminates in '*videlhamukti*' (i.e. *mukti* after death). The following passage from the Chandogyopanishad (6.14.2) is quoted both by the '*jivanmukti-vadins*' and '*ideha-mukti-vadins*' to support their own theories: 'As a person who had been blindfolded is released from his bandage and told: "The *Gandhara*-village is in that direction, go in that direction", being informed and capable of judgement, would be asking his way from village to village and arrive at the *Gandhara*-village. Exactly in the same way does a person here who has a teacher know, "I shall live here only so long as I shall not attain *moksha* (*vimoksye*); afterwards I shall attain (*moksha, mukti*)".' For the ancient Indians who were crushed under the weight of 'rebirth-belief', this hope of *mukti* through God-experience (*Brahma-anubhava*) was a great solace; for, it was believed that *Brahma-jnana* will reduce to ashes all the rebirth – causing *karma* – residues that have accumulated in the soul through its past actions: 'All the (past) karmas are destroyed by the intuitive vision of *Brahman*, the basis and zenith of all . . . And the *Chandogyopanishad* (5.24.3: 4.14.3) speaks of the soul shaking off its karmas (accumulated karma-effects in the soul) as a horse shakes its manes or as the moon liberates itself from

*Rahu*, the vicious serpent, during the eclipse. The liberated person is declared by the Upanishads as 'transcending the realm of good and evil', and as 'untouched by his *karmas*'.

## (B) Upanishadic texts on *moksa*

1 *From the* Brhadaranyakopanishad:

'Lead me from the unreal to the Real; lead me from darkness to Light; lead me from death to Immortality' (1.3.28).

2 *From the* Isopanishad:

'Demonic indeed are these worlds and enveloped in blinding darkness; into those worlds will go those *Atman*-killers after '*Atman* killers': those who kill the *Atman*, that is, sinners or those who commit suicide.'

'To the sage who has attained the unity-vision, what delusion, what sorrow, is there? Because in him all beings have become his very *ātman*'. 'Into blinding darkness will enter those who worship ignorance. Into still greater darkness will enter those who pride in their knowledge'. 'O Pusan [Sun-God], the face of truth is hidden by a golden disc; kindly remove that veil for me so that I may see the Truth and *Dharma*'.

'O Pusan, the sole Seer, the Controller, the Sun, the Son of Prajapati, Send forth your rays, and manifest your radiant Light so that I may see your most lovely form. The person over there in the Sun am I too'. 'May my life-breath enter into the Immortal Spirit, though this body will soon be reduced to ashes. O my mind, recollect, remember your past deeds'.

'O Fiery God, lead us, along the auspicious path to spiritual well-being. O God, you know all our actions. Remove from us all our harmful iniquity. We will offer you praises in abundance'[18].

3 *From the* Kathopanishad:

'Having reached the imperishable, celestial beings [saints], what mortal fellow here below will find delight in the transient pleasures of this life or in a long mundane existence?' (1.28).

'One thing is the good, and another thing is the pleasant; both have different goals; they both present themselves to each person. It will be well with the person who chooses the good instead of the pleasant;

whereas the person who chooses the pleasant will stray away without ever reaching the goal' (2.1).

'Fools residing in the midst of *avidya* [ignorance] and yet vainly fancying themselves to be wise and learned, go round and round staggering like the blind men led by the blind' (2.5).

'This *Atman* cannot be grasped if taught by an unenlightened person; nor is the *Atman* easily attained because there are very many erroneous opinions circulated among men.' 'The *Paramatman* cannot be obtained by logical skill; when guided by a qualified person [*guru*] he is easily grasped' (2.8.–9).

4 *From the* Svetasvatara-Upanishad:

'He (God) is beginningless and endless; He is the Creator (*srasta*) in the midst of chaos [i.e. He establishes order through His cosmic creation from the chaotic materials]; He is multiform, still the sole encompasser of the universe; one who knows Him (experientially) gets freed from all bondages' (5.13).

'There is the One different from, or beyond, the samsara-tree [mundane existence]; in Him the universe revolves; He, the Lord, is the bestower of merit (*dharma*) and the remover of sin (*papa-nudam*); one who knows Him as the eternal Indweller and immortal world-ground (attains ever lasting bliss)' (6.6).

'Him we know as the Supreme Lord of all lords, the Highest Deity, King of kings, the Transcendent One, the adorable God, Master of the universe' (6.7). 'He, of His own accord, covers Himself like a spider with threads made of materials of this world. May He grant us Eternal Deliverance (*Brahma-pyayam, Brahma-nirvanam*)' (6.10). 'He, in times past, created Brahma, the Demiurgue (Hiranyagarbha) and entrusted to him the Vedas (Holy Scripture). He is the Light of my soul and intellect. I, eager for eternal liberation, fall at His feet and worship Him' (6.18). 'This profound mystery [recorded] in the Upanishad, this inspired doctrine declared [to the sages] of old, should not be revealed to one whose passions are not controlled, nor to one who is not a son or a disciple' (6.22).

## IV LIBERATION IN THE *GITA*

The *Bhagavadgita* has a rather complex doctrine on *mukti*, or liberation. In line with the devotional literature of India, the *Gita* also presents *mukti* as the culmination of *bhakti*. All the same the Gita speaks also, in passing as it were, about a sort of heaven and demonic worlds. This is so probably because the *Gita* shares the Heaven-Hell concept of early Hinduism along with the later doctrine of salvation through God-experience. We read for instance in the *Kathopanishad* (1.12): 'In the Heavenly world (*svarge loke*) there is neither fear nor old age nor death. There, people experience no hunger, no thirst, no sorrow; there they rejoice'. And the *Isopanishad* warns those sinners against the demonic world of blinding darkness: 'Devilish indeed are those worlds enveloped by blinding darkness. It is into these worlds that those who commit suicide (or sin against the *Atman*) fall after their death' (Isa. 3). In similar vein, the Gita too describes Heaven and Hell. Heaven is described to be terminable whereas the demonic world seems to be eternal. 'The knowers of the three Vedas, worshipping Me by *yajna*, drinking the soma, and thus being purified from sin, pray for a passage to Heaven (*svarga-gati*); reaching the holy world of the Lord of the Devas (*surendra-lokam*), they enjoy in heaven the divine pleasures of the gods'. 'Having enjoyed the vast *Svarga-loka*, they enter the mortal world, on the exhaustion of their merit. Thus, abiding by the injunctions of the three Vedas' desires, they come and go [undergo repeated rebirths]' (9.20–1), 'Having attained to the worlds of the righteous, and dwelling there for everlasting years, one fallen from *yoga* (spiritual life) undergoes repeated births in the home of the pure and the prosperous' (6.41). 'Bewildered by many fancies, entangled by the meshes of delusion, addicted to the gratification of lust, those unholy people will fall down into the Hell' (16.16). 'Malicious, wicked people hate me in their own bodies and in those of others' (16.18). 'Those wicked and cruel evil-doers, most depraved of men, I hurl perpetually into the wombs of Asuras [demons] only, during their repeated births' 16.19). 'Lust-Anger-Greed: this is the triple gate of Hell (*naraka-dvaram*), destructive of the soul; shun this' (16.21). 'A person freed from this triple Hell-gate can work out his salvation and attain his Supreme Goal' (16.22).

## (A) Liberation from sin and through union with God

Besides describing Heaven as a terminable Paradise, the *Gita* sets forth its important doctrine on eternal liberation through perfect union with the Lord in ecstatic experience; and for this ecstatic experience, one necessary pre-requisite is liberation from sin: 'Relinquishing all duties take refuge in Me alone; I will liberate you from all sins; don't be sorry' (18.66). And spiritual practices aimed at a total self-surrender of the aspirant to the Lord culminate in intimate union with the Lord: 'Occupy your mind with Me, be devoted to Me, sacrifice to Me, worship Me. You will reach Me; I give you my word. You are dear to Me' (18.65). Such total self-commitment will lead the devotee to the highest ecstatic experience of the Lord: 'When the fully controlled mind rests serenely in the *Atman* alone, freed from all hankering after desires, then is called a person "*yukta*" or "integrated"' (6.18). 'As a lamp stands in a windless spot unflickering' – such has been the simile used for a *Yogi* of controlled mind, practising self-integration (6.19). 'When the mind, absolutely restrained by the practice of concentration, comes to rest, and when of oneself one sees the *Paramatman* and finds joy therein – that is the bliss that surpasses all the senses and understanding. Having obtained this bliss, the yogi regards no other gain superior to that; and therein he firmly stands unmoved by any suffering however grievous it may be. This he should know to be what is meant by '*yoga*' (union) – the loosing of the bond with suffering and pain. The *yoga* must be diligently practised with firm resolve and steady mind' (6.20–3; and the rest of ch. 6; 2.15–71; 5.7, 3.15,30,42; 5.18–20; 6.7,8,9,29). In these passages the yogī is said to become *Brahman* and attain perfect liberation.

## (B) Spiritual exercises

For the *Gita*, *moksha*, or liberation, is the goal of all spiritual exercises. The *Gita* teaches: 'The wise man of equanimity is eligible for immortality' (2.15). Wise men of enlightenment, freed from karmas and rebirths, reach the Supreme Abode (2.51)! Freed from all turbulent passions, people of calm obtain serenity of mind (2.64); 'they win the highest peace' (2.70); it is through the spiritual knowledge that they win the highest peace (4.39; cf. 5.12; 5.29; 6.15). People who are unselfish and desireless attain peace and divine nature (1.71–2; 2.39; 4.19).

## (C) Liberation from the trammels of *karma*

The *Gita* proposes liberation also as freedom from the trammels of work and work-results (*karma*) (4.19; 2.39); it is freedom from old-age and death as well (7.2; 8.16); a *yogi* enjoys internal joy; he becomes *Brahman* and attains '*Brahman*'s rest' or *Brahma-nirvana* (5.24). The Buddhist term '*Nirvana*' implies both a state of freedom from misery and a state of positive bliss. Scholars point out that the *Gita* is influenced in its concept of *mukti* by the Buddhist concept of 'nirvana'. The *Gita* says also that the perfect man (*sthita-prajna*) sees his *atman* as the very *atman* of all contingent beings (5.7; 6.29; 4.35); he stands unmoved (6.22). And yet for the *Gita* the human soul is essentially dependent on the Supreme Soul, the gracious Lord to whom *bhakti* is due. The following verses from the *Gita* throw further light on the *Gita*-concept of *mukti*: 'With their sins destroyed, doubts dispelled, senses subdued, delighted in the good of all beings, the sages obtain *Brahma-nirvana*' (5.25). 'With senses, mind and soul restrained, the silent sage on deliverance intent, who has forever banished fear, anger, and desire, is truly liberated (*mukta*). Knowing Me to be the proper object of sacrifice and mortification, great Lord of all the worlds, friend of all contingent beings the yogi reaches Peace' (5.27–29).

## CONCLUSION

The Indian longing for eternal liberation from the bondage of mundane existence is certainly impressive. The *Parama-purusartha* or the Supreme Goal of human existence for the Indian religio-philosophic system – is the attainment of 'infinite and abiding happiness' – as Spinoza would say. And the importance of the acquisition of experiential knowledge or mystic vision or God-experience (*Brahma-jnana* or *anubhuti*) is insisted upon by all these systems and their different schools as necessary means for salvation. Even the '*Bhakti-margis*' stress the importance of the knowledge of the Supreme Reality. Along with experiential knowledge of the Supreme Reality or as a condition for it, all the religio-philosophic Indian systems emphasize the necessity of living a moral–ethical life (*dharma*). The idea of salvation through right knowledge is not foreign to the Bible either. See the following passages: 'Jesus said to the Jews who had believed in him: "If you obey my teaching, you are really my disciples; and you will *know the truth and the truth will liberate* you" (John 8.31–2). 'Eternal life consists in *knowing you* [*Father*] the only true God, and *knowing Jesus Christ* whom you sent' (John 17.3). And in the Book of Genesis the devilish serpent's insinuation that 'God commanded you not to eat those fruits because *He knows* that when you eat of these fruits of that tree, *you will be like God and know what is good and bad*' (Gen. 3.5) alludes to the 'liberation-through-knowledge' theory. In the Gospel passages quoted above (i.e. John 8.31–2), Christ lays great stress on the obeying of His teachings to 'know the truth', probably to know God experientially. And according to St Thomas Aquinas, Beatific Vision of the Blessed in Heaven is the possession of God through the vision of ennobled intellectual faculties. Another important feature of the Indian religious philosophies is their persistent insistence on Salvation *'hic et nunc'* or here and now rather than a post-mortem affair. Christianity also teaches that Salvation is not merely a posthumous experience, but starts here in this life on earth; the life of grace is incipient already in our earthly sojourn; it sprouts here though it blossoms and fructifies in heaven; the relation between the 'this-worldly life of grace' and 'the next-world life of Vision' is that of the seed and the tree. Of course, there are beliefs and practices – such as the *karma-samsara*-theory and practice of idol-worship – that are unacceptable to Christianity, Judaism and Islam. At the same time we must remember that Christianity can certainly benefit from the deep religious consciousness and the refined and penetrating philosophies of Indian religions. And Christianity can indeed enrich the Indian religions by offering Christ and His love to these religions.

Publisher's note: the diacritical marks in the original have not been retained here: thus, for example, *moksha* in place of *mokṣa*, *nirvana* for *nirvāṇa*.

## NOTES

1   A. L. Basham, *The Wonder that was India* (London, Fontana, 1974; Calcutta, Rupa Co., 1967), p. 239.

2   *The Hymns of the Rigveda*, vols I and II, translated with a popular commentary by R. T. H. Griffith (Benares, E. J. Lazarus, 1920 and 1926).

3   *Vedic Hymns*, translated from the Regveda with introduction and notes by E. J. Thomas (London, John Murray, 1923).

# 28

# On Developing Liberation Theology in Islam

This essay has been chosen to show how people of other faiths use their sacred
texts to respond to the questions of poverty and oppression, and seek to work
out a theology of liberation in their own terms. The implications of this for
inter-faith dialogue are incalculable.

The essay is taken from *Focus* (6, 3, 1986), a Pakistani quarterly, and is
available from Pastoral Institute, GPO 288, Multan, Pakistan, 60000.

Asghar Ali Engineer is the Director of the Institute of Islamic Studies,
Bombay, India. He has published articles on communalism, Islamic theology,
etc.

## INTRODUCTION

I propose to throw light on developing liberation theology in Islam. If
we do not treat the Islamic theology as developed by the 'ulama' during
the medieval ages to suit their time and conditions as sacrosanct,
immutable and unalterable, as is often assumed, Islam, in my opinion,
has great potential for lending itself to develop liberation. Liberation
theology, it must be understood, is much more than rational theology.

Rational theology views the religious teachings and institutions in
the light of reason and advocates freedom of reinterpretation of the
scriptural text. It has great appeal for the modern elite as, more often
than not, rational theology subserves the ends of this elite. However,
this rational approach may not appeal to the masses as they hardly feel
any need for rational theology. In the present social structure which
imposes severe constraints on the economic as well as intellectual
progress of the masses and compels them to remain backward, a
rational or book view of religion with its transcendental complex does
not enthuse them. In this state of backwardness, what appeals to them
is folk religion with its attendant rituals. Religion, in this form, serves

their psychological need to bear the hard conditions of life, miseries which would be difficult to bear without such a psychological prop.

However, liberation theology does not confine itself to the arena of pure and speculative reasoning: it widens its scope to become a most powerful instrument for emancipating the masses from the clutches of their masters and exploiters and inspires them to act with revolutionary zeal to fight against tyranny, exploitation and persecution. Thus liberation theology enables them to change their condition for the better and transforms religion into a powerful instrument of militant struggle and revolutionary change.

## HISTORICAL GENESIS OF ISLAM

Islam has great potential for developing a liberation theology. The historical genesis of Islam can help us understand its revolutionary potential. Mecca, birth place of Islam, was a centre of international commerce at the time of its origin. There had emerged on the social scene of Mecca powerful merchants specialising in complex international financial operations and commercial transactions. Due to these developments, the institution of private property which was absent in the tribal society began to consolidate itself. The rich merchants had formed intertribal corporations to carry on and monopolise trade with the regions of the Byzantine empire and accumulated profits without distributing a part of it to the poor and needy of their tribes. This went against the tribal norms and caused social malaise in Mecca.

The Prophet felt the acute social tensions developing in the Meccan society due to the widening gap between the rich and poor and the violent conflict it could lead to if these tensions were not resolved. He addressed himself to the powerful merchants of Mecca and exhorted them not to hoard their wealth but to take care of the poor, orphans, and the needy. The Meccan verses revealed to the Prophet sharply condemn the practice of accumulation of wealth and warn the Meccan merchants of the dangerous consequence which will follow if they do not spend their wealth in the way of Allah. It is said in one of the Meccan verses:

[Woe unto] who has gathered wealth and sedulously hoards it, thinking that their riches will render them immortal!

By no means! They shall be flung to the destroying flame. Would that you knew what the destroying flame is like. It is Allah's own kindled fire, which will rise up to the hearts of men. It will close them from every side, in towering columns (Qur'an, 104.2–9).

And again: Worldly affluence has made you oblivious [of consequences] until you come to the graves.

But you shall know, you shall before long come to know. Indeed, if you knew the truth with certainty, you would see the fire of hell: you would see it with your very eyes. Then, on that day, you shall be questioned about your joy (Qur'an, 102.1–8).

Thus we see that in the verses quoted above hoarding of wealth and worldly affluence is condemned in no uncertain terms. Significantly, in the latter verse it is said that preoccupation with the piling up of wealth makes one oblivious of all the consequences until they meet their graves. It is further predicted that if they remain preoccupied with joys of life they would soon see hell fire (i.e. people's wrath who are deprived of their just and legitimate share), and they would certainly be confronted with this wrath and then they will be questioned about their joys.

It was primarily for this reason that the powerful merchants of Mecca opposed the Prophet and became his sworn enemies. These were the vested interests the Prophet had to fight against in Mecca. First, the Meccan rich offered inducements to the Prophet if only he stopped preaching his egalitarian doctrine. The Prophet refused to compromise with the rich and so they began to severely persecute him. The Meccan rich who also commanded the leadership of the society (there was no regular government or state machinery as such in Mecca at that time) like the rich in any other society, were not much perturbed with the religious doctrines preached by the Prophet. They were seriously concerned with the socio-economic consequences of his teachings and the attack he launched on their wealth and privileges. The Qur'an attacked their power which was a result of concentration of wealth and monopoly of trade established by them.

It can thus be seen that the Prophet initiated a process of profound change in Arabian society which brought about the downfall of the powerful vested interests which had emerged on the Meccan scene. The Prophet of Islam was seriously concerned with the fate of the downtrodden in Mecca and this concern burst forth in the verses revealed during this period. Some of the terms often used in the Qur'an will have to be redefined while developing liberation theology in the light of this consideration. Islam naturally began as a religious movement and these terms, therefore, have acquired deep religious connotations. However, Islam, as pointed out above, was not only concerned with the spiritual, but also equally with the worldly side of life. It took the project of establishing a just society here on earth quite seriously and repeatedly emphasised this approach.

## SOCIO-ECONOMIC PERSPECTIVE

The terms we are referring to will, therefore, have to be seen in a socio-economic perspective also. A liberation theology cannot confine these terms to their religious connotations only; they must be reinterpreted to bring out their socio-economic import. Islam gives a concept of society which is free of exploitation, oppression, domination and injustice in any form. Also, it emphasises progress and change in harmony with the laws of God who is merciful and just. The God of Qur'an, it must be remembered, is not only merciful but is also mighty and powerful. He approved of those oppressed avenging themselves.

## THE QURANIC CONCEPT OF JUSTICE

The true quranic spirit would make it necessary to devise new institutions other than mere almsgiving to ensure social justice. Socialist concepts and institutions come much nearer to this quranic spirit. In a socialist economy distributive justice is as much important as production of wealth. According to the quranic concept of justice it is the producers who have the right of ownership over the wealth produced by them. It is very clearly stated in the Qur'an that no one shall bear the burden of others (Qur'an 53.38). It is a clear denial of the right of extracting labour without fully compensating for it as is sanctioned by feudal or capitalist systems in one form or the other. The Qur'an also says that man shall get what he strives for (Qur'an 53.39). Both the above quranic verses put together are clear enunciation of the principle of ownership of wealth based on one's labour. In other words, Islam does not recognise ownership based on exploitation of labour by way of appropriation of surplus labour or by way of speculation and future trading in commodities. It is in this spirit that speculation and future trading in commodities has been categorically banned in Islam. Liberation theology, needless to say, would give great emphasis to the principle of ownership based on labour or work – a principle which has been neglected by medieval theology.

## PRIVATE PROPERTY IN ISLAM

This brings us to the most important question of right of private property in Islam. The traditional theologian considers the institution of property as sacred and inviolable. An Islamic conference held in Mecca in 1976 opposed the concept of nationalisation as against the teachings of Islam. It emphasised man's trusteeship of natural re-sources and of social and economic institutions. State intervention in their view should not extend beyond supervising the economic growth for realisation of ideological objectives. However, taking the true spirit of Islam into account, the 'ulama' are not justified in treating private property *per se* as sacred: 'Those who do oppress [others] will come to know by what a [great] reverse they will be overturned' (Qur'an 26.227).

The God of the Qur'an also declares his sympathy in no uncertain terms in favour of the oppressed and the weak:

> And we desired to show favour unto those who were oppressed in the earth, and to make them leaders of mankind and to make them inheritors [of this earth] (Qur'an 27.5).

When the Qur'an categorically condemns oppression and injustice, its concern for the social health and egalitarian social structure cannot be denied and hence the quranic terms would have, apart from religious import, socio-economic connotations also. Thus a con-demnatory term like *kafir* would not only connote religious disbelief, as is the case in traditional theology, but would also imply obstruction in the creation of a just and egalitarian society free of all forms of exploitation and oppression. Thus a *kafir* is one who does not believe in God and actively opposes with all his might an honest attempt to restructure a society in order to eliminate concentration of wealth, exploitation and other forms of injustice.

*Kufr* (disbelief) would not be determined, as far as liberation theology is concerned, by more formal denial of faith in God; one who formally professes faith in God but indulges in accumulation of wealth by exploiting others and goes in for conspicuous consumption while others starve in the neighbourhood would also commit *kufr*, and thus incur the displeasure of God. The Qur'an says in one of the Meccan suras:

> Have you observed him who belies the religious? It is he who turns away the orphan and does not urge others to feed the poor. Woe to those who pray but are heedless in their prayer; who make a show of piety and obstruct the needy from necessities (Qur'an 107).

Thus it is clear that those who profess their faith in religion and make show of their piety, but deprive the orphans and destitutes of their rights are not real believers. Thus to be a believer or a true Muslim one has to act in a way so as to create a just society that takes care of the orphans, the destitute and the needy. The medieval theologians emphasised giving of alms but a liberation theologian in a modern society would interpret it to mean creation of a just society. A property acquired by exploitation, speculation or by any means other than by one's own labour cannot have any sanction in Islam.

There are clear traditions of the Prophet prohibiting share cropping or owning the land which is not cultivated by the owner himself. All the standard works on *hadith* (traditions), that is, *Muwatta* of Iman Malik, Sahih Bukhari, Sahih Muslim, etc., have included a number of traditions of the Prophet against giving the land on share cropping or on rent. These traditions have been narrated by six companions of the Prophet who are considered highly reliable. According to a tradition in Sahih Muslim narrated by Jabir bin, 'Abdallah the Prophet said that one who possesses land should cultivate it himself, and if he is unable to do so he should give (that portion of the land or whole piece of land which he cannot cultivate) without taking any compensation.

## TAWHIDI SOCIETY

The other central concept of Islam is *tawhid* which, as far as traditional theology is concerned, means unity of Godhood. *Shirk* (i.e. associating another with Allah) has been strongly condemned by the Qur'an. Liberation theology, while accepting the concept of the unity of godhood, strives to broaden the scope of *tawhid*. *Tawhid* in liberation theology implies not only unity of God but also unity of mankind in all aspects. The *mujahiddin* of Iran are engaged in a liberation struggle and they are giving new interpretations to the quranic concepts like *tawhid*, *kufr*, etc. A truly *tawhidi* society is one which ensures complete unity among mankind, and for that it is necessary to create a classless society. Unity of godhood must ensure complete unity of society and such a society cannot admit of any division, not even class division. There cannot be true solidarity of the faithful unless all racial, national and socio-economic divisions are done away with. Thus such a concept of *tawhid* acquires primary importance in developing liberation theology. Class divisions would imply domination of the strong over the weak. Such a domination is the very denial of the creation of a just society.

## REINTERPRETING THE QUR'AN

These are some of the most important considerations in reinterpreting the Holy Qur'an for developing a liberation theology of Islam.

The Qur'an, it is important to note, opposes in categorical terms all oppressive establishments. Most of the prophets mentioned in it are from amongst the masses and fight against tyrants and oppressive rulers. The prophets came from among the people, not from among the rulers of ruling establishments. The Qur'an declares:

> It is he who has sent forth apostles from amongst the people to recite to them his revelations, to purify them, and to impart to them wisdom and knowledge of the scripture . . . (62.2).

This is made quite clear by the Qur'an that apostles are selected from amongst the people themselves and they impart wisdom to them and guide them to fight against oppression and exploitation. The prophet Moses is projected by the Qur'an as a liberator of the Israelis who were being oppressed by pharaoh. The Israelis were the oppressed and weak *mustad'ifun* on earth. Moses was the man of the people who fought for their liberation from the oppressive establishment.

Another important concept in Islam is that of *jihad*, which literally means struggle. This concept also needs to be reinterpreted in the context of liberation theology. A propounder of liberation theology has to emphasise (as the Qur'an does) to wage struggle (*jihad*) for eliminating exploitation, corruption and *zulm* (wrong-doing, tyranny) in all their varied forms and this struggle will continue until these corrupting influences are completely eliminated from the earth. The Qur'an declares unambiguously:

> And fight them until persecution is no more, and religion is all for Allah. But
> if they cease, then Lo: Allah is seer of what they do (8.39).

Thus it is very clear that Allah desires that the faithful fight until
persecution ceases on earth. And seen in a proper context, the real
import of a 'religion is all for Allah' is the creation of a society where
there would no more be persecution and exploitation of man by man. It
is the basic duty of every believer to wage struggle until this divine
objective is realised.

The Qur'an does not approve of people sitting idly by when others
are being persecuted. It says:

> Why should you not fight for the cause of Allah and of the weak among men
> and of the women and the children who are crying: 'Our Lord! Deliver us
> from this town of which the people are oppressors! Oh, give us from thy
> presence some protecting friend! Oh! give us from thy presence some
> defender!

It is thus clear that the Qur'an wants the faithful to fight for the cause
of the weak among men, women and children who pray to be delivered
from the clutches of the oppressors. And it must be noted that to fight
for this cause is to fight for the cause of Allah. The Qur'an also makes it
clear that an oppressor cannot be entrusted with the leadership of the
people even if he belongs to the progeny of a prophet. When the
prophet Abraham is told that he would be appointed the leader of the
people he inquires about the status of his offspring. He is told in no
uncertain terms that this covenant does not include the wrongdoers:

> And of my offspring (will there be leaders)? He said: My covenant includes
> no oppressors (Qur'an 4.75).

Thus the whole emphasis of the Qur'an is on liberation of mankind
from exploitation and oppression. The liberation theology in Islam
derives its strength from such qur'anic injunctions. Those who do not
fight for the liberation of the oppressed and the weak cannot claim to
be really faithful by mere profession of faith verbally. The Qur'an says:

> Do men imagine that they will be left because they say, 'We believe' and will
> not be tested (in action). Lo! We tested those who were before you (29.2).

The prophetic tradition also says that 'the best form of *jihad* is telling
the truth in the face of tyrants'. Today most of the Muslim countries
happen to be in the Third World and are exploited by imperialist
forces. Thus it would be their duty to wage struggle against the

imperialist forces and it is in this light that the struggles of the peoples of Palestine, Iran and other countries should be seen. Liberation theology would urge every Muslim to fight against exploiters and oppressors within the country they belong to, and outside the country by joining hands with all anti imperialist forces.

## THE REAL AND THE POSSIBLE

A perceptive observer of the social scene knows that there is always tension between the real and the possible. A traditional theology tries to resolve this tension by compromising with the real and coming to terms with it. As against this, liberation theology seeks to intensify tension between the real and the possible by putting greater emphasis on the possible and by waging struggle against that which exists today in order to bring it closer to the possible. The attainment of the possible, liberation theology emphasises, can be brought about by increasing degrees of freedom both for individuals and collectively (a group, a community or a nation), reducing economic exploitation (by socialising instruments of production, prohibiting accumulation of wealth, severely penalising practice of usury, creating appropriate institutions to ensure satisfaction of basic needs of all the people, etc.), waging unceasing struggles against those who have a vested interest in maintaining the status quo and interpreting the quranic injunctions in such a way as to ensure continuous progress of humanity. Liberation theology is, therefore, essentially the theology of the possible.

Liberation theology stands for unity of mankind and does not admit of any division based on caste, creed, class or race. It continuously strives to achieve this unity by eliminating all such differences. Even the differences based on religion are more apparent than real. The Qur'an says:

> For each we have appointed a divine law and a way (of worshipping). Had Allah willed he could have made you one community. But that he may try you by that which he has given you. So vie with one another for good deeds (5.15).

Thus the real emphasis is on good deeds and on the ways of worshipping (which may differ from community to community). Liberation theology also lays a good deal of emphasis on justice, which is one of the most important quranic doctrines.

## CONCLUSION

Thus justice is of primary importance for liberation theology in Islam. One must not be carried away by passions as it would lead to oppression (*zulm*), injuring the cause of justice which Islam upholds so dearly and, therefore, liberation theology also has to make it a matter of central concern. The traditional theologians have, more often than not, remained preoccupied with metaphysical questions and *ibadat* (prayer, fasting, etc.), relegating the question of social justice and this worldly existence to a secondary position. Liberation theology seeks to re-emphasise the central concern of Islam with social justice and its fundamental emphasis on liberating the weaker sections and the oppressed masses and radically restructuring society to eliminate all the vested interests, which would ultimately lead to the creation of a classless society which is the real purpose of *tawhidi* society. It is needless to point out that liberation theology is opposed to the fundamentalist movement as it seeks to re-emphasise traditional issues and seeks to give new lease of life to traditional theology without concerning itself with the problems of the modern world.

# PART FIVE

# *People as Exegetes*

'It's our business,' she said. 'You know your Bible. We know people.'

'The Bible is people,' he said.

(Harold Robbins *Spellbinder*)

# 29

# A Malawian Example: The Bible and Non-literate Communities

## PATRICK A. KALILOMBE

Re-reading of the Bible assumes literacy. But how does one use the Bible in a non-literate context? A Malawian tries to provide some hermeneutical clues as to how to tackle this problem.

This essay is the revised version of the paper presented at the International Congress on Africa and the Bible, August 1988, Cairo.

Bishop Patrick Kalilombe is the Director of the Centre for Black and White Christian Partnership, Selly Oak Colleges, Birmingham, UK.

African theology, as the Ecumenical Association for African Theologians (EAAT) would want to practise it, must be a tool for human liberation in obedience to the Word of God as revealed in the Scriptures. This is why EAAT's inaugural declaration indicated as the first source of theology the Bible and Christian Heritage, saying:

> The Bible is the basic source of African theology, because it is the primary witness of God's revelation in Jesus Christ. No theology can retain its Christian identity apart from Scripture. . . . Through a re-reading of this Scripture in the social context of our struggle for our humanity, God speaks to us in the midst of our troublesome situation.[1]

But it is not just any use of the Bible that serves the purposes of liberation. As Mesters has reminded us: 'The Bible is ambiguous. It can be a force for liberation or a force for oppression. If it is treated like a finished monument that cannot be touched, that must be taken literally as it is, then it will be an oppressive force.'[2] In the past the Bible has often been invoked in such a way as to legitimize the most obvious social, economic or political injustices, to discourage stirrings of revolt against oppressive or discriminatory practices, and to promote attitudes of resignation and compliance in the face of exploitative manipulations of power-holders.

Even today there seems to be an intensified invasion of certain types of biblical interpretation which can only be characterized as simplistic and distracting. They centre so much on the spiritual and interior needs of the people that the connection between the Word of God and the realities of every day becomes secondary, almost irrelevant. Ominously this kind of biblical faith is being promoted with particular effect in countries of the Third World, that is, precisely among those peoples for whom the facts of material deprivation, violations of human rights and sheer exploitation are the most pressing concerns. In such circumstances the Bible is hardly a credible liberating power, and can even become a tool for continued enslavement.

It is, however, in these same areas of the Third World that special efforts are currently being made to discover and employ the power of the Bible for people's full liberation. There are conditions for this liberating force to come out. Advocates of liberation theology have been studying, as a matter of urgency, this question of the use and misuse of the Scriptures, acknowledging that what might be called a 'political' reading of the Bible is not only legitimate, but highly desirable.[3] These investigations are useful and enlightening. And yet they are at such a level of scholarly sophistication that it is not immediately evident how useful they can be when we consider the problems of biblical usage by ordinary people engaged in the project of liberation at the grassroots.

Liberation theology is of practical use only in the measure in which it is practised by these ordinary people; otherwise it remains a merely intellectual activity indulged in by comfortable academics. By the same token a liberative handling of the Bible becomes effective only when the people themselves are practising it in their own struggle. It is necessary, therefore, to examine carefully how the people at the grassroots actually use the Scriptures and how this use can relate to their liberation.

## THE SPECIAL PREDICAMENT OF THE NON-LITERATE

When Mesters warns against the possible oppressive use of the Bible, it is clear that the central issue is that of interpretation: what meaning do we give to the text of the Scriptures? This assumes that the biblical text is itself available to the people and can therefore become the object of interpretation.

My interest is with a more radical situation. What happens when the text of the Bible is not available, or when its availability to one section of the community is controlled and regulated by another section? This is the case when part of the community is illiterate and cannot therefore have direct contact with the written Word of God. Such people are at the mercy of their literate neighbours if they wish to know what the Bible has to say.

Those who can read and write are in a position to share with their less fortunate brothers and sisters the contents of the Holy Book. But they have also the possibility of withholding parts of the contents and distorting what they report from the Bible. They may choose to share only some selections and leave out others, according as they themselves judge good or opportune. They could very well leave out those parts that they think useless, ambiguous, or dangerous. This is not simply a matter of quantity. It is also a question of interpretation. What the readers of the text choose to share is determined very much by their own judgment, interests, or objectives. The illiterate hearers have very little scope of judging for themselves. Therefore their understanding of God's Word and their capacity to reflect on it and use it for their own lives are to a large extent controlled by others.

When, then, we discuss the importance of the Bible for doing theology in Africa, we are raising some quite vexing questions. This theology is meant to be a liberating tool, especially for those who are underprivileged or oppressed. In our developing countries the illiterate are surely among such disadvantaged people. What possibility is there for them to take an active and fair part in hearing the Word of God and reflecting on it in the light of their own experience? Are they reduced to having others do theology for them? Such questions are of special relevance in a continent like Africa.

## LITERACY AND ILLITERACY IN AFRICA: EXAMPLE OF MALAWIAN CATHOLICS

It is important to remember that, in general, Africa is largely non-literate. In more than half of the countries less than half of the population above 15 years of age know how to read and write, and in about all the countries literacy among the female population is far below that among the male.[4] Let it be said in passing that this last fact is, as far as religion is concerned, of tremendous consequence since in general the more active and practising members in any community are often women. And in many communities, especially among matrilineal people, the female role (mother, sister, grandmother) is most decisive as far as religious development and practice are concerned. It is legitimate, therefore, to assume that African life is, in general, less literate and more oral, auricular, and visual.

Christianity would normally be expected to be influenced by this factor. Only where literacy has been seen as in some way a precondition for membership in the Church would one expect the majority of believers to belong to the literate sector. This has been the case for most Protestant churches in Africa. If that constitutes an advantage as far as contact with the Bible is concerned, it also spells out the danger of a serious constraint in evangelization: only those with a certain degree of modern education will feel at home in the Church. In other words, conversion and fidelity to the Christian faith would be conditioned by acceptance of modern culture. That certainly leaves out a large part of the African population, those people who for one reason or another have not had the chance of a meaningful education and live largely within the confines of traditional life. This is the case for many people in the rural areas; and even in urban and semi-urban areas the proportion of people who live a non-literate culture is greater than one might be led to imagine.[5]

I am less acquainted with communities where literacy is preponderant, and where therefore the use of the Bible as a written word presents no special problem. My experience has been mainly with communities for whom reading and writing were peripheral in daily life: in acquiring and communicating knowledge and in passing on information. Among them there were admittedly persons who had been to school and could read and write more or less fluently. One hoped that more schooling would become available to them; and indeed heroic efforts in education were being made in these areas. Still, for the time being, their ordinary way of life was not dependent on literacy. When we imagine such people using the Bible for their Christian life, for 'doing theology at the grassroots', are we just dreaming? Is there no way these people can come into real contact with the Scriptures?

I shall take the case of my own country: Malawi; and more precisely, I am thinking of the Catholic population there. Although statistics indicate that 49.9 per cent of the population above 15 years of age are literate,[6] among Catholics this percentage would be too high. For reasons that are due mainly to history, the Catholic Church in Malawi has been successful mainly among the more traditional and less Westernized communities. As Linden pointed out: 'On the whole their [Catholic missionaries'] converts came from the edges of African society, the marginal men and late-comers to Nyasaland [former name of Malawi] like the immigrant Alomwe and Sena.'[7]

A large proportion of Malawian Catholics are therefore either illiterate or semi-literate, and belong to the oral tradition rather than the literary one. As such, the Bible as written word still remains unfamiliar and marginal to their life as believers. When you watch Catholics going to church or to other services, very few will be carrying literature of any kind. A few may be bringing along their hymn- and/or prayer-books, or perhaps a catechism or some devotional book. But hardly any will be carrying the Bible, not even the New Testament text! They know in advance that the standard Catholic service does not require the general faithful to read written texts for themselves. Why is this so?

The historical fact of a majority of non-literate members has been reinforced by what seems to be traditional Catholic practice. In standard Catholic ideology the faith expression of believers and their practical response to God's Word do not derive directly from the Bible, but from the teaching authority of the Church: the *magisterium*. It is understood, of course, that the *magisterium* itself is informed by the Scriptures, and to that extent the faith of the believers rests in the final analysis on the authority of the Bible. But the Bible is read and interpreted, not necessarily by each individual believer, but within the 'Tradition' of the Church. Sometimes this ideology has been unfairly and incorrectly expressed as though for Catholics the faith derives from two distinct sources: the Scriptures *and* Tradition. The more correct way of putting the matter is this: Faith derives from God's revelation, and this revelation reaches us through the Bible within tradition. Vatican Council II, in its Constitution on Divine Revelation, has attempted to express more satisfactorily the relation between these two complementary aspects of God's revelation. 'Sacred Tradition and Sacred Scripture', it says, 'make up a single deposit of the Word of God, which is entrusted to the Church'.[8]

Whether or not this Constitution has succeeded in shedding new light around the Reformation contention about *Sola Scriptura* is a different matter which is not our direct concern here. What comes out clearly, however, is the crucial importance of two elements: Tradition and Community. The need for Catholics to read Scripture *within*

*Tradition* makes this Tradition the *practically* decisive hermeneutical authority. If this principle is taken to its bitter logical conclusion, it would be quite normal for the believers to be satisfied with Tradition's presentation of the Scriptures without the necessity to read and examine personally the letter itself of the Bible. The biblical witness, content, selection, and interpretation would come to them through the various organs whereby Tradition addresses itself concretely to the believer. Such are, for example, the catechism, the pronouncements of the *magisterium* (Pope, Councils, Bishops, Synods, etc.), the liturgy (including rituals, preaching, hymnody, iconography . . .), and indeed also popular piety and devotions. Here lies the special power of Catholic faith, but also the source of problems which we shall need to examine later on.

Until quite recently direct contact with the Bible was a rare phenomenon among Catholics, certainly among the ordinary faithful in Malawi. Since Vatican II things have begun to change, and it is fair to say that heroic efforts are being made to bring the scriptures to the people.[9] Since the coming of the use of vernacular languages in the liturgy, more and more biblical texts are heard by the faithful at Mass and other services. In many areas, as complete Bibles or portions of Scripture become available to the faithful, suggestions for daily Scripture readings are being proposed, often with accompanying aids of an exegetical or spiritual nature. The possibility, then, for a widespread contact with the Scriptures is now there in Malawi.

## THE CRUCIAL PROBLEM: BRINGING THE BIBLE TO NON-LITERATE PEOPLE

But does this solve the problem of the use of Scripture among our Catholic faithful? Not automatically. The crucial point is that even here the methods being used assume largely a literary culture which the majority of the people are not accustomed to. For a people of a non-literate way of life, the mere availability of the written Word is not enough to bring the Scriptures into their life. The Word of God must first become 'incarnated' in their own specific way of hearing and responding. In other words: the Bible needs to come to them in non-literate ways.

In communities where reading and writing are marginal ways for learning, communicating, assimilating knowledge and values, and expressing them, there exist other media which are, for those people, much more familiar and effective. *Hearing* appropriately formulated inputs and *seeing* culturally adapted messages take the place of reading as means for taking in and assimilating information and knowledge. To match the value of the ever-present written text (to which the readers can always return if they forget), non-literate people employ mnemonic devices like *repetition* or *variation* of analogous visual aids. In order to interpret and apply to life what is being taken in, they have such potent tools as *acting, retelling* in their own words, or *responding* through gestures or emotion-filled expressions. Through these appropriate methods, messages and instructions are passed around, selected, interpreted and evaluated, and then assimilated so that they influence people's lives.

There is no reason why the Bible could not be made to reach the non-literate through these ways with the same efficacy that the written word reaches the literate. If all of them cannot read the Bible text for themselves, they surely can hear it read to them, provided care is taken to make this reading as effective as possible. In a community of mostly illiterate folk there might be two or more who are able to read. By reading out the text to the group these few would enable their brothers and sisters to hear the Word ('Faith cometh by hearing, and hearing by the word of God', Rom. 10.17). Reading out or 'proclaiming' the Scriptures could thus become a value ministry for the few literates among our people. If need be, the readers would be requested to repeat the text or parts of it for the benefit of the audience. In our modern times when such technical instruments as tape-recorders are no longer rarities even in the remote villages, much use can be made of recorded biblical tapes. Our Muslim neighbours know this only too well: have you not heard hoisted loudspeakers blaring out recorded Qur'anic surahs from up the mosque tower in the market-place? Christians could learn to make such a resourceful use of these modern devices.

Reading out biblical texts could very easily become a new version of the traditional art of the story-teller. Our people do enjoy story-telling: children and adults alike. In all sorts of formal (ritual, courts) or informal occasions people are ever eager to hear 'nkhani' (story or narrative). They crowd around the public place where cases are being tried; they surround the newly arrived visitor who brings fresh news and messages from relatives or friends, or who simply describes the wonders of faraway places and peoples; they regale one another with wise sayings, parables, fables or riddles. The spoken and heard word is very central. It fulfils the functions of newspapers, reviews, books, or advertisements in literate communities. That is why the radio has become a favourite toy in the villages. The Bible would come effectively to the non-literate if the skills of the spoken word were used judiciously, and if the power of this word were put at the service of the Scriptures.

The role of music and singing in non-literate societies is likewise great. Often the song accompanies dancing, but it should not be thought of simply as a means of entertainment. Singing serves to express interior sentiments, to underline and reinforce values, to praise or to ridicule, to exalt or to debase. In ritual and religion, singing is often used as a means of arousing and communicating appropriate attitudes of mind and soul. As with the spoken word, so also the incantation has effective power. The song is also a vehicle of information and teaching, all the more effective because it is easy to remember and to reproduce. In traditional rituals singing was a favourite tool for instruction, for admonition, and for passing on traditional lore: history, customs, or the art of living.

With a bit of imagination, singing could be used for bringing the Bible to the people. A lot of the Scripture text was originally for singing – for example, the psalms and the numerous canticles and hymns which scholars discover in various books of the Bible (Revelation seems to be full of them). Our hymn-books offer quantities of fine hymns. Some of them are more or less directly biblical in origin and inspiration. But a large number are not. This is principally because in standard congregational practice the hymns are simply a commentary on, or an accompaniment or reinforcement of, the Bible text that is supposed to be read during the service. But where reading is not possible, or is marginal, why should the song itself not replace the reading of the written word?

Important texts would be put to music (e.g. the Beatitudes, the Sermon on the Mount, the parables). Thus the singing itself could constitute a direct contact with God's Word, thus abolishing the unfair discrimination whereby the Bible is unduly restricted to the literate. In sessions for Christian instruction, and even in Bible discussion groups, the song could thus serve as the Scripture text. There are enough gifted people in the local congregations for whom composing tunes is not a problem. All they need is to be given the Bible text. One can imagine a special ministry for such people whereby they could gradually build up a home-made repertoire of biblical portions in local music.

The part played by the *visual media* in non-literate societies should also be taken into account. Much information and many important messages circulate through what people are able to see and to handle. Students of the so-called African art are wont to say that the objects that Western sensibility classifies as 'art' are actually very functional tools in the society, be they sculptures, paintings, pottery, vestments and 'ornamentation', architecture, and even weapons and utensils. They are not there simply as an embodiment of the aesthetic spirit. First and foremost they are saying something and are meant to produce useful results for the needs of the community. As with the gestures and words that are usually associated with these objects, we are dealing here with 'symbols', understood in the strong sense of conventional signs which are meant to effect what they signify. Symbolism is a central force in non-literate societies. The visual object, by virtue of the evocative and associational power of its shape, design, texture and colours, becomes a medium for expressing values, recalling stories, fables or parables, and often also for evoking meaningful history.

Christian churches still need to learn to exploit the vast resources of our people's visual media in the religious field. The schools, especially at the primary level, have always recognized the importance of visual aids. Just as much contact with the Bible can be established through hearing (e.g. tapes), so also can the eyes capture what the Scriptures are saying through words. A picture depicting a biblical scene is able to bring the message quite powerfully to those who are unable to read. Often the illustrations in a book convey the essential points of the text. Paintings, sketches, statues, or artistic arrangements in the place of worship have been used traditionally for more than mere decorative purposes: they were often the text-book of the illiterate. How much biblical instruction could be done with the help of slides, videos or films for non-literate audiences! In recent years catechetical centres have been providing material of this kind. The biblical apostolate should make more use of such visual aids.

## EXPLOITING LOCAL RESOURCES

There is, of course, the objection that this type of material is often prohibitively expensive, and in many cases there is need for sophisticated equipment which simple people would neither possess nor be in a position to handle efficiently. And again, some material is foreign and ill-adapted for use among Africans. That is sometimes true. Well-meaning people, when they set out to meet the needs of non-literate communities, tend to introduce resources that have to be sought from outside. This is not helpful: it simply prolongs, often even aggravates, the dependence of these disadvantaged people on outside help.

But there is no reason why locally available resources should not be exploited. Simple ordinary material, which the people use in their daily life, can be easily turned into effective illustrations for biblical communication. The people are able to attach didactic value to what they possess. They do not need exotic equipment for that. They can resort to the various symbols in their culture which express values and meanings in line with the biblical message: symbols of birth, life, death, purification, joy, humility. These can be used anew to stand for one or the other biblical message.

In this connection the symbolic value of colours, insignia, or ritual objects comes to mind. If the people themselves establish this connection between their culture and the Bible, there can slowly grow up an inventory of visual symbolism through which the Bible message can be interpreted, evoked and made use of. At any rate, it is counterproductive to create the impression that progress is being made because the local needs are being met with 'modern' means.

## HOW TO INTERPRET AND APPLY
## THE BIBLICAL MESSAGE

Through auditory and visual media, biblical material is able to be taken in by people who are not of a written tradition. The objective, however, is not simply to receive and take in what Scripture offers. As they receive the Bible message, the people should at the same time have the capacity *to react* to the input, to *interpret it*, that is: give it their own understanding, and then to *apply it* to their life as believers. This is a decisive stage, for it is only in this way that the non-literate actually do their own theologizing with the means that are familiar to them. They allow the Word of God to meet and challenge their ordinary experience. In ways and idioms proper to their culture, they take the initiative to reflect on this Word, asking themselves what it means to them. They evaluate its significance and relevancy to their lives, and then apply it.

There are several ways whereby non-literate people appropriate and interpret inputs. One of these is *repeating in their own words* what they hear, see or experience. The exercise of re-telling or putting in one's own words forces the person to say what in the input was worth retaining. It is therefore an exercise in personal *selection* of the meaningful: for in a given input not everything is equally relevant to everyone. By the same token it is an exercise in *interpretation* and assessment of value: for one remarks and retains only those points that are significant for one (personal) reason or another.

The value of retelling is enhanced when several people *exchange and discuss* what they have retained singly. By so doing they enlarge the extent of the meaningful, one person's points being enriched by points from the others. At the same time this makes possible mutual challenges and criticism. Questions will come as to whether one heard correctly or missed out on an important point. There will be questions about the real meaning of this or that word or expression. And then there is the wider area of discussion about how the biblical message applies to individual or common living. By engaging in a discussion of this type the group is actually constructing their 'theology': a reasoned reflection on their experience in the light of God's Word.

Another powerful means of selecting, interpreting and applying inputs is what we may call *drama* or re-enacting. When the audience proceeds to act out what they have taken in, they inevitably select what struck them, and automatically express *why* and in what way it struck them. By reproducing it through drama they are also applying the meaning to their familiar world in familiar idiom. Even when only one part of the community does the acting, while the others look on, there is possibility of mutual exchange and 'discussion'. The reactions of the onlookers can be affirmative, interrogatory, encouraging, reinforcing (e.g. through applause), or, on the contrary, cool, disapproving, or indifferent. It has been said that the preaching in some churches, where the congregation is expected to manifest its response, is a version of this kind of drama. It is not the preacher alone who interprets and expresses the message. Through their responses and reactions, the 'audience' take part in directing the content, affecting the flow of delivery, and giving it shape. This too is a group-type of theologizing.

In this context of a religious gathering, another effective way of interpreting and applying God's Word is *prayer*. When people pray after hearing the Word of God, they automatically express what meaning the Word has for them, and usually they go on to apply it to their lives. The Word will have enlightened them, questioned their assumptions, rebuked their conduct, or given them guidance and encouragement. All this usually transpires through prayer, which then becomes a response to the challenge of God's Word. We know how enriching shared prayer can be. Different members simply say aloud what the Word has done to them; and as divers responses flow into one another the assembly shares in an ever-enriched pool of understandings and applications.

In some congregations there is the practice of *testimony*. Here individuals attempt to put in communicable words their experience of God's activity in their lives. Often these testimonies are veritable biblical commentaries made in simple terms by ordinary people.

We can see, then, that much scope exists even for the non-literate to receive the biblical message, to interpret and apply it, even if they do not themselves read the written text.


## A LIBERATING THEOLOGY FROM THE UNDERSIDE OF HISTORY

What is the point in all this discussion about the Bible and non-literate people? Our concern is for the integrity of the kind of Third World theologies which our Ecumenical Association of African Theologians has been attempting to formulate and promote in the past ten years of its existence. In numerous discussions and exchanges, the gist of which can be found in the written works produced by both EATWOT and EAAT, several basic characteristics of this type of theology have emerged.

I would like to recall three of them. First, it is a committed and liberating theology, as was stressed at the very inaugural assembly of the Ecumenical Association for Third World Theologians (EATWOT):

> We reject as irrelevant an academic type of theology that is divorced from action. We are prepared for a radical break in epistemology which makes commitment the first act of theology and engages in critical reflection on the reality of the Third World.[10]

Second, this liberation must be achieved ultimately by the oppressed themselves, and not on their behalf, even though others will join them in this commitment. The Asian theologians expressed this felicitously when they said:

> To be truly liberating, this theology must arise from the Asian poor with a liberated consciousness. It is articulated and expressed by the oppressed community using the technical skills of biblical scholars, social scientists, psychologists, anthropologists, and others. It can be expressed in many ways, in art forms, drama, literature, folk stories, and native wisdom, as well as in doctrinal–pastoral statements.[11]

Third, the basic source of this liberating theology is the Bible.[12]

If the Bible is the source of liberating theology, those who would engage in doing such a theology must have the Bible realistically available to them, and they must be in a position to reflect on it, not by procuration, but in their own right. Clearly this poses a question for those who cannot read and write, since the Bible offers itself to us today primarily as a written text. Normally only those who are literate will be able to study it directly and base their reflection on this Word of God. Those who are unable to read are in the unenviable position of depending on others.

Unless there is a radical change in methodology, it is not realistic to expect such people to take a creative part in doing theology. Their knowledge of the Scriptures risks being from mere hearsay and to consist only of bits and pieces that are kindly made available to them by those who can read. As we said, the interpretation itself is affected by this dependence. The non-literate would not have full confidence in their own understanding of the Bible, as they would not know whether or not they had all that was required for an informed interpretation. Those who have direct access to the Scriptures would always be tempted to act as judges, with the very real risk of presenting their own interests and viewpoints as the only valid and correct norm of God's Word. The literate would thus have a decided advantage over the non-literate as far as the Bible is concerned.

In the present situation in the Third World, literacy is a key for access to resources of knowledge, power and wealth; and inversely, illiteracy usually bars people from all these. It is natural, therefore, that, all things being equal, the non-literate will tend to be among the less advantaged, among the powerless and those most likely to be oppressed and exploited. If then, they are incapable of taking an active part in reflecting over the Bible; the project of a liberating theology is largely in vain. There is the frightening possibility that theology, dominated by the more advantaged, will not be really for the liberation of those on the underside of history.

## CONCLUSION

The gravity of this situation becomes evident in the case of a continent like Africa where illiteracy is so high. And taking the example of Malawi, we saw that the predicament of the Catholic population was quite tragic. The conclusion seems to be, then, that a major concern for those interested in developing an effective theology in Africa should be to make sure that literacy is not the only condition for access to Holy Scripture.

This paper attempted to suggest how this could be done: how the Bible could very well become accessible to non-literate people through the media adapted to their way of life. It does not pretend to offer elaborate recipes or ready-made prescriptions. All we are saying is that there is need to liberate ourselves from the idea that only those who have the advantage of modern education can take part in developing the kind of liberating theology that Africa needs today.

## NOTES

1  'Final Communiqué: Pan-African Conference of Third World Theologians: Dec. 17–23, 1977', in K. Appiah-Kubi and S. Torres (eds), *African Theology en Route* (Maryknoll, NY, Orbis Books, 1979), pp. 192–3.

2  C. Mesters, 'The Use of the Bible in Christian Communities of the Common People', in N. K. Gottwald (ed.), *The Bible and Liberation* (Maryknoll, NY, Orbis Books, 1983), p. 124.

3  The collective work, ed. N. K. Gottwald, *The Bible and Liberation* (cf. note 2), is a good example of such studies. J. Severino Croatto's penetrating study, 'Biblical Hermeneutics in the Theologies of Liberation', ed. V. Fabella and S. Torres, *Irruption of the Third World* (Maryknoll, NY, Orbis Books, 1983), pp. 140–68, will be familiar to EATWOT members.

4  cf. *1987 Britannica Book of the Year* (Chicago, Encyclopaedia Britannica, 1987), pp. 914–19. Of 55 African countries, 30 have an adult literacy of less than 50 per cent. Except for Lesotho (62 per cent male: 84.5 per cent female), in all other countries the female literacy is below that of the male, sometimes very dramatically so – for example, Chad (35.63 per cent male: 0.5 per cent female).

5    D. B. Barrett (cf. *Schism and Renewal in Africa*, Oxford, Oxford University Press, 1968) has rightly established, in the case of Africa, a correlation between literacy and availability of the Scriptures in the local language on the one hand and the growth of Church independency on the other. But he surely did not imply that all meaningful contact with the Bible is through direct reading of the Book. The question, then, of liberative or non-liberative use of Scripture is not exactly the same as that of the growth of independency.

6    cf. *1987 Britannica Book of the Year*. ibid.

7    I. Linden with J. Linden, *Catholics, Peasants, and Chewa Resistance in Nyasaland* (Berkeley and Los Angeles, University of California Press, 1974), p. 8.

8    'Dogmatic Constitution on Divine Revelation', n. 10; cf. *Vatican Council II*, vol. I, ed. A. Flannery (Northport, NY, Costello Publishing Co., 1984), p. 755.

9    Many new translations of the Bible or portions thereof in African languages have been made or are in progress (cf. J. S. Mbiti, *Bible and Theology in African Christianity* (Nairobi, Oxford University Press, 1986, esp. pp. 22–5)). The Catholic Symposium of Episcopal Conferences in Africa and Madagascar (SECAM) has set up a biblical apostolate centre in Nairobi with the objective of promoting Bible knowledge among Catholics in Africa.

10    S. Torres and V. Fabella (eds), *The Emergent Gospel: Theology from the Underside of History* (Maryknoll, NY, Orbis books, 1978), p. 269.

11    V. Fabella (ed.), *Asia's Struggle for Full Humanity*, Maryknoll, NY, Orbis Books, 1980), pp. 156–7.

12    cf. note 1.

# 30

# A Nicaraguan Example: The Alabaster Bottle – Matthew 26.6–13

A new phenomenon to come out of Latin America in recent years is the establishment of grassroots Christian communities. One such community that became famous was at Solentiname in Nicaragua. Its popularity was the result of two factors. One was its involvement in the revolutionary struggles, and the other the biblical commentaries that came out of its weekly worship meetings. The community gathered weekly to study the Bible under the leadership of Ernesto Cardenal (the 'I' of this passage). Hermeneutics was undertaken in the face of the torture, death and terror practised by the national guards of Samosa's army.

This piece is reproduced from the fourth volume of the collection – *The Gospel in Solentiname* (Maryknoll, NY Orbis Books, 1982).

It was in Bethany. When they were sitting at the table a girl approached Jesus and poured perfume on his head.

*When the disciples saw this, they were angry and they began to say: 'Why this waste? This could have been sold for much money to help the poor.'*

WILLIAM:  Maybe they were thinking she was bewitching him.

OSCAR:  If they'd sold it, it would have gone to only a small number of the poor, and the poor of the world are countless. On the other hand, when she offered it to Jesus, she was giving it, in his person, to all the poor. That made it clear it was Jesus we believe in. And believing in Jesus makes us concerned about other people, and we'll even get to create a society where there'll be no poor. Because if we're Christians there shouldn't be any poor.

I:  John, in telling this, says that the one who was criticizing was Judas, and he says that Judas said it because he was in charge of the money and that he was a 'thief.' And he also adds that Judas calculated that it was worth about 300 denarii (which is about 1,000 pesos).

OLIVIA:   It would seem that the one who said that said it sincerely, but it was hypocrisy, because he wasn't going to give it to the poor. Just like now, what an abundance of things there are, and the poor don't even get a whiff of anything.

WILLIAM:   Everything should really have been given to the poor, not just that perfume, so there was no reason for criticism.

GLORIA:   Maybe if she'd poured the perfume on herself nobody would have criticized her.

TERESITA:   It's possible that he'd done her some favor, some miracle, and the only way she found of thanking him was to perfume him.

I:   It seems that this girl, who John in his version calls Mary, is the same Mary Magdalene out of whom Jesus cast seven devils.

ALEJANDRO:   An expensive prostitute, it seems she was, one of the expensive ones.

WILLIAM:   Yes, because she was carrying a very precious bottle.

ALEJANDRO:   Possibly she saw herself as a slave, an exploited one, and saw in him her liberation.

TERESITA:   But why does she have to have been middle class? She could have been a poor prostitute, a working girl.

WILLIAM:   But all that perfume. And the bottle. The alabaster bottle!

I:   The alabaster bottle was sealed, and it had to be broken to use the perfume. The perfume could be used only once. And the Gospel says the whole house was filled with the fragrance of nard. It's believed that nard was an ointment that came from India.

TERESITA:   Maybe a smuggler paid her with that.

MARIA:   Jesus was a poor man, too, and he too deserved to have the perfume poured on him.

I:   And worse off than poor, for they were going to kill him two days later. In the passage before this, Jesus said that it was two days to Passover. And in the following passage it's told that Judas went away from there to make the bargain to sell him.

A STUDENT FROM MANAGUA:   The Magdalene was used to that perfumed life, and things like that, and so she's being grateful according to her way of life. She's accustomed to a life of perfumes, jewels, carousing. And she pours perfume on him because that's the life she led, she thinks that's logical.

WILLIAM: She's accustomed to squander everything on the man she loves. And she doesn't have that economical mentality of the others. She squanders it right there. And she's not making economical calculations, like Judas.

DONALD: The criticism must have been because that perfume was one of the most costly, but for her it was still cheap to spend it on Jesus, because of what Jesus had done for her earlier. She wasn't paying even a quarter of what she owed him.

JOSE (*Maria's husband, who works in the San José Bank*): But Jesus hasn't forgotten the poor, because notice that in the following verse he says they will always have the poor among them. He means that if they want to help the poor they can be helping them a lot, later. They'll have the opportunity to give everything to the poor.

> *Jesus heard this and said to them:*
> *'Why do you bother this woman?*
> *This thing that she has done is a good thing.*
> *The poor you will always have among you,*
> *but you will not always have me.'*

BOSCO: That's stupid.

LAUREANO: That's a pretty weak answer because to say you're always going to have the poor is pretty silly.

I: But isn't it true that we've always had them?

LAUREANO: But we're not always *going* to have them.

WILLIAM: This is a phrase much used by reactionaries to say there'll always have to be poor people, because Christ said so. The world can't change, because according to Jesus there'll always have to be rich and poor.

I: He doesn't say there'll always be poor. Let's read it again.

MYRIAM (*reads*): The poor you will always have among you.

WILLIAM: And the 'always'? How must we interpret that 'always'?

I: Very simply. As long as there are poor, they will always be among us, we shall not be separated from them. Because the Christian community must be with the poor.

WILLIAM: But there's that 'always.' Are there always going to be poor people? That's what disturbs me.

I: He says they are never going to be separated from the poor. That's not the same as saying there'll never stop being poor people. As long as there are poor, they'll always have them at their side, and among them.

TOMAS PEÑA: When there's no more poor they won't.

A STUDENT: I've got it! He says 'among you.' He's referring to *them*, to his disciples, but that doesn't mean there'll never fail to be poor; he's not talking to all of humanity.

LAUREANO: Well, it *was* the disciples that he was saying that to. The disciples always have to be among the poor; they couldn't be among the rich.

TOMAS PEÑA: There's lots of ways of being poor: a poor person can be somebody with an arm missing. A poor person is somebody born stupid, or an orphan child, without parents. These will be in the community. There'll always be people like that in need, but of course if we're Christians they won't be poor, in poverty; if they're among us, that is, we won't let them perish.

NATALIA: Like what's happened in Cuba, where they treat the orphan children with enormous affection, and the insane, the old folks, the crippled, the widows. They're all cared for.

OLIVIA: It could also be that he was telling them instead, it seems to me, that there wouldn't be rich people, that everybody had to become poor. That there must be only poor people. That's what socialism claims. The revolution isn't so we'll all be rich but so we'll all be poor, so there'll be enough for everybody. Not disastrous poor but comfortable poor, tidy, clean, with medicine, with human dignity.

　　Or is it maybe that since there'll always be progress there'll always be new needs and there'll always be people that are needy? Those would be the poor.

I: That's what the reactionaries say. That even though there may be a lot of progress in humanity there'll always be a difference between rich and poor. That there'll never be a perfect society, a society all equal.

FELIPE:   It seems that if things are well distributed there can't be any rich; then everybody's poor.

I:   Jesus is referring to the beggars. It's for the beggars that, according to Judas, they should have sold the perfume. And it seems to me that's not a good prophecy of Jesus, and that it contradicts his announcement of the kingdom of heaven, saying that we'd always have beggars with us. I think what he's saying is that he's going away but that in place of him the poor are left. What that woman was doing with him, they'd have to do later with the poor, because he wasn't going to be there any longer, or rather, we were going to have his presence in the poor. But can it be forever that he'll not be there? The Gospel speaks of a second coming. He was going away and he was coming back.

FELIPE:   When there's that society that we dream about, that's when he's coming back, and we'll have him, and there won't be any poor people.

I:   Helpless orphans, people who have to go begging, or that sleep under a tree, or die in the streets the way the consumptives die in Managua, that's what's not going to exist when he comes. People for whom you ought to sell a bottle of perfume if you have one. All this now has disappeared in Cuba, and in all the other socialist countries. What supporters of capitalistic inequality say, that there will always be poor, has already stopped being true in socialist countries.

ELVIS:   Then there'll be no need to sell any bottles of perfume, and people can use those perfumes, like that alabaster bottle, if they think it's useful to use those perfumes.

MYRIAM:   And pouring perfume on anybody will be the same as pouring it on Christ.

I:   So you can answer these people who defend inequality: there will always be poor people as long as Jesus isn't here. But when there's only equality and justice, and no needy, no beggars, Jesus will be with us again.

WILLIAM:   This passage has also been used to justify big spending for luxury in churches. Because Jesus accepted the pouring of perfume on him. But right here it says that afterwards we'd have to do that with the poor; we couldn't do it to him in church because he wasn't going to be with us in person.

OSCAR:   He wasn't going to be with us in person? He was going to be with us in the person of others.

OLIVIA:   What that woman did was a lesson for us, and a reminder, so that what's spent in great temples that are good for nothing can be better spent on people, on the poor people he left behind. Now we do have to give to the poor, because the poor are present with us. What she had present was Jesus, his person; now we have him present but in the person of the poor.

FELIPE:   Those who now want to spend a lot on church buildings and not on the poor, they're repeating what Judas did in opposing pouring perfume on Jesus. Judas did it because he wanted to get the money, and the people that now want all the spending for the churches, it's for the same reason, because they live off that money. They're thieves.

WILLIAM:   What he's trying to tell them is that they're worrying about something silly, and they're not worrying about all the perfume that's been poured onto other stupid things.

I:   And that they're going to go on having poor people. And besides, they're not going to do anything for them.

WILLIAM:   He's telling them they don't do a damned thing for the poor.

OLIVIA:   I also see there, in that woman's attitude, the change in her. It seems to me that for that woman the most valuable thing she's found among her possessions is that alabaster. She's changed her attitude and from that day on she's begun to love, and she's given up the best thing she has. It seems to me that it's also a very good lesson for the bourgeoisie, because poor people don't have anything to give, only love; but for people that do have, Magdalene's lesson is very important: give up what you have, and it's no good to be beating your chest and giving lots of charity to a church, and not give what you have to the poor. She looked at Jesus, she saw him humbler than herself, and more deserving to use that alabaster, that fragrance, and she put the perfume on Jesus. It seems to me that she intended to give herself, all of herself, with that perfume. She looked at him: Jesus looked like a poor man, like a proletarian, because he never was in those big mansions with rich clothes or anything; so she saw him with that simplicity and that humility, and he deserved the best there was.

ALEJANDRO:   Besides, he must have needed that cleaning up.

I:   That perfume that they poured on people was like a deodorant, because there was no running water then; people weren't always bathing. And Jesus must have been, we might say, just a little smelly.

> *What this woman has done,*
> *in pouring this perfumed oil on my body,*
> *is to prepare me for my burial.*

FELIPE:   Maybe because they wouldn't pour any on him when they killed him.

I:   He is predicting his violent death, without a normal burial. He really wasn't embalmed. When the women arrived with ointments on the third day (and this Mary was with them), he was no longer there. And could it not be that she was doing this on purpose, foreseeing what was soon going to happen to him, and Jesus understood her purpose? Because in the previous passage Jesus had told his friends that it was two days until Passover, and that he was going to be delivered up to the Romans.

> *In truth I tell you,*
> *that wherever this good news*
> *is announced throughout the world,*
> *what this woman did will also be told,*
> *so that you may remember her.*

I:   But at the same time he foresees his immediate death, he foresees that his good news about liberation will be announced throughout the whole world. And that whenever his violent death is remembered, with no funeral, like the death of any subversive, they will remember what that woman did, as part of the good news.

OLIVIA:   It seems to me that the remembering is for us also to do what she did. So that we do it now, not to him anymore, but to the poor. Or to him in the person of the poor. That's why we must remember her. That woman gave up a luxury. She was used to that kind of life, to those luxuries. As I see it, when she poured that very expensive perfume on Jesus she was giving up all her luxuries and squanderings and that's why Jesus defended her from the criticism. You ought to see how the bourgeois live and what they spend on perfumes and clothes and on the mansions they live in and on their automobiles. And her example and the lesson that Jesus is giving is that you have to give now to the poor.

And people like us who don't have perfumes or luxurious things to give because we're poor?

FELIPE: We can give other valuable things that we have.

LAUREANO: We can offer our lives as Jesus did. Then it'll be also for us, that perfume that the woman poured on Jesus.

# 31

# An Indonesian Example: The Miraculous Catch – Luke 5.1–11

Inspired by the Nicaraguan example, the editor of the *International Review of Mission* invited several grassroot communities to send in their comments on selected passages. These were published in the October 1977 issue. These are the reflections of community workers, both professionals and volunteers, who were actively involved in the welfare of those marginalized in Solo, Indonesia. The group included a Muslim. The printed pages may not convey the smiles, anger, surprise and joy that this group experienced but, in spite of this limitation, this example shows how people in different situations appropriate the word with vigour and freshness.

*One of the group read the first three verses of the text:*

> One time Jesus was standing on the shore of Lake Gennesaret while the people pushed their way up to him to listen to the word of God. He saw two boats pulled up on the beach; the fishermen had left them and gone off to wash the nets. Jesus got into one of the boats – it belonged to Simon – and asked him to push off a little from the shore. Jesus sat in the boat and taught the crowd (Luke 5.1–3).

MRS ARIS (*the rural case worker, listens thoughtfully and says*):   In verse 2, Jesus gives us an example of how he conducted his ministry without using any elaborate facilities. He taught from an ordinary boat and not always in the temple. We ought to educate the people to use their simple facilities and not just wait for better ones.

ONE OF THE WOMEN AGREES:   You're right. We have to educate the people, even though we do it in an open field. Jesus worked outside more often than inside the temple.

BAMBANG (*another rural case worker*):   If Jesus had taught more often in the temple, people wouldn't have believed him. They'd have hated him. But he taught in the midst of the people, outside the temple, and they believed.

*He continues with the reading:*
When he finished speaking, he said to Simon, 'Push the boat out further to the deep water, and you and your partners let your nets down for a catch.' 'Master', Simon answered, 'we worked hard all night long and caught nothing. But if you say so, I will let down the nets.' They let the nets down and caught such a large number of fish that the nets were about to break. So they motioned to their partners in the other boat to come and help them. They came and filled both boats so full of fish that they were about to sink (Luke 5.4–7).

A VILLAGE TEACHER:   In verse 5 you can see that the disciples obeyed Jesus.

MISS YATI (*the administrator of community development projects*):
Although our job is hard, even risky, we have to obey the Lord's words.

MISS DEBORA (*a labour organizer*):   But we shouldn't feel desperate as we face our job. Often, in our most discouraged moments when we're feeling frail and weak, the Lord comes to help us.

MISS ANNA (*a Muslim law student*):   You know, it's interesting. Peter didn't catch all those fish for himself; he shared them with his friends, so that others, too, might feel the blessing of the Lord.

ANOTHER STUDENT:   One point interested me: In verses 1–3 Jesus taught and preached. In verses 4–7, he did what he taught. Words were followed by deeds.

BAMBANG:   Peter and the other disciples helped each other. That means that we have to be able to work together and cooperate with all kinds of groups in society to improve the mutual welfare.

ONE OF THE WOMEN ADDS:   If we work among the people, we can feel their suffering. Like Peter – he knew the distress of his friends who caught no fish.

MRS ARIS:   At night Peter failed to catch fish but after he served Jesus, there was a ray of hope. So often the Holy Spirit comes upon us just at the moment we fail. That's what happened to Peter.

MISS ANNA:   Was Peter's catch a matter of fate?

YANIS (*the pastor*):   In verses 6 and 7 we see a case of income equality and a spirit in Peter that shows no egotism. But if he hadn't shared with his friends, his ship would have sunk and his friends would have had no fish.

BAMBANG: If the other disciples hadn't come to help Peter, they would not have gotten any fish.

MISS DEBORA (*speaking from her experience as a labour organizer*): It seems to happen just the other way round in our society. For instance, foreign employers drain our fish and our properties for their own profit without sharing or making any adequate compensation.

MISS ANNA: It's a case of the strong against the weak.

YANIS (*reads*):

> When Simon Peter saw what had happened, he fell on his knees before Jesus and said, 'Go away from me, Lord, for I am a sinful man!' He and all the others with him were amazed at the large number of fish they had caught. The same was true of Simon's partners, James and John, the sons of Zebedee. Jesus said to Simon, 'Don't be afraid; from now on you will be catching men.' They pulled the boats on the beach, left everything and followed Jesus (Luke 5.8–11).

MISS DEBORA: Our organization doesn't work long in one spot, but leaves after a certain time, to let people go forward and grow by themselves.

MRS RIBKAH: Perhaps we should say instead that we dare to abandon *our* stake in *them*; we free them from it.

YANIS: There are here, it seems to me, three steps to follow: confession, repentance and then mission.

MISS ANNA: Verse 5 simply stated a matter of fact. That's the way it is, and for us, too: we've already been toiling.

MISS YATI: And it was clear in verse 7 that in that work there was danger.

YANIS: One important thing in verse 7 is that the load of fish was shared equally between the two boats so that both were loaded. We are very much concerned, not for those who have, but rather for the have-nots. We never send funds to, let's say, one of the well-known pre-schools in our city, but, instead, to the children of families of village people for their education.

# 32

# A South African Example: Jesus' Teaching at Nazareth – Luke 4.14–30

This is the other example introduced in the last essay. Here are the reflections of a group from Claremont, Cape Town. It consisted of Blacks, Coloureds and Whites. The names are fictitious. Most of them were involved in some form of social action. Squatters and black unrest were the heremeneutical backdrop for their reflections.

MAG (*after introducing the study*):   Maybe we could pretend we are going to make a television film of the incident, first as it happened, then, later, as it might appear in our situation.

REB (*the theological student, read Luke 4.14–21*):

Then Jesus went to Nazareth, where he had been brought up, and on the Sabbath day he went as usual to the meeting house. He stood up to read the Scriptures, and was handed the book of the prophet Isaiah. He unrolled the scroll and found the place where it is written:

'The Spirit of the Lord is upon me.
He has anointed me to preach the Good News to the poor,
He has sent me to proclaim liberty to the captives,
And recovery of sight to the blind,
To set free the oppressed,
To announce the year when the Lord will save his people!'

Jesus rolled up the scroll, gave it back to the attendant, and sat down. All the people in the meeting house had their eyes fixed on him. He began speaking to them: 'This passage of scripture has come true today, as you heard it being read.'

MAG:   Who are the people we need for the film? What are they like?

SALLY (*the ex-nun*):   Typical religious congregation . . . upholders of the *status quo* . . . like the local authority officials we are dealing with.

REB:   No, like ANY church congregation, like the people in the church I went to a few weeks ago to talk about squatters, and they got very uptight and some of them went off to another parish where they wouldn't get this sort of thing.

MAG:   Were they workers?

WILL (*the community worker*):   Yes, they were Nazareth people so they were shepherds and workers, and they knew Jesus from long ago.

LIN (*who works for the Anglican social responsibility board*):   And there were visitors, too, probably, because it says Jesus was well known and popular in Galilee.

MAG:   Do you think the locals welcomed the visitors?

ANN (*a student*):   'Perhaps they weren't too keen on them, especially if they caused a disturbance.

(*Nobody mentions Jesus as a character in the film. We all take him for granted.*)

MAG:   So what happened?

ANN:   He went into the synagogue and during the service he was given the scroll and he read from it.

WILL:   He chose that bit of prophecy from Isaiah about the deliverer who would set the people free.

MAG:   Were they free in Jesus' time?

REB:   No, they were under the Romans and they were probably very disappointed in Jesus that he wasn't going to lead a revolution against the Romans, but only give them spiritual liberation.

SALLY:   But it wasn't just spiritual . . . he did do things like giving sight to the blind.

REB:   But he didn't liberate captives.

MAG:   Didn't he?

REB:   Well, it depends what you mean by captives, because he did set people free from their lusts and selfishness and attitudes like that.

SALLY:   Yes, and he gave them hope that things would be better.

WILL:　But he was saying that today the prophecy was fulfilled and things were still the same, so they must have been disappointed.

LIN:　It depends what your concepts are of how change comes about. He wasn't just promising something invisible and internal that would leave outside things the same.

MAG:　Let's look at the different actions promised.

SALLY:　He said he would heal the brokenhearted . . . he comforts people and encourages them.

REB:　And he gives them insight, helps them to see the things they can't see, or don't want to see.

LIN:　He's exposing the truth, exposing people to the truth.

WILL:　But people don't always want that.

ANN:　They probably reacted in different ways then – some of them enthusiastic and others skeptical.

MAG:　The skeptical ones would have been particularly put off by the last bit about the acceptable year of the Lord because the Jubilee Year, every fiftieth year when slaves were to be set free and everything shared out again, never really happened.

REB:　Some of the people could have felt threatened because he was saying things were going to change. He attracted people and so he could be taking away some of their power.

SALLY:　Others would be glad because he was offering them something.

*After reading Luke 4.22–30:*

> They were all well impressed with him, and marveled at the beautiful words that he spoke. They said, 'Isn't he the son of Joseph?' He said to them: 'I am sure that you will quote the proverb to me, "Doctor, heal yourself." You will also say to me, "Do here in your own home town the same things we were told happened in Capernaum." I tell you this', Jesus added: 'A prophet is never welcomed in his own home town. Listen to me: it is true that there were many widows in Israel during the time of Elijah, when there was no rain for three and a half years and there was a great famine throughout the whole land. Yet Elijah was not sent to a single one of them, but only to a widow of Zarephath, in the territory of Sidon. And there were many lepers in Israel during the time of the prophet Elisha; yet not one of them was made clean, but only Naaman the Syrian.' All the people in the meeting house were filled with anger when they heard this. They rose up, dragged Jesus

out of town, and took him to the top of the hill on which their town was built, to throw him over the cliff. But he walked through the middle of the crowd and went his way.

SALLY: I'm reminded of that little boy from one of our townships here who made good as a singing star and the others acted as if it wasn't anything special. One boy said, 'I knew him when he ran round the streets without any pants on when he was two years old', as if that made any difference to the boy's success now.

WILL: Yes, people don't accept a person for what he is, they always want to classify him.

ANN: When people are familiar we take them for granted. They said Jesus was just Joseph's son, as if that meant they didn't need to listen to him.

MAG: How did Jesus react to their rejection?

WILL: He challenged them. Mentioning Capernaum wasn't very tactful, there was probably rivalry between the villages.

REB: He really confronted them; he used their history to give them examples of other situations of rejection ... that widow, and Naaman the leper, who was a foreigner.

MAG: Did he upset everybody?

SALLY: No, the 'groupies' were there, the ones who had followed him round, and they were probably on his side.

LIN: And when some wanted to throw him over the hill, others made it difficult and he got away.

MAG: So it wasn't just a quiet Sabbath service?

REB: Far from it; he really caused a disturbance and stirred them all up.

MAG: Perhaps at this point we could turn to the modern situation and look at the parallels like ...

SALLY: The officials we have to deal with.

REB: And the ordinary church congregations.

WILL: And the people who support the *status quo*.

ANN: And the oppressed who want change and are looking for leadership.

MAG: Who plays the Jesus role in our situations?

REB: The one who tells the truth, especially to the oppressors.

ANN: Anyone who stands up for what is right.

LIN: The people who attack unjust structures.

MAG: You mean people like us here!

REB: Well, yes, though I don't suppose we quite like to put it that way.

SALLY: But that is what we are trying to do.

MAG: So, how do we avoid falling into the trap of self-righteousness?

SALLY: That's where other people come in, why we must be in community, so that we can expose one another to the truth.

REB: We need mutual correction, we can take criticism from people we trust.

LIN: Does that mean we can only expose the truth to people we already trust? Can't we go and confront the officials who are upholding an unjust system?

REB: Yes, but we mustn't be on our own, we need all the time to be checking out with one another.

MAG: What does this say about our churches, where the pattern is: one talks and the rest listen?

WILL: That's all wrong, of course, because we need something different.

REB: Yes, we have to be sharing with one another.

SALLY: We need to be close to people we can trust and be talking with them.

MAG: So, is there a danger of group self-righteousness?

REB AND SALLY: Oh yes, we can easily fall into that. That's why we have to be working with different kinds of people and organizations like the ones who were with us last night [at a meeting about squatters].

LIN: But how did you react to that chap who was giving that great story about volunteers and how he wanted everybody to be coordinated and helping the committee?

REB: We don't want people to work for the [coordinating] committee. We want them to be themselves in their own situation, to get to see the truth and do something about it.

MAG:  So, could we look at the meaning in our situation of those actions Jesus quoted?

REB:  People are captives to the idea that they must be like somebody else or that they must follow a certain programme; but they need internal liberation and then the other things will follow. It doesn't matter which power rules, people need internal liberation. After we get majority rule, there will still be oppression – if people don't change inside.

LIN:  But is that enough? Can you be free inside if the situation is still bad?

REB:  People want quite simple things, like a chap I worked with on a building site who just wanted to save enough money to buy a plot of land to settle on with his family.

ANN:  We want deliverance from oppression.

WILL:  We want to live freely as we used to before the white man came. When I was a small boy, my grandfather had land, cattle, sheep, goats, plenty of land that they tilled and could reap good harvests and had cows to milk. And life was good. You felt you had what you wanted. But they took the land away from him; something to do with title deeds and white farmers, and that happened to other blacks as well, and the men had to work for the white farmers or come to town to work. So that's how we came here.

MAG:  But is that idea of a farm of your own what you want or are you a town man?

WILL:  No, I am a town man, I want to live freely in town.

ANN:  We want to be accepted as human beings, want the right to be here, live here, have comfortable homes.

WILL:  And share in the government of the country.

LIN:  Will there still be rich and poor?

WILL:  Yes, but not on lines of race.

MAG:  Will the country as a whole be changed after, say, ten to twenty years of majority rule?

SALLY:  It makes me think of the early church and the way they shared everything and no one was in want.

REB:  Political change won't bring that about. There will still be exploitation unless people change inside.

428

MAG:   Can the ideal or principle of sharing apply to a wider society?'

LIN:   We're in the process of getting concessions towards multi-racial integration, but this could just mean that in twenty years' time the Nationalist Party will still be ruling the country on the basis of Progressive Party policy.

WILL:   Blacks can be just as oppressive as whites.

REB:   Black slaves in the USA used to sublimate their hopes and sing songs about heaven, and blacks tend to do that here.

ANN:   But, lately, at the funerals we have noticed that when we sing the hymns, the words of the first verse are traditional, and then the second verse has different words that the youth have composed, and then, maybe, the third verse is traditional, and so on. And after a while the older people join in with the new words as well as the traditional ones and you can see from their faces that they are sharing the feelings and aspirations of the youth.

LIN:   Have these songs been written down? What ideas are being expressed?

ANN:   No, it hasn't gone that far.

WILL:   It's rather spontaneous.

MAG:   So, have we any clearer idea of what good news to the poor means in our situation?

ANN:   It means that they will have the chance to share and be accepted as full human beings.

REB:   I come back to those early Christians and their experiment. Communal life is possible under any regime – it's a matter of the spirit and just getting on with it.

SALLY:   We must live the sharing.

LIN:   But we'll go on externally just the same, with war on the border and all the rest of it?

REB:   No, things would change. We must clear the communication channels. This sharing life isn't just passive, the togetherness is active and reaches out to other people.

SALLY:   You mean it's catchy, infectious?

REB:   We must actively persuade people by our example and by our challenging of their values.

MAG:   How does this sound to the blacks? Do you think, Will, that black youth would go for what Reb is saying?

WILL:   In the black consciousness movement, there is a strong stress on communalism and egalitarianism. We want the kind of society in which there is sharing.

MAG:   Does the black consciousness movement rely on education and persuasion or on political action and confrontation too?

WILL:   Black community programmes are putting the philosophy into practice, educating people in what communalism means.

MAG:   Isn't there a double thrust, educational and political, BCP and BPC (Black People's Convention)? Isn't it a matter of walking on two legs?

WILL:   Yes.

LIN:   I like that expression, walking on two legs. We need both emphases, on the internal change and on the external confrontation with structures. Otherwise we can end up like some people I know on a rural commune about 200 km from here. They are very happy on their farm, sharing with one another, but they are completely irrelevant to the rest of our situation.

# 33

# A Chinese Example: 'The Silences of the Bible'

## K. H. TING

Different people seek different things in the Bible. Here is an attempt to introduce the Bible to new and younger Chinese Christians. This piece, reprinted from Ting's book, *How to Study the Bible* (Hong Kong, Tao Fong Shan Ecumenical Centre, 1981), is a reminder that one has to listen not only to the voices, but also to the silences, in the Bible, in order to discern the word.

Bishop Ting is an internationally known and eminent leader in the Chinese Christian community. A collection of his writings has been published under the title, *No Longer Strangers* (Maryknoll, NY, Orbis Books, 1989).

## THE SILENCES OF THE BIBLE

We must listen to what the Bible says to us; we must also pay attention to what the Bible does not say to us. There are some things which the Bible does not say and there are good reasons for this.

In that famous painting entitled 'The Light of the World,' Jesus, holding a lamp in one hand, is knocking on the door of a house. There were those who noticed that there was no handle on the door and they raised this point with the artist. The artist said it wasn't that he had forgotten it but that he wanted to use this to tell us that Jesus is standing sorrowfully outside the house knocking on the door. But this door may only be opened from the inside, if the person inside is willing.

In the same way, there are some things which the Bible does not mention, but this is not due to God's forgetting them. In those things which are not mentioned there is also a message which he wants to tell us.

For example, how does the parable of the Prodigal Son end? Does the older brother finally listen to his father's exhortations and return home to make peace with his brother? Or does he continue in his arrogant behavior, remaining outside the house, unwilling to enter? No one knows. This parable ends suddenly just at the point where our interest is greatest. Why? Because we are that elder brother; whether we finally enter the house or remain outside depends on us. The blank space after Luke 15.32 is for each of us to fill in.

In the entire Bible, there is one book which concludes with a question mark. This is the Book of Jonah. God asks Jonah a question but the Bible does not tell us Jonah's reply and the Book of Jonah ends here. And why is this? We must realize, this is not only a question God asked of Jonah. Even more so, he is asking it of us. And he is waiting eagerly for our answer.

The silences in the Bible are important. In its silences, there are also tiny voices speaking in our souls, exhorting us.

Of the sixty-six books in the Bible, there is one – the Book of Esther – which does not once mention God, from beginning to end. What is this particular silence telling us?

Esther is a young woman who accomplished a very wise and courageous thing for the well-being of her people. The book makes clear that God's hand is moving in the affairs of the world, even though God is never mentioned. God himself was glad about what Esther did for her people, and was willing to have this book among those in the Bible.

That the Bible has in it a book which doesn't even mention God, is clearly telling us that the things which God cares for far surpass what we term 'religion.' God does not place importance on mere words. Esther's courageous action, done out of passionate love for her country and people, is not outside God's care and providence.

Therefore, we can say that while whatever is written in the Bible is naturally important, there is also a message in whatever silences the Bible keeps.

Biblical silence has yet another important function. It is like a red light, telling us that we should go no further.

Someone once asked Jesus: 'Lord, will those who are saved be few?' (Luke 13.23.) Jesus answered neither 'many' nor 'few.' he said, 'Strive to enter by the narrow gate.' Peter asked, 'Lord, what about this man?' (John 21.21.) Jesus didn't answer this either. He just said, 'What is that to you? Follow me!'

The disciples begged Jesus to tell them about the day when he would come again (Matt. 24.3), but Jesus said to them: 'But of that day and hour no one knows, not even the angels of heaven, nor the son, but the Father only' (v. 36). Later the disciples again asked, 'Will you at this time restore the Kingdom to Israel?' (Acts 1.6.) Still, Jesus said, 'It is not for you to know times or seasons which the Father has fixed by his own authority. But you shall receive power when the Holy Spirit has come upon you; . . . and be my witnesses.' We can see that Christ does not want us to probe deeply into certain questions. When we do ask these questions he answers us with silence, at the same time reminding us to take care of our own responsibilities, to do our present tasks. The Bible tells us, 'the secret things belong to the Lord our God; but the things that are revealed belong to us and to our children for ever, that we may do all the words of this law' (Deut. 29.29). It is obvious that, as human beings, we must recognize that there are some things which we have to be agnostic about.

The conclusion of the Gospel of John says, 'But there are also many other things which Jesus did; were every one of them to be written, I suppose that the world itself could not contain the books that would be written.' Fortunately the Bible was not written to satisfy our curiosity, but to allow those who hunger and thirst for righteousness to know Jesus and to seek to become holy. The Bible offers us sufficient and clear guidance for this goal. We really have no reason to desire more.

What, then, is the truth which the Lord wants us to enter into, and what are the things he does not want us to probe?

Whatever God is willing to reveal to us – the truth which he wants us to enter into – is whatever can help us to become better children of God. Whatever will not aid us in becoming better children of God is, then, not the Biblical truth which God wants us to enter into. In his prayer to the Father, Jesus says: 'Sanctify them in the truth; thy word is truth' (John 17.17).

Sadly, there are times when we are not willing to follow the Spirit humbly, when we are not willing to respect the silences of the Spirit, but, stiff-necked, insist on knowing those things that God does not yet want us to know. Some take human ways of reckoning and presumptuous understanding to be Biblical truth and pass them on to others. They even use them to build themselves up to the point of attacking those loyal, humble souls who do not dare to be wildly arrogant. This is extremely dangerous.

# Postscript: Achievements and Items for a Future Agenda

## R. S. SUGIRTHARAJAH

The essays assembled here are representative examples of the hermeneutical trek of a people attempting to make sense of their faith and their scriptural text in the light of their context. None of these hermeneuts would wish to claim that their articulations are definitive exegetical statements, or the products of a 'school'. They represent the hermeneutical odyssey of a loosely knit but deeply committed people, sharing common causes, and trying to regain their humanity and selfhood and a sense of purpose for their lives.

What these essays demonstrate is that all biblical interpretations are contextual and arise out of life experience, and are intrinsically tied to the milieu in which they are produced and articulated. They underline the fact that a contextual approach is the key to the recovery of the Bible. A contextual reading of the Bible strengthens the view that the meaning of the biblical message is retrievable when it is read from a concrete situation. For the underprivileged, the blacks, women, and Christians who live amidst adherents of other faiths, reading the Bible from their own perspective does not threaten its catholicity; rather, it releases the word of God from its timeless neutrality and ideological abstraction, and helps to bring out its multifaceted concrete and novel dimensions.

What then are these hermeneuts trying to do apart from giving a voice to the voiceless? What do the expositions of this marginal minority highlight? One can itemize the following, not necessarily in this order, as major achievements of the hermeneutics of the marginalized.

## 1 The repossession of the Christian Scripture by ordinary people

One of the major achievements of this approach has been to place the

Bible where it belongs – in the hands of the people. The Bible, in Paul's reckoning, is their book and was written for them (1 Cor. 10.11). It is about them, and it contains their stories, songs, hopes, disappointments, etc. In the course of time, the Bible, which was the product of and belonged to the category of popular literature, came to be regarded as an expert's book. The academy and the biblical critics have made the Bible the preserve of professionals, and have made biblical interpretation a complicated art. The array of technical skills and the mastery of many languages required to decipher the biblical narratives leaves an ordinary person with the notion that the Bible is only for the experts with the special knowledge to decode it. Often the hermeneutical pronouncements of a biblical scholar will overawe a reader. The attitude of the ordinary reader becomes: who am I to challenge and question the exegetical verdicts of giants like Bultmann or Käsemann? The aura that surrounds the professional exegete deters the uninitiated from working out their own interpretations, and tempts them to relinquish their judgement in favour of 'expert opinion'.

But now the peasants, fisherfolk, tradespeople, and housewives not only claim that the Bible is their book, but also, more importantly, have broken their dependency on others for their interpretations. The fact that ordinary people have become owners and interpreters of the Bible is something of a revolution. During the medieval period, the Christian Church used to burn and excommunicate those who attempted to translate the Bible into the languages lay people could understand. But now the Bible has been restored to the people. As the examples reproduced in Part Five indicate, they see new and exciting things in the biblical texts. More importantly, they have begun to detect parallels between their lives and those of the biblical communities. This enables them to discover new dimensions to their own lives as well as fresh understandings of the Bible. In the words of Carlos Mesters, the Dutch biblical scholar, who has pioneered the people's exegesis in base Christian communities in Brazil, 'The people are beginning to see in the Bible not only an account of past history but also a reflection of current history of which they are a part.'[1]

## 2 Solidarity and performative interpretation as ways of overcoming the hermeneutical gap

Another significant step has been the attempts of these hermeneuts to bridge what in biblical-theology circles is known as the hermeneutical gap. One of the vexing problems of biblical interpretation is how to make the interpretative trek from the biblical milieu to the present day. This problem is specifically the creation of the historical–critical methods. Historical criticism tends to introduce into the task of interpretation a division of labour between the exegete and the expositor, between the scholar and the preacher, and between biblical scholarship and theological enterprise. This is the original sin of the historical–critical method. It sees the historian's task as taking up facts and handing them over to the theologian, as if it is a relay race and the theologian's task is to complete the final lap.

These essayists, on the other hand, envisage their hermeneutical task in a dialectical fashion – a dynamic interaction between text and context, between theory and praxis, between understanding and accomplishment. For them, the role of an exegete and that of an expositor are indistinguishable. They see their task not only as seeking the authentic meaning of a text or uncovering the hidden meaning in a narrative, but also as concretizing the Word in the context. They seek to overcome the historical distance between the text and their context in two ways. First, through the criterion of solidarity, and then, through analogously participating in similar historical struggles of the people. The criterion of solidarity enables the interpreter to identify with people and their oppression, thus making the historical distance between the text and the context less conspicuous. Linked with this understanding of interpretation is the idea of enacting the Word in the context. 'In the last instance,' Gustavo Gutierrez says, 'our exegesis of the word to which theology hopes to contribute, occurs in deed.'[2] In other words, they perceive hermeneutics as an activity aimed at transforming society. Thus the quest for the historical Jesus lies not only in finding the truth about the man from Nazareth, but also in fighting for the truth that will liberate humankind. The biblical concept of resurrection becomes clear only when one brings new hope and love to people who have no hope and love. Jesus' proclamation of God's rule becomes real only when the ideals of the kingdom – love, justice and mercy – are put into practice.

## 3 The underprivileged as the hermeneutical focus

Another major achievement has been that these hermeneuts have on their own initiative and very persuasively put the needs of the people at the head of the criteria of biblical interpretation. Every new situation discloses a new hermeneutical category which the earlier interpreters had either overlooked or neglected. The claims of the poor, the blacks and women were largely ignored by the dominant biblical approaches. When the Euro-American exegetes confront these issues, they (a) spiritualize (b) neutralize or (c) patronize. The attitude is generally one of benevolent sentimentality or moral conceptualization of the causes of poverty, or denigration of the status of women and blacks.

Asian, Latin American and black hermeneuts, on the other hand, do not begin with theories or concepts, but with a praxiological commitment to redress poverty and the oppressive status of women and blacks. The experience and the concerns of the poor, women and blacks become the privileged hermeneutical focus. It is from the perspective of the losers of history that the biblical materials are read and re-read and re-heard. Identification with the underprivileged becomes the first step in understanding the Christian Scripture. Such a concentrated effort to interpret the Bible from the standpoint of the disadvantaged is new in biblical theology. In fact, the poor as the hermeneutical focus must be the starting point for any theology.

## 4 Fruitful fusion of struggles and scholarship

The exegetical efforts of these hermeneuts draw attention to the fact that academic rigour and advocacy on behalf of the weak and the needy can go hand in hand. The examples published here indicate that campaigning for contextual causes does not necessarily undermine scholarly sharpness. These expositors have very successfully opened a new relationship between the common causes of the people and biblical scholarship. The dominant biblical scholarship tends to withdraw from harsh economic realities and social problems by taking refuge in the study of the biblical past. The essayists here make a compelling case for biblical scholars to come to grips with the everyday problems that people face such as malnutrition, rape, dowry, debts, racism, hunger, bad housing, unemployment, etc.

The Euro-American biblical scholars use critical methods to unravel mysteries such as the synoptic problem or the puzzling and abrupt ending of Mark's Gospel. For a Euro-American exegete, these are tools that can make the biblical narratives meaningful to secularized people unsure of their faith. Their counterparts in the South make use of these very methods to make sense of the biblical traditions to people who are exploited but have not given up their faith. These hermeneuts have shown that these tools can also be marshalled effectively for a liberative reading of the biblical materials. Their exegetical works not only demonstrate the social responsibility of these scholars, but also show that it is possible to fuse the struggles of the common people with sophisticated scholarly enquiry.

## 5 The importance of social location and exposure of 'value-free' reading

These biblical expositions very acutely underline the significance of the socio-cultural context of the interpreter. The form-critical school has relentlessly emphasized the importance of the context of the text. The hermeneutical inputs of biblical scholars who represent the marginal minorities, and who themselves are marginal to mainline scholarship, show the significance of the context of the interpreter, especially his or her social location. All interpreters bring their own political, gender, racial and ideological and religious biases to the text.

'Objectivity', 'impartiality' and 'academic detachment' are the sacred words in the lexicon of Euro-American interpreters, but these hermeneuts openly, unapologetically and consciously declare that they take sides. They admit that only in critical solidarity with the weak and the vulnerable can they engage in the interpretative task. Their whole enterprise not only exposes the so-called objective exegesis of Euro-American exegetes, but also challenges them to reflect critically on their own unconscious prejudices, their class, gender and ideological interests. Hermeneutical neutrality is impossible in a divided world – either you are part of the solution or you are going to be part of the problem.

## 6 Setting goals – transforming the world

This approach adds an important dimension to the interpretative task; namely, it highlights the need for interpreters to have goals. Liberation hermeneutics has forced interpreters to address themselves constantly to the question of specific goals. For them, interpretation is undertaken not primarily to solve intellectual queries: the paramount concern of hermeneutics is to transform society. They see liberation as the goal of hermeneutics. The goal emerges out of one's faith, in its existential and praxiological dimensions. The goal may differ somewhat from context to context, but the important thing is to identify it in the light of the word one hears in the context.

## ITEMS FOR A FUTURE AGENDA

Where do we go from here? What are the future tasks and issues that continue to concern us?

### 1 Re-oralizing and Re-casting the message

Asian, Latin American and black hermeneuts face twin constituencies. On the one hand, they have to address the literary minority who are educated and urbanized, and on the other they have to speak to the oral majority whose way of life is not necessarily determined by a literary mode of thinking. The task, then, for these hermeneuts is not only to analyse the written word, but also to help people to hear the spoken word behind the text. After all, the Gospels originated as an oral tradition.

The way hermeneutics is undertaken today indicates that authority is invested in the written text. This reflects the current bias towards the printed word and its analysis. Both attitudes are relatively new. The written text became prominent in Europe, partly because of the Protestant need for an alternative authority, and partly as a result of the invention of printing. Historical and literary study of the text by professional exegetes is less than 200 years old and was a product of the bourgeois class of Europe and America.

In all faith traditions, including Christianity, the original authority is not the text but the word that is heard. Hindus classify their scriptural texts into two categories – *Śruti* (that which is heard) and *Smṛti* (that which is remembered). For them *Śruti* has more authority than *Smṛti*. Thus the oral word takes precedence over the written word. It also has the power to sensitize people. When the Jesus movement wrote down the words of Jesus, the prime purpose was to read them aloud publicly to assembled gatherings, and they were not meant to be read privately in a closed study. So also with the letters of Paul and other compositions of the Jesus movement. Recently, Vincent Wimbush has reminded us how the Afro-Americans who were denied the opportunity to learn, read and 'write letters', and so were denied access to the biblical texts, kept their faith and Christian tradition alive. 'What became important was the *telling* and *re-telling* [italics his], the hearing and re-hearing of biblical stories – stories of perseverance, of strength in weakness and under oppressive burdens, of hope in hopeless situations.'[3]

Along with the study of texts and their transmission, the task that lies ahead for Asian, Latin American and black hermeneuts is to open the way for a greater oral potency of the word. The oral word is more effective in conscientizing people. The written word tends to be rigid and inflexible, and stifles the spirit, tone and mood in which it is presented. Asian, Latin American and black hermeneuts in their future exegetical enterprise will need to enable the oral experience of the word and critical analysis of its written form to illuminate each other in a reciprocal solidarity. This will empower the word to come alive.

There is also the need for hermeneuts to try to share their articulations through other mediations. Besides giving expression to their cogitations in erudite language and scientific analysis, these hermeneuts need to engage in non-verbal hermeneutics. Along with the use of the written word, contextual hermeneutics should utilize other art forms such as drama, dance, song, sculpture, etc. These media may help us to discover the deeper symbolism of biblical narratives, which mere intellectual and logical approaches may not bring out. Here again, there are sporadic attempts. Two examples come immediately to mind. One is of the ever-resourceful Solentiname community. Fresh after the revolution, the peasants, who earlier had tried to articulate the biblical materials in a verbal form, have attempted to capture the biblical message through painting.[4] The other is of an Indian artist, Jyoti Sahi. Sahi has used Indian artistic conventions as a vehicle to communicate the meaning of biblical materials.[5]

## 2 Multi-faith hermeneutics

The comparative study of biblical narratives and other sacred texts is another task that awaits hermeneuts who are part of multi-religious communities. In many instances, the other faith traditions have used their sacred texts as a source of strength and inspiration in their resistance to oppression and degradation. These texts have been God's accomplices in defending human dignity and offering solace to countless millions of other religious adherents.

Comparative hermeneutics is not an entirely new enterprise. There have been earlier attempts, but they were prompted by missionary apologetics, where Christian texts were set over the others as prior, and ethically and spiritually superior. But in a changed theological climate, where other religious texts exert a great influence, the task is not to be combative, but to complement each other's textual resources. At a time when no one text can claim total and exclusive possession of the truth, and as every sacred text has spiritual wealth to enrich the others, one needs to engage in a different comparative exegetical discourse.

A recent example is that of Ishand Vempeny's work. In his book, *Krsna and Christ*,[6] based on the textual study of the New Testament and the *Bhagavad Gita*, he offers valuable insights to both faith communities – Hindu and Christian. He presents Jesus to Hindus without any proselytizing intention and also he uses texts from both traditions to remind Hindus of the forgotten Hindu ethics of socio-economic involvement on behalf of the poor and the oppressed. Similarly, he renders a very valuable service to Christians. He presents one of the colourful religious personalities, *Krsna* through the texts of the *Gita*, and so reminds them how they have lost the Christian aspect of *ananda* – joy. There is still room for such exegetical enterprise.

Linked to such comparative exegetical studies is another task, that of looking for influences and borrowings between different sacred texts. One of the fruitful insights of historical criticism is that various religious traditions are inter-dependent. It has shown how different religious traditions of the Mediterranean world are historically, culturally and theologically interrelated. It has shown that Christian faith was a development from Judaism and Judaism in turn grew out of and was enriched by the Near Eastern religions.

It is time for hermeneuts from Asia to engage in an interpretative enterprise that will go beyond the identification of the influences of Jewish and Greek thinking on the faith of the early Christians, and detect possible Hindu or Buddhist elements in the faith articulations of the early Christian movement. There have been some attempts by Euro-American scholars from the nineteenth century on, but this interest lost its momentum after the 1930s.[7] Recently, Roy C. Amore has suggested that both Christianity and Buddhism share a common message, though they may use different metaphors from their diverse cultural backgrounds. He demonstrates this possibility by showing that the Q source, which was widely used by Luke and Matthew, could have been influenced by Buddhist texts. Historical records show commercial links between India and Palestine at that time. Amore reckons that, along with the exchange of mercantile goods, one can assume the possibility of Indian thought-patterns influencing the cultural milieu where the early Christian faith germinated.[8]

The task of Asian scholars is to pursue this matter further and detect similarities and possible influences and borrowing between different traditions. The purpose is not to minimize the truth-claims of any one tradition, but to show that religious traditions are earthly, relative and do not exist in complete isolation, and that they cannot grow rejecting one another. Such an exegetical undertaking can also serve to point to the universal resonances of different sacred texts. More importantly, it can help to remove religious bigotry and communal tension caused by the alleged superiority and uniqueness of one faith tradition over another.

## 3 Blacks and biblical antiquity

A similar task awaits black hermeneuts. They need to look afresh at biblical antiquity. Recent studies have revolutionized our perception of Egypt and its relationship with other parts of Africa. The eminent position of Egypt in the ancient world and her influence on Greek thought, and the fact that some Egyptians were of black extraction, provide a new framework for a critical assessment of the status of blacks and the question of race in biblical antiquity.[9] Black hermeneuts can take a cue from feminist interpreters. Just as feminist hermeneutics has exposed sexism in many texts, interpretations and translations, black exegetes need to look at the biblical data again for potential and latent racism. This again is not quite virgin soil, and there have been a few attempts. Cain Felder, using biblical and extra-biblical data, overlooked by Western commentators, has demonstrated the identity of the Queen of Sheba as black.[10] Clarice J. Martin has retrieved the story of the conversion of the black Ethiopian (Acts 8.26–40) as culturally affirming and empowering. Expanding on the 'hermeneutics of suspicion' in her study, she points out how white biblical interpreters ignore and minimize the ethnographic data and fail to inform their readers that in the Greco-Roman world 'Ethiopian' was a generic term used to denote dark-skinned people.[11] A future task for blacks is to recover biblical impulses that can enhance their self-esteem and self-dignity.

## 4 Networking and talking to each other

The time has come for Asian, Latin American and black hermeneuts to start conversing among themselves. This is probably one of the most urgent tasks before them. To date, in their hermeneutical discourses they have been either addressing the challenges or critiquing the interpretations of Euro-American scholars. Seldom have they talked to each other, let alone admired each other's work. The dialogue is necessary on at least two grounds.

First, it could help to clarify some of the undeclared tensions in their approach. One such issue that I have identified is the status and authority that is accorded to the Bible. Some regard it as the referent point for faith, and acknowledge that it contains norms and sources for Christian faith. This is the general view among Latin Americans and Africans. But the hermeneuts who come from multi-religious contexts, mainly Asians, tend to take a different view. For them the Christian Scripture has only an illuminative character that could be either complemented or corrected by other sacred texts. The task then is to resolve this tension without assuming that either a biblical text or the context of a particular interpreter has universal validity.

Secondly, dialogue among these hermeneuts can help to de-absolutize their hermeneutical interests. The temptation for a hermeneut is to totemize his or her contextual concerns. For instance, Latin Americans tend to absolutize class, blacks emphasize race, and feminists point out gender prejudices. Consequently, they look only for these elements in the biblical narratives. Preoccupation with their own concerns makes them insular, and cuts them off from other equally important and pressing hermeneutical issues and interests. By talking to each other as partners in a common cause, they can mutually challenge and correct each other's enterprise. This will not only enhance their task, but also widen their horizons to other hermeneutical possibilities.

There may be other tasks and fresh challenges as we struggle along to create a more human world. Indian sages when they embark on a spiritual odyssey take with them a mantra to keep alive their quest and vision. What one of Salman Rushdie's characters said in his novel *The Satanic Verses* could be our mantra as we face these new questions. 'A poet's work is to name the unnameable, to point at frauds, to take sides; start arguments, shape the world and stop it from going to sleep.'

## NOTES

1  C. Mesters, *Defenseless Flowers: A Reading of the Bible* (Maryknoll, NY, Orbis Books; London, CIIR, 1989), p. 101.

2  G. Gutierrez, 'The Hope of Liberation' (*WorldView*, June 1974), p. 23.

3  V. L. Wimbush, 'Biblical Historical Study as Liberation: Toward an Afro-Christian Hermeneutic' (*The Journal of Religious Thought*, 42, 2, 1985–6), pp. 10, 11.

4  P. and S. Scharper, *The Gospel in Art by the Peasants of Solentiname* (Maryknoll, NY, Orbis Books, 1984).

5  J. Sahi, 'An Artist looks at the Fourth Gospel', and 'A Comparison between the Johannine Structure of Image Sign and the Buddhist–Hindu Mandala', in C. Duraisingh and C. Hargreaves (eds), *India's Search for Reality and the Relevance of the Gospel of John* (Delhi, ISPCK, 1975), pp. 78–80 and 84–92.

6  I. Vempeny, *Kṛṣṇa and Christ* (Pune, India, Ishvani Kendra, 1988).

7  R. C. Amore, *Two Masters, One Message: The Lives and Teachings of Gautama and Jesus* (Nashville, Abingdon Press, 1978), pp. 96–136.

8  ibid.

9  M. Bernal, *Black Athena: The Afroasiatic Roots of Classical Civilization*, vol. 1, 'The Fabrication of Ancient Greece 1785–1985' (London, Free Association Books, 1987; New Brunswick, Rutgers University Press, 1987).

10  C. H. Felder, *Troubling Biblical Waters: Race, Class and Family* (Maryknoll, NY, Orbis Books, 1989), pp. 22–36.

11  C. J. Martin, 'A Chamberlain's Journey and the Challenge of Interpretation for Liberation' (*Semeia*, 47, 1989), pp. 105–35.

# INDEX OF
# SCRIPTURE REFERENCES

**Genesis**
1.2 118
1.6 118
1.9–10 118
1.20–3 118
1.26 371
1.27–8 306
2. 210
2.7 370
3. 64–5
3.5 384
3.20 120
5.32 186n
6.1 211
6.10 186n
7.13 186n
8.20–2 174
9.1–17 174
9.18 174–5
9.18–19 186n
9.18–27 173–6
9.19 174
9.20–7 174, 186n
9.22 175
9.23 175
9.24 175
9.25 175
9.28 174
9.29 174
10.177–8
10.1 186n, 187n
10.2 187n
10.6 187n
10.7. 177
10.21 187n
10.21–31 178
10.28 177
12.3 235
15.13 290
15.14 290
15.18–21 290
47.13–26 234

**Exodus**
2.11–15 232
3. 244
3.1–14 243
3.6 244
3.7 135, 243–4
3.12 244
3.14 244
3.14–15 231
3.16 237
3.17 290
6.2–6 231
6.2–7 162
6.6–7 163
7.1–5 238
12.12–14 259
12.38 231
12.43 231
12.48 231
15.1 123
15.5 123
15.20 162
15.21–2 259
19.4–6 163
20.2–3 230
21.1 194
21.16 194
22.21 152, 290
22.21–4 159
22.25 153
22.26 153
23.6–8 153
23.10 153
23.11 151
23. 31–3 291
30.15 150, 153
34.6 358

**Leviticus**
14.21 153
19.9 153
19.9–10 151

19.10 159
25.1–7 153
25.8–17 153
25.25–8 151
25.36–8 153

**Numbers**
12.1 178
12.10 178
12.1–16 174
14.11 119
27.17 89

**Deuteronomy**
1.25 158
1.35 158
3.25 158
4.6–8 163
6.18 158
6.20–3 162
6.21 259
7.1 291
7.2. 291
7.6–8 180
7.7–8 237
8.7–10 158
10.15 180
10.16–18 232
10.17–19 159
10.18 152
14.29 137
15.1–11 159
15.1–18 153
15.4 158
15.7–11 151
23.19 153
24.7 194
24.10–13 153
24.14 151, 159
24.14–18 151
24.17 159
24.19–22 153

445

**Deuteronomy** – *cont.*
26.5–9 162
29.29 433

**Joshua**
24.2–13 162

**Judges**
8.2.3 240n

**Ruth**
3.2 109

**1 Samuel**
2.8 150
7.14 214
8.1–22 164
8.5 219, 235
8.11–17 219
13.19 108
23.1 109
23.1–5 216

**2 Samuel**
2.1–14 216
3.1 150
5.1–5 216
6.6 109
7. 53
9–20 190
11.1–5 191
11.8 192
11.9 192
11.10 192
11.13 192
11.25 192
11.27 199
12.1 151, 199
12.1–7 193
12.5 194
12.9 192, 194
12.10 192
12.13 192, 194
12.15 201
12.16. 18, 201
12.19–21 201
12.22–3 201
12. 24–5 201
12.25 191
13–20 195
18.21–32 179
20.23 112
22.28 158

**1 Kings**
1–2 190, 195, 216
4.1–19 216
4.7–19 216–17
4.16 217
4.22–8 217

4.26 218
4.27 216
5.3–8 217
5.10–11 215
5.12 214–15
5.13–15 217
9.15–19 217
9.26–8 219
10.1–10 219
10.28 219
11.28 217
11.29 218
17. 219
22.10 109

**2 Kings**
10. 219
19.9 179

**1 Chronicles**
1.4 186n
1.17–34 177
27. 1–21 111

**2 Chronicles**
9.25 218

**Job**
7.11 140
16.2 141
16.3 141
19.25–7 133, 144n
28.19 180
34.28 150
36.6 158

**Psalms**
10.2 158
12.5 158
14.6 159
18.28 158
22. 135
22.1–3 135
22.1–4 135, 159
22.4–5 135
22.6–8 136
22.14–17 136
22.22–3 137
22. 23–31 143n
22.24 136, 153
22.26 136
22.27–8 137
31.5 137
34.6 153
35.10 151, 158
37.14 151, 158
66. 259
68.5. 152
68.31 180
69.5 159

69.34–5 132
72. 195
72.2 153
72.4 153, 166
73. 92
76.9 159, 166
78. 259
82.3 150–2, 158
86.1 153
105. 259
109.16 158
109.30–1 132
112. 154
113.7 150
140.12–13 153
146.7–9 159
146.9 152
147.6 158

**Proverbs**
6.6–11 152, 157
10.4 157
13.23 153, 158
14.20 151
14.21 159
14.31 150, 159
16.9 201
18.23 151
19.17 159
20.24 202
21.13 159
21.17 152, 157
21.31 202
22.2 151
22.16 159
22.22 150, 153
22.23 159
23.21 152, 157
28.6 151
28.8 159
28.27 159
29.7 153
30.14 158
31.8–9 5

**Isaiah**
1.16 164
3.13–15 159, 164
3.14 153, 158
3.15 159
5.1–7 164, 221
5.7 221
5.8–10 158
5.8–24 222
10.1–4 159, 164, 222
10.2. 150–1, 153, 158
11.2–9 164
11.4 150, 153, 158–9
11.9 170
11.11 180

12.3 123
13.13–15 159
14.30 150
18.7 180
19.18 235
24.4 159
25.4 156
26.5 158
29.19 151
32.7 158
37.9 179
40.6–8 261
41.17–20 153, 260
42.1–5 132
42.10 133
43.16–21 260
43.20 180
43.21 182
45.14 180
49.6 235
49.13 153, 158, 166
51.2 158
51.21 153, 158
51.22 159
52.4–6 260
54.11–14 153
58.1–12 159
58.5–9 153
61. 266n
65.9 180
65.12–25 164
66.25 170
66.2 153

**Jeremiah**
1.4–10 130
1.10 222
2.3 180
5.4 150
5.28 153
7.5–7 159
7.6 152
20.13 132
22.3 195
22.13 159
22.16 159
31.12 127n
38.7–13 179
39.15–18 179
46.9 179

**Ezekiel**
16. 260
16.3–9 260
16.49 151, 153, 159
18.12 153
22.29 153, 158
34.1–24 159
34.5 89

**Hosea**
2.16–17 260
11.1 259
14.7 127n

**Amos**
2.6 150, 153
2.6–7 221
2.6–8 159, 164
2.7 150–1
4.1 150, 158
4.1–3 159, 164
5.11 153
5.12 150, 153
5.7–12 164
5.12 153
6.4–8 159
8.4 151
8.4–6 158, 164
8.6 150, 153
9.13 127n

**Micah**
2.1 112
2.1–3 159, 164, 221
3.1–4 164
3.2 113
4.1 115
4.6 115
5.2 115
6.9–16 164
7.8 115

**Habakkuk**
1.2–4 220
3.7 187n
3.14 158

**Zephaniah**
1.1 180
3.10 180
3.12 151, 153, 159, 164

**Zechariah**
7.10 152–3, 159

**Malachi**
3.5 152

**Judith**
16.2 132

**The Wisdom of Solomon**
1. 17 362

**The Wisdom of Jesus the Son of Sirach**
18.32 152, 157
24.6 362

**Baruch**
29.5 127n

**Matthew**
5.3 97, 150, 154
5.3–10 155
5.8 48
5.11 154
5.17 171
5.21 342
5.21–44 341
5.23–4 78
5.27 342
5.33 342
5.38 342
5.43 342
5.46–8 94
6.7 94
6.24 161
8.20 164
8.29 121
10.5 94
10.8 131
10.42 103n
11.5 154–5
11.9 94
11.19 91, 93–4
11.25 68
11.28 97
11.30 138
12.28 342
13.12 73
17.2 103n
18.6–7 97
21.32 91
22.14 182
24.3 432
24.36 432
27.46 135

**Mark**
1.15 101
1.16–20 164
1.22 86
1.24 121
1.30 86
1.32 86
1.33 86, 156
1.37 86
1.44 86
1.45 86, 156
2.2 86
2.4 86, 88
2.4–6 89
2.5 95–6

**Mark** – *cont.*
2.10 341
2.11 95
2.13 88–9, 164
2.13–17 88, 90–1, 164
2.14 91, 96
2. 16–17 94
2.17 96
2.18 103n
2.23 341
2.27 97, 340
3.1 95
3.2–21 89
3.8 86
3.9 88
3.18 94
3.20 88
3.31–5 164
3.32 88
3.34 89
3.35 90
4.1 88–9
4.11–12 89
4.13 102n
4.35–42 102n
4.36 88
5.7 121
5.19 95
5.21 88
5.24 88, 156
5.31 88
5.34 95
5.35 95
5.36 95
6.3 164
6.14 346
6.34 89, 91, 102n, 156
6.46 88
6.51 102n
7.1 96
7.2 96
7.4 89
7.5 96
7.6 86
7.14 96–7
7.15 96–7, 103n 341
7.17 88
7.24 95
7.33 88
8.1 88, 91, 102n
8.1–2 156
8.2 90
8.8 123
8.26 95
8.31 341
8.32 102n
8.34 88
8.38 339–40
8.37 350n
9.14 88

9.23 95
9.32 102n
9.37 97
9.42 103n
10.1 88–9
10.9 333
10.13–15 97
10.17–22 165
10.18 341, 343
10.21 154
10.32 102n
10.45 341
10.46 88
10.52 95
11.18 89
11.27 89
11.32 89
12.12 89
12.41 91, 159
12.42 154
12.44 160–1
13.18b 90
14.2 86
15.8 89
15.15 89
15.34 135
15.43 165

**Luke**
1.3 188n
1.52 160
3.36 176
4.14–21 423
4.16–21 266n
4.18 154–5
4.18–19 280
4.22–30 425
5.1–3 420
5.4–7 421
5.8–11 422
5.29 91
5.33–9 125
6.15 165
6.20 154–5
6.20–6 159–60
6.36 358
7.2 188n
7.22 154
9.48 97
12.13–21 160
12.15 161
13.2 95
13.23 432
14.5 154
14.12–14 159–60
14.13 154
14.21 154
15.1 93
15.1–2 164
15.2 96

15.7–10 94
15.18 94
15.32 432
16.10–14 161
16.19–31 73, 159–60
16.20 154
16.22 154
17.1–2 97
17.21 350n
17.10 34
17.24 340
19.1 165
19.8 154
19.47 99
21.2 154
22.66 99
23.46 137
24.27 126

**John**
1.1 316
1.3 316
1.12 347n
1.14 119, 316
1.16 122, 316
1.26 126
1.29 126
2.1 118
2.2 119
2.3 121
2.5 121
2.6 122
2.7 122
2.11 118, 126, 127n
3.1 165
3.5 184
3.25 126
4.10 126
4.54 127n
5.2–9 127n
6.14 127n
6.37 347n
6.53 126
7.6 121
7.30 121
7.38 126
8.20 121
8.28 260
8.31–2 383–4
9.1 92, 95
9.16 127n
10.14–15 335
12.18 127n
12.23 121
12.27 121
12.49 335
13.1 121
13.10 124
13.29 154
14.6 134

14.9 336
14.10 335
14.17 345
15.3 124
15.13 335
16.13 345
17.3 383
17.17 433
17.21 335
17.21–3 335
17.26 260
19.25–7 119
19.26 121
21.21 432

**Acts**
1.1 188n
1.6 432
2. 188n
4.8 99
4.34 154
8.26–40 183–4
8.37 184
9.1–19 354
10.1 188n
10.12–48 184
10.22 188n
10.34–43 184
11.26 185
12. 188n
13.1 184–5
17. 188n
22.4–16 354
23.5 99
26.9–19 354
28. 183, 188n

**Romans**
2.4 356
6.4 359
7. 355
7.17 333
8.4 336
8.9 336
8.10 346, 350n
8.15–17 357
8.29 357
9.11 181
10.17 403
11.2 181
11.11 181
11.25 182
11.28 181
11.29 181
12.2 356
13.1–5 188n
15.18 332, 347n

15.26 154
15.28 183

**1 Corinthians**
1.4 334
1.18 138
1.25 138
1.26–8 165
1.26–9 138
1.27 182
1.28 182
2.16 34
7.10–12 333
8.1 207
8.4 208
10.18 181
10.23 208
11.2 210
11.2–16 205–7
11.4 206–7
11.5 207
11.6 207
11.9 207
11.11 211
11.12 211
11.14 207
11.16 210
12. 346, 348n, 350n
12.3 335, 345
12.10 34
12.13 182
14.34 66
14.37 332–3
15.10 334, 348n

**2 Corinthians**
4.6 333, 347n
5.16 87
5.17 334, 346
5.20 332
6.10 154, 159
7.9–10 356
8.9 159
9.9 154
12.21 356
13.3 332

**Galatians**
1.1 333
1.6 335
1.11–17 354
1.12 357
1.14 356
1.15–16 347n
1.16 345–6
1.20 347n
2.10 154

2.19 332
2.20 333–4, 341, 346, 351n
3.28 182
4.6 141
4.9 154
6.16 181

**Ephesians**
5.22–4 66

**Philippians**
1.21 333, 335
2.13 335, 343
3.6 356
3.10 356
3.12 354

**Colossians**
1.19 122
2.9 122
3.11 182
3.12 182

**1 Timothy**
2.5 57

**Hebrews**
5.7–10 138

**James**
2.1–6 159–60
2.2–6 154
2.5 160, 182
5.1–6 160
5.7 170

**1 Peter**
2.9 182

**1 John**
5.4 146n
5.6–8 184

**Revelation**
3.17 154
7.9 87, 185
7.17 146n
13.16 159
19.1 87
19.6 87
21.1–4 166
21.3–4 170
21.5 133

**1 Clement**
5.7 183, 187n

# SELECT INDEX OF
# NAMES AND SUBJECTS

Abraham, K. C. 44
African Americans 287–8
Ahn Byung-Mu 308
Allah 386–7
Allen, H. N. 247–8
American Indians 287
Amida Buddha 340, 345
Amore, A. C. 362, 441–2
*Analects* 38, 40, 302
*ananda* 441
*'ānī 'ānāw* 150–1, 154, 157–8
*anubhava* 40, 49n
Apenzeller, H. 248
*apocalypse* 207
Aquinas, St Thomas 384
Aquino, C. C. 224–5
ápiru (habiru) 240n, 242, 255n
Asian christian theology 41
Asian women theologians 306–7
atheism 337
Atler, R. 193
Atman 377, 379, 380–3
*Aum* 40
Auschwitz 139, 145n
*Avatar* 361
Ayacucho 129, 140, 145n

Barrett, C. K. 125
Barth, K. 301, 360
beatitudes: spiritualization of 73, 155
*Bhagavadgītā* (Gita) 5, 37–8, 121, 126, 328,
    352, 361–2, 380–1, 441; and *mukti*
    381–2
*bhakta* 117
Bhutto, B. 212
Bible, the: Chinese woman's perspective
    300, 309–13; evangelization 251;
    deposit of truth 43; hierarchy within
    10; 'historical memory of the poor' 63;
    ideological use of 324; Latin
    American Woman's perspective
    67–70; marginalization of women

62–3; oppressive use of 397–8; as
    peoples' book 435; as ruling class
    document 115; and racism 173;
    silences in 432; source of Asian
    biblical interpretation 42; source of
    Black theology 52; as written word
    400–1
    *see also* Word of God
biblical authority 64–5
biblical interpretation: Asia 37–41, 304–5;
    Africa 51–9; Chinese 303; contextual
    434; as re-enacting 407; as re-telling
    407, 440; and sociological study 147;
    as testimony 408; task of 362–3; and
    visual media 405, 440
biblical scholarship and struggle 437–8
biblicism 43–4
Black biblical hermeneutics 59
Black experience 52–3
Black theology: exegetical bondage 53–4;
    of liberation 55, 115; problem of
    universality and plurality 55–9; and
    Word of God 52–3
Black people 173, 179
Bloch, E. 74
Boesak, A. 55
Borg, M. 357
*Brahman* 377–8, 382–3
Brandon, S. G. F. 24
Bruce, F. F. 354
Brueggemann, W. 114
Buck, H. M. 359
Buddhism 38, 246, 331, 346; Mahayana
    344; Pure Land 340; Zen 337
Bultmann, R. 87, 97, 155, 181, 339, 359
Butchers' Liberation Movement 250
Buthelezi, M. 57–8

Cabral, A. 58
Cardenal, E. 360, 412
Carlston, C. E. 362
Cannon, K. G. 304, 311

# Index

canon: closure of 19, 311; issue of 310–11
Central America 145n
Chao, T. C. 299, 301
Chaney, M. 109, 111–12
Childs, B. 292
Chinese Christians 299–300
Christ, C. 310–11
Christology: Antiochean 336; Alexandrian 336; Johannine 337; pluralistic 331
Christian Conference of Asia 42
Christian Scriptures: exclusive claims of 47
Christian women 66
Christian writings, the: functions of 30
class: in the Bible 148; in Marxist understanding 149
comparative exegesis 361, 441
Cone, J. 51–2, 56; view of Bible 52
Confucianism 37–8; Neo-Confucianism 246–7, 303
Confucianists 247
Confucius 38–40, 203, 302
contextual hermeneutics 3
Contrast Community 163–4, 171n
conversion 353; Ethiopian Finance Minister 183–7; Paul's 354–9; as transformation 356–7
'correspondence of relationships' 27–33
'correspondence of terms' 23–6
Croatto, J. 79
Culler, J. 310
Cullmann, O. 24

dal 150, 154, 157
David 109–12, 190–203, 216
Derrida, J. 312
Detweiler, R. 309–10
Deuteronomic code 42
De Geus, C. H. J. 107
De Vaux, R. 112
dharma 383
dharma yuddha 38
Dhvani 117
dialogical approach 356–9
dialogical imagination 304–5, 312
Dictionary of Biblical Interpretation, A 2
Dilthey, W. 12
'discernment of the spirits' 81
Dodd, C. H. 286
Dwane, S. 53

Eagleton, T. 113
Eaton, J. 362
ebyôn 150, 154, 157–8
Ecumenical Association of African Theologians (EAAT) 397, 408
Ecumenical Association of Third World Theologians (EATWOT) 42, 316, 408, 410n
'Egyptian captivity' 254

Eisler, R. 24
election: Israel 180–1
    Paul's understanding of 181–2
'enacted interpretation' 77
endees 154
Engels, F. 55, 74
'eschatalogical reversal' 76, 160
Euro-American biblical scholars 4, 437
Euro-American feminist scripture scholars 2
exegetes: Euro-Americans 437; African 4; Afro-American 4; Asian 4; Latin American 4
Exodus, the: passim
exousia 206

Felder, C. H. 442
Fiorenza, E. S. 66, 311–12
First World radical feminists 65
Foucault, M. 300
Francis of Assisi, St 127

Gadamer, H. G. 11–12
Gallup, G. 306
Galtung, J. 220, 224
Gandhi, M. K. 38, 328, 352
genealogies 177–8
George, A. 157
God: after Auschwitz 139; of the Bible 229; gratuitousness 131–4; justice of 133; as liberator 231, 244; of missionary preaching 257; as Mother 120; preferential option for the oppressed 232, 243
Gottwald, N. K. 105, 108, 111–12, 167–8, 215, 217, 289
Gqubule, S. 56–7
grass-root communities 63–4
Gregory the Great, 141
Gutierrez, G. 292, 436

Haenchen, E. 184
Ham 173, 175, 177; curse of 174, 258
Hangul 248, 250–1
Hauer Jr, C. E. 218
Hauerwas, S. 292
Hebrews, the 31, 234, 236, 238, 241–5, 373; origins of 172–3; see also ápiru; Israel
Heidegger, M. 13
Hengel, M. 24
hermeneutic circle 13–17
'hermeneutic competency' 19, 30
hermeneutic improvisation 14
'hermeneutic mediation' 18
hermeneutic positivism 33
'hermeneutic watchfulness' 21
hermeneutical gap 435–6
'hermeneutical millenarianism' 17
hermeneutical neutrality 438

hermeneutics: *passim*
hermeneutics of liberation: materialist
    method 105
'hermeneutics of suspicion' 1, 442
hermeneuts 5, 435, 438, 443; Asia
    439–40; black 439–40; Latin America
    439–40
Hisamatsu Shin-ichi 337–9
historical-critical methods 4, 117, 436
historical-critical tools 4, 85
Holy Spirit 32, 433
Hopkins, D. D. 110–11
Hsieh Fu Ya 302
Hutchison, W. R. 303
Hu Tsan Yün 302

ideology: of ruling class 54
'ideological suspicion' 72–3
'ideological suspicions' 69–70
imperialism 223–4
Indian spirituality 325–6
Indra 125
*ipsissma verba Jesu* 27
Israel: origins of 233–5; as special people
    of God 237 *see also* ápiru, Hebrews

Jainism 372
Jeremias, J. 73, 92
Jesus: attitude towards *ochlos* 89–90;
    gospel of 65; history of 164; and
    kingdom of God 97; messianic
    consciousness 331, 339; Son of Man
    339–40, 331; rich and poor 73–4;
    resurrection of 345–6; as
    revolutionary 303
Jesus Movement 4, 168, 361, 439
*jihad* 391–2
Joll, J. 54
Joseph narrative, the 198–9
Justin Martyr 366–7

Kamba 46
karma 158, 382
Kautsky, K. 74, 147
kephale 206
Kim Yong-Bock 42, 307
Korean Christians 251–3; depoliticizing of
    252
Koyama, K. 304
Kraemer, H. 301
Kraft, C. 45
kṛṣṇa 441
Kummel, W. G. 97

*laos* 86, 98–9, 308 *see also ochlos*
Lao-tse 121
Lao Tzu 38, 40–1
Latin America 61, 68–9, 134, 139–40,
    145n; 324 reading of the Bible 68;
    talking about God 140

Latin American liberation hermeneutics 352
Latin American liberation theologians 1,
    292, 353, 359, 363
Laxmi 125
Lee Humphreys, W. 198
Lee, S. H. 308
Lewis, N. B. 307
Liberation: in Vedas 373
liberation theology 53–4, 63, 385–6,
    393–4, 398; exegesis 147, 288;
    hermeneutical contribution of 148;
    Latin American 59, 129; Native
    American 287; Palestinian 280–1; in
    Islam 386–94
liberation theologians 44, 69
Lindbeck, G. 292
Logos 366–7

MacRae, R. 357
Mafeje, A. 116
magisterium 401–2
Manson, T. W. 155, 339
Marcos, F. 224
Martin, C. J. 442
Marx, K. 51, 55, 71–2, 113, 149, 156, 170
Mary: and ganga 119–20; and water
    119–21
materialist biblical hermeneutics 106
materialist method 104–5
Mecca 386–7, 389
Mendenhall, G. E. 168
Mesters, C. 397–8, 435
Metz, J. B. 139
Mgojo, E. K. M. 56
Minjung 42, 98, 100–2, 241, 244, 246,
    248–9, 307–8, 310–12 *see also ochlos*
*miskēn* 151, 154, 157
mode of production: in premonarchic
    Israel 105–9; after David's conquest
    109–13
Moffett, S. A. 251
moksha 372, 376–7, 382
Moltmann, J. 261–2
Moore, G. F. 181
Mott, J. R. 301
*Mount Fuji and Mount Sinai* 304
Mukti 372, 376–8
multi-faith hermeneutics 5, 362, 440

Native Americans 287–9, 294
Native American theology of liberation 287
neighbourly relationships 47
Nicaragua 5, 145n
*nirvana* 372, 383

*ochlos* 86–8, 308; attitude of Jesus 89–90,
    96; characteristics of 88–9;
    composition of 90–6; Mark's use of
    100–2; as Minjung 101–3 *see also laos*
oikoumene 37, 47

# Index

pacifism 24
Palestinians 280–1
Palestinian Christians 280–3; and canon of hermeneutic 285
Parks, S. 305
Paul: contradictions in his writings 66; election 181; head covering 207–12, and historical Jesus 87; 'I' in 332
*penēs* 154
Pharisees 92, 103n
Pieris, A. 3
*pleroma* 122
*plousios* 159
Po Ch'en Kuang 302
Pongudom, M. 306
poor: as concern of Yahweh 159; as a dialectical group 157–61; as a dynamic group 161–66; liberation of 159 *see also* preferential option for the oppressed;
praxis 77; of Christians 256; interreligious 292
preferential option for the poor 44, 68
Promised Land 79
Prophet, the 386–7, 390
*ptōchos* 150, 154–5, 159
Puebla 134, 142n
*purdah* (veil) 208

Qur'an 5, 38, 46, 387, 391–2
concept of justice 388
God of 388–9

Radhakrishnan, R. 37
Ramanuja 37
*Rāmāyana* 46
rāsh 151, 154, 157
Ratzinger, J. 123
Remonstrating Counsellors 196
remonstrator: in Chinese and Hebrew tradition 190
re-read 325, 353
re-reading 323–5, 353
Revelation 19, 301
Rice, G. 178
Ricoeur, P. 12
Rig Ved(a) 128n, 373
Rose, G. 134
Rostagno, S. 54–5
Ruether, R. R. 311–12
Rushdie, S. 443

*Sabda* 40
Sacralization: definition of 173; example of 178; racial implications of 179
Saddharma Pundarika (Lotus of the Good Law) 38
*sadiq* 150
salvation: biblical notion of 258; as right knowledge 383

*Satanic Verses, The* 443
Satpatha Brahmana 118
Schleiermacher, F. 12
Scriptures: heritage of all humankind 47; as *Pothumarai* (common scripture) 362; non-ideological pre-supposition 52, relation with reading community 17; and tradition 401–2; traditions of 46 *see also* the Bible
Scriptures of other religions 37, 46; impact on Christian Scriptures 46–7
secularization: definition of 173; example of 183–5
Seebass, H. 180
semantic positivism 14–15
*sensus plenior* 31
*shalom* 214, 220, 222
Shankaracharya (Sankara) 37, 121, 377
signs 119
Simon, U. 194–5
Smith, C. W. 353
*Smriti* 40, 439
*Sola Scriptura* 401
Song, C. S. 306
Song of Miriam 162
spiritualization of texts 44
*Sruti* 40, 439
Stech-Wheeler, T. 108
Stendahl, K. 355
Suk Nam Dong 308

Takizawa, K. 330, 344–6
*tawhid* 390–1, 394
*Tears of Lady Meng, The* 306
*Tell Us Our Names* 306
Tertullian 361
texts: antiwomen 68; legitimizing women's inferiority 65; 'macho' 68
Theissen, G. 167
Third World 79, 302, 325, 392, 398, 409;: definition of 2–3
'Third World' hermeneutics 6
'Third worldness' 3
Thistlewaite, S. B. 305
*Tirukural* 361
Tiwari, T. K. 354
*Tonghak* rebellion 249–50, 253
Torah 47
Torres, C. 78
Toynbee, A. J. 281–2
'transcendent presence' 309
*Tribes of Yahweh, The* 105
Tulsidas 46

Underwood, M. G. 248
Upanishads 37–8, 316, 377–9

Valmiki 46
Vempeny, I. 362, 441

Vielhauer, P. 339
von Rad, G. 104, 180, 199–200

Waldbaum, J. C. 108
water: in Genesis 118; in St John 118; and Mary 119
Weber, M. 73
Wei Cheng 196–8
West, C. 52, 53, 59
Westermann, C. 174–5
Williams, D. 311
Wimbush, V. 439
Wink, W. 4

Word of God 14, 29, 52–6, 283–5, 303, 319–21, 402; Black theology's notion of 52–3
working class 55; conversion of 249
Wu, Y. T. 302–3

*yang ban* 247–9
*yoga* 382

zealotism 24
Zealots 24, 101
Zen: buddhism 337; meditation 331
Zionists 285